THE OFFICIAL®

PRICE GUIDE TO

STAR TREK®
and
STAR WARS®

COLLECTIBLES

THE OFFICIAL®

PRICE GUIDE TO

STAR TREK®
and
STAR WARS®

COLLECTIBLES

By Sue Cornwell and Mike Kott

SECOND EDITION

THE HOUSE OF COLLECTIBLES
NEW YORK, NEW YORK 10022

TABLE OF CONTENTS

Star Trek

Star Wars

ACKNOWLEDGMENTS

We wish to express our sincere thanks to the following individuals who have taken the time and effort to help make this book possible: Virginia Acker, TX; Dee Anne Ackermann; Peter Arnone Jr., NY; Deborah Jean Barkley, PA; Scott Bingham, CA; Dianne Boldt, Kenner Toys; James Booska, VT; Brent A. Bradley, FL; Buddy Brown, Battlestar Enterprises, RI; Kevin Brown, CA; Martha J. Brown, NH; Jim and Julie Cabler, CA; Eric Carlson, TX; Sherry Charvat, OH; Melinda Collins, VA; Ken Cross, NY; Lisa D'Addeo, CT; Jody Davies, NY; Gregg E. Davis, LA; Stan Day, NM; Jim Dietz, PA; Noreen Doyle, ME; H. Elseman, CA; Micheline England, IL; Dave Esposito, OH; Mark Ezell, MD; David Godfrey, IL; Melanie Guttierrez, LA; Aaron Finch, VA; Lenny Frederick, GA; Phyllis Gould, Remco Corp., NJ; Travis Groat, IL; Carol and Chuck Hale, CA; Darryl Hale, MO; Don Harden, GA; Charles Hayes, CA; Karen Heidemann, CA; T.F. Herrmann, SD; Dan Holder, IA; Huckleberry Designs, NY; Jay Jengo, NJ; Duncan Jenkins, MO; David Jessup, NY; Galen Johnson, NC; Glenn Johnson, NJ; Louyse Jolin, Canada; Jill Kadron, MD; Dan Kaiser, NE; Gail Kelly, PA; Tom Kennedy, MI; Steve Kinzler, ND; Kirtl Kundurazieff, CA; Dawn E. Law, NY; Bob Likes, ID; John Lowig, Belgium; Shirley S. Maiewski, MA; Joseph Marcel, MI; Darren Margolis, MD; Bill Mason, PA; Robert Mattingly, MO; Donna May, AR; The McNeal Family, OR; Shane Morrissey, Australia; Karen Mostafa, Arista Designs, CA; Phyllis A. Murrel, KY; Thomas C. Nelson, WV; Eric Nett, WA; Bob Ostrowski, AZ; Frank Owens, KS; Frank Pagoria, KY; Ross Paris, AL; Bill Perkins, WA; Mark Phipps, SC; Joseph Portelli, MI; Laura Powell, VA; Gary R. Quick, NY; Christopher Raffeld, SC; Karin Rhodes, FL; Pam Robertson, Kenner Corp., OH; Elliott L. Roden, AL; Kevin C. Rooker, IL; Danillo Rose, CA; Rostirasa, NY; Timarie Seneca, CA; Anita Severance, WY; Tom Shaeffer, OR; Ronald Shafer, AZ; Lita Sheldon, AZ; Theresa Sledge, FL; Robert Smith, VA; Ellie Smith, VA; William H. Smith IV, CA; Scott Spies, MD; E. Steinmeyer, CA; Eric Stillwell, OR; Walter Stuben, PA; Brent W. Studer, IA; J. Blair Tarleton, NC; Steven Tauber, NY; Kasey Vandenberg, TN; Eileen D. Walton, CA; Jeffrey White, NY; Michael Wilcoxon, NM; Suzie Wolin, AZ; Susan Zizza, Inter Audio Studios, NY.

Special thanks to Jeff Maynard, New Eye Studio, CT; Harry Freidenberg, H & R Records, CA; Jeff Killian, KS; Kathe Walker, CO; and Jamie LaMoreaux, Intergalactic Trading Co., FL.

BECOME A CONTRIBUTOR!

EXPERIENCED COLLECTORS—Lend us the benefit of your knowledge to improve, update, and expand this book. By doing so, you are helping your fellow collectors and insuring that the hobby keeps growing. If you know of items not in this book or have new information on items already included, send a full outline plus your return address and phone number to: Sue Cornwell, P.O. Box 1516, Longwood, FL 32750 (no phone calls, please). If your contribution is accepted, your name will appear on the contribution page as a participating member of our editorial team.

NOTE TO READERS

MARKET REVIEW

Stated simply, the Star Trek market is in the middle of an unprecedented boom. Defying the rule that says sequels aren't as good as the original, *Star Trek IV* was an unquestioned success. So successful, in fact, that not only is *Star Trek V* in the planning stages, but a new Star Trek TV show, tentatively titled "Star Trek: The New Generation," is in the works for the 1987–88 television season. Though the cast will be different, many of the production people who created the atmosphere and feel of the original series are coming back for this new venture.

How will this affect the market? Hopefully, with an influx of new products. There are several new items in this book from *Star Trek IV,* many, if not most of them, of interest to the serious collector.

There has been a definite change from the past when major companies produced large amounts of licensed goods from movies. Studios used to charge a lower fee for licensing and made their profits on the royalties if the item was a success. Nowadays the regular licensing fee is out of reach of all but the largest companies, and most of them are not willing to take the risk. As a reesult, most *Star Trek IV* items were produced under "limited" licenses, restricting the manufacturer to specialty markets. The result is less merchandise than the hungry market can absorb—virtually instant collectibles!

The longevity of Star Trek also means a constantly expanding market, with new buyers for decreasing amounts of older collectibles keeping prices steady.

Items of special note in the Star Trek market are the second and third series 8″ Mego TV dolls. These dolls, always high-priced items, have been climbing in value rapidly this past year, and at present no end is in sight as to how high they will go. Prices collectors winced at only six months ago would seem like bargains today!

Other trends concern a greater demand for more obscure items, as the advanced collectors in the market seek out those oddities missing from their collections and, with the continuation of the Star Trek movies, any sort of production items from the Star Trek film sets.

In the Star Wars field, as predicted, the dwindling mass market supply has boosted into the collectibles market many items that only a year or so ago would have been thought of as common. Kenner, the largest manufacturer of licensed Star Wars items, has discontinued this entire line, even those items based on the "Ewoks" and "Droids" animated series of only a year ago.

The newest trend seems to lie in the area of the small action figures and related toys. There was once a huge variety of these items, and now that they are no longer available in stores, people are turning to the collectors' market to complete their sets.

It should be noted that 1987 was the tenth anniversary of *Star Wars,* resulting in some merchandising, though probably of the restricted kind mentioned before and not by major manufacturers.

Also of interest to the collector is the rumor that George Lucas is planning another movie in the *Star Wars* series, definitely a boost to an already booming collectors' market!

One continuing trend that is worth reviewing is the one toward "mint in the box" items, especially toys. Items in this condition are bringing two or even three times the price of the same piece in identical condition out of the box. While we'll concede that a box always makes an item more desirable, this seems a little extreme, more so than in other collectibles fields. A wise investor in collectibles might look to buying mint condition pieces in less-than-perfect boxes or with no box at all, looking to the future when scarcity of the items in general might close the price gap to something more reasonable.

Happy collecting!

STAR TREK: FROM THE BEGINNING

When thinking about *Star Trek,* most of us can picture clearly what we know to be the form and substance of the TV series. We tend to forget the chameleon character of the program and how it metamorphosed continuously from its inception until its cancellation. We picture Dr. McCoy hovering solicitously over Captain Kirk's shoulder and Mr. Spock lifting his eyebrow in silent contempt while the Captain smiles benignly at his two friends and comrades. We forget, or perhaps were not even aware, that the interaction of these personalities and many other "regular" features did not originally exist. In fact, in the first show filmed (but not the first to be seen on TV) the captain was played by Jeffrey Hunter, not William Shatner, and the captain's name was Christopher Pike.

In 1964, Gene Roddenberry, an experienced and already successful screenwriter, developed a 16-page synopsis of an idea for a science fiction TV series called *Star Trek.* For those fans who would like to read the second version of this outline, it is printed in the book, *The Making of Star Trek.* Very few of the names we associate with the series were in either of these drafts; for example, the starship was called the S.S. Yorktown instead of the Enterprise.

When the synopsis was presented to Metro-Goldwyn-Mayer, the producers seemed intrigued, but did not follow up with any offer. When the Desilu Company was approached, it contracted with Gene Roddenberry to develop and produce television pilots based on the synopsis during the following three years. This agreement was reached only a month after Roddenberry had completed the outline.

The vice-president for Desilu, Oscar Katz, offered the series to CBS first, but it was NBC which provided payment to Roddenberry and the go-ahead to write three story outlines. From these outlines, the network chose the story "The Cage" as the series' pilot. The story outline, dated June 29, 1964, can be found in full, printed in *The Making Of Star Trek*. The title was later changed to "The Menagerie."

The first pilot was filmed during late November and December of that same year although some of the special optical effects were filmed as early as September.

The greatest challenge for the producers was devising special effects that were not phony looking. Since the most important effect was the starship, much effort was expended towards the design of a realistic one. The final design was a combination of several different styles. The Howard A. Anderson Company, which specializes in optical effects, contracted to make the models. Twenty technicians were assigned to this difficult project.

Three miniature models were constructed—the first being a wooden scale model only four inches long, the second a more detailed work three feet long, and the third a fourteen foot model. The largest piece required hundreds of hours of work. Made mostly from sheet plastic, the nacelles were tooled from hardwood. Today, this model is displayed in the Air and Space Museum of the Smithsonian. In this model, the dome was larger and rounder than the ship that eventually became familiar to Trek fans. There are several other differences, particularly with the nacelles.

The largest of the models was placed on a pipe which led down to a pedestal on a tripod mount. This device allowed the model to be turned or tilted during the filming. For the scenes where the Enterprise is seen zooming through space, both the model and camera were in motion to create the effect of great speed. It is uncertain as to how many of these models were eventually constructed or what their sizes were.

During this period, there were few of the special effects that we are so familiar with today. The technology available to today's producers offers greater freedom in creating spectacular sights and sounds. But these techniques were not available for the producers of *Star Trek.* Besides production costs, the deadlines for a TV series limited their options as compared to a full-length movie film.

Another special effect which required great care and innovation was the transporter. Difficulty arose from the need to produce something spectacular, but affordable, week after week. After much experimentation, they devised a method where they photographed the actors on the transporter platform, stopped the camera while they stepped off, then shot the empty platform. By placing a duplicated negative print of the footage, they could create a matte of the subject. This matte allowed the actors to be dissolved out of the scene. Later, the glitter effect was added.

In February 1965, the completed pilot was submitted to NBC. The network turned the work down, but commissioned a second pilot to be filmed. Many characters in the original script were cut; NBC requested that Mr. Spock also be dropped from the series, but Gene Roddenberry insisted that he remain.

At this time, first draft scripts for three different stories were written. Roddenberry wrote two of these: "The Omega Glory," and "Mudd's Women." Novelist and screenwriter Samuel Peeples wrote the third one, "Where No Man Has Gone Before." When the three rough drafts were submitted in June 1965, NBC chose the third script even though this particular story line involved more expense and presented a greater challenge in production. Since Jeffrey Hunter was unavailable for the shooting of this second pilot, another actor had to be found for the part. William Shatner had already proven himself an able actor with many impressive credits, and he was offered the role.

James Doohan joined the staff in this episode because of his ability to recreate different accents. Roddenberry was captivated by his Scottish brogue, since he had not completely formulated the personality of the Chief Engineer prior to Doohan's reading.

Sulu also appeared in this early Trek show, but had a part that required only two lines. In this episode, the ship's doctor was a Dr. Piper played by actor Paul Fix. At this point, the relationship between the doctor and the captain was of no importance, although the first pilot has a Dr. Boyce who is supportive of the emotional stress faced by the Captain.

Many other changes occurred. The costumes were redesigned, Spock's makeup was modified to give him a more exotic appearance, and many of the props were revamped. Animation was used to provide special effects for glowing eyes, phaser blasts, and showers of light and energy releases.

The second version was submitted to NBC in January 1966; a month and a half later, NBC accepted *Star Trek* as a series. The original version of this show has never been televised. Although the story line and the action are basically the same, the variations are sufficient to be noticeable.

Modifications continued with most of the major cast changes being made during the first season. Dr. McCoy, Lieutenant Uhura, and Yeoman Janice Rand were added to the cast. But the last of the eight major characters, Mr. Chekov, didn't join the show until the beginning of the second season.

Star Trek appeared on TV from September 1966 to September 1969. The show inspired little enthusiasm from the media and received mixed reviews. Some thought it to be a show strictly for children. And in fact, many of its viewers were in their teens or early twenties. Because of the weak ratings, NBC announced its intention to cancel the series. The Star Trek fans responded with vehement protests—thousands of letters deluged the NBC offices with pleas that the series be continued. In an unprecedented move, NBC reversed its former decision and continued the show for another season. Unfortunately, the series was moved to a time slot unfavorable for its particular audience—Friday night. Since most of its viewers were young, most of them were on dates or at the movies on Friday evenings. Even so, the series garnered more and more devoted fans, though the Nielsen ratings indicated that it lacked popularity. At this time, the first of the Star Trek fanzines emerged, further increasing the number of followers (see Fanzine section).

During its first season, *Star Trek* was nominated for five Emmy awards: as the best dramatic series, for the best dramatic actor (Leonard Nimoy), special photographic effects, special mechanical effects, and film and sound editing. Despite these honors, NBC again contemplated cancelling the series during its second season. Again, fans organized an impressive writing campaign. The fans were fearful that the show would either be cancelled or converted into a kiddie format. Fans even wrote up a guideline "How To Write Effective Letters To Save Star Trek" targeting the people and agencies to send these letters to.

Apparently, this convinced NBC to continue with the series—the network announced that 115,893 letters had been received from *Star Trek* fans.

At the start of the third season, there were rumors that the series would be moved to a time-slot geared to its audience, but at the last moment it was announced that the series would be stuck in the 10 to 11 P.M. slot on Friday. This was worse than the second season.

Over the three seasons, a change of producers evolved. For the first 12 episodes, creator/writer Gene Roddenberry as producer was closely involved with all aspects of the show. At that point, Roddenberry became executive producer with Gene L. Coon taking the reins of producer. Although the two conferred often, Roddenberry's direct participation had come to an end.

During the second season, John Meredyth Lucas followed Coon as the producer. Again, in the third season, a new producer was chosen— Fred Freilberger. Although no one will deny that some outstanding episodes were made in the last season, some fans felt that the important ingredients that had made the series worthwhile were missing in some of the shows. Most of the criticism was directed at situations in which Mr. Spock uncharacteristically showed excessive emotion. When he is forced to laugh in "Plato's Stepchildren," plays in a jam session in "The Way To Eden," and conspires against the Captain in "The Turnabout Intruder," it goes against his persona so obviously that the fans resented the lack of continuity.

On June 3, 1969, the last network episode, "The Turnabout Intruder," was shown. But fans adamantly refused to let their favorite series disappear unforgotten. The number of fanzines grew; they supplied an outpouring of poetry, original stories, artwork, trivia questions, and suppositions about the actors and characters.

At first, NBC syndicated *Star Trek* only to its affiliate stations all over the United States. But eventually, they prepared a promotional package, touting the enthusiastic public response from its fans. By 1978, *Star Trek* was one of the most successful syndications in TV history. It had been translated into 42 languages, appearing in 51 countries. The series was being shown 300 times per day across the world. Within the United States alone, the show had 134 different outlets.

Syndication led to a continual increase in the number of followers. Fan clubs, fanzines, and collectible objects increased to meet the need. By 1978, there were 371 fan clubs, 431 fanzines, innumerable collectibles, and some 30 annual conventions.

From 1972 to 1974, an animated version of *Star Trek* was shown on

Saturday mornings as part of the usual kiddie cartoons. There were 22 of these. Although the voices were those of the original actors, the animation was stilted and uninspiring. But it did garner more fans for the series.

THE STAR TREK MOVIES

Since 1972, when the first *Star Trek* convention drew 3,000 people, rumors circulated that the series would be brought back to TV as a new production, with the original cast. Tentative announcements from Paramount from time-to-time that production preparations were under way encouraged the fans to keep hoping. During the mid-1970s, Paramount was working with Gene Roddenberry on a feature film for television. Even though the sets were built and the story outline completed, they had a good reason to change their plans.

After the overwhelming success of *Star Wars,* Paramount decided that the day of the big-budgeted science fiction film had arrived. A decade after the cancellation of the TV series in 1969, *Star Trek: The Motion Picture* was released.

The original cast is present with several new faces added. Not only are those familiar faces older, but the time and budget for a full-length film gave the producers, writers, and director a much greater range of freedom to make *Star Trek* different in many respects. Also, the innovative work on special effects pioneered by George Lucas in *Star Wars* opened up an entirely new way of adding excitement that was previously unavailable.

During the TV series, fans had been accustomed to seeing minor changes in the appearance in the Enterprise, the props, and quite often the characters. But for the movies, an entirely new ship was built. It was eight feet long, four feet wide, and weighed 70 pounds. The ship was built around an aluminum frame which allowed it to be supported in five different places. The ability to change the points of support meant that the Enterprise could be filmed from any angle. As much detail as was possible was added—individual plates are visible on the outer surface, and there were miniature lights inside.

The set for the bridge was changed. The chairs were restyled and the instrument panels were more complicated and larger. A security station and an electronic map of the ship were new features.

All the areas familiar to *Star Trek* fans—sick bay, the engineering areas, the recreation deck, the officers' quarters, the hallways, and the transporter—were also transformed. All were made larger, more elaborate in detail, and much more technical in appearance. Even the costumes were changed—not only were the standard uniforms redesigned, but a larger variety of outfits were used. One-piece fatigues, specialized uniforms, and working uniforms gave the crew a more realistic appearance.

Unfortunately, the reviews were not outstanding and there was some dissatisfaction on the part of the audience: the dramatic characterizations, and the warm interactions between the major characters which was so vital to the TV series seemed to be missing in the motion picture. There seemed to be too much emphasis on special effects, fast-paced action, and breath-taking scenes. Despite these flaws, the first film earned over $175 million dollars. And when the sequel was released, the fans flocked to see *Star Trek II: The Wrath Of Khan* in the hope that the old charm and essence of the TV series had been recaptured. In the second film, their hopes were realized.

Filming for *The Wrath Of Khan* began in November 1981. Again, there were thoughts of producing a film for television which might possibly be released in theaters at a later time.

Harve Bennett, a talented and experienced TV producer, was offered the executive producer's position. He was the one responsible for developing the story line. After watching all 79 episodes of the TV series, he not only zeroed in on what ingredients were missing in the first film, but became fascinated with further developing a particular episode, "Space Seed," into the major plot. The episode was about Khan, the diabolical, genetic superman who was out to destroy Captain Kirk, and was a worthy adversary to oppose the crew of the Enterprise. The only problem was that Khan had been played by Ricardo Montalban, and it was thought that his role in the popular TV series *Fantasy Island* would prevent him from being in the film. Fortunately, this was not the case. Montalban loved the part of Khan and wanted to play it again in the movie. To have someone else play Khan was never considered—fans know the characters in all the episodes too well for that to be acceptable.

Nicholas Meyer was named the director. He also realized the life and death questions that were lacking in the first film, and incorporated the idealistic, humanistic striving, the loyalty and deep friendships which made fans care about the Enterprise and her crew. He was more concerned with portraying a story about human beings, struggling with their conflicts—internal and external—and facing the consequences of their actions, not a story about whizzing space ships and extravagant space battles.

The plot centers around the three major characters—Kirk, Spock, and Dr. McCoy—just as the TV series did. And they are faced with a frightening, powerful, and evil foe.

Only 43 days were allotted for shooting. The set was closed to anyone not involved in producing the film. The security was as tight as possible. All cast and production members were sworn to secrecy; no one divulged the plot. All members were required to wear I.D. badges with their photos. In spite of these precautions, props were stolen from the set continuously. Cast members found that they had to be careful about putting down even their I.D. badges—or they were stolen, too.

Halfway through the filming, rumors leaked out that the character Spock would die. A wave of protest erupted from fans. Although Leonard Nimoy had no say-so as to what would happen to Spock in the film, some of the anger from the fans was directed at him. In an attempt to alleviate his unenviable position, director Nick Meyer concocted a list of the different possible ways that the film could end (some in which Spock would not die). Rumors about the multiple endings dissipated the strident clamorings.

Since all of *Star Trek II* was filmed inside Paramount studios, the designers had a menagerie of sets to create: the bridges for three different space ships, a space station, a desert, an Eden cave, and various planetary settings. This task fell to Joe Jennings, Designer, Mike Minor, Art Director, and Lee Cole, Graphics Designer.

Their first chore was to redesign the bridge of the Enterprise. There were several problems with the bridge used in the first movie. The first bridge was constructed of one piece which limited the mobility of the camera, and the characters were often crowded into a very confining area. These problems were resolved by taking all of the 11 sections apart. This allowed the camera to move in close or to be placed in a number of locations. With the maneuverability of the camera, the bridge appears larger and the shots are much more interesting and poignant.

In the first film, the monitors on the bridge were 8 mm and 16 mm film loops. This caused two problems: the projectors that were used to run them were too noisy (all of the dialogue had to be dubbed in later), and very dim light was necessary when filming in order for the objects on the monitors to show up at all. Also, the monitors had to be filmed from a straight-on position, so the camera was limited in its movement. The result was a dreary, uninteresting bridge in the first movie.

For the second film, all the film loops were transferred to videotape. When video images are filmed by a motion picture camera, they appear to be vibrating and a special technique was utilized to overcome this obstacle. Not only did this allow for more lighting and camera movement, but the videotapes eliminated the need to replay an entire film loop every time there was a retake.

The bridge of the Enterprise was revamped into three different versions. In one scene, it is the Enterprise bridge; in another scene, it is the bridge of its sister ship, the USS Reliant; and in the beginning of the show, it appears as the simulator room in the Starfleet cockpit.

The Enterprise bridge was partially converted to the Reliant bridge by placing partitions in front of an elevator and a console. In the scene where Khan blows up the bridge of the Reliant, the designers created partitions for these sections made of paper, balsa wood, and gel. Paper decals and blinking lights behind gave the fragile frames the appearance of realism. These flimsy sections blew up quite convincingly during the scene.

More is seen of the Enterprise during the second movie and more attention was given to creating the illusion of a busy, bustling ship. For the first time, the audience sees the torpedo room and the inner rooms of the sick bay. Kirk's quarters were redesigned to look less sterile, to look more lived-in with a nautical-type of decor. The same set was used for Mr. Spock's quarters, but with a spiritual appearance, almost austere. Both of these sets were styled to match the well-known personality traits of these two characters.

The most difficult sets were the desert planet and the Eden cave. For the desert, they built 60-foot sand dunes which dropped off at a 45-degree angle. Frames were constructed, then packed with fuller's earth. This was covered with a sand substance which was blown about with large fans. During the filming on the desert set, the production crew wore goggles, surgical masks, and protective clothing. Also, on this set, they had to create Khan's living quarters which had to be used as an interior and an exterior set. Khan's quarters were decorated with objects that would have been available after the "Space Seed" episode.

Constructing the Eden set posed a puzzling situation. In the show, the Eden cave is a subterranean paradise, a product of Dr. Marcus' Project Genesis. A huge bubble-like structure was made to look like an onyx stone. It was designed so it could be composited with large matte paintings.

Throughout the filming, Dr. Richard Green of NASA's Jet Propulsion Laboratory, who aided Harve Bennett with the science logistics for the story line, continued to provide guidance. He reviewed all aspects of the show—the script, the designs, and the actual production in order to make sure that everything corresponded to current scientific thought.

For the special effects, director Nick Meyer chose to use the top-notch experts at the Industrial Light and Magic Company (ILM) first set up by George Lucas to produce the effects for *Star Wars*. All of the space battles, take-offs, and other spectacular scenes, which totaled 150, were done by ILM.

Normally, special effects are created after the live action has been filmed. But because of Star Trek's tight schedule, both were done at the same time by working from duplicate story boards. When necessary, ILM's camera crew would go down to Paramount Studios in Hollywood (from their San Francisco location) to film background plates of the various sets. This footage was composited with the special effects.

With a budget one third that of the first Star Trek movie, *The Wrath Of Khan* recreated once again the magic of the legendary TV series—and more, it added a tantalizing vista with spectacular effects never possible more than a decade ago.

Star Trek III: The Search For Spock began almost as a comedy of errors. Harve Bennett, the writer/producer of *Star Trek III,* wanted to use Leonard Nimoy as director for the new film but was given the erroneous impression that Leonard's prior contract from *The Wrath Of Khan* precluded him from working on *Star Trek III.* That he, in fact, would be "dead." During a casual conversation Harve mentioned to Leonard that he would have loved to have had him take a shot at directing the new film, but it was a shame that the contract stated he couldn't. Leonard didn't know what Harve was talking about, so Harve sent for a copy of the contract. No such mention was found. Harve then offered Leonard the job of director, and he accepted.

Leonard's extensive background in films and on stage more than qualified him for the task. Fans were also delighted with the prospect of having Leonard direct. Here, at last, we would have a director completely familiar with the "feel" of the original series. There was an additional bonus having Leonard direct. He knew the cast. This allowed for kind of a "short hand" in direction because Leonard already knew the skills and range of the actors. Because of this the film was brought in ahead of schedule and within the budget.

One difficulty with the new film concerned replacing actress Kirstie Alley, who played Lt. Saavik, with newcomer Robin Curtis. Fans generally felt that thought Robin did a good job in a difficult situation, Kirstie would have been a stronger screen presence.

The use of one word—*remember*—just before Spock's death in *The Wrath Of Khan,* successfully links the two films together and allows for the regeneration of a new Spock via the Genesis effect. Nimoy has expressed on several occasions the great personal emotional pain he felt during the filming of his death scene. He said it was very difficult for him to do and he was very happy to be, as it were, reborn.

Christopher Lloyd's performance as the Klingon commander Kruge was particularly outstanding.

Several new ships were introduced in this film, including: the Grissom research ship, the hybrid Klingon-Romulan Bird of Prey scout ship, the transwarp-drive Excelsior, and the Merchantman.

During the filming of *Star Trek III,* a great fire struck the Paramount lot, destroying the famous "New York street" that had been used in countless films for decades. Science fiction fans will remember it from the George Pal production of *War of the Worlds.* There was great fear that the fire could spread to Stage 15, where many of the complex Star Trek sets were housed. Yet even with fire burning, filming continued and the day's shooting was completed successfully.

Special effects were once again handled capably by the team at ILM who, this time around, produced the most convincing planetary explosion this writer has seen since *When Worlds Collide.*

Though *The Search For Spock* is loaded with special effects, the story centers around the characters as Kirk fights to save, but loses, his son, at the same time trying to prevent the capture of the Genesis process and deal with an unstable planet, an equally unstable McCoy, his hijacking of the Enterprise, the possible regeneration of his closest friend Spock, the destruction of the Enterprise, and a very angry Federation. Whew! The film ends with the destruction of the Enterprise and the saving of a regenerated Spock—but at what cost—and we must remember Saavik's haunting words . . . "And what is yet to come."

Strangely, there was almost no merchandising associated with this film and the fans were left hungry for toys and other merchandise. It is possible that the toy companies, badly burned by *Star Trek: The Motion Picture,* didn't want to take the risk. The FASA Company did produce a successful line of games linked to the later films. For collectors it meant turning their attention back to the TV toys that had been produced in great variety. These still have very strong investment potential, particularly since at about this time the Mego Corporation went out of business.

As effective as *Star Trek II* and *III* had been in attempting to recapture the feel of the *Star Trek* TV series, it wasn't until *Star Trek IV: The Voyage Home* that the effort really succeeded. Here at last was the real humor and spirit of the original show. The terrific script was a co-effort of Harve Bennett and Leonard Nimoy. The story dealt directly with serious 20th-century problems but contained the most humor and warmth of any of the Star Trek films.

Leonard Nimoy was once again faced with the twin burden of being both actor and director in the same film. And once again he brought the picture in on time.

Star Trek IV saw the return of Mark Leonard as Ambassador Sarek (Spock's father), Jane Wyatt as Amanda (Spock's mother), and Grace Lee Whitney as Yeoman Rand. The film also featured actress Catherine Hicks, whose performance as marine biologist Gillian Taylor helped make the film a success.

The film's only weak spot occurs in the beginning when yet another probe-spaceship comes from deep space to threaten earth. This overused plot device immediately makes one think of Nomad from the TV series and V'ger from *Star Trek: The Motion Picture.* However, once past this weak point the picture soars.

Unlike the other Star Trek films, which were shot entirely at the studio, *Star Trek IV* went on location in San Francisco, San Diego, and Monterey, California. Leonard, while continuing from the trilogy, wanted to give this film a completely different look.

The shooting of any quality film requiring large numbers of special effects is an enormous undertaking. This film had the additional problem of having to create believable-looking whales. Since no one, as yet, has an aquarium large enough to hold a full-size humpback whale, the whales had to be created.

A brilliant team of artists created the world's first free-swimming model of a whale. This four-foot model allowed greater freedom in shooting the underwater shots. The small whale was so well designed that the water pump designed to propel it forward wasn't needed; the swimming motion so perfectly copied the real thing that it swam by itself. The pump was used only when the whale had to dive or surface.

Where it was necessary to have larger whale models, the film crew used the astronaut training tank at McDonnel Douglas. One of the models was thirty feet long. When the small model was filmed at high speed and the film played back at normal speed, the whale looked real. When a human had to be in the same shot with a whale, larger life-size sections (models) were used.

One of the more difficult scenes was shot just after the Klingon Bird of Prey crash-lands in San Francisco Bay after a harrowing time-travel sequence. If you drive in the front gate at Paramount, directly ahead of you is a huge, painted sky. At the foot of this is the sunken parking lot that was flooded (after first removing the cars, of course) to create the aftermath of the crash. Wave and wind machines combined to produce a terrible and convincing storm. Added to this was a giant mechanical whale.

Another complex matte shot was filmed on the runway at Oakland Airport. This is the brief scene of the starbase at San Francisco with the Golden Gate Bridge in the background.

Still another complex sequence was created for the time-travel dream in which the actors' faces seem to float up from a fog and change before our eyes to other people. These effects were created by a company called Cyberware in Monterey, California. By using a slit scan technique and computers, they can create a styrofoam duplicate of a person's face in a few hours. The heads were then lighted to create dreamlike color and photographed, all with computers. It took a total of two weeks to complete this effect.

To create the new Enterprise used at the end of the film, it was necessary to repair the old model (destroyed in *The Search For Spock*). The model had been painted with a coating of rubber cement and spray painted black with pieces of foil to give it a ripped and torn look. This all had to be removed and the ship repainted with the new numbers added. The old bridge had a bit of reworking done to it for the final bridge shot.

In *Star Trek IV,* each of the original cast had their moment on-screen without it feeling forced. In all, this was a warm, wonderful film, very well received by both fans and the general public.

Once again, however, with the exception of a few reprints of old books and fan merchandise, almost no new products were offered to the public. Someone, again, was missing the boat.

THE CREATION OF STAR WARS

After six years, over 10 million dollars, and the work of hundreds of artists and technicians, George Lucas unleashed his spectacular film, *Star Wars.* In his early thirties, Lucas drew on his childhood love of *Flash Gordon,* fantastic science fiction, Westerns, mythology, and samurai movies to write and direct a movie which combines the excitement and adventure found in all of these forms. He created the type of film he wanted to see as a child—not based on science and logic, as many of the more recent science fiction shows are, but one based on sheer fantasy, a modern fairy tale where good confronts the forces of evil and wins. The story occurs in another galaxy far away from our own, and in a time long before our existence. This ploy allows Lucas to bring into being a unique universe where our laws of physics and aerodynamics could be ignored.

Following his tremendous success with *American Graffiti,* Lucas tried to buy the rights to produce a film based on the old TV series *Flash Gordon.* When he was unable to do so, he decided he would write his own fantasy adventure. Despite his box-office success with his first major film, Universal Studios turned down Lucas' proposal for a science fiction film. But Twentieth Century–Fox, which had been successful with its film *Planet of the Apes,* willingly backed him. After two years, Lucas had produced a script he was happy with.

In casting, he chose fairly unknown actors—Mark Hamill and Harrison Ford had very little experience. But each possessed the qualities that Lucas had envisioned for these characters. Ford had an arrogant, roguish appearance which suited Han Solo, and Mark Hamill had the wistful look of a youth yearning for adventure that was essential for Luke Skywalker. Even though Lucas' close friend Cindy Williams wanted the role of Princess Leia, Carrie Fisher was chosen because she possessed the combination of regal beauty and combative toughness necessary for the part.

Although Lucas balked at the thought of working with a big name actor, Twentieth Century–Fox insisted that one be selected in order to increase the film's box-office appeal. Talented veteran Alec Guiness eliminated any of Lucas' reservations of working with a big star: Guiness was found to be an invaluable asset and quite easy to work with.

One of the first steps to translating ideas of a fantastic nature on to film is to have a visualizer transform them into pictures. Numerous artists worked with George Lucas, but Ralph McQuarrie was the main one. His chores included the designing of the characters, costumes, props, and scenery to suit Lucas' ideas. From rough charcoal sketches to completed, polished story boards, McQuarrie provided the details of R-2 D-2, Threepio, The Jawas, the Death Star, and various landscapes of planets.

The visualizer creates a detailed sketch for every scene—showing the costumes, the comparative sizes of people and objects, and any special lighting. McQuarrie achieved Lucas' objective—a blend of the fantastic with the realism of a documentary.

The shooting began in the desert of Tunisia. Although Lucas was aiming for a documentary appearance, the lighting problems inherent in the desert led to artistic touches. Working on location caused a variety of problems as is often the case. The continually bad weather slowed the shooting, and the chief makeup artist, Stuart Freeborn, had to be hospitalized from food poisoning by the time they returned to London for further shooting. This meant that he was unavailable during the shooting of Mos Eisley's bar—the humorous, raucous scene with the largest and strongest collection of aliens shown in the film. Later, parts of this were reshot on the Utah desert with the expertise of makeup artist Rick Baker, making for a much more satisfying scene.

There were other problems: making Banthas, the mammoth-like creatures ridden by the sand people, that looked realistic, and building a transporter for the Jawas that was large enough. A compromise ended with only the lower portion being built and the remainder painted on matte backdrops.

Intermingled with days of exhilaration and a sense of accomplishment were days of frustration and depression. *Star Wars* took much more time and much more money than Lucas had anticipated. He felt that, despite the years and billions of dollars, he was constantly having to compromise—accepting a scene that wasn't quite the way he wanted it, cutting corners whenever possible. Lucas' involvement with the film was total—seven days a week, long working hours, week after week with painstaking care and attention to all details. Unlike more mature directors, Lucas was accustomed to controlling all aspects of his films, and this cost him in time and energy.

Besides all these obstacles, there were the overwhelming challenges of superimposing the special effects on to the film. Lucas and his producer, Gary Kurtz, understood the importance of impressive but believable effects.

Lucas set up the Industrial Light and Magic Company (ILM) to produce the special effects for *Star Wars.* It was originally located in Los Angeles, but was moved to San Francisco in 1978 when *The Empire Strikes Back* was being shot. ILM continues to produce the special effects for various major films, including *Star Trek II: The Wrath Of Khan, Raiders Of The Lost Ark,* and *Dragonslayer.*

During the filming of *Star Wars,* the optical department worked 24 hours a day, six days a week. Although Lucas selected more mature members for the operations, the artists, engineers, technicians, model-makers, and cinematographers were for the most part unusually young. Their average age was below 30.

In order to achieve the stunning and exciting effects that Lucas was after, hundreds of hours were necessary and these often resulted in only a few seconds for the film.

The most difficult challenge for special effects was the large space battle in *Star Wars* which takes up the last 20 minutes of the film. In order to acquire the authentic appearance of an aerial fight, Lucas and Kurtz videotaped a number of dogfights out of World War II movies. From these, they selected portions and transformed them on to a black and white 16 mm film. This patched-together sequence was used as a guideline to their battle scene. This film was converted to storyboards and the special effects people worked arduously to recreate the battle on film.

Special effects had to produce footage where there was an appearance of continuous motion, a number of ships banking and rolling, explosions, plus planets and stars in the background. The motion control camera created the illusions of tremendous speed. ILM has four of these computer-controlled cameras, but only two were used for *Star Wars.* The models are actually still during the filming. Instead, the cameras move at various speeds with numerous types of movements—the model can appear to bank, roll, and twist in innumerable styles and speeds.

A computer recorded each move so that any action could be duplicated if need be. The use of a lighted backdrop with a blue light and a red filter over the camera lens allowed for other objects or images to be superimposed onto the scene until everything was included.

Stop-motion animation was used extensively in *The Empire Strikes Back* although only briefly in *Star Wars* for the chess game sequence. The movements of the Tauntaun and the AT-AT Walker portions were accomplished by this method. This technique was similar to that used in animation except that each shot involves the model placed in a different pose.

Special effects also included the model-makers—to design the different types of space ships, the special creatures, such as Yoda and the Tauntaun; and the matte painters who produced the realistic backgrounds; the designers and builders of the special equipment; and the programmers for the computer software.

The scenes where charts are shown on monitors or screens, such as when the Rebel Pilots read the printouts of the Death Star, involved special effects people programming the machines to draw the diagrams. This technology allowed these to be produced much faster than if they had been done by hand. Still, months of work often resulted in only a few minutes of the film.

Certainly, the effects used in these films were revolutionary—new techniques that explored the possibilities available with our new advanced technology. Lucas was viewed as the pioneer in special effects.

The matching of a film with appropriate music which adds to the drama or humor offered an important challenge. Lucas chose the talented John Williams to write the score—an award-winning composer who had done the scores for all of Steven Spielberg's films, plus many other major pictures.

Lucas had already decided that he wanted an expansive score—one that had a sense of high adventure, strength, and soaring hope. Williams worked on the music for over a year, finally recording the 90 minute score in 14 different recording sessions with the London Symphony Orchestra. As Williams conducted the orchestra, the appropriate sequences of the film were shown on a screen behind the orchestra. This allowed him to match the speed of the music with the action and to know when to give the music extra emphasis. Of course, all this time and attention paid off: The *Star Wars* album as well as several of the singles from it became big hits.

The sound effects, recognized by fans as an integral and important aspect of the movie, were created by expert Ben Burtt. Most films average 200 sound effects; *Star Wars* has about 2000. Burtt provided alien languages (most of which are really nonsense, but several are actually Peruvian Inca dialect), the animalistic sounds of a Wookie, and the eerie buzzing noise of a light saber. Most of these were a blend of sounds, so that each was realistic, but unearthly.

Although there was no attempt at designing scientifically-sound space ships, there was great effort to make each and every one believable—as was true with all features in *Star Wars.* The strange silence of space so accurately portrayed in *2001* was abandoned for the more emotionally satisfying screeches of space ships zooming past each other, the deadly hum of laser guns, and the resulting explosions. The audience's sense of what an aerial war should look and sound like were fulfilled.

Another aspect of *Star Wars* completely different from other science fiction films is the usual appearance of a sterile, almost-perfect environment. In *Star Wars,* Lucas conjures up a universe which shows evidence of being recycled—Jawas collect and sell scrap metal, the Millennium Falcon shows signs of being patched and repaired. And the choice of ships seems to be as varied as our vehicles are today. Ships are designed for specialized tasks—speed, maneuverability, power, transportation, or heavy armament.

Even when the majority of the work was finished, Lucas balked, wanting to reshoot some of it again. When Twentieth Century–Fox said no to this request, Lucas and his editors cut and spliced the film together. The resulting show ran two hours.

REVENGE (RETURN) OF THE JEDI

The trilogy was completed by the release of *Return Of The Jedi* but somehow, it seems the Star Wars saga is far from over. The elements that changed the way movies were made began with Star Wars and by the third film, Lucas had perfected his formula. The dazzling effects, the aura of space and the realistic portrayal of healthy, robust heroes combined to make yet another blockbuster film.

To the collector's delight, the market has been deluged with articles pertaining to the third sequel. Because many of the toys from the first and second movies have been removed from the stores to make way for paraphernalia from *Return Of The Jedi,* many of these primary collectibles have been changing hands on the secondary market. Since many of these products are only three or four years old, most are in excellent condition and all of these factors produce a very lucrative market.

Furthermore, a most interesting change of mind has created the most valuable Star Wars collectible yet. Initially known as *Revenge Of The Jedi,* the movie began production with all of the props and incidentals printed with this title. Promotional packages, posters, crew jackets, scripts, clothing labels and more were manufactured by the hundreds.

Lucas and Twentieth Century felt, after getting into the filming, that the title connotated a negative image for the heroic warriors of The Jedi. The change was made to *Return of The Jedi,* and instantly a major collectible was born.

Since *Return of the Jedi* ended the movie trilogy, Lucasfilm concentrated on the television medium for the continuation of the *Star Wars* saga. There have been two Ewok television movies and two animated shows, "Ewoks" and "Droids."

There are two noticeable differences between *Star Wars* in this medium compared to how it was presented in the theatrical movies. The first one is production values. Television can't support the high costs for sets, makeup, special effects, etc. that a major motion picture can, and the Ewok movies reflect this lower standard. Animation, of course, is inherently cheaper to produce.

The second difference is that the television offerings seem aimed at a distinctly different audience, a much younger one, than those that were attracted to the movies. The major characters of the Ewok films are young children and both the animated series are standard Saturday morning cartoons, the traditional kiddie time slot.

It is unclear whether this shift in audience appeal was intentional or if the powers behind *Star Wars* never fully understood their original fan following, but the response on the part of merchandise manufacturers was definitly lukewarm. Very few licensees were prepared to risk their capital on the part of these new *Star Wars* ventures.

BUILDING A COLLECTION

Collecting *Star Trek* and *Star Wars* articles is a relatively new hobby. The oldest are no more than 20 years old; and most of the objects have been around for only a few years, or in some cases, just a few months. In most collecting fields, the objects are scores, or even hundreds of years old, with hobbyists having collected the objects for many, many years. Guidelines for grading condition, quality and value have usually been well established. With *Star Trek* and *Star Wars* collectibles, this is not the case.

Already, there are some entrenched ideas about what is valuable and what isn't, and many questions are still fluctuating. Collectors are well-advised to look to the future. Eventually, many of the accepted ideas in related fields will probably become part of the *Star Trek* and *Star Wars* hobby. For example, toys should be valued and cared for as toys;

the same with trading cards, paper objects, books, records, and cloth-ing.

For the beginner collector, it is best to arm yourself with as much knowledge as possible—about the shows and their productions, as well as the collectibles derived from them. Only through study and experi-ence will you be able to avoid the major pitfall faced by all collectors: paying too much for an item. Everyone does it eventually, even the most expert collectors and dealers. Don't let this discourage you. Accept your mistakes, but try to gain the expertise to keep these to a minimum.

With the field still so young, you will often gather contradictory infor-mation. At this point, you can either try to verify what you've learned or rely on your logic. The more books that are written about *Star Trek* and *Star Wars* collectibles, the more accurate the information will become. This has certainly been true in other fields.

The beginner collector should proceed slowly at first. For the most part, authenticity is not a problem for *Star Wars* collectors. *Star Trek* fans have a completely different set of circumstances: many unauthor-ized objects and duplicates of the original props are sold as being authentic.

Even without this problem, the beginner will find it wiser to take his time in order to let his collecting take some direction before accumulat-ing a number of items. As your collecting progresses, you'll find that certain items are out of place in your collection or that your interest in them has waned. But this varies from collector to collector. Some hobbyists will want to possess all the *Star Wars* items; others will find that they are only interested in certain types of objects, such as the books or the models. Whether you build a general or specialized collec-tion depends on you; both types of collections will be valuable. But if your budget limits you, you may find a specialized collection more suitable.

For the majority of items, dealers are the most viable source for older items. Also, there are a number of companies which create and sell authorized articles from current Star Trek projects.

For any articles which you can't locate in stores, science fiction dealers who specialize in *Star Trek* and *Star Wars* are ideal. They can provide you with the largest selection of items, including fan-produced and authorized articles. These dealers usually carry objects which date back to the beginning of the collecting phenomena for either of these productions.

Since there is not a great number of science fiction dealers who specialize in *Star Trek* and *Star Wars,* you probably won't be able to find one within driving distance unless you live in one of the larger cities. Still, call or visit any dealers in your area who carry science fiction articles, toys, books, trading cards, or paper collectibles, such as photographs and posters. Quite often, they will have a few *Star Trek* and *Star Wars* objects. Besides, they may be able to guide you to other dealers who would be helpful.

This book provides ample sources for locating dealers through magazines (in the listings), fanzines, etc. Subscriptions to these publications will be worthwhile. Not only are they fun to read, but they offer important information for collectors. Most of these have ads run by dealers or private collectors who are either looking to buy or sell *Star Trek* and *Star Wars* objects. Some even list their prices for certain objects. By comparing these prices with those in this price guide, you will be able to determine which dealers run high and which run low.

You may want to study several issues of the same publication before you decide to order from a particular dealer. Although most dealers are scrupulous, you should be wary. Many people out to make a quick buck look for the inexperienced and naive customer. If a particular dealer has consistently advertised in the same publication over a period of time, you can surmise that he is probably reputable.

Read the ad carefully. If descriptions of the articles are vague, you might be better off phoning and getting any information you need. Some of these dealers offer detailed lists or catalogs which require at least a self-addressed, stamped envelope, if not a nominal fee. Before ordering, make sure you know what their procedures involve. Will they give a refund if you are dissatisfied with an object and want to return it? You should buy only from dealers who give you that option. But prepare to be reasonable: returnables should be sent back within three days, packaged carefully, and in the same condition as when you received them.

If you don't want to encounter any delays, a money order will expedite your order, since most dealers will not ship anything to a first-time customer until their check clears the bank. If you show yourself to be a reliable and regular customer, the dealer may become less stringent about this. Some of them may accept credit cards, but you may have to inquire about this.

Because of the relative newness of these collectibles, you should make an effort to purchase objects only in outstanding condition. The exceptions should be original props, scripts or other objects that you would expect to show signs of wear and tear.

Instead of providing price lists, some dealers will ask you to send a want list. Since most dealers don't know which pieces they will have available from one month to the next, many of them prefer taking want lists instead of running large ads listing their entire stock, or publishing their own catalogs. The want lists are particularly helpful to the more advanced collector who is looking for some hard-to-find items.

Your want lists should include your name, address, and phone number, plus a full description of what pieces you want. Indicate what you want by name and any identification numbers or dates. If you are looking for a particular size, variation, or color, include this information, also. The dealer will check his stock. If he has the piece or pieces, he'll inform you of his prices and terms of sale. Obviously, you should not list a large number of articles you're not seriously intending to purchase. This type of list will discourage the dealer from helping you or taking you seriously. It would be much better to list several pieces that you want and maybe several alternatives if these are not available.

If the dealer doesn't have any of the pieces that you want, he'll probably inform you that he has placed your list in his file. Then, if he receives a piece that is on your want list, he will contact you. As to whether he will keep the piece for you until he hears from you depends on whether or not you've been a long-standing customer of his. This really varies from dealer to dealer. Sometimes, the dealer will know of someone who has the piece for sale and can secure it for you. He may charge you a commission for such a sale, so be sure to find out beforehand. The more dealers you work with, the greater the chance you will have of finding the pieces you want.

When you find a dealer who provides satisfactory service, you can use him as your main source for collectibles. But as your collection grows, you will begin to want more to gather the difficult-to-find articles. There are various ways to expand your resources.

Private parties—either collectors or persons disposing of items no longer wanted—can be a source of great bargains, but the risks are much greater than with most other sources. A collector or private party may be unwilling to guarantee satisfaction and may be more likely to misjudge condition. Quite often, a private party will have only a few pieces he wants to sell and will know very little about them. His ad may not include pertinent information, because he doesn't realize it is of importance. Obviously, such persons may be willing to sell their pieces for well under the market price either because of ignorance or inexperience. Collectors can also be a great supply of bargains. Sometimes they must sell their collections quick in order to raise cash for an emergency. They don't have the time to wait for a good offer in such cases.

There may come a time when you will want to or need to sell your collectibles—either a few pieces or an entire collection. Just as in buying, there are various avenues open to you, each with its advantages and disadvantages. Your circumstances and how many items you have to sell may dictate the method you choose. If you are forced to sell your items quickly because you need to raise cash in a hurry, you should anticipate a loss, though this is not always the case. Any time you have to sell a collectible of any type quickly, you dramatically decrease your chances of selling the item at a profit or breaking even. It takes time to sell a collectible—time to shop around for an eager buyer who is willing to pay close to book price or higher. To sell a collectible at a profit, you normally need to hold on to an article for years (to let it appreciate in value) and sell it at your leisure.

The most common ways to sell science fiction collectibles are to a dealer outright, on consignment, through an auction, to private collectors through advertising (either with a stated price or with a mail bid), and by answering want ads. The easiest way to sell is through an auction, but this method is suitable only for large collections of the more prestigious collectibles.

If you're in a great hurry to raise cash, selling to a dealer is the quickest method, but you will be disappointed if you expect to receive the full value for your articles. Buying from the public is the best source of collectibles for dealers. But before you take the time to pack your items off to a shop, you should call to find out if they carry science fiction articles. Some dealers will have little interest in such items, so you would just be wasting your time. A dealer specializing in the field is more likely to offer a higher amount for your collection than a local dealer who doesn't specialize.

Try to arrange to visit the shop at the hours they're least likely to be busy. Pack each piece carefully—not only for protection, but to impress the dealer with the idea that you value your pieces. If he thinks you just want to get rid of them in a hurry, he'll assume he can buy them from you at a bargain. It's probably best not to appear to be overly eager or anxious about obtaining immediate cash for the same reason. With a large collection, you could take in just several pieces; then, if the dealer is interested in the entire collection, he may very well visit your home to give you an estimate of his buying price.

You'll have greater success for a satisfactory sale when you can take your time. Get estimates from a number of dealers—their offers can vary greatly. You never know if a dealer has a customer eager to purchase the exact pieces you have or whether he has only a few customers for these particular types of objects. There can be numerous reasons why one dealer will offer you a low price while another will offer you considerably more. One dealer might have exceeded his budget for buying from the public or be overstocked at the moment. Another might have a low inventory and be looking for something to fill his shelves. You never can know until you've taken the time to talk to them and receive an estimate. Their offers will reflect their particular business and their clientele.

Just remember: You may have to pay 80% to 100% of the market value for a piece, but a dealer couldn't do that and stay in business. He will rarely offer you more than 40% to 60% of book price. And you will rarely receive a better percentage from a dealer by trying to haggle with him, because he has usually figured out just how much he must make on his articles in order to pay his overhead and still make a small profit.

If it irks you to receive only half of the book price for your items, you could place them with a dealer on consignment though most dealers won't bother with smaller items. This is a much slower method, but you will receive a higher price. If you don't mind waiting months for your pieces to sell, you can set the price yourself. Make sure you know the market value of your item before you agree on a selling price. If you agree to let a dealer sell an item for $50 when it is really worth $75, he could easily sell it for the $75 and pocket the extra $25 without you ever being the wiser.

You should insist upon a written agreement which stipulates the selling price, how long you agree to leave it on consignment, the amount for his commission (which will probably be about 20%), and for how much he will insure your item from damage or theft. Your regular insurance will not cover your piece when it is in a dealer's shop.

If you are determined to obtain full book value on your items, advertising in a collector's publication with national distribution is an effective method, but one which can be very time consuming. You will probably get faster results than if you place items on consignment with a dealer, but you must expect to put in quite a bit of effort. By reaching a large, but select readership, you will increase your chances for some excellent sales. But even if you sell your articles at full book price, you will have expenses which will detract from your profit.

Except for the most common pieces, many articles that are priced at market value or slightly under will sell immediately after the publication comes out—some by telephone perhaps even that very afternoon. Common pieces that you price below market value may be snatched up quickly, also. Some items may take weeks to sell; whereas some pieces will not attract any offers at all.

You can choose to either state prices for each piece or offer to take mail bids. Either way, be sure to state your terms of sale clearly and fully. You will need to list enough information so that the readers can determine exactly which pieces and variations you have. List the names, any numbers or dates, the sizes, colors and any trademarks. You will attract a greater response if your ad is easy to read, includes all necessary information, and looks professional. Many advertisements are poorly written because the advertiser was trying to save space (and thus, advertising money) or was just plain careless. You can try to conserve space and still present a professional-looking ad. If you have a number of pieces of the same size, group them under a head indicating the size. The same method can be done with other important traits. If all of your pieces are in top condition, you can just state that once in the ad; but if most of your pieces are in top condition, with some in less than mint, you could place asterisks next to those works and state that the asterisks indicate pieces in less than mint condition. Experiment with what you will include in your ad; try writing it in several different ways. If you leave out some crucial information, such as your address (which has been done), you will have incurred the cost of an ad without the benefits. This will cut into the profit you will make on selling your collectibles.

As the checks arrive, deposit them in your bank account and allow ten days to make sure they clear before shipping any pieces off. It might be a good idea to put this stipulation in your ad. With money orders and drafts, you will not need to wait. Duplicate checks which arrive late or bids that didn't win should be returned immediately. You should expect to receive inquiries as well as offers to buy by phone and by mail. So keep a full list of all pertinent information handy to the phone. And make sure you have enough time set aside to answer written queries.

Some collectors sell their items by answering want ads in national collector publications. Usually, these ads are run by people who are looking for specific pieces. They quite often receive offers from people selling pieces at very low prices who are trying to dispose of their collections quickly and easily. But sometimes, these advertisers are searching for scarce or rare pieces that they have been unable to find and are willing to pay well above book price for such items.

The method you choose will depend on how quickly you need to sell your collectibles, how much you need to obtain from a sale, and just how much time and risk you're willing to take.

When buying, the best sources are the conventions. Both science fiction or *Star Trek* conventions are enjoyable and stimulating for the collector. *Star Trek* and *Star Wars* objects can be found at any of these affairs. All popular science fiction conventions are publicized in the publications mentioned earlier.

The major activity at the cons is buying and selling. In fact, many of the dealers that attend the conventions subsist completely by selling their wares at such affairs. You will find a larger variety of *Star Trek* and *Star Wars* collectibles than you have probably seen previously. Some of the rarest items will be on display.

The best advice is to proceed with caution. Often, beginners will be so excited about coming across a desirable item that they will pay whatever price is asked without scanning any other booths to see if it can be bought at a better price. Quite often, patience pays off. Remember: many of the major science fiction dealers will be present. Many scarce items will show up at one or more of the dealers' booths. So use your judgment and take the time to find the best deal.

Probably, the most sought-after objects are original props from any of the productions. Unless you know a dealer is reputable, plan to skip this kind of purchase. Original props are very easy to duplicate and very difficult to authenticate.

Most of the original props are from the *Star Trek* productions, but apparently there are *Star Wars* objects also. Prior to the release of *Star Wars,* several thousand film stills, transparencies, posters, and other *Star Wars* objects, such as space ship models, were stolen from the company's office. Little has been heard of these, though you can be sure that they have been sold to collectors.

The most valuable *Star Trek* props are from the TV series, but ones from the movies are also desirable. Even though there was tight security on the set during the shooting of *The Wrath Of Khan,* numerous props were taken. Some of the props are sold by the actors or other people involved in the production. A charity auction in Stamford,

Connecticut at the premiere of *The Wrath Of Khan* offered original production art and sketches, photographs, oil paintings, uniform insignias, jewelry, belts, and phasers. Spock's ears (there are a number of these since new ones were used when they were reapplied) sold for $1025, preproduction art pieces for around $400, and phasers for $200.

Props also include scripts, writers' guides, Tribbles, costumes, and any other objects used during the production. Original scripts are favorites with collectors; they were used by the actors and production people.

Fans love these, particularly if they have any markings. The TV series was done with such a tight deadline that changes in dialogue were often penciled right on the script. Actors often made notations as to where they were to stand and walk, and any ideas on how to interpret certain passages. Some of the stars from the show have even given dealers permission to sell their personal scripts. Walter Koening wrote a handwritten note on each title page of his scripts, declaring them to be authentic.

"The Star Trek Bible," which was a guide for writers of the TV series, is also popular. This is a twenty-page, mimeographed leaflet (not photocopied) which spells out *Star Trek* folklore—background of the characters, definitions of terms, and a general description of the *Star Trek* universe. Additional pages were added as the series progressed.

Due to various circumstances, there are other articles which are highly desirable. Fan-produced materials for *Star Wars* is very limited due to the stringent enforcement of copyright laws. These articles are valued by many fans. Some imitations of the *Star Wars* robots were imported from the Orient, but it is uncertain as to whether these are collected for their *Star Wars* qualities or not. Presently, any articles with the title *The Revenge of the Jedi* (which was finally changed to *The Return Of The Jedi*) will have much higher values than many similar items due to their rarity. These include any promotional materials, posters, and patches.

When buying *Star Trek* and *Star Wars* items, you will probably find that the earliest and the first of any objects are some of the most valuable. For example, the program booklet for the first *Star Trek* convention in 1972 is considered to be rare and valuable, as is the first printing of the book *The Making Of Star Trek*.

Whatever your goals are in collecting—accumulating a massive amount (some fans have a warehouse full), or just a few special items for decorative purposes, the extent of your delight can match your efforts and ambitions. This is still an open field where new items are still being uncovered and great bargains still abound.

CONDITION AND CARE

In collecting *Star Trek* and *Star Wars* items, condition is of great importance. You should not buy any items which are not in the best of condition. The only exceptions are original props and very rare items. With original props, condition is of no importance whatsoever; they are expected to show signs of use. With rare items, you should still attempt to purchase high quality material, but when this is impossible be ready to accept what is available.

Since the hobby is relatively new, articles in mint condition or very close to that standard, are readily available. In all of the collecting hobbies, condition has dictated a vast difference in value—the same items can be either very valuable or worthless, because of their condition. In the future, this probably will be the case with *Star Trek* and *Star Wars* articles.

For toys or items which come encased in boxes, most avid collectors leave them unopened. This is especially true of the models. This may seem somewhat strange to the novice, but if you think of an item's possible value in the future, you'll understand the importance of such precautions. If you wanted to buy one of the starship models ten or even twenty years from now, you would most likely be willing to pay more for the models in an unopened box than a model already opened and put together. Most collecting fields have always given a premium to items that were identical to their state when they left the factory. If this seems an unsatisfactory manner in which to collect, you could compromise by buying one model to keep encased, and another to open and enjoy.

If you do open your boxed articles or purchase one which has a box, be sure to keep the box. An item with its original box will have more value than one without and often the box is worth more than the article. In the future, these may be important to collectors because of the wealth of information about the toys that are printed on the panels.

An operating toy or object will have a somewhat greater value than a nonworking one. Most collectors don't play with their toys or objects, so they usually will work. If you have a toy or object which doesn't operate, you could consider having it repaired. If the repair causes damage to the finish or any of the parts, this will detract from the value.

Of course, repairing it yourself could easily make scratches, or dents if you don't know what you're doing. So, have someone who is skilled at this sort of thing make the repair if you feel you aren't adept at it.

For most articles, it is very important that all the components are present. If you're not sure, check any information on the boxes if available. You should also check for any signs of chips, scratches, or even very small nicks. Look at each item from all angles—the original factory finish should still be present.

Collectibles made of paper present other problems. Age and abuse can deteriorate paper items quite easily. Once deterioration occurs, any repair can only restore its appearance (possibly), but not the item's value. So it is of great importance that you purchase articles that are still in good condition, because they will deteriorate some no matter what you do. Some of the earlier booklets or promotional materials can be expected to show signs of age, but don't bother with recent articles that have frayed edges or are even slightly dog-eared.

Storing paper items properly will keep them in the best possible condition. Keep them away from direct sunlight, moisture, and dust. Although it is quite common for collectors and dealers to store cards stacked with a rubber band wrapped around them, this is not a good idea since this will damage them after a period of time. Cards are best kept in special albums (see Baseball Hobby publications). Posters are best framed or shrink wrapped, and books and magazines should be kept in glass-encased shelves or in special plastic covers. Be sure to buy the type available in hobby shops or hobby publications—regular plastic can adhere to paper after a period of time. Also, be sure to never use any kind of tape on any paper collectibles in order to secure them into albums.

Try to store or display your collectibles where they are free from any detrimental effects of the environment. Care taken now to keep them in the best possible condition will benefit you later—your collection will retain its charm as well as its value.

CONVENTIONS

In the early 70s, before *Star Trek* conventions became separate entities, there had been a growing *Star Trek* following at comic and science fiction conventions. In 1972 the first convention devoted entirely to *Star Trek* was held in New York City. It was an overwhelming success. The organizers at this first convention were a mixture of professional convention organizers and dedicated fans. The convention became an annual affair and grew steadily until in 1974 a break occurred between the professional and fan organizers, each setting up their own convention. In the meantime, other individuals around the country, both fan and professional organizers, had been saying to themselves "Hey, I can do that too!" The convention phenomenon has grown steadily, until today there is a convention virtually every weekend in some part of the country.

Today conventions are generally mixed media in nature reflecting the diverse interests of today's fan. (Lucasfilm does not allow the name *Star Wars* to be used in conjunction with a convention.) Actors and other personalities associated with *Star Trek* and other TV shows and movies are present as guests at the larger conventions. In addition *Star Trek* episodes and movies as well as other films are shown on 16 mm film and/or videotape and there are usually other activities, trivia contests, costume contests, and of course there is the dealers room. The dealers room at a large convention can be one of the best places to buy, sell and trade collectibles. You can inspect the items first hand and prices are sometimes more flexible.

The hardest thing about going to a convention is finding one! With very few exceptions thers are no annual shows held predictably at the same time each year. Conventions are generally unique events with different organizers, even within the same city, and having no association with each other. If you have a local comic book or science fiction bookstore, they can often supply you with information on upcoming conventions in your area. You may be disapointed in these, however, if you are looking for a large show with guests and an extensive dealers room. Local conventions are often little more than informal fan gatherings with no guests and only one or two local dealers. To find a large convention the best sources are the various national science fiction oriented magazines. These often have a convention listing and/or ads for upcoming conventions. It should be noted that the larger conventions are confined almost entirely to bigger cities that have the facilities and population needed to support such activity. So if you don't live near a major city you may need to travel to a convention once you find one!

DEALER DIRECTORY

Acme Space Products
2430 West Shore Rd.
Warwick, RI 02888

Alternate Worlds
ST & SW
6017 Snowdens Run Rd.
Sykesville, MD 21784

Bags Unlimited
Collection, Protection, and
Storage Devices
53 Canal St.
Rochester, NY 14608

Bud Plant Inc.
New Book Seller
P.O. Box 1886
Grass Valley, CA 95945

Fandom Computer Services
The Fandom Directory
P.O. Box 4278
Norton AFB, CA 92409

FASA Corp
ST Games
P.O. Box 6930
Chicago, IL 60680

H & R Records
ST & SW Dealer
717 Lilian Way
Los Angeles, CA 90038

**Intergalactic Comics &
Collectibles**
109 Semoran Rd.
Fern Park, FL 32730

**Intergalactic Trading Company
Inc.**
ST & SW Dealer
P.O. Box 1516
Longwood, FL 32750

**Jerry Ohlingers Movie Material
Store, Inc.**
ST & SW Film Stills and
Photos
120 W. 3rd St.
New York, NY 10012

John F Green
Model Kits from ST
1872 Carol Dr.
Fullerton, CA 92633

Lincoln Enterprises
Licensed Commercial Items for
ST
P.O. Box 69470
Los Angeles, CA 90069

Mark Macaluso
Gum Card Sets
43 Texas St.
Rochester, NY 14606

New Eye Studio
ST & SW Dealer
P.O. Box 632
Willimatic, CT 06110

Southern Fantasies
ST Dealer
3377-B Lawrenceville Hwy.
Tucker, GA 30084

Star Fleet Printing Office
ST Dealer
P.O. Box 20215
Baltimore, MD 21204

Star Land
ST & SW
P.O. Box 19413
Denver, CO 80219

Star Tech
ST & SW Dealer
P.O. Box 456
Dunlap, TN 37327

Starpost Enterprise
ST
RR #1, Box 744
New York, NY 10022

Starstation Aurora
ST Dealer
P.O. Box 750
Holyoke, MA 01040

T-K Graphics
ST Paraphernalia
P.O. Box 1951
Baltimore, MD 21203

TKRP the Best in the Galaxy
SW Licensed Merchandise
P.O. Box 23114
Lansing, MI 48909

Trek Clipping Exchange
ST Services
2829 Frankel Blvd.
Merrick, NY 11566

PUBLICATIONS

Comic Buyers Guide
700 E. State St.
Iola, WI 54990

Datazine
P.O. Box 19413
Denver, CO 80219

Intergalactic News
P.O. Box 1516
Longwood, FL 32750

L'Affiche
2352 S. Osage
Wichita, KS 67213

The Official Star Trek Fan Club
P.O. Box 111000
Aurora, CO 80011

Starlog Magazine
475 Park Ave. South
New York, NY 10016

ABOUT THE PRICES IN THIS BOOK

Thousands of collectibles are listed with prices. A price range is given for each article. This range shows the lowest and highest selling prices for this particular piece at the time this book was compiled. These prices are retail selling prices—what dealers sell these items for to the public. Prices were determined by averaging the prices of actual sales or sale offers from across the country. Sales at secondary sources, such as flea markets and garage sales, which can be much higher or much lower, were not included in the averaging of prices.

These prices should be used as guidelines and not as set laws. Just as in buying other articles, you can find differences in prices by shopping around. You will discover prices much higher and much lower than these averages, but these will be exceptions, not the rule. It is not unusual for very high or very low prices to be paid at auctions. Also, the prices dealers charge will vary depending on their volume of business, their overhead, and the type of customers they have. A dealer who pays high rent for an attractively situated shop may have to charge more to meet his high overhead; another dealer may have such a large number of customers that he can afford to make a smaller margin of profit on each piece, so his prices may be lower.

Also, a 20% to 30% variation from these prices might indicate a changing trend for that particular piece, especially if you keep encountering prices consistently higher or lower. In fact, you should remain aware of any fluctuations in prices as this may affect your strategy as to what you'll purchase, and when.

These prices are those at which dealers sell *Star Trek* and *Star Wars* collectibles to the public. Dealers will not buy them from you at these prices. In order to meet their overhead expenses and still make a profit, dealers buy at wholesale—which is about 40% to 60% of the retail price. This can vary, too, depending on the dealer's circumstances.

HOW TO USE THIS BOOK

The articles in this book are divided into two major sections: *Star Trek* and *Star Wars* collectibles. Under each section, items are listed in groups alphabetically by type of item, such as button, poster, toy. The Table of Contents lists each topic grouping. Within the group, each individual item is listed either alphabetically by its most common name or short descriptive term, chronologically by issuing date, or alphabetically by manufacturer. Thorough descriptions are given when possible in order to aid you in positively identifying your pieces. Manufacturer (when known) is given, with color, size, date and any other pertinent information.

Star Trek

STAR TREK LISTINGS

ACTION FIGURES

This section is divided into two categories: large and small action figures. The two categories are organized chronologically by TV show and movie. Values listed are for dolls in their original packaging. Values for unpackaged dolls are 50% to 75% of that for packaged ones.

LARGE ACTION FIGURES

Star Trek **TV action figures:** 8″ tall, Mego Corporation, 1975. These were issued in 3 different series and values are based on scarcity of each series. A small hoard of first series dolls surfaced in Canada in 1985, keeping these values artificially low until the supply has been depleted. All are fully costumed with movable joints and hand equipment.

FIRST SERIES:

	Price Range	
☐ **Captain Kirk,** with phaser, communicator & belt	15.00	25.00
☐ **Mr. Spock,** with phaser, communicator, belt and tricorder	15.00	25.00
☐ **Dr. McCoy,** with tricorder	30.00	50.00
☐ **Mr. Scott,** with phaser, communicator & belt	40.00	60.00
☐ **Lt. Uhura,** with tricorder	25.00	40.00
☐ **Klingon,** with phaser, communicator & belt	20.00	30.00

SECOND SERIES:

☐ **Cheron,** black and white alien	65.00	100.00
☐ **Gorn,** reptilian alien	85.00	125.00

McCoy, 8″ TV Action Figure

	Price Range	
☐ **The Keeper,** blue, barefooted alien in light colored robe	65.00	100.00
☐ **Neptunian,** green amphibian with webbed feet and hands..............................	75.00	100.00

THIRD SERIES: The price on these dolls has risen astronomically, especially for those in original packaging.

☐ **Andorian,** blue, antennaed alien	150.00	300.00
☐ **Mugato,** horned head alien	150.00	250.00
☐ **Romulan,** with gold helmet	150.00	300.00
☐ **Talosian,** yellow robe and boots	150.00	200.00

Star Trek: The Motion Picture **figures:** 12″ tall, Mego Corporation, 1979. All are fully costumed with posable joints and hand equipment.

☐ **Captain Kirk,** with phaser and belt buckle ...	40.00	50.00
☐ **Mr. Spock,** with phaser and belt buckle	40.00	50.00

Decker—Large STTMP Action Figure, from Mego

	Price Range	
☐ **Decker,** with phaser and belt buckle	75.00	125.00
☐ **Ilia,** with white shoes and necklace	30.00	45.00
☐ **Arcturian,** fleshy head, beige uniform	30.00	45.00
☐ **Klingon,** ridged head, uniform	45.00	65.00

SMALL ACTION FIGURES

Star Trek: The Motion Picture, Mego Corporation, 1979, 3¾" tall, fully posable.

FIRST SERIES:	Price Range	
☐ **Captain Kirk**	5.00	10.00
☐ **Mr. Spock**	5.00	10.00
☐ **Ilia**	8.00	15.00
☐ **Decker**	8.00	15.00
☐ **Dr. McCoy**	10.00	25.00
☐ **Scotty**	8.00	15.00

SECOND SERIES: Made primarily for overseas markets. Some were available in the U.S. through Sears mail-order.

☐ **Betelgeusian,** blue-snooted alien with black hat	30.00	100.00
☐ **Megante,** multi-lipped alien with black hood ..	30.00	100.00
☐ **Klingon**	30.00	100.00
☐ **Rigellian,** purple alien	30.00	100.00
☐ **Zarante,** insectoid creature	30.00	100.00
☐ **Arcturian,** fleshy-faced alien	30.00	100.00

Star Trek III: The Search for Spock, ERTL Corporation, 1984, 3¾" tall, fully posable with hand equipment.

☐ **Captain Kirk,** with communicator	4.00	5.00
☐ **Mr. Spock,** with phaser	5.00	6.00
☐ **Mr. Scott,** with phaser	3.00	4.00
☐ **Klingon leader,** with pet	3.00	4.00

ARTWORK

It would be improper to write a book about collectibles without mentioning original works of art. At the same time, it is impossible to catalog art because it is by nature unique. When considering Star Trek art as a collectible it is, first of all, best to use the same criteria you would use for any other category: does it appeal to you? This might be both difficult and easy at the same time because Star Trek art is so diverse. The word *art* means a painting to most people, but this overlooks a vast assortment of skills and crafts. At a large Star Trek convention you can find sculptures, ceramics, jewelry, needlepoint, leatherwork, and much more that fits into the category of art.

When buying an item with an eye toward future collectibility, however, you may wish to consider a few things. Is the piece well made? Is the person that made it a good craftsman as well as a good artist? Does the piece have a unique quality? Does it fit in with your other collectibles? Is the artist well known in his or her field? Has the work ever been published, say as a book cover?

Some very well-known artists in the fantasy and science fiction art field have done artwork for published Star Trek items.

Prices range from a few cents for a fan-made craft item to several thousand dollars for a painting by a nationally known artist.

BLUEPRINTS

	Price Range	
☐ **Almeida Class Heavy Cruiser-Freighter,** M. Morrissette, five sheets, 8″ x 22″	4.00	5.00
☐ **Animated Freighter Blueprint Set,** Geoffrey Mandel, 12 sheet set	4.00	6.00
☐ **Aurora,** alien vessels from *Star Trek,* the TV show, set of two sheets, 16″ x 22″	4.00	6.00
☐ **Avenger Class,** 1983, D.J. Nielsen, 6 sheet set, Reliant	8.00	10.00
☐ **Bridge Blueprints,** M. McMaster, 1st edition, vertical cover format, blue ink	20.00	30.00
☐ **2nd Edition,** horizontal format, red and blue cover	10.00	15.00
☐ **3rd Edition,** black ink, horizontal format cover	10.00	12.00
☐ **Caracal Class Command Cruiser,** T. Guenther, shows interiors and exteriors, twelve sheets, 8½″ x 28″	10.00	15.00
☐ **Decater,** Starstation Aurora, one sheet, several different ships	3.00	4.00
☐ **Detroyat Class Heavy Destroyer,** M. Morrissette, general plans, six sheets, 10½″ x 28″	5.00	6.00

	Price Range	
☐ **Dreadnought,** Allie C. Peed III, ten sheets . . .	10.00	12.00
☐ **Drone Blueprints,** four sheets, shows sensor carrying drone which has ability to travel at light velocity and defend or self destruct as needed	5.00	6.00
☐ **Durance Cargo Tug Class Starship,** T. Guenther, exterior and cutaway views, five sheets, 8″ x 17″	5.00	6.00
☐ **DY 500,** Starstation Aurora, one sheet	3.00	4.00
☐ **Enterprise,** pilot film version from television show, two sheet set, shows detailed exterior	6.00	8.00
☐ **Enterprise,** regular season from television show, two sheet set	6.00	8.00
☐ **Enterprise Blueprints,** Franz Joseph, rolled edition, few produced prior to professional production by Ballantine Books, desirable collectible	150.00	175.00

Enterprise Blueprints, Ballantine Books

	Price Range	
☐ **Enterprise Blueprints,** Professional Edition, Franz Joseph, Ballantine Books, Brown Pouch	40.00	75.00
☐ **Enterprise Blueprints,** from "Star Trek—The Role Playing Game," boxed, with book of description, set of nine, 22″ x 33″, F.A.S.A.	15.00	20.00
☐ **Enterprise Construction Plans,** A. Everhart, four sheets, shows deck plans for the construction in outer space of the U.S.S. Enterprise, 18″ x 24″	6.00	8.00
☐ **Enterprise Exterior Profiles,** 24″ x 60″, Starcraft Productions	6.00	8.00
☐ **Excelsior,** Starstation Aurora, eight sheets, white plastic pouch, blue cover sheet	9.00	11.00
☐ **Federation Reference Series,** Vol. 1 Starfleet Printing Office, fan made, Booklet form	4.00	6.00
☐ **Federation Reference Series,** Vol. 2 Starfleet Printing Office, fan made, Booklet form	4.00	6.00
☐ **Federation Reference Series,** Vol. 3 Starfleet Printing Office, fan made, Booklet form	4.00	6.00
☐ **Federation Reference Series,** Vol. 4 Starfleet Printing Office, fan made, Booklet form	4.00	6.00
☐ **Federation Size Comparison Charts,** Special Edition, 2 sheets, Starstation Aurora	6.00	8.00
☐ **As above, Volume II**	6.00	8.00
☐ **Galileo Shuttlecraft Plans,** A. Everhart, 2 sheets, exterior and cutaway views, 18″ x 24″	3.00	4.00
☐ **Glenn Class Fleet Survey Vessel,** four sheets	5.00	8.00
☐ **Gorn Blueprints,** depicts exterior of the Gorn ship, two sheets, 8½″ x 14″	4.00	6.00
☐ **Hornet Class Starship,** fan produced, 7 sheets	10.00	12.00
☐ **Katanga Class Klingon Vessel,** exterior profile, Starcraft Productions	7.00	9.00
☐ **Klingon Blueprints,** M. McMaster, supplement detail sheet, exterior and interior, all levels and decks, set of eight, 13″ x 29″	8.00	10.00
☐ **Klingon D-7 Blueprints,** from "Star Trek—The Role Playing Game," boxed, with book of description, set of six, 22″ x 33″, F.A.S.A.	11.00	13.00

	Price Range	
☐ **Klingon K'torr Blueprints,** interior and exterior plans	9.00	10.00
☐ **Klingon Scout Vessel,** from Star Trek III: The Search for Spock, fan produced, 6 sheets	10.00	12.00
☐ **Merchantman,** five sheets	6.00	9.00
☐ **Regula I Space Station,** fan produced, 5 sheets	8.00	10.00
☐ **Renner,** four sheets	4.00	6.00
☐ **Romulan Bird of Prey Cruiser,** M. McMaster, fan produced, five sheets	6.00	8.00
☐ **Saladin Class Destroyer Scout,** deck by deck plans, Jeffries tube plans, inside view of space warp propulsion unit, set of nine sheets, Starcraft Productions	8.00	9.00
☐ **Size Comparison Chart,** showing the exterior designs of all the ships of Star Trek, includes: Romulan, Tholian, Klingon D-7, Enterprise	3.00	4.00
☐ **Star Trek: The Motion Picture Blueprints,** by David Kimble, shows exterior detail only of the Enterprise bridge, Klingon ship and bridge, Vulcan shuttle, travel pod and more, blue pack, out of print	15.00	30.00
☐ **Star Trek: The Motion Picture Blueprints,** unauthorized reprint, comes in paper envelope	7.00	12.00
☐ **Vadenda Class Freighter Plans,** very large 12 page blueprint set of a new ship in the Star Trek Universe	10.00	12.00
☐ **Warp Drive Blueprints,** 1984	2.00	3.00
☐ **Weapons And Field Equipment,** Volume I, 1983, The Noron Group, five sheets, features phasers, communicator and phaser rifle	8.00	10.00
☐ **Weapons And Field Equipment,** Volume II, by The Noron Group	8.00	10.00
☐ **Weapons And Field Equipment,** Volume III, by The Noron Group	8.00	10.00

BOOKS

Price Range

☐ **Abode Of Life, The,** L. Correy, Captain Kirk must try to help the hostile citizens of Mercan against their own sun, paperback, Pocket Books, 1982 .... 2.00 3.00

☐ **Battlestations!,** sequel to *Dreadnought!,* novel by Diane Carey, Pocket Books, 1986 .... 3.00 5.00

☐ **Best Of Trek, The,** W. Irwin and G. B. Love, volume #1, interviews, convention close-ups, close-up on special effects, compiled from *Trek,* the magazine for Star Trek fans, 1974 3.00 4.00

☐ **Best Of Trek, The,** W. Irwin and G.B. Love, volume #2, The Rise and Fall of the Federation, Captain Kirk's Black Book, Spock's past, compiled from magazine for Star Trek fans, 1977 3.00 4.00

☐ **Best Of Trek, The,** W. Irwin and G.B. Love, volume #3, Sulu's profile, genealogy, alternate universes, plus an in-depth look at the movie, compiled from magazine for Star Trek fans, 1979 .... 3.00 4.00

☐ **Best Of Trek, The,** W. Irwin and G.B. Love, volume #4, 1981 .... 3.00 4.00

☐ **Best Of Trek, The,** W. Irwin and G.B. Love, volume #5, 1982 .... 3.00 4.00

☐ **The Best Of Trek #6,** September 1983, Signet Books 3.00 4.00

☐ **The Best Of Trek #7,** June 1984, Signet Books 3.00 4.00

☐ **Best of Trek #8,** March, 1985, Signet Books, paperback 3.00 4.00

☐ **Best of Trek #9,** 1985 Signet Books, paperback 3.00 4.00

☐ **Black Fire,** Sonni Cooper, novel about sabotage aboard the Enterprise, Timescape Pocket Books, paperback, 1982 .... 2.00 3.00

☐ **Chain of Attack,** novel by Gene DeWeese, Pocket Books, 1987 .... 3.00 5.00

Price Range

☐ **Chekov's Enterprise,** W. Koenig, a personal journal of the making of Star Trek: The Motion Picture, the off-camera camaraderie of the cast and crew in a personal on-the-set-diary, paperback, Pocket Books, 1980 .... 10.00 25.00

☐ **Come And Be With Me,** L. Nimoy, poetry, Blue Mountain Arts, paperback 10.00 25.00

☐ **Corona,** Greg Bear, Pocket Books, 1984 .... 2.00 3.00

☐ **Covenant Of The Crown, The,** H. Weinstein, The Galaxy's hope to live long and prosper falls under the shadow of the Klingons, paperback, Pocket Books, 1981 .... 2.00 3.00

☐ **Crisis on Centaurus,** novel by Brad Ferguson, Pocket Books, 1986 .... 3.00 5.00

☐ **Death's Angel,** K. Sky, Star Trek novel, paperback, Bantam Books, April, 1981 .... 10.00 15.00

☐ **Death's Angel,** 1984 reprint 2.00 3.00

☐ **Demons,** novel by J.M. Dillard, Pocket Books, 1986 .... 3.00 5.00

☐ **Devil World,** Gordon Eklund, Star Trek novel, Bantam Books, paperback, 1979 .... 8.00 12.00

☐ **As above,** 1984 reprint 2.00 3.00

☐ **Dreadnought!,** novel by Diane Carey, Pocket Books, 1986 .... 3.00 5.00

☐ **Dwellers in the Crucible,** Margaret W. Bonanno, paperback, Pocket Books, 1985 ..... 3.00 4.00

☐ **Enterprise Flight Manual,** 1978, fan produced 4.00 6.00

☐ **Enterprise:** The First Adventure, novel by Vonda McIntyre, The Enterprise's first adventure with Kirk, Spock, etc., Pocket Books, 1986 3.00 5.00

☐ **Enterprise Officers Manual,** Geoffrey Mandel, Technical Model-Training for Starfleet Personnel, spiral-bound, 8½″ x 11″, 110 pages, currently available 10.00 12.00

☐ **Enterprise Officers Manual,** revised edition, 120 pages, squarebound 12.00 15.00

	Price Range	
☐ **Entropy Effect, The,** V. McIntyre, Spock must travel back in time to change history or the world will perish, paperback, 1980	2.00	3.00
☐ **Fandom Triumph,** Geoffrey Mandel, Doug Drexler, and Ron Barlow, contains detailed production information of Star Trek: The Motion Picture, fanzine	6.00	10.00
☐ **Fate Of The Phoenix, The,** S. Marshak and M. Culbreath, the most dangerous villain, Omne, is back again in a sequel to *The Price of the Phoenix,* paperback, Bantam, 1979	6.00	8.00
☐ **Fate Of The Phoenix,** 1984 reprint	2.00	3.00
☐ **The Final Reflection,** Pocket Books	2.00	3.00
☐ **Foto Novels,** Mandala Productions, color scenes from complete episodes of the television series, series of 12.		
☐ **Vol. #1,** City on the Edge of Forever, Nov. 1977	10.00	15.00
☐ **Vol. #2,** Where No Man Has Gone Before, Nov. 1977	10.00	15.00
☐ **Vol. #3,** The Trouble with Tribbles, Dec. 1977	10.00	15.00
☐ **Vol. #4,** A Taste of Armageddon, Jan. 1978	10.00	15.00
☐ **Vol. #5,** Metamorphosis, Feb. 1978	10.00	15.00
☐ **Vol. #6,** All Our Yesterdays, March 1978	10.00	15.00
☐ **Vol. #7,** The Galileo 7, May 1978	12.00	18.00
☐ **Vol. #8,** A Piece of the Action, June 1978 . . .	12.00	18.00
☐ **Vol. #9,** Devil in the Dark, July 1978	15.00	20.00
☐ **Vol. #10,** Day of The Dove, August 1978 . . .	12.00	18.00
☐ **Vol. #11,** The Deadly Years, Sept. 1978	12.00	18.00
☐ **Vol. #12,** Amok Time, Oct. 1978	18.00	24.00
☐ **From The Files Of Star Fleet Command,** sequel to Enterprise Officer's Manual, December 1980, Interstellar Associates	5.00	7.00
☐ **Galactic Whirlpool, The,** D. Gerrold, a strange people, isolated for centuries, is being sucked into a whirlpool and Kirk must save them, paperback, Bantam, 1980	4.00	6.00

	Price	Range
☐ **Galactic Whirlpool,** 1984 reprint	2.00	3.00
☐ **Gorn Guidebook,** produced by fans	3.00	4.00
☐ **I Am Not Spock,** Leonard Nimoy, autobiography of the Spock/Nimoy connection, oversized paperback, Celestial Arts, 1976	35.00	60.00
☐ **As above, Ballantine Books**	15.00	30.00
☐ **Ishmael,** Barbara Hambly, Star Trek novel, paperback, Pocket Books, 1985	3.00	4.00
☐ **Killing Time,** Della Van Hise, Star Trek novel, paperback, Pocket Books, 1985. First version originally released with passages objected to by Paramount.	10.00	15.00
☐ **As above,** Second version, both versions say first printing	3.00	4.00
☐ **Klingon Dictionary,** Mark Okrand, English/Klingon and Klingon/English, paperback, Pocket Books, 1985	4.00	5.00
☐ **Klingon Gambit, The,** R. Vardeman, the crew of the Enterprise is losing their minds and the Klingons are hungry for war, paperback, Pocket Books, 1981	2.00	3.00
☐ **Letters To Star Trek,** S. Sackett, paperback, Ballantine Books, Jan. 1977	8.00	12.00
☐ **Making Of Star Trek, The,** G. Roddenberry, a complete and authorized history of the television series, how it was conceived, written, produced and sold, paperback, Ballantine Books, 1968.		
☐ **First edition**	10.00	25.00
☐ **Later editions**	5.00	10.00
☐ **Current edition, 22nd edition**	4.00	5.00
☐ **Making Of Star Trek: The Motion Picture, The,** Susan Sackett with Gene Roddenberry, inside story of how the picture was made, soft cover, Wallaby Books, 1980	20.00	30.00

Price Range

☐ **Making Of Star Trek II: The Wrath of Khan, The,** Allan Asherman, behind-the-scenes story of Star Trek's greatest adventure, paperback, Pocket Books, 1982 .... 15.00 20.00

☐ **Making Of The Trek Conventions, The,** Joan Winston, hardcover, photographs, behind-the-scene view of producing conventions, humorous, paperback, published by Playboy.

☐ **Hardcover** (Doubleday) 15.00 20.00

☐ **Paperback** 5.00 8.00

☐ **Meaning in Star Trek,** Karen Blair, explains Star Trek's popularity through Jungian psychology, Warner Books, 1977.

☐ **Hardcover** 10.00 12.00

☐ **Paperback** 5.00 8.00

☐ **Mindshadow,** J.M. Dillard, Star Trek novel, paperback, Pocket Books, 1986 .... 3.00 4.00

☐ **Mirror Friend, Mirror Foe,** G. Takei, Playboy Press, original science fiction 5.00 10.00

☐ **Monsters of Star Trek, The,** D. Cohen, paperback, Pocket Books, Jan. 1980 .... 3.00 5.00

☐ **Mr. Scott's Guide to the Enterprise,** Shane Johnson, Simon & Schuster, 1987 .... 10.00 12.00

☐ **Mudd's Angels,** J. A. Lawrence, Star Trek novel, paperback, Bantam Books 10.00 15.00

☐ **As above,** 1984 reprint 2.00 3.00

☐ **Mutiny On The Enterprise,** Robert Vardeman, Pocket Books, 1983 .... 2.00 3.00

☐ **My Stars,** M.C. Goodwin, collector of comic strips about Star Trek and the Enterprise, soft cover, Vulcan Books, 1980 .... 10.00 15.00

☐ **My Enemy, My Ally,** by Diane Duane, July 1984, Pocket Books 2.00 3.00

☐ **Official Star Trek Cooking Manual,** Ann Piccard, Bantam, 1978 .... 40.00 60.00

☐ **Official Star Trek Quiz Book, The,** Mitchell Magilo, paperback, 256 pages, Pocket Books, 1986 .... 6.00 8.00

	Price Range	
☐ **Official Star Trek Trivia Book,** hardcover, 205 pages	10.00	15.00
☐ **Official Star Trek Trivia Book, The,** R. Needleman, paperback, Pocket Books, Jan. 1980	6.00	10.00
☐ **On The Good Ship Enterprise,** Bjo Trimble, cover is purple with cartoon figures of the crew riding in the Enterprise, Starblaze Special Edition, Donning Company, 1982, paperback	6.00	8.00
☐ **Pawns and Symbols,** Majliss Larson, Star Trek novel, paperback, Pocket Books, 1985	3.00	4.00
☐ **Perry's Planet,** J. Haldeman II, The Klingons are back and ruled by a "human" that's been dead for 300 years but is waging war against the Enterprise, paperback, Bantam, 1980	8.00	12.00
☐ **1984 Reprint**	2.00	3.00
☐ **Phaser Fight,** "Which-Way book" #24, Archway, 1986	2.00	4.00
☐ **Planet Of Judgment,** Joe Haldeman, Star Trek novel, paperback, Bantam Books	6.00	10.00
☐ **As above,** 1984 reprint	2.00	3.00
☐ **Price Of The Phoenix, The,** S. Marshak and M. Culbreath, Captain Kirk dies and is miraculously reborn, Spock is forced against Omne, paperback, Bantam, 1977	6.00	8.00
☐ **1984 Reprint**	2.00	3.00
☐ **Prometheus Design, The,** S. Marshak and M. Culbreath, a mysterious wave of violence is overtaking the universe and the Enterprise, paperback, Pocket Books, 1982	2.00	3.00
☐ **Shatner: Where No Man . . .,** W. Shatner with S. Marshak and M. Culbreath	50.00	75.00
☐ **Shadow Lord,** by Laurence Yep, Star Trek novel, 1985, paperback	3.00	4.00
☐ **Sing A Song Of Trekkin,** glossy cover, songs, cartoons, art, folksong book	4.00	6.00

	Price Range	
☐ **Six Science Fiction Plays,** Roger Elwood, editor, includes television script for "The City On The Edge of Forever" episode, Pocket Books, 1976, paperback	10.00	15.00
☐ **Spaceflight Chronology,** S. Goldstein and F. Goldstein, the evolution of space flight from the 20th to the 23rd century, soft cover, Pocket Books, 1980	15.00	25.00
☐ **Spock Must Die,** J. Blish, Star Trek novel, paperback, Bantam, 1970	4.00	6.00
☐ **1984 Reprint**	2.00	3.00
☐ **Spock, Messiah!** Theodore Cogswell and Charles Spano, Bantam, 1976.	4.00	6.00
☐ **As above,** 1984 Reprint	2.00	3.00
☐ **Star Fleet,** Bartender's Guide	2.00	3.00
☐ **Star Fleet Code Book,** 1978	2.00	3.00
☐ **Starfleet Officer Requirements,** fan produced book, 1985	12.00	15.00
☐ **Starfleet Officer Requirements, Vol. 2,** fan produced, 1986	9.00	11.00
☐ **Star Fleet Hand Weapon Familiarization Handbook**	4.00	5.00
☐ **Star Fleet,** Marriage Manual	3.00	5.00
☐ **Star Fleet Ship,** Recognition Manual	8.00	10.00
☐ **Starfleet Uniform Recognition Manual,** Shane Johnson, Noron Group, 1985	12.00	13.00
☐ **Starless World, The,** G. Eklund, Star Trek novel, paperback, Bantam, 1978	8.00	12.00
☐ **As above,** 1984 reprint	2.00	3.00
☐ **Starship Design,** Starstation Aurora, fan produced technical journal of the future, 1984 ..	9.00	10.00
☐ **Startoons,** Joan Winston, Playboy Press, Dec. 1979	6.00	8.00
☐ **Star Trek,** compilation of issues No. 7, No. 10 and No. 12 from the Marvel Comics Series, Marvel Illustrated Books, 1980–81, paperback	2.00	3.00

	Price Range	
☐ **Star Trek Annual,** BBC Productions, a series, 1972 to date, comics and other articles, hard cover, Western Publishing.	20.00	30.00
☐ **1973–75**	15.00	20.00
☐ **1976–80**	12.00	15.00
☐ **1981–83**	10.00	12.00
☐ **1984–86**	6.00	10.00
☐ **Star Trek Buyer's Guide,** addresses of companies that sell Star Trek products, 1980, April Publications	3.00	5.00
☐ **Star Trek Catalog,** Gerry Turnbull, large size, Grosset & Dunlap, 1979	7.00	10.00
☐ **Same as above,** small size	4.00	6.00
☐ **Star Trek Compendium,** Allan Asherman, Articles on Beginnings, T.V. show to the Motion Picture, paperback, A. Wallaby Books, 1981	10.00	12.00
☐ **As above,** revised 20th anniversary edition, Pocket Books, 1986, updated	9.00	11.00
☐ **Star Trek Concordance,** B. Trimble, story lines of television series, glossary to all characters, dates, happenings, plus an easy reference circle index, long out of print.		
☐ **Fan Edition**	10.00	15.00
☐ **Mass Market Edition,** with wheel on cover	50.00	120.00
☐ **Star Trek Files, Vol. 1,** Where No Man Has Gone Before, John Peel, New Media, 1985	10.00	15.00
☐ **Reprint, Pt. 1**	6.00	8.00
☐ **Reprint, Pt. 2**	6.00	8.00
☐ **As above,** The Early Voyages, John Peel, New Media, 1985	5.00	6.00
☐ **Reprint, Pt. 1**	6.00	8.00
☐ **Reprint, Pt. 2**	6.00	8.00
☐ **As above, Vol. 2,** Time Passages, John Peel, New Media, 1985	5.00	6.00
☐ **As above, Vol. 3,** A Taste of Paradise, John Peel, New Media, 1985	5.00	6.00
☐ **As above, Vol. 4,** On the Edge of Forever, John Peel, New Media, 1985	5.00	6.00

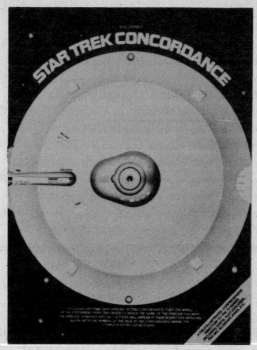

Star Trek Concordance, Ballantine Books

	Price Range	
☐ **As above, Vol. 5,** Mission Year Two, John Peel, New Media, 1987	**10.00**	**12.00**
☐ **As above, Vol. 6,** Journey to Eternity, John Peel, New Media, 1986	**6.00**	**8.00**
☐ **As above, Vol. 7,** The Deadly Years, John Peel, New Media, 1986	**6.00**	**8.00**
☐ **As above, Vol. 8,** Return to Tomorrow, John Peel, New Media, 1986	**6.00**	**8.00**
☐ **As above, Vol. 9,** Assignment Earth, John Peel, New Media, 1986	**6.00**	**8.00**
☐ **As above, Vol. 10,** Enterprise Incident, John Peel, New Media, 1986	**6.00**	**8.00**
☐ **As above, Vol. 11,** Tholian Web, John Peel, New Media, 1986	**6.00**	**8.00**

Price Range

☐ **As above, Vol. 12,** Whom Gods Destroy, John
   Peel, New Media, 1986 .... 6.00   8.00
☐ **As above, Vol. 13,** All Our Yesterdays, John
   Peel, New Media, 1986 .... 6.00   8.00
☐ **As above, Vol. 15,** The Animated Voyages
   Begin, John Peel, New Media 6.00   8.00
☐ **As above, Vol. 16,** The Animated Voyages
   End, John Peel, New Media 6.00   8.00
☐ **As above,** Star Trek: The Motion Picture, John
   Peel, New Media 6.00   8.00
☐ **As above,** Star Trek: The Wrath of Khan, John
   Peel, New Media 6.00   8.00
☐ **As above,** Star Trek: The Search for Spock,
   John Peel, New Media 6.00   8.00
☐ **As above,** Star Trek: 20th Anniversary Tribute,
   John Peel, New Media 7.00   9.00
☐ **Star Trek Intergalactic Puzzles,** James Razzi,
   series one, large silver and black paperback,
   Bantam Books, 1977 .... 10.00   12.00
☐ **As above,** small paperback version 6.00   8.00
☐ **Star Trek Lives,** S. Marshak, J. Winston and J.
   Lichtenberg, all about Star Trek, articles from
   Fanzines, Bantam, 1975 .... 5.00   10.00
☐ **Star Trek Log One,*** adapted by Alan Dean
   Foster from the animated Star Trek episodes,
   published by Ballantine, June 1974, 184 pp. 3.00   5.00
☐ **Log Two,** September 1974, 177 pp. 3.00   5.00
☐ **Log Three,** January 1975, 215 pp. 3.00   5.00
☐ **Log Four,** March 1975, 215 pp. 3.00   5.00
☐ **Log Five,** August 1975, 195 pp. 3.00   5.00
☐ **Log Six,** March 1976, 195 pp. 3.00   5.00
☐ **Log Seven,** June 1976, 182 pp. 6.00   10.00
☐ **Log Eight,** August 1976, 183 pp., each 6.00   12.00
☐ **Log Nine,** February 1977, 183 pp. 8.00   15.00
☐ **Log Ten,** published by Del Rey/Ballantine,
   January 1978, 250 pp. 8.00   20.00

*Logs 1–6 have now been reprinted and are currently available.

	Price Range	
☐ **Star Trek Maps,** an introduction to navigation, Jeff Maynard, background and technical material about navigating with the Enterprise, four charts of the Federation, Klingon, and Romulan Zones, in portfolio, Bantam Books, 1980	75.00	150.00
☐ **Star Trek Medical Reference Manual,** Eileen Palestine, a reference to Vulcan Physiology; Medical time line, chart of Diseases and Drugs, Ballantine Books, 1977.		
☐ **Fan Edition,** white cover	50.00	60.00
☐ **Blue Edition,** mass market	7.00	10.00
☐ **Star Trek New Voyages I,** S. Marshak and M. Culbreath, collection of new Star Trek adventures, paperback, Bantam, 1976	4.00	6.00

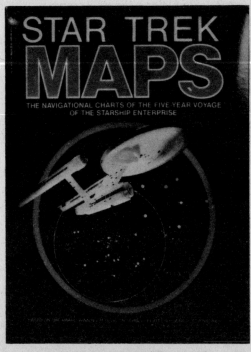

Star Trek Maps, Bantam

	Price Range	
☐ **1984 Reprint**	2.00	3.00
☐ **Star Trek: The New Voyages II,** S. Marshak and M. Culbreath, collection of eight new adventures, Bantam, 1977	4.00	6.00
☐ **1984 Reprint**	2.00	3.00
☐ **Star Trek Primer,** Phil Foglio, cartoonist, Hugo Award Winner, first issue	6.00	10.00
☐ **Star Trek Puzzle Manual,** J. Razzi, officially approved by Training Command: Star Fleet Academy, a collection of puzzles, mazes and trivia, Bantam, 1976	10.00	12.00
☐ **Star Trek Puzzle Manual,** J. Razzi, second of series, Bantam Books, 1978	8.00	10.00
☐ **Star Trek Quiz Book,** by B. Andrews with B. Dunning, June, 1977, Signet Books	10.00	12.00
☐ **Star Trek Reader, The,** J. Blish, adaptations of the television stories including Arena, Tomorrow is Yesterday, 20 stories in all, 1970, hardcover	10.00	25.00
☐ **Vol. II,** J. Blish, collection of 20 television stories, including Charlie's Law, Dagger of the Mind and The Immunity Syndrome, 1972	10.00	25.00
☐ **Vol. III,** collection of stories adapted from the television show including: Whom Gods Destroy, The Tholian Web, Elaan of Troyius, 1973	10.00	25.00
☐ **Vol. IV,** J. Blish, series of stories from the television show, includes Spock Must Die, 1974	10.00	25.00
☐ **Star Trek Series Adaptions,** by James Blish. Many different printings, earlier ones tend to be more valuable.		
☐ **No.1,** January, 1967	2.00	3.00
☐ **No.2,** February, 1968	2.00	3.00
☐ **No.3,** April, 1969	2.00	3.00
☐ **No.4,** July, 1971	2.00	3.00
☐ **No.5,** February, 1972	2.00	3.00
☐ **No.6,** April, 1972	2.00	3.00
☐ **No.7,** July 1972	2.00	3.00
☐ **No.8,** November 1972	2.00	3.00

	Price Range	
☐ **No.9,** August, 1973	2.00	3.00
☐ **No.10,** February, 1974	2.00	3.00
☐ **No.11,** April, 1975	5.00	8.00
☐ **No.12,** November, 1977	12.00	20.00
☐ **Star Trek Speaks,** S. Sackett, Fred Goldstein and S. Goldstein, Anthology of Trek's Philosophies, and Universal Truths, soft cover, Paramount Pictures, 1979	3.00	5.00
☐ **Star Trek Star Fleet Technical Manual,** Franz Joseph, oversize soft cover book in rigid black binder, Ballantine Books, 1975	40.00	100.00
☐ **As above,** 20th anniversary reprint, Ballantine Books, 1986, same as above with new soft cover, no binder	10.00	12.00
☐ **Star Trek: The Motion Picture,** British novelization with color inserts, published by Futura, 1979	3.00	4.00
☐ **Star Trek: The Motion Picture,** G. Roddenberry, the original screenplay adapted to this novel about the reunion of the crew of The Enterprise, paperback, Pocket Books, 1979	3.00	4.00
☐ **As above,** hardcover book club edition	5.00	10.00
☐ **As above,** special hardcover edition with slipcase, autographed by G. Roddenberry, limited to 500	15.00	35.00
☐ **Star Trek: The Motion Picture,** Marvel Comics, compilation of issues No. 1, No. 2 and No. 3 from the Marvel Comics series, Stan Lee full-color version, Marvel Comics, 1979–80, paperback	2.00	3.00
☐ **Star Trek: The Motion Picture Peel-Off Graphics Book,** Lee Cole, contains peel-off stickers of signs and designs from movie, Wallaby Books, 1979	15.00	25.00
☐ **Star Trek: The Motion Picture Photo Story,** R. Nobile, the story of the first famous movie in hundreds of color photos, paperback, 1980	12.00	20.00

Price Range

☐ **Star Trek, TV And Movie Tie-Ins,** James A. Lely, green and blue cover with cartoon drawing of Enterprise in a black circle, Creative Education Publishers, 1979, paperback 4.00 6.00

☐ **Star Trek II—Biographies,** William Rotsler, biographies of all the major characters on Star Trek, Wanderer Books, 1982, paperback 4.00 6.00

☐ **Star Trek II—Distress Call,** William Rotsler, a plot-your-own adventure story, Wanderer Books, 1982, paperback 3.00 4.00

☐ **Star Trek II—Short Stories,** William Rotsler, Enterprise inverted on cover, six short stories, Wanderer Books, 1982, paperback 3.00 4.00

☐ **Star Trek II: The Wrath Of Khan,** hardcover, book club edition 8.00 10.00

☐ **As above,** paperback 2.00 3.00

☐ **Star Trek III Movie Trivia,** William Rotsler, trivia book with pen that reveals answers, Wanderer, 1984. . . . . 3.00 4.00

☐ **Star Trek III—Plot It Yourself Adventure Stories,** William Rotsler, oversized paperback, adventure of the Vulcan Treasure, Wanderer Books, 1984. . . . . 3.00 4.00

☐ **Star Trek III Post Card Book,** Simon & Schuster, 1984 . . . . 5.00 7.00

☐ **Star Trek III-Short Stories,** William Rotsler, oversized paperback with five short stories, Wanderer Books, 1984. . . . . 3.00 4.00

☐ **Star Trek III: The Search for Spock,** Vonda McIntyre, movie adaptation, paperback, Pocket Books, 1984. . . . . 3.00 4.00

☐ **Star Trek III: The Search for Spock Storybook,** by Lawrence Weinberg, includes 61 color photos, published by Simon and Schuster 6.00 8.00

☐ **Star Trek III Novel,** Vonda McIntyre, book club edition, hardback, 1984. . . . . 6.00 8.00

☐ **Star Trek IV: The Voyage Home,** movie novelization by Vonda McIntyre, Pocket Books, 1986 3.00 5.00

	Price Range	
☐ **Star Trek IV: The Voyage Home,** photostory, Wanderer, 91 pp.	5.00	7.00
☐ **Star Trek, Voyage to Adventure,** "Which-Way Book" #15, Archway, 1984	2.00	4.00
☐ **Star Wars, Star Trek and the 21st Century Christians,** Winkie Pratney, Bible Voice, 1978	4.00	6.00
☐ **Strange and Amazing Facts About Star Trek,** Simon & Schuster, 1986	2.00	4.00
☐ **Tears of the Singers,** Melinda Snodgrass, Star Trek novel, paperback, Pocket Books, 1984	3.00	4.00
☐ **Thank You For Your Love,** L. Nimoy, poetry, Blue Mountain Arts	10.00	25.00
☐ **These Words Are For You,** L. Nimoy, poetry, Blue Mountain Arts	10.00	25.00
☐ **Trek Memorabilia Price Guide,** 1983, fan produced	12.00	15.00
☐ **Trek or Treat,** T. Flanagan and E. Ehrhardt, humorous look at outer space with Kirk, Spock and McCoy, Paramount Pictures, Ballantine Books, 1977	3.00	5.00
☐ **Trek To Madworld,** S. Golden, Star Trek novel, paperback, Bantam Books	8.00	12.00
☐ **As above,** 1984 reprint	2.00	3.00
☐ **Trekkie Quiz Book,** B. Andrews, B. Durning, originally entitled "Star Trek Quiz Book," paperback, Signet	4.00	6.00
☐ **The Trellisane Confrontation,** by David Dvorkin, Pocket Books, 1984	3.00	4.00
☐ **Triangle,** Sandra Marshak and Myrna Culbreath, Star Trek novel, Timescape Pocket Books, paperback, 1983	3.00	4.00
☐ **Trivia Mania,** Star Trek Edition, Xavier Einstein, Zebra Books.	2.00	4.00
☐ **Trouble With Tribbles,** D. Gerrold, complete story of T.V. script, photos, paperback, Ballantine Books, 1977	6.00	8.00
☐ **Uhura's Song,** Jane Kagan, Star Trek novel, paperback, Pocket Books, 1985	3.00	4.00

Price Range

☐ **USS Discovery Officer's Manual,** fan produced, manual for mythical ship in Star Fleet   4.00   6.00

☐ **U.S.S. Enterprise Bridge Punch-Out Book,** Jor Lokvig, illustrated by Chuck Murphy, allows the owner to build an elaborate 360° bridge of The Enterprise, superior design, blue cover, Wanderer Books 10.00   15.00

☐ **U.S.S. Enterprise Punch-Out Book,** STTMP Red Cover, Wanderer Books 10.00   20.00

☐ **Vulcan!,** Kathleen Sky, Star Trek novel, paperback, Bantam 10.00   14.00

☐ **1984 Reprint** 2.00   3.00

☐ **Vulcan Academy Murders,** Jean Lorrah, Star Trek novel, paperback, Pocket Books, 1984   3.00   4.00

☐ **Vulcan Language Guide,** dialects, pronunciation, names and more, fan produced 2.00   3.00

☐ **Warmed By Love,** by Leonard Nimoy, 1983, Blue Mountain Press 15.00   20.00

☐ **We Are All Children Searching For Love,** L. Nimoy, an anthology of poetry by the actor who plays the famous Mr. Spock, paperback, Blue Mountain Arts, 1977 ....   10.00   20.00

☐ **Web Of The Romulans,** M.S. Murdock, Star Trek novel, Timescape Pocket Books, paperback, 1983. ....   2.00   3.00

☐ **Who Was That Monolith I Saw You With?,** by Michael Goodwin, 1976, Heritage 10.00   15.00

☐ **Who's Who in Star Trek,** a comprehensive encyclopedia of the contributors to Star Trek including the actors, writers, directors, production, fan authors 4.00   5.00

☐ **Will I Think Of You,** L. Nimoy, poetry, Celestial Arts, 1974, first edition 10.00   25.00

☐ **World of Star Trek,** D. Gerrold, the show, original conception, writers, stars, technicians, fans and more, paperback, Ballantine Books, 1973   6.00   10.00

Price Range

☐ **World of Star Trek,** D. Gerrold, updated version of 1973 original includes information from Star Trek III, Bluejay Books, 1984 . . . . 8.00 10.00

☐ **World Without End,** J. Haldeman, an adventure novel about the crew of The Enterprise at Chatalia, an artificial world inhabited by furry winged creatures, paperback, Bantam, 1979 6.00 8.00

☐ **As above,** 1984 reprint 2.00 3.00

☐ **Wounded Sky, The,** by Diane Duane, Pocket Books, 1983 . . . . 3.00 4.00

☐ **Wounded Sky, The,** Diane Duane, hardback book club edition, 1983. . . . . 6.00 8.00

☐ **Wrath Of Khan Photo Story,** R.J. Anobile, hundreds of action scenes from Star Trek, second feature film, black and white, paperback, Pocket Books, 1982 . . . . 3.00 4.00

☐ **Wrath Of Khan, The,** Vonda McIntyre, based on the screenplay, Pocket Books, 1982 . . . . . 3.00 4.00

☐ **Writer's Guide,** G. Roddenberry, professional guide with vital information on the characters, the Enterprise, and other data 4.00 6.00

☐ **Writings of Surak,** fan produced Vulcan philosophy book. 2.00 3.00

☐ **Yesterday's Son,** A.C. Crispin, hardback book club edition, 1983. . . . . 6.00 8.00

☐ **Yesterday's Son,** A.C. Crispin, Spock discovers his own son living 5,000 years in the past, Timescape Pocket Books, paperback, 1983 3.00 4.00

☐ **You And I,** L. Nimoy, poetry, Celestial Arts . . 10.00 15.00

BOOKS—CHILDREN

☐ **A Bomb in Time/The Psychocrystals,** Whitman Comic Book, 1976 . . . . 5.00 6.00

☐ **Coloring Book,** Lincoln Enterprises, contains 24 scenes from the cartoon show, high grade, suitable for mounting 3.00 4.00

	Price Range	
☐ **Coloring Books,** Merrigold Press, series of six.		
☐ **#1306, Planet Ecnal's Dilemma**	2.00	3.00
☐ **#1307, Rescue At Raylo**	2.00	3.00
☐ **#1308, Futuristic Fun**	2.00	3.00
☐ **#1309, Far Out Fun**	2.00	3.00
☐ **#1310, A Blast of Activities**	2.00	3.00
☐ **#1311, A Launch into Fun**	2.00	3.00
☐ **Crier In The Emptyness, The,** Peter Pan Publishing, book and record, set	4.00	8.00
☐ **Dinosaur Planet,** Peter Pan Publishing, book and record, 1979, set	4.00	8.00
☐ **The Evictors/The Choice,** Whitman Comic Book, 1976	3.00	4.00
☐ **Futuristic Fun,** Whitman/Western, children's activity book	2.00	3.00
☐ **Giant In The Universe,** Random House, television story of Kirk versus The Giant, in three dimensions, a pop-up book, 1977	20.00	40.00
☐ **Incredible Intergalactic Crossword Puzzle,** Running Press	4.00	6.00
☐ **Jeopardy At Jutterdon,** Whitman/Western juvenile sticker book	3.00	4.00
☐ **Make-A-Game Book,** B. Nash and G. Nash, The Klingons are approaching, punch out this game and save The Enterprise, Wanderer Books	10.00	20.00
☐ **Make Your Own Costume Book,** background historical data, photos and patterns to make costumes, Wallaby Books, 1979.		
☐ **Hardcover**	10.00	12.00
☐ **Softcover**	6.00	8.00
☐ **Mirror For Futility And The Time Stealer,** Peter Pan, book and record set	4.00	8.00
☐ **Mission to Horatius,** M. Reynolds, a children's novel about The Enterprise and its crew, Western Publishing, 1968, hardcover	15.00	30.00
☐ **Passage To Moauv,** Peter Pan Publishing, book and record set, 1975	7.00	12.00

Giant in the Universe Pop-Up Book

	Price Range	
☐ **Planet Ecnal's Dilemma,** Whitman Coloring Book, 1978	1.00	2.00
☐ **Pop Up Book,** Wanderer Publications, the story of Star Trek: The Motion Picture, in three dimensions	8.00	10.00
☐ **Prisoner Of Vega,** R. Swanson, Random, hardcover	15.00	20.00
☐ **Same as above,** but with Gibraltar Library Binding.	20.00	25.00
☐ **Punch Out And Play Album,** from Star Trek, the television show	10.00	12.00
☐ **Rescue At Raylo,** Whitman Western Publishing, coloring book	1.00	2.00
☐ **Robot Masters, The,** Peter Pan Publishing, book and record set, 1979	3.00	5.00

	Price Range	
☐ **Star Trek Action Toy Book,** J. Razzi, large format, full color, punch-out book, Random House	7.00	15.00
☐ **Star Trek Coloring Book No.1,** Saalfield Publishing	1.00	2.00
☐ **Star Trek Coloring Book No.2,** Saalfield Publishing	1.00	2.00
☐ **Star Trek, Giant Story Coloring, Vol. 1 and Vol. 2, The Motion Picture,** Wanderer, coloring book	2.00	4.00
☐ **Star Trek, Giant Story Coloring Book,** "The Uncharted World," 1978, Parkes Run Publishing	3.00	5.00
☐ **Star Trek III:** The Search for Spock Story Book, L. Weinberg, Little Simon Publishing, 1984	6.00	8.00
☐ **Trillions Of Trillig,** Random House, pop-up book of television show, in three dimensions, 1977	20.00	40.00
☐ **Truth Machine, The,** S. Lerner, children's book, Random House, 1977	15.00	20.00
☐ **Same as above,** with Gibraltar Library Binding	20.00	25.00

BUMPER STICKERS

	Price Range	
☐ **Beam Me Up Mr. Spock,** Avia Enterprises, blue and white printed on orange.	2.00	3.00
☐ **Bring Back The Enterprise,** Lincoln Enterprises	1.00	2.00
☐ **Don't Honk! I Can Only Do Warp 2**	1.00	2.00
☐ **Don't Tailgate, This Is A Klingon War Cruiser,** Lincoln Enterprises	1.00	2.00
☐ **Dr. McCoy Doesn't Make House Calls,** Aviva Enterprises, blue and white printed on orange	2.00	3.00
☐ **Earther Beware! Klingon Battlecruiser**	1.00	2.00
☐ **Federation Shuttlecraft**	1.00	2.00
☐ **Federation Vehicle Official Use Only,** Aviva, 1979	2.00	3.00

	Price Range	
☐ Follow Me Where No Man Has Gone Before	1.00	2.00
☐ Government Vehicle, Vulcan Embassy, Lincoln Enterprises	1.00	2.00
☐ Graduate of Star Fleet Academy	1.00	2.00
☐ The Human Adventure Is Just Beginning, Lincoln Enterprises	1.00	2.00
☐ I Am A Carbon Unit, Lincoln Enterprises	1.00	2.00
☐ I Am A Trekkie, Aviva, 1979	2.00	3.00
☐ I Grok Spock Lincoln Enterprises, black lettering with fluorescent background	1.00	2.00
☐ I Have A One Trek Mind	1.00	2.00
☐ I Operate On Impulse Power	1.00	2.00
☐ I Study Horta Culture, Fasson, shows Spock examining a horta with magnifying glass	1.00	2.00
☐ Jaws Is A Klingon Minnow (with picture) Lincoln Enterprises	1.00	2.00
☐ Live Long And Prosper, Aviva, 1979	2.00	3.00
☐ Live Long And Prosper, Lincoln Enterprises, black lettering with fluorescent background ..	1.00	2.00
☐ Mr. Spock For President, Lincoln Enterprises	1.00	2.00
☐ Mr. Spock Phone Home, Lincoln Enterprises	1.00	2.00
☐ Phasers on Stun	1.00	2.00
☐ Powered By Tribbles	1.00	2.00
☐ Smile (picture) If You Like Star Trek	1.00	2.00
☐ Space ... The Final Frontier	1.00	2.00
☐ Spock For President	1.00	2.00
☐ Spock Is Dead? Long Live Star Trek	1.00	2.00
☐ Spock Is Dying To Be In Star Trek III, 2½″ x 11″	1.00	2.00
☐ Spock Lives, Fan produced, 2½″ x 11″	1.00	2.00
☐ Star Trek Fans Make Better Lovers	1.00	2.00
☐ Star Trek Lives, Lincoln Enterprises, black lettering with fluorescent background	1.00	2.00
☐ Star Trek: The Motion Picture, Aviva, 1979	2.00	3.00
☐ Starfleet The Human Adventure Continues, 2½″ x 11″	1.00	2.00

	Price Range	
☐ **Support The Right To Arm Klingons,** Lincoln Enterprises	1.00	2.00
☐ **This Is Illogical**	1.00	2.00
☐ **Vote Yes On Star Trek,** Lincoln Enterprises	1.00	2.00
☐ **We Want Star Trek III,** Lincoln Enterprises ..	1.00	2.00
☐ **We're One Happy Fleet,** 2½" x 11", fan produced	1.00	2.00
☐ **Enterprise, License Plate,** fan produced, artwork of the Enterprise on metal plate	3.00	5.00
☐ **License Plate,** NCC-1701/USS Enterprise, 6" x 12", fan produced	3.00	5.00
☐ **License Plate,** USS Enterprise, 4" x 12", fan produced	3.00	5.00

BUTTONS

The primary thing to consider when collecting buttons is the ease of manufacture. Button-making machines are available to the hobbyist for about $20. In addition there are companies that will produce relatively small quantities of buttons for a modest price. Word buttons are particularly easy. They can be hand-lettered or run off cheaply at any local printer. As for picture buttons, it is easy and perfectly legal to cut any picture out of a magazine and incorporate it into a button. For this reason we are only including those button series which had sheets printed in large quantities for the specific purpose of making buttons. It is arguable whether certain other buttons may have collector's value, especially those from conventions, but because they could be so easily duplicated it is unlikely they would ever become very valuable.

	Price Range	
☐ **Button,** Lincoln Enterprises, says "I Am A Trekkie," light blue background, black lettering, 1976, diameter 1¼"	1.00	2.00
☐ **Promotional Button,** pictures Spock, "Star Trek: The Only Logical Books to Read." Pocket Books	1.00	2.00

	Price Range	
☐ **Star Trek: The Motion Picture,** Group shot on the bridge, 2¼″, Aviva	**2.00**	**3.00**
☐ **As above,** Kirk in grey uniform	**2.00**	**3.00**
☐ **As above,** Kirk, standing, blue background, 2¼″	**2.00**	**3.00**
☐ **As above,** Kirk, Spock and McCoy, 2¼″	**2.00**	**3.00**
☐ **As above,** Spock, in uniform, 2¼″	**2.00**	**3.00**
☐ **As above,** Spock, in Vulcan attire, 2¼″	**2.00**	**3.00**

Langley & Associates was an early manufacturer of licensed merchandise, now out of business

☐ **Button With Captain Kirk,** Langley Associates, close-up of head, diameter 2¼″	**1.00**	**2.00**
☐ **Button With Captain Kirk,** Langley Associates, in dress uniform, diameter 2¼″	**1.00**	**2.00**
☐ **Button With Captain Kirk,** Langley Associates, in The Trouble with Tribbles, diameter 2¼″	**1.00**	**2.00**
☐ **Button With Captain Kirk,** Langley Associates, ready to beam down, diameter 2¼″	**1.00**	**2.00**
☐ **Button With Captain Kirk,** Langley Associates, with communicator, diameter 2¼″	**1.00**	**2.00**
☐ **Captain Kirk,** close-up of head, Langley Associates, 2¼″	**1.00**	**2.00**
☐ **Captain Kirk,** in dress uniform, Langley Associates, 2¼″	**1.00**	**2.00**
☐ **Captain Kirk,** in The Trouble with Tribbles, Langley Associates, 2¼″	**1.00**	**2.00**
☐ **Captain Kirk,** ready to beam down, Langley Associates, 2¼″	**1.00**	**2.00**
☐ **Captain Kirk,** with communicator, Langley Associates, 2¼″	**1.00**	**2.00**
☐ **Captain Kirk,** hand reaching out through cell bars, Langley Associates, 2¼″	**1.00**	**2.00**
☐ **Captain Pike,** the original commander of the Enterprise, Langley Associates, 2¼″	**1.00**	**2.00**

Price Range

☐ **Button With Captain Pike,** Langley Associates, the original commander of the Enterprise,
diameter 2¼" 1.00   2.00

☐ **Button With Dr. McCoy,** Langley Associates,
close-up of face, diameter 2¼" 1.00   2.00

☐ **Button With Dr. McCoy,** Langley Associates,
looking puzzled, diameter 2¼" 1.00   2.00

☐ **Button With Dr. McCoy,** Langley Associates,
speaking, diameter 2¼" 1.00   2.00

☐ **Button With Enterprise,** Langley Associates,
captioned "Star Trek," diameter 2¼" 1.00   2.00

☐ **Button With Enterprise,** Langley Associates,
looming over planet, diameter 2¼" 1.00   2.00

☐ **Button With The Enterprise,** Langley Associates, rear view, diameter 2¼" 1.00   2.00

☐ **Button With The Enterprise,** Langley Associates, shooting phasers, diameter 2¼" 1.00   2.00

☐ **Button With The Enterprise,** Langley Associates, with red planet, diameter 2¼" 1.00   2.00

☐ **Button With Khan,** Langley Associates, original evil character, diameter 2¼" 1.00   2.00

☐ **Button With Klingon Ship,** Langley Associates, overhead shot, diameter 2¼" 1.00   2.00

☐ **Button With Lt. Uhura,** Langley Associates,
leaning on communicator's equipment, diame-
ter 2¼" 1.00   2.00

☐ **Button With Lt. Uhura,** Langley Associates,
with headset on, diameter 2¼" 1.00   2.00

☐ **Button With Mr. Chekov,** Langley Associates,
flanked by crew, diameter 2¼" 1.00   2.00

☐ **Button With Mr. Chekov,** Langley Associates,
in a deep frown, diameter 2¼" 1.00   2.00

☐ **Button With Mr. Chekov,** Langley Associates,
on the bridge, diameter 2¼" 1.00   2.00

☐ **Button With Mr. Chekov,** Langley Associates,
smiling, diameter 2¼" 1.00   2.00

☐ **Button With Mr. Scott,** Langley Associates,
close-up of head, diameter 2¼" 1.00   2.00

	Price Range	
☐ **Button With Mr. Spock,** Langley Associates, as Science Officer, diameter 2¼"	1.00	2.00
☐ **Button With Mr. Spock,** Langley Associates, close-up profile, diameter 2¼"	1.00	2.00
☐ **Button With Mr. Spock,** Langley Associates, in a rare laugh, diameter 2¼"	1.00	2.00
☐ **Button With Mr. Spock,** Langley Associates, looking logical, diameter 2¼"	1.00	2.00
☐ **Button With Mr. Spock,** Langley Associates, smiling, diameter 2¼"	1.00	2.00
☐ **Button With Mr. Spock,** Langley Associates, talking on the bridge, diameter 2¼"	1.00	2.00
☐ **Button With Mr. Spock,** Langley Associates, tight close-up of head, diameter 2¼"	1.00	2.00
☐ **Button With Mr. Spock,** Langley Associates, with beard, diameter 2¼"	1.00	2.00
☐ **Button With Mr. Sulu,** Langley Associates, as the navigator, diameter 2¼"	1.00	2.00
☐ **Button With Mr. Sulu,** Langley Associates, close-up shot of head, diameter 2¼"	1.00	2.00
☐ **Button With Mr. Sulu,** Langley Associates, looking up, diameter 2¼"	1.00	2.00
☐ **Button With Nurse Chapel,** Langley Associates, close-up shot, diameter 2¼"	1.00	2.00
☐ **Button With Yeoman Rand,** Langley Associates, with plaited hair, diameter 2¼"	1.00	2.00

Star Trek Galore was a manufacturer of unlicensed merchandise, now out of business.

	Price Range	
☐ **Button With Captain Kirk,** Star Trek Galore, in full dress uniform	1.00	2.00
☐ **Button With Chekov And Sulu,** Star Trek Galore, on bridge	1.00	2.00
☐ **Button With The Crew Of The Enterprise,** Star Trek Galore, on the bridge	1.00	2.00
☐ **Button With Enterprise,** Star Trek Galore, firing phasers	1.00	2.00

	Price Range	
☐ **Button With Galileo,** Star Trek Galore, the Enterprise's mini transport	1.00	2.00
☐ **Button With Kirk, Spock and McCoy,** Star Trek Galore, on bridge	1.00	2.00
☐ **Button With Kirk,** Star Trek Galore, with hand on chin	1.00	2.00
☐ **Button With Kirk,** Star Trek Galore, with the Trouble and Tribbles	1.00	2.00
☐ **Button With Scotty,** Star Trek Galore, looking worried	1.00	2.00
☐ **Button With Scotty,** Star Trek Galore, portrait type	1.00	2.00
☐ **Button,** "Spock Lives," black print on yellow, limited to 400	1.00	2.00
☐ **Button,** "Spock Lives," yellow print on black, limited to 400	1.00	2.00
☐ **Button With Spock,** Star Trek Galore, aiming phaser	1.00	2.00
☐ **Button With Spock,** Star Trek Galore, giving hand signal	1.00	2.00
☐ **Button With Spock,** Star Trek Galore, in rare display of emotion	1.00	2.00
☐ **Button With Spock,** Star Trek Galore, making point	1.00	2.00
☐ **Button With Spock,** Star Trek Galore, with beard	1.00	2.00
☐ **Button With Spock,** Star Trek Galore, with child Vulcan	1.00	2.00
☐ **Button With Spock,** Star Trek Galore, with harp	1.00	2.00
☐ **Button With Spock,** Star Trek Galore, with three-dimensional chess game	1.00	2.00
☐ **Button With Uhura,** Star Trek Galore, The Enterprise's Communication Officer	1.00	2.00
☐ **Button With Spock,** from animated series . . .	1.00	2.00
☐ **Button With Kirk,** glitter button, black background, 2½"	1.00	2.00

	Price Range	
☐ **Button With McCoy,** glitter button, black background, 2½"	1.00	2.00

Image Products, **Star Trek: The Wrath of Khan,** 3" buttons.

☐ **Enterprise**	1.00	2.00
☐ **Group shot**	1.00	2.00
☐ **Khan**	1.00	2.00
☐ **Kirk**	1.00	2.00
☐ **Spock**	1.00	2.00
☐ **Button,** fan produced, says "Vulcans never bluff," diameter 2¼"	1.00	2.00
☐ **Button,** fan produced, says "Vulcan power," diameter 2¼"	1.00	2.00
☐ **Button,** fan produced, says "Be logical"	1.00	2.00
☐ **Button,** fan produced, says "Don't underestimate the Romulans"	1.00	2.00
☐ **Button,** fan produced, says "Dr. McCoy doesn't make house calls"	1.00	2.00
☐ **Button,** fan produced, says "I'm from a class M planet"	1.00	2.00
☐ **Button,** fan produced, says "Klingons need loving too"	1.00	2.00
☐ **Button,** fan produced, says "Meet me in the transporter room"	1.00	2.00
☐ **Button,** fan produced, says "Q-12 Starfleet Captain"	1.00	2.00
☐ **Button,** fan produced, says "Star Trek lives"	1.00	2.00
☐ **Button,** fan produced, says "Transporter technician"	1.00	2.00
☐ **Button,** fan produced, says "What's a Sulu?"	1.00	2.00
☐ **Button,** fan produced, says "Beam me up," diameter 2¼"	1.00	2.00
☐ **Button,** fan produced, says "Closet Trekkie," diameter 2¼"	1.00	2.00
☐ **Button,** fan produced, says "I Grok Spock," diameter 2¼"	1.00	2.00
☐ **Button,** fan produced, says "Illogical but fascinating," diameter 2¼"	1.00	2.00

	Price Range	
☐ **Button,** fan produced, says "Live long and prosper," diameter 2¼"	1.00	2.00
☐ **Captain Kirk,** close-up of head, from TV series, Button-up, 1½"	1.00	2.00
☐ **Captain Kirk,** close-up of head, from Star Trek III, Button-up, 1½"	1.00	2.00
☐ **Captain Kirk,** head and shoulders shot, from Star Trek III, Button-up, 1½"	1.00	2.00
☐ **Commander Checkov,** close-up of head, from Star Trek III, Button-up, 1½"	1.00	2.00
☐ **Commander Sulu,** close-up of head, from Star Trek III, Button-up, 1½"	1.00	2.00
☐ **Commander Uhura,** holding a phaser, from Star Trek III, Button-up, 1½"	1.00	2.00
☐ **Crew member,** from Star Trek III, Button-up, 1½"	1.00	2.00
☐ **David Marcus,** head and shoulders shot, from Star Trek III, Button-up, 1½"	1.00	2.00
☐ **Enterprise,** picture of the Enterprise from the TV show, Button-up, 1½"	1.00	2.00
☐ **Group Shot,** Dr. McCoy, Lt. Uhura and Checkov, from TV series, Button-up, 1½" ...	1.00	2.00
☐ **Group Shot,** Captain Kirk, Dr. McCoy and Mr. Spock, from TV series, Button-up, 1½"	1.00	2.00
☐ **Kruge,** Klingon, close-up of head, from Star Trek III, Button-up, 1½"	1.00	2.00
☐ **Kirk and Dr. McCoy,** head shots, from TV series, Button-up, 1½"	1.00	2.00
☐ **Kirk and Mr. Spock,** close-up from Errand of Mercy, from TV show, Button-up, 1½"	1.00	2.00
☐ **Lt. Saavik,** close-up of head, from Star Trek III, Button-up, 1½"	1.00	2.00
☐ **Lt. Sulu,** close-up of head, from TV series, Button-up, 1½".............................	1.00	2.00
☐ **Logo from Star Trek III,** Button-up, 1½".	1.00	2.00
☐ **Spock, in Vulcan garb,** from Star Trek II, Button-up, 1½"	1.00	2.00

	Price Range	
☐ **Starships,** The Enterprise and Constellation, from the TV series, Button-up, 1½″	1.00	2.00

CALENDARS

Some of the earlier calendars came packaged in boxes. Calendars with their original boxes are worth about 25% more. Values here are for calendars that have not been written in. Ones with writing are worth 25–50% of values listed, depending on the amount of writing.

	Price Range	
☐ **1973,** Lincoln Enterprises, color TV pictures ..	10.00	15.00
☐ **1974,** Lincoln Enterprises, animated pictures	10.00	15.00
☐ **1976–1978, Three-Year Calendar,** Lincoln Enterprises, color TV photos	6.00	8.00

1976 Star Trek Calendar, Ballantine Books

	Price Range	
☐ **Star Trek Comedy Calendar,** Lincoln Enterprises	3.00	4.00
☐ **1976,** Ballantine Books, photos from the TV series, color, boxed	25.00	45.00
☐ **1977,** Ballantine Books, TV photos, boxed ...	20.00	30.00
☐ **1977,** Franco, cloth hanging, in envelope	30.00	50.00
☐ **1978,** Ballantine Books, color TV photos, boxed	20.00	30.00
☐ **1979,** Ballantine Books, color TV photos, boxed	20.00	30.00
☐ **1980,** Pocket Books, color movie photos, boxed	15.00	25.00
☐ **1980,** Blue Mountain Press, nature, art & poems by Leonard Nimoy, Nimoy on cover	10.00	15.00
☐ **1981,** Pocket Books, color photos from first movie	12.00	20.00
☐ **1982,** Pocket Books, color photos from first movie	15.00	25.00
☐ **1983,** Pocket Books, color photos from second movie	10.00	15.00
☐ **1984,** Pocket Books, color photos from TV show	10.00	15.00
☐ **1985,** Pocket Books, color photos from third movie	8.00	12.00
☐ **1985 Historical Calendar,** Datazine, cartoons and dates pertinent to Star Trek	5.00	6.00
☐ **1986,** Pocket Books, color portraits from movies	8.00	9.00
☐ **1986 Historical Calendar,** Datazine, cartoons and dates pertinent to Star Trek	5.00	6.00
☐ **1987,** Pocket Books, stars favorite episodes, TV pictures. *Note:* This calendar apparently had a very short print run and may become an excellent collectible in the future	8.00	12.00
☐ **1987,** Historical calendar, Datazine, Star Trek IV cartoons	5.00	6.00

CELS AND STORYBOARDS

Cels are the transparencies on which the action parts of an animated film are printed. Storyboards are the preliminary sketches made for an animated story. There are hundreds of storyboards and thousands of cels for each half hour of an animated Star Trek episode. An original storyboard should sell for between $10.00 and $40.00; an original cel for $15.00 to $75.00 depending on subject matter. When buying a cel for a collection, desirable features are large, well-centered, complete figures. Main characters and group shots are always in demand. There were some reproductions of original cels made for collectors. These are listed below.

	Price Range	
☐ **Handpainted Cels,** limited edition with studio authentication seal, numbered, set of 14 from the animated show, set	250.00	350.00
☐ **1A The Crew Of The Enterprise**	20.00	45.00
☐ **5 Yesteryear**	20.00	45.00
☐ **6 More Tribbles, More Troubles**	20.00	45.00
☐ **9 The Ambergris Element**	20.00	45.00
☐ **11 Jihad,** composite of aliens	20.00	45.00
☐ **12 Spock,** the boy atop L'Chaya	20.00	45.00
☐ **14 The Time Trap**	20.00	45.00
☐ **15 The Enterprise And The Aqua Shuttle**	20.00	45.00
☐ **16 Beyond The Farthest Star**	20.00	45.00
☐ **20 Kukupkan And The Enterprise**	20.00	45.00
☐ **22 Time Warp**	20.00	45.00
☐ **23 About To Battle A Klingon**	20.00	45.00
☐ **25 The Counter Clock Incident**	20.00	45.00
☐ **00 Title Scene From Star Trek**	20.00	45.00

4″ x 8″ copies of character cels, Lincoln Enterprises.

☐ **Chapel**	2.00	3.00
☐ **Enterprise**	2.00	3.00
☐ **Kirk**	2.00	3.00
☐ **Lt. Arex**	2.00	3.00
☐ **Lt. M'Hress**	2.00	3.00
☐ **McCoy**	2.00	3.00
☐ **Scotty**	2.00	3.00

	Price Range	
☐ **Spock**	2.00	3.00
☐ **Sulu**	2.00	3.00
☐ **Uhura**	2.00	3.00

CERAMICS

ERNST COLLECTIBLES BY ARTIST SUSIE MORTON

PLATES

	Price Range	
☐ **Beam Us Down Compilation Collector's Plate,** 8½"	30.00	35.00
☐ **Captain Kirk Collector's Plate,** 8½"	30.00	35.00
☐ **Chekov Collector's Plate,** 8½"	30.00	35.00
☐ **Enterprise Collector's Plate,** 10¼"	40.00	50.00
☐ **McCoy Collector's Plate,** 8½"	30.00	35.00
☐ **Mirror, Mirror Collector's Plate,** second in series of scene plates	30.00	35.00
☐ **Scotty Collector's Plate,** 8½"	30.00	35.00
☐ **Spock Collector's Plate,** 8½"	30.00	35.00
☐ **Sulu Collector's Plate,** 8½"	30.00	35.00
☐ **Trouble With Tribbles Collector's Plate,** 8½", this is the first in a series of Star Trek action scenes scheduled for 1987–88	30.00	35.00
☐ **Uhura Collector's Plate**	30.00	35.00

MUGS (1986)

☐ **Beam Us Down**	5.00	8.00
☐ **Captain Kirk**	5.00	8.00
☐ **Chekov**	5.00	8.00
☐ **McCoy**	5.00	8.00
☐ **Scotty**	5.00	8.00
☐ **Spock**	5.00	8.00
☐ **Sulu**	5.00	8.00
☐ **Uhura**	5.00	8.00

OTHER

	Price Range	
☐ **Enterprise Collector's Plate,** signed by cast	**45.00**	**60.00**
☐ **Mugs,** The Official Star Trek Fan Club 20th Anniversary and fan club logos, 1986	**10.00**	**12.00**
☐ **Mugs,** The Wrath of Khan, Image Products, 1982		
Khan	**50.00**	**75.00**
Kirk	**35.00**	**50.00**
Spock	**25.00**	**50.00**
☐ **Steins,** 6¼″ tall, sepia tone, Ernst Collectibles, 1986		
Kirk	**20.00**	**25.00**
Spock	**20.00**	**25.00**

CERTIFICATES AND DIPLOMAS

CERTIFICATES

	Price Range	
☐ **Deltan Oath Of Celibacy**	**1.00**	**3.00**
☐ **Federation Birth Certificate,** 22K borders, heavy gauge bond	**1.00**	**3.00**
☐ **Only Vulcan Spoken Here,** 22K borders, heavy gauge bond	**1.00**	**3.00**
☐ **Tribble Pedigree,** 22K borders, heavy gauge bond	**1.00**	**3.00**
☐ **Vulcan Birth Certificate,** 22K borders, heavy gauge bond	**1.00**	**3.00**
☐ **Vulcan Kolinahar Discipline,** 22K borders, heavy gauge bond	**1.00**	**3.00**
☐ **Vulcan Land Deed,** 22K borders, heavy gauge bond	**1.00**	**3.00**
☐ **Vulcan Marriage License,** 22K borders, heavy gauge bond	**1.00**	**3.00**
☐ **U.S.S. Enterprise Crew,** 22K borders, heavy gauge bond	**1.00**	**3.00**

	Price Range	
☐ **Star Fleet Officers Club,** 22K borders, heavy gauge bond	1.00	3.00
☐ **Vulcan Officers Club,** 22K borders, heavy gauge bond	1.00	3.00
☐ **Deluxe Flight Deck Certificate,** Lincoln Enterprises, blue, Enterprise superimposed on background, on parchment-like paper, two-color ribbon, insignia sticker, signed by William Shatner and Gene Roddenberry	1.00	3.00
☐ **Flight Deck Certificate,** Lincoln Enterprises, blue, picture of Enterprise superimposed on background, signed by William Shatner and Gene Roddenberry	1.00	3.00

DIPLOMAS

☐ **Doctorate Of Space Medicine,** 22K borders, heavy gauge bond	1.00	2.00
☐ **From The Klingon Academy,** 22K borders, heavy gauge bond	1.00	2.00
☐ **Klingon,** academy diploma	1.00	2.00
☐ **Klingon Captain,** 22K borders, heavy gauge bond	1.00	2.00
☐ **Phaser Marksman,** 22K borders, heavy gauge bond	1.00	2.00
☐ **Star Fleet Academy,** 22K borders, heavy gauge bond	1.00	2.00
☐ **Star Fleet Admiral,** 22K borders, heavy gauge bond	1.00	2.00
☐ **Star Fleet Captain Certification,** 22K borders, heavy gauge bond	1.00	2.00
☐ **Star Fleet Operations Officers,** 22K borders, heavy gauge bond	1.00	2.00
☐ **Vulcan Academy Of Science,** 22K borders, heavy gauge bond	1.00	2.00
☐ **Vulcan Master,** 22K borders, heavy gauge bond	1.00	2.00

CLOTHING AND ACCESSORIES

	Price Range	
☐ **Belt,** Star Trek: The Motion Picture, stretch cloth with "Star Trek" woven in, Lee	10.00	15.00
☐ **Belt Pouch,** Star Fleet Academy with UFP Janus head, silk-screened vinyl, T-K Graphics, 6″ x 9″	4.00	5.00
☐ **As above,** Star Fleet Headquarters Tactical Operations Center, T-K Graphics, 6″ x 9″ ...	4.00	5.00
☐ **As above,** UFP Diplomatic Service, T-K Graphics, 6″ x 9″	4.00	5.00
☐ **As above,** USS Enterprise/NCC-1701, T-K Graphics, 6″ x 9″	4.00	5.00
☐ **As above,** Enterprise schematic, T-K Graphics, 6″ x 9″	4.00	5.00
☐ **As above,** Vulcan Science Academy, T-K Graphics, 6″ x 9″	4.00	5.00
☐ **Cap,** Star Trek III, baseball cap with embroidered patch, Lincoln Enterprises	10.00	12.00
☐ **Cap,** Star Trek IV, beige corduroy red, embroidered with logo, Official Star Trek Fan Club, 1986	12.00	15.00
☐ **Cap,** Star Trek 20th Anniversary embroidered patch on baseball cap, Lincoln Enterprises, 1986	10.00	15.00
☐ **Cap,** USS Enterprise, baseball cap with embroidered patch and command star, Thinking Cap Co.	7.00	9.00
☐ **Cap,** United Federation of Planets, baseball cap with embroidered patch, Thinking Cap Co.	8.00	10.00
☐ **Cap,** Vulcan ear hat, rubber pointed ears attached, Thinking Cap Co.	8.00	12.00
☐ **Cap,** Star Trek II: Wrath of Khan, silkscreened baseball cap, Thinking Cap Co.	6.00	8.00
☐ **Checkbook Cover,** Star Fleet Academy, vinyl silkscreened, T-K Graphics	2.00	3.00
☐ **As above,** Star Fleet Hqts. Tac. Ops. Ctr. ...	2.00	3.00
☐ **As above,** UFP Diplomatic Service	2.00	3.00

Star Trek II: The Wrath of Khan Cap

	Price Range	
☐ **As above,** USS Enterprise/NCC-1701	2.00	3.00
☐ **As above,** Vulcan Science Academy	2.00	3.00
☐ **Iron-On Transfer,** Enterprise, Lincoln Enterprises	1.00	2.00
☐ **As above,** Group shot from "Patterns of Force"	1.00	2.00
☐ **As above,** Kirk from TV series	1.00	2.00
☐ **As above,** Kirk & Spock from TV series	1.00	2.00
☐ **As above,** Kirk & Spock with phaser from TV series	1.00	2.00
☐ **As above,** Kirk & Spock from "Patterns of Force"	1.00	2.00
☐ **As above,** Kirk & Spock from "Spock's Brain"	1.00	2.00
☐ **As above,** Kirk with phaser from TV series ..	1.00	2.00
☐ **As above,** Spock with Vulcan salute	1.00	2.00
☐ **As above,** Star Trek III: Search for Spock logo	1.00	2.00
☐ **As above,** USS Enterprise, in white or blue ..	1.00	2.00
☐ **Iron-On Transfer,** Klingon Battlecruiser, Mego Corp.	2.00	4.00

	Price Range	
☐ **As above,** "Star Trek Lives," Mego Corp. ...	2.00	4.00
☐ **Iron-On Transfer,** Wrath of Khan logo, Pacific Transfer	1.00	2.00
☐ **As above,** Kirk from Wrath of Khan, Pacific Transfer	1.00	2.00
☐ **As above,** Spock from Wrath of Khan, Pacific Transfer	1.00	2.00
☐ **As above,** Khan from Wrath of Khan, Pacific Transfer	1.00	2.00
☐ **Iron-On Transfer,** "Pet Me, I'm a Tribble," fan produced	1.00	2.00
☐ **Iron-On Transfer,** "How's Your Tribble?," fan produced	1.00	2.00
☐ **Iron-On Transfer,** "Keep on Trekkin" with character stepping out, fan produced	1.00	2.00
☐ **Iron-On Transfer,** "Keep on Trekkin" with Enterprise and planet	1.00	2.00
☐ **Iron-On Transfer,** "Vulcan Power"	1.00	2.00
☐ **Jacket,** TV show, silver with UFP patch, Great Lakes, 1974	25.00	35.00
☐ **Jacket,** lightweight with built-in flashing LEDs, Starlog, 1976	75.00	100.00
☐ **As above,** deluxe version, lined with UFP patch, movie logo and Enterprise on back ...	100.00	125.00
☐ **Jacket,** embroidered Star Trek III patch on front, black nylon, Lincoln Enterprises	40.00	50.00
☐ **As above,** in white or blue satinique with words "USS Enterprise" on back	40.00	50.00
☐ **Jacket,** with 20th Anniversary patch, 1986 ...	40.00	50.00
☐ **Jacket,** white, fully embroidered design on back with Star Trek IV and Scene of Enterprise over San Francisco	125.00	150.00
☐ **Jacket,** silver, two-color Star Trek IV logo on back, Official Star Trek Fan Club, 1986	40.00	50.00
☐ **Pajamas,** PCA, permanent press, picturing Spock	6.00	8.00
☐ **Shopping Bag,** canvas, blue, open, with handles, uniform insignia on front	9.00	11.00

Price Range

☐ **Socks,** John Batts Inc., TV show, Kirk or Spock, iron-on white material, 1976	10.00	15.00
☐ **Tote Bag,** dark blue, with carrying strap, decal on front of Enterprise, 1979, Aviva Enterprises	15.00	25.00
☐ **As above,** dark blue, with carrying strap, decal on front pictures Kirk, Aviva Enterprises, 1979	15.00	25.00
☐ **As above,** dark blue, with carrying strap, decal on front pictures Spock, Aviva Enterprises, 1979	15.00	25.00
☐ **Tote Bag,** white canvas with carrying strap, decal on front reads "Star Fleet Space Shuttle" with TV series uniform insignia, c. 1976	10.00	15.00

Note: Because of the current trend in the T-shirt industry toward inexpensive silkscreened T-shirts, available in relatively small quantities, unlicensed Star Trek shirts have become very common. The shirts listed here are all either promotional or licensed items. While some of the unlicensed products are very attractive, it is unlikely they will ever become collectible.

☐ **T-Shirt,** Boston Star Trek Convention, 1976	8.00	10.00
☐ **T-Shirt,** Star Trek Lives, silkscreened, Lincoln Enterprises	6.00	8.00
☐ **T-Shirt,** early NBC Star Trek TV promo art on tank top, Lincoln Enterprises	6.00	8.00
☐ **T-Shirt,** Bloom Country, silkscreened characters in "Star Trek" phase with caption "Ahead Warp Zillion" Lin-Tex, 1986	10.00	15.00
☐ **T-Shirt,** Funky Winkerbean, silkscreened, "Beam Me Up Scotty. . . .", Datazine, 1986 . .	10.00	15.00
☐ **T-Shirt,** Star Trek IV, logo on black shirt, Official Star Trek Fan Club, 1986	8.00	10.00
☐ **T-Shirt,** "The Next Generation," silkscreened, silver letters on black. Came in early promo kit from Paramount, 1986	10.00	20.00
☐ **T-Shirt,** 20th Anniversary logo, early version, Paramount, 1986	10.00	20.00

	Price Range	
☐ **T-Shirt,** 20th Anniversary logo, later version, Official Star Trek Fan Club, 1986 . . . . ⸗	10.00	15.00
☐ **Underwear,** Nazareth Hills, Star Trek, The Motion Picture, T-shirt and underwear set, boys, 1979	2.00	5.00

COMIC BOOKS

STAR TREK

DAN CURTIS GIVEAWAYS

Set of 6 small comics. Two were Star Trek.

	Price Range	
☐ **#2,** Enterprise Mutiny	2.00	4.00
☐ **#6,** Dark Traveler	2.00	4.00

D.C. COMICS

☐ **Star Trek, #1–8**	1.50	2.50
☐ **Star Trek, #9–40**	1.00	1.50
☐ **Star Trek Annual, #1**	2.00	3.00
☐ **Star Trek Annual, #2**	2.00	3.00
☐ **Star Trek III,** Movie Special #1, July 1984 . .	2.00	3.00
☐ **Star Trek IV,** Movie Special #2	2.00	3.00
☐ **Who's Who in Star Trek, #1**	1.50	2.50
☐ **Who's Who in Star Trek, #2**	1.50	2.50

DIMENSION GRAPHICS

☐ **Elf Trek,** Part 1, Star Trek parody, 1986	1.50	2.00
☐ **Elf Trek,** Part 2, 1986	1.50	2.50

GOLD KEY COMICS, 1967–79

☐ **1,** K-G Planet of Death, pictures Spock with beeper, Kirk and Sulu, rare	25.00	50.00
☐ **2–6**	10.00	20.00
☐ **7–12**	8.00	12.00

Star Trek Gold Key Comic #1

	Price	Range
☐ **13–22**	5.00	10.00
☐ **23–30**	4.00	8.00
☐ **31–40**	4.00	6.00
☐ **41–56**	3.00	5.00
☐ **56–61**	5.00	7.00

STAR TREK: THE ENTERPRISE LOGS

Golden Press; a Boston warehouse fire destroyed half of the U.S. supply. This item could become highly collectible in the future.

	Price	Range
☐ **1–8,** collection of comic strips from Gold Key, 1976, 224 pp	10.00	20.00

	Price Range	
☐ **9–17,** Volume 2, Western Publishing Company, 1976, 224 pp	10.00	20.00
☐ **18–26,** Volume 3, 1977, 224 pp	10.00	20.00
☐ **21, 28, 30–36, 38,** Volume 4, 1977, 224 pp ..	10.00	20.00

STAR TREK: THE MOTION PICTURE

MARVEL COMICS GROUP

☐ **1**	.50	1.50
☐ **2–10**	.50	1.00
☐ **11–17**	.50	1.00
☐ **18**	2.00	4.00

CONVENTION PROGRAM BOOKS

In the early days of Star Trek conventions it was common practice to produce souvenir program books. Rising costs have discouraged them in recent years.

	Price Range	
☐ **1972 International Star Trek Convention Program Book,** small size black cover with picture of Enterprise, black and white pictures inside, rare	15.00	30.00
☐ **1973 International Star Trek Convention Program Book,** second New York convention, Doohan, Takei guests, color cover	10.00	15.00
☐ **1974 International Star Trek Convention Program Book,** New York, full color, Spock cover, Kelly, Koenig, Nichols and Takei guests, full of photos, 48 pages	5.00	10.00
☐ **1974 New York Star Trek Convention Program**	5.00	10.00
☐ **1975 International Star Trek Convention Program Book,** New York, full color cover of Spock, Kirk and McCoy, Shatner, Doohan and Koenig guests, 24 pages, 8½″ x 11″	3.00	6.00

	Price Range	
☐ **1975 New York Star Trek Convention Program**	3.00	6.00
☐ **1975 Miamicon I Convention Program Book,** Miami, cover by Jack Kirby, art by Adams, Kirby and Bode, Jimmy Doohan guest, 36 pages, 8½" x 11"	3.00	6.00
☐ **1975 International Star Trek Convention Program Book,** Philadelphia, Spock cover, lots of pictures inside	3.00	6.00
☐ **1975 Trekon I Program Book,** West Palm Beach, Beck cover, Takei, Kelly Freas and Noel Neill guests, 32 pages	3.00	6.00
☐ **1976 Bicentennial 10 Convention Program Book,** New York, Shatner, Kelly, Doohan, Nichols, Takei, Koenig and Grace Lee Whitney guests, 8½" x 11"	3.00	6.00
☐ **1976 Boston Star Trek Convention Program Book,** full color wraparound cover, Doohan, Kelly, Koenig, Nichols and Takei guests, 48 pages	3.00	6.00
☐ **1976 Omnicon Program Book,** Kelley guest, program guides for Star Trek, Outer Limits, UNCLE, more	8.00	12.00
☐ **1977 Space-Con 4 Program Book,** Los Angeles, color wraparound cover, Shatner, Kelly, Whitney and Harlan Ellison, 48 pages, 8½" x 11"	2.00	4.00
☐ **1978 Odyssey One Convention Program Book,** Milwaukee, full color covers, Takei and Koenig guests, 12 pages	2.00	4.00
☐ **1978 Space-Con 7 Program Book,** Los Angeles, Shatner, Takei, Nichols and Ellison guests, 30 pages, 8½" x 11"	2.00	4.00
☐ **1979 Star Con Program Book,** Dallas, Grace Lee Whitney guest, 48 pages	2.00	4.00
☐ **1982 Ultimate Fantasy Program Book,** Houston, billed as "The" Star Trek con of all time	5.00	6.00

COSTUMES AND UNIFORMS

There is a great deal of interest in authentic Star Trek costumes. With the exception of Star Fleet Uniforms, no one has manufactured ready-to-wear authentic uniforms. Individuals continue to make their own however, often with excellent results. Original costumes are of course extremely rare and anyone having one for sale could virtually name their own price. For example, a pair of Leonard Nimoy's ear tips worn in Star Trek II went for $1000.00 at auction at the time of the movie's release.

	Price Range	
☐ **Uniform,** Star Trek TV shirt, adult sizes only, in gold, blue or red, Starfleet Uniforms	20.00	30.00
☐ **Uniform,** Star Trek: The Motion Picture shirt, white, short sleeve, authentic reproduction, adult sizes only, Starfleet Uniforms	15.00	25.00
☐ **Halloween Costume,** Mr. Spock, Collegeoille Costumes, #217, 1967	20.00	40.00
☐ **Halloween Costume,** Kirk, cloth costume plus plastic mask, came in small, medium, or large, boxed, Ben Cooper, 1975	15.00	25.00
☐ **As above,** Klingon	15.00	25.00
☐ **As above,** Spock	15.00	25.00
☐ **Mask,** Kirk from Star Trek: TMP, Don Post Studios	40.00	60.00
☐ **As above,** Spock from Star Trek: TMP, Don Post Studios	40.00	60.00
☐ **As above,** Klingon from Star Trek: TMP, Don Post Studios	40.00	60.00
☐ **As above,** Vulcan Master from Star Trek: TMP, Don Post Studios	40.00	50.00
☐ **Pattern,** Men's TV uniform shirt, Lincoln Enterprises	4.00	5.00
☐ **As above,** Women's TV uniform dress, Lincoln Enterprises	4.00	5.00
☐ **As above,** Jacket from Star Trek II–IV, Men's, Lincoln Enterprises	7.00	8.00
☐ **As above,** Women's jacket from Star Trek II–IV, Lincoln Enterprises	7.00	8.00

	Price Range	
☐ **As above,** Trousers from Star Trek II–IV, Lincoln Enterprises	5.00	6.00
☐ **As above,** Turtleneck undershirt from Star Trek II–IV, Lincoln Enterprises	5.00	6.00
☐ **As above,** Recreational Jumpsuit from Star Trek II–IV, Lincoln Enterprises	7.00	8.00
☐ **Spock Ears,** from Star Trek: TMP, soft plastic, Aviva Enterprises	10.00	15.00
☐ **As above,** from Wrath of Khan, Don Post Studios	6.00	10.00
☐ **As above,** promotional giveaway from Ballantine Books, came with 20th Anniversary logo stickers	2.00	3.00
☐ **Vulcan Ear Tips,** professional quality latex, applied with spirit gum, Star Fleet Command	10.00	15.00

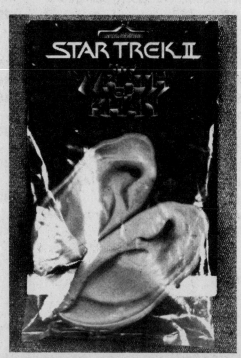

Star Trek II Ears, Don Post Studios

SEE SECTIONS ON JEWELRY AND PATCHES FOR UNIFORM ACCESSORIES.

DECALS AND STICKERS

	Price Range	
☐ **Decal Sheet, No. 1,** Lincoln Enterprises, three different insignia designs, two-color, water mount	.75	1.00
☐ **Decal Sheet, No. 2,** Lincoln Enterprises, decals of the Enterprise, the Klingon fighter, Galileo	.75	1.00
☐ **Decal Sheet, No. 3,** Lincoln Enterprises, decals of a communicator, a phaser, and 3-D chess game	.75	1.00
☐ **Federation Seal Sticker,** blue on white, Star Fleet Academy	1.00	1.50
☐ **Puffy Sticker Sets,** Star Trek: The Motion Picture, two sets, features characters and ships	1.00	2.00
☐ **Star Trek Stamp Album,** 1977, by Celebrity Stamps, all stamps included, six packets, each set featuring Kirk, Spock, Enterprise, aliens, space ships, weapons and action scenes, each packet	5.00	10.00
☐ **Complete sets**	25.00	40.00
☐ **Album**	6.00	10.00
☐ **Assembled albums**	20.00	25.00
☐ **Star Trek: The Motion Picture,** peel-off graphics book, large stickers including Kirk, Spock, Ilia, Klingon and phasers, Wallaby, 1979	15.00	25.00
☐ **Sticker,** Star Trek: The Motion Picture, instant stained glass stickers, Admiral Kirk, Aviva Enterprises, 1979	1.00	4.00
☐ **As above,** Enterprise	1.00	4.00
☐ **As above,** Spock	1.00	4.00
☐ **As above,** Spock giving Vulcan Salute	1.00	4.00
☐ **As above,** Spock with Science Symbol	1.00	4.00

	Price Range	
☐ **As above,** The Vulcan Salute	1.00	4.00
☐ **Sticker,** Promotional, Blue and yellow "Star Trek 20th Anniversary, the only logical books to read!", Pocket Books	1.00	2.00
☐ **Vending Capsule Decals,** Paramount Pictures, Inc., set of four color peel-back stickers of Spock, Kirk, and The Enterprise, 1979, McDonald's Promotion	6.00	12.00
☐ **Vulcan Sticker,** black lettering with green heart, says "Even Vulcans love Star Trek" . .	2.50	4.00
☐ **Window Sticker,** Star-fleet Academy	1.00	3.00
☐ **Window Sticker,** Vulcan Science Academy . .	1.00	3.00
☐ **Walls Ice Cream Stickers,** New Zealand, set of six, Captain Kirk, Mr. Spock, Khan, Sulu, Uhura, 1982	10.00	15.00

FAN CLUBS

The following is a partial list of fan clubs devoted to Star Trek. Most are soliciting new members. Don't forget your SASE when writing for information.

DOMESTIC

Allegiance For DeForest Kelley
Sandra Keel
RT 3 Box 48
Lafayette, AL 36862

Alliance For William Shatner
Sandra Keel, RT 3 Box 48
Lafayette, AL 36862

Allies For Star Trek
David Jackson
P.O. Box 27191
Memphis, TN 38127

Atlanta Star Trek Society
Owen Ogletree
454 Huff St. #9
Lawrenceville, GA 30245

Eastside Star Trekkers
Janis Worrell
25450 Fall City Hwy.
Redmond, WA 98052

George Takei International Fan Club
Mai Sanchez
1211 Hi Point St.
Los Angeles, CA 90035

The Information Center
Frances Bloomer
522 W. Oak
Round Rock, TX 78664

**The James Doohan
International Fan Club**
Mrs. Anna Hreha
1519 N.W. 204th Street
Seattle, WA 98177

Leonard Nimoy Fan Club
Barbara Walker
17 Gateway Dr.
Batavia, NY 14020

Leonard Nimoy Fan Club
Sandra Keel
RT 3 Box 48
Lafayette, AL 36862

Shatner Calls
June Tisdale
304 N. Leavitt
Brazil, IN 47832

Starbase 2
270 Robincroft Dr.
Pasadena, CA 91104

Starbase 3
Art Harrison
8613 S. Levergne
Burbank, IL 60459

Star Fleet Academy
Joseph M. Portelli
24640 Orchard
Taylor, MI 48180

Starfleet, Region 1
Stephen Thomas
7301 River Rd. #117
Newport News, VA 23607

Starfleet, Region 2
Linda Taylor
829 Heron Rd.
Coca, FL 32926

Starfleet, Region 3
Mary Helm
6914 Country Dawn
San Antonio, TX 78240

Starfleet, Region 4
Pamela DuPrey
142 S. Wilton Dr.
Los Angeles, CA 90004

Starfleet, Region 5
Michael Martinez
5239 21st Ave. N5
Seattle, WA 98105

Starfleet, Region 6
Frank Jungers
428 S. Lincoln
Sioux Falls, SD 57104

Starfleet, Region 7
Bryan Ackermann
3321 Ave. P
Brooklyn, NY 11234

Starfleet, Region 7
Irene Hightower
739 Hill Ave.
Pittsburgh, PA 15221

Starfleet, Region 12
Suzanne Harris
2217 Denver
Kansas City, MO 64127

Starfleet, Region 14
John Supranovich
224 Larkin St.
Bangor, ME 04401

Starfleet, Region 14
Mike Diegnan
33 Moreland Ave.
Providence, RI 02908

Starfleet, Region 15
Jack Fields
3141 Sudbury Rd.
Cameron Park, CA 95682

Starfleet, Region 16
John Hoffstrom
PC 1 USS San Jose AFS-7
FPO San Francisco, CA 96678

Starfleet, Region 17
Charles Brown
15 N. Estes St.
Lakewood, CO 80226

Starfleet, Region 18
Sebetha
32936 Kelly Lane
Yucaipa, CA 92399

Starfleet, U.S.S. Achernar
T'Pam
142 S. Wilton Dr.
Los Angeles, CA 90004

Starfleet, U.S.S. Carson
Karen Emerson
35 E. Lincoln Way
Sparks, NM 89431

Starfleet, U.S.S. Defiance
Robert Lerman
P.O. Box 554
Fair Oaks, CA 95682

Starfleet, U.S.S. Eagle
Eugene Craig
1663 Longspur Ave
Sunnyvale, CA 94114

Starfleet, U.S.S. Endurance
Martin McClure
P.O.Box 5499
Richmond, CA 94805

Starfleet, U.S.S. Hannibal
Mark Ernst
Clearview Park 9, RT. 28
Epsom, NH 03234

Starfleet, Minnesota
Kelly Huffman
157-15 Place Victory Village
Mankato, MN 56001

Starfleet, U.S.S. Vigilant
Andrea Wright
1151 Sanchez
San Francisco, CA 94114

Star Trek Association For Revival (STAR)
OKC
P.O. Box 565
Bethany, OK 73008

Star Trek Association Of Fans
1721 Blake Ave.
Racine, WI 53404

Star Trek Enterprises
59 Hillside Ave.
New Rochelle, NY 10801

Star Trek: The Official Fan Club
Dan Madden
P.O. Box 111000
Aurora, CO 80011

Star Trek Welcommittee/ Office Of The Publisher Of The Directory
Kay Johnson
301 Porte Cimi Pas
Kansas City, MO 64114

Star Trek Welcommittee (STW)
Shirley Maiewski,
Chairman
481 Main St.
Hatfield, MA 01038

The Tholian Web
R.A. Mitchell
200 Niagara St. #302
Buffalo, NY 14201

Trek Clipping Exchange
2829 Frankel Blvd.
Merrick, NY 11566

Trek-A-Teers
Anita Severance
430 Tschirgi
Sheridan, WY 82801

Trekkers In The Wilderness
Carolyne McClayne
1665 Hwy 418 W.
Silsbee, TX 77656

United Trekkers Of America
Joey Mandala
P.O. Box 755
Barnsville, NC 28714

U.S.S. Starfleet Command
Steve Mehallo
477 Beech Ave.
San Bruno, CA 94006

U.S.S. Voyager, NCC 20621
Daniel Maack
Box 9284
Huntington, WV 25704

Walter Koenig International
Carolyn Atkinson
2017 Kentucky Ave.
Ft. Wayne, IN 48605

Warp Nine
Jeff Bolognese
303 Adams Way
Ambler, PA 19002

Where No Fan Has Gone Before
Joe Ames
RD #2 Box 208
New Ringgold, PA 17960

William Shatner Letter Exchange
Pamela Igo
6001 Arlington Blvd. #918
Falls Church, VA

FOREIGN

Starfleet, Region 8
Pam Clarke
154 Colston Benwell
Newcastle Upon Tyne
NE 4 BUN
Great Britain

Starfleet, Region 9
Petra Vasseur
Quinkestrass 46
69 Heidelburg, West Germany

Starfleet, Region 10
Elisabeth Rose
209-8540 Citation Dr.
Richmond, BC V6Y 3A3
Canada

Starfleet, Region 11
Diane Marchant
2 Margaret St.
Morialoc
3195 Victoria, Australia

Starfleet, Region 12
Greg Young
706-2080 Rembina Way
Winnipeg, MB R2T 2G9
Canada

FANZINES

Fanzines are fan-written magazines containing stories, poetry, artwork and comments. Star Trek fanzines started in the mid–seventies and were generally passed among fans at conventions, with less than a hundred copies being printed. Although fanzines can still be found at Star Trek Conventions today, most fanzines are now sold through the mail and have print runs of up to a thousand copies.

Most early fanzines were produced on mimeograph machines and as such were produced in a rainbow of ink colors and on low quality paper. They were often bound using braids to facilitate putting them in ringed binders to protect them. With the advent of copy machines and larger print runs, stapled and bound fanzines became more common and mimeographed fanzines have become a thing of the past. Current fanzines are usually offset printed with card stock covers. Cover art has become an important part of modern fanzines and covers range from the simple borders on "Echoes of The Empire" to the full color portraits on "Vault of Tomorrow." ZineEds (a short term for Fanzine Editors) have become aware that great cover art can actually help the sale of their zines. A lot more attention is also being paid to the way the interior of the zine is laid out. With the use of border tapes, rub-off lettering and fancy type styles, today's fanzines are taking on a much more professional look. Many ZineEds now use computers to edit and print out their fanzines—so computer print is quite common. Although fanzines have greatly improved from their early predecessors, they are still considered non-profit ventures.

Because of the small print runs, most fanzines may seem relatively expensive when compared to professional publications. Fanzines are available directly from the publishers for an average price of $8.00 per 100 pages. Different types of binding and cover stock can affect the overall price as well as whether you purchase the fanzine from the original publisher. Information on currently available fanzines can be found in the publication DATAZINE, PO Box 19413, Denver, CO 80219. DATAZINE has a TV Guide format and is available by subscription. Older fanzines can be found at conventions and through fanzine auctions listed in DATAZINE.

In STAR TREK fanzines there are basically four different themes: Action/Adventure (AA), Love/Romance (LR), Mixed Media (MM), and Adult (Adult or K/S for Kirk/Spock Relationship). Fanzines with a love/romance theme are sometimes referred to as "Mary Sue" stories, because typically the heroine of the story is the only one who can save the Enterprise, be Captain Kirk's or Mr. Spock's only TRUE love, and/or save the galaxy from total destruction. Fanzines with adult themes cover the entire spectrum from gentle romance to hard core sex. Some contain explicit Kirk/Spock love stories or detailed hurt/comfort themes. Most sexually explicit fanzines require an age statement before you can purchase them. Zines with love/romance and adult themes command the highest prices and seem to hold the greatest value over time, although certain older action/adventure fanzines still sell for relatively high prices.

What makes a fanzine a collectible? It is really up to the individual reader. If a fanzine has a particular story in it that really appeals to you, then you would probably want to keep the zine for your collection. Some fanzines, however, have earned certain honors because they have broken new ground or appealed to a large number of fans. There are now two awards given to fanzines that are awarded by readers, The Trekstar

Awards (for Star Trek fanzines) and FanQ Awards. If a fanzine has received either of those awards, you can count on it being one of the better fanzines in its category.

Below are some of the more collectible fanzines; some are currently available, others are long out of print. The prices listed are for single issues of original issue copies only.

	Price Range	
☐ **Accumulated Leave,** by Yeoman Press (AA)	10.00	12.00
☐ **Alternate Universe,** # 1–2 by Shirley Maiewski (AA)	18.00	20.00
☐ **Archives,** by Yeoman Press (AA)	12.00	15.00
☐ **As I Do Thee,** Series by A. Gelfand (K/S)	15.00	18.00
☐ **Babel,** by Laura and Margaret Basta (AA)	25.00	50.00
☐ **Berengaria,** by V. Kirlin (AA)	8.00	10.00
☐ **Bloodstone,** by C. Frisbie (Adult)	20.00	25.00
☐ **Broken Images,** by V. Clark (K/S)	20.00	25.00
☐ **Castaways (The),** by V. Kirlin (AA)	15.00	18.00
☐ **Cheap Thrills,** by Carol Hunterton (K/S)	18.00	20.00
☐ **Contact,** by Bev Volker and Nancy Kippax (Adult) # 1–# 4	35.00	40.00
☐ **# 5/ # 6**	25.00	30.00
☐ **Companion,** Series by Carol Hunterton (K/S)	25.00	30.00
☐ **Courts of Honor,** by Syn Ferguson (Adult)	18.00	20.00
☐ **Daring Attempt,** Series by W. Rathbone (K/S)	15.00	18.00
☐ **Delta Triad,** Series by Melinda Reynolds (AA)	18.00	20.00
☐ **Diamonds and Rust,** by Cheryl Rice (LR)	15.00	18.00
☐ **Displaced,** Series by L. Welling (LR)	10.00	15.00
☐ **Don't Tell It to the Captain,** by M. Lamski (AA)	15.00	20.00
☐ **Duet,** edited by D. Dabinett (K/S)	25.00	30.00
☐ **Echoes of the Empire,** Series by J. Thompson (Adult)	15.00	18.00
☐ **Epilogue,** by Jean Lorrah (AA)	12.00	15.00
☐ **Eridani Triad # 1–5,** by Judith Brownlee (AA)	10.00	12.00
☐ **Fesarius Series,** by T.J. Burnside (AA)	16.00	18.00
☐ **Full Moon Rising,** by Jean Lorrah (LR)	8.00	10.00
☐ **Furaha,** by Virginia Walker (AA)	12.00	15.00
☐ **Grup,** Series by Carrie Brennan (Adult)	25.00	30.00

Price Range

☐ **Handful of Snowflakes,** by M.L. Steve Barnes
(AA) 12.00   15.00
☐ **Honorable Sacrifice,** by B. Zuk (Adult) 15.00   18.00
☐ **In a Different Reality,** by M. Krause (AA) ...   15.00   18.00
☐ **It Takes Time on Impulse,** by H. Stallings
(Adult) 15.00   20.00
☐ **Interphase!,** by Connie Faddis (Series) (AA)   35.00   40.00
☐ **Kraith Collected Series,** by Carol Lynn (AA)   15.00   20.00
☐ **Masiform-D,** by Devra Langsam (AA) 8.00   10.00
☐ **Menagerie,** by Sharon Ferraro and Paula Smith
(AA) 8.00   10.00
☐ **Mirrors of Mind and Flesh,** by Gayle Feyrer
(K/S) 18.00   20.00
☐ **Mixed Metaphors,** by D. Barry (AA) 18.00   20.00
☐ **Naked Times,** Series by Pon Farr Press (K/S)   15.00   20.00

Interphase! Fanzine

	Price Range	
☐ **Night of the Twin Moons,** by Jean Lorrah (LR)	8.00	10.00
☐ **Nome Series,** by V. Clark and B. Storey (K/S)	30.00	35.00
☐ **Nu Ormenel,** Series by F. Marder (Adult)	18.00	20.00
☐ **Nuage Series,** by K. Bates (AA/LR)	12.00	15.00
☐ **Obsession,** by M. Lowe and K. Scarrett (LR)	12.00	15.00
☐ **Odyssey Series,** by Ingrid Cross (AA/LR) ...	15.00	18.00
☐ **OSC'Zine,** by T'Kuhtian (Adult)	18.00	20.00
☐ **One Way Mirror,** by Barbara Wenk (LR)	18.00	20.00
☐ **Out of Bounds,** Series by P. Rose and L. Shell (K/S)	20.00	25.00
☐ **Penumbra,** by M. Arvizu (AA)	12.00	15.00
☐ **Perfect Object,** by Yeoman Press (Adult) ...	12.00	15.00
☐ **Pledge,** by C. Davis (LR)	12.00	15.00
☐ **Precessional,** by Laurie Huff (AA)	15.00	18.00
☐ **Price and the Prize,** by Gayle Feyrer (K/S) ..	20.00	25.00
☐ **R & R,** by Yeoman Press (Adult) #1–#5	12.00	15.00
☐ **Sahaj Series,** by Leslie Lilker (AA)	35.00	40.00
☐ **Sensuous Vulcan,** by D.T. Steiner (Adult) ...	45.00	50.00
☐ **Showcase #1,** by Sharon Emily (LR)	20.00	25.00
☐ **Sol Plus,** by Jackie Bielowicz (AA)	10.00	12.00
☐ **Spock Enslaved,** by D.T. Steiner (Adult)	35.00	40.00
☐ **Spockinalia** #1–5, by Devra Langsam (AA)	20.00	15.00
☐ **Stardate Unknown:,** #1–#5, by Gerry Downes (AA)	20.00	25.00
☐ **Sun and Shadow,** by C. Frisbie (Adult)	18.00	20.00
☐ **T'Hy'La Series,** by Kathleen Resch (Adult) ..	18.00	20.00
☐ **Tales of Feldman,** (Series) by Mindy Glazer (AA)	18.00	20.00
☐ **Thrust,** by C. Frisbie (K/S)	45.00	50.00
☐ **T–Negative,** by Ruth Berman (AA)	5.00	8.00
☐ **Vault of Tomorrow Series,** by Marion McChesney (AA/LR)	15.00	20.00
☐ **Warped Space,** by T'Kuhtian Press (AA)	10.00	15.00
☐ **Weight, The,** by Leslie Fish (AA/Adult)	18.00	20.00

The list below is only partially representative of the short stories, novels, newsletters, commentaries, and correspondence circulating around the world of Star Trek. If you would like to contact any on this list, please enclose a self-addressed stamped envelope for ordering or submitting information.

Accumulated Leave R & R Collected
Yeoman Press
5465 Valles Avenue
Bronx, NY 10471

The Adventure Continues
Our Trash Press
P.O. Box 3742
Ontario, CA 91764

Alkarin Warlord
M'Pingo Press
P.O. Box 206
New Rochelle, NY 10804

Ainitah
Joyce Cluett
3 Antonia Close
Raunds, Wellingborough,
NN9 6EA, England

Alpha-Omega
Tina Angel Bennett
1936 W. Jefferson St.
Louisville, KY 40203

Alpha Touch
Box 103
Queens, NY 11418

Alternate Universe 4
Shirley Malewski, et al.
481 Main Street
Hatfield, MA 01038

Alternative Factor
Star Empire Press
205 Katherine Ave.
Salinas, CA 93901

And Starry Skies
Ruth Berman
5620 Edgewater Blvd.
Minneapolis, MN 55417

Antithesis
Triad Publications
687 East Market Street
Marietta, PA 17547

Arakeyno
Fern Marder, Carol Walske
342 East 53rd Street, #40
New York, NY 10022

Archives
Yeoman Press
5465 Valles Avenue
Bronx, NY 10471

Berengaria
Vicki Kirlin
13018 Emiline
Omaha, NE 68137

The Bridge
Polaris Productions
P.O. Box 109
Lindenwold, NJ 08021

Captain's Log
Sylvia Billings
49 Southampton Rd.
Far Cotton, Northampton
NN4 9EA, England

Captain's Log
Richard Pollet
37–45 59th St.
Woodside, NY 11377

Carbon Based Life
C.J. Andrus
4717 Densmore N.
Seattle, WA 93101

Companion-The Rest Of The Story
Ellen Kobrin
3 Jetmore Pl.
Massapequa, NY 11758

Computer Playback
Janet Hunt
54 Foxhunter Drive
Cadby, Liecester
LE2 5FE England

Conquest
Shona Jackson
The Klingon Embassy
261 Grove St. #43
Waterbury, CT 06710
(Convention listings for New York, New England)

Contact
Bev Volker, Nancy Kippax
5657 Utrecht Road
Baltimore, MD 21206

Cordrazine
Skye Press
4455 Baldwin Ave.
Montreal, Quebec
H1K 3A7, Canada

Changeling
Carolyn Meridith
221 S. Bernard St. #44
State College, PA 16801

The Child Within Us
Danielle Dubois
from John Spires
5550 Trent, #307
Cote St. Luc, Quebec,
H4W 2B9 Canada

Chrysalis
Karl Troeller
P.O. Box 214
S. Bound Brook, NJ 08880

The City On The Edge Of Whatever, Coloring Book
T'Kuhtian Press
5132 Jo-Don Drive
East Lansing, MI 48823

The Clipper Trade Ship
Jim and Melody Rondeau
1853 Fall Brook Ave.
San Jose, CA 91530

Communicator
Joseph M. Portelli
24640 Orchard
Taylor, MI 48180

Creator Of Yesterday
Andrea Bennett
From Starfleet Entertainment
P.O. Box BB
Southgate, MI 48195

Crisis At Kahlel-Den
LexPression
Rt 1 Box 184AA
Keysville, GA 30816

Deck Five Digest
Terry Martin
1126 Highland
Houston, TX 77009

Dedication
Sasasher Press
Leslye Lilker
61 Union Place
Lynbrook, NY 11563

Delta Triad
Melinda Reynolds
Anneta Rd., Box 216
Lietchfield, KY 42759

Destiny's Children
Florence Butler
8030 14th St.
Washington, DC 20012

Dilithium Crystals
Jacqueline Edwards
P.O. Box 137
Bennington, NE 68007

Diversifier Paragon
C.C. Clingan
P.O. Box 1836
Oroville, CA 95965

Dreadnought Explorations Collected
Canadian Contingent Press
1068 Bathgate Dr.
Gloucester, Ontario
K1J 8E8, Canada

Dreamworlds
T'Kuhtian Press
5132 Jo-Don Drive
East Lansing, MI 48823

Echerni-The Lightfleet Letters
Shirley Malewski
481 Main St.
Hatfield, MA 01038

Echoes From The Past
Rebecca Hoffman
205 Pine St.
Greer, SC 29651

Eclipse
Wendy Rathbone
14156 Tobiasson Rd.
Poway, CA 92064

EE Miniar
Deborah Layman
1495 Grandville Ave.
Pontiac, MI 48005

Enter-Comm
Canadian Contingent Press
1068 Bathgate Dr.
Gloucester, Ontario
K1J 8E8, Canada

Enterprise
APA for S.T. Fans:
Mark Ernst
Clearview Park #9,
Route 28
Epsom, NH 03234

Enterprise Log Entries
Shiela Clark
Scot Press
6 Craigmill Cottages
Strathmartine-by-Dundee
Scotland

Epilogue
Jean Lorrah
301 S. 15th St.
Murray, KY 42071

Fanattic
Melissa James
3820 Penhurst Ave.
Baltimore, MD 21215

Fandom Directory
Harry Hopkins
P.O. Box 863
Langley AFB, VA 23665

Fanfare
C.A. Wiggins
745 Drewry St.
Atlanta, GA 30306

The Farthest Star
Pat Nolan
3284 Hull Ave.
Bronx, NY 10467

Federation Report
Michael Brantley
17 Oakdale Dr.
Monevallo, AL 35115

Final Frontier
Tiberius Press
6472 Cascade St.
San Diego, CA 92112

Forget The Dawn
Jean LeCreste
1315 John St.
Evansville, IN 47714

Forum
Kathe Donnelly
6302 S. Spotswood St.
Littleton, CO 80120

Friends And Strangers Near And Far
Jane Freitag
3940 W. Lisbon Ave. #305
Milwaukee, WI

From Hell's Heart
Lee Pennell
Phoenix Press
2203 Sandtown Rd.
Marietta, GA 30060

Full Moon Rising
Jean Lorrah
from Yeoman Press
5465 Valles Ave.
Bronx, NY 10471

Future Wings
Jeanette Eilke
CFPO 5056
Belleville, Ontario
K0K 3R0, Canada

G: Galactic Discourses
Laurie Huff
1156 E. 57th Street
Chicago, IL 60637

Gateway
Martha Bonds
5905 Yorkwood Rd.
Baltimore, MD 21239

Gemini Lynx
Mary Schmidt
from T'Kuhtian Press
5132 Jo-Don Dr.
East Lansing, MI 48823

Gempath
Karen Baily, Wendy Klug
P.O. Box 34
Brighton, MA 02135

Genesis
Ann Becker
14 Hallock Rd.
Patchogue, NY 11772

Genesis Aftermath
ShiKahr Press
P.O. Box 13756
St. Paul, MN 55113

Golden Oldies And New Delights
4 Play Press
P.O. Box 4106
Cave Creek, AZ 85331

Greater California K/S
Noel Silva
674 Clarinada Ave.
Daly City, CA 94015

Grip
Roberta Rogow
P.O. Box 124
Fairlawn, NJ 07410
(Features new writers)

Grope
Ann Looker
46 Bryn Road
Mrynmill, Swansea,
W. Glam
SA2 OAP, Wales

Guardian
Mazeltough Press
Linda Deneroff
1800 Ocean Parkway #E2
Brooklyn, NY 11223

A Handful Of Snowflakes
M.L. Barnes
from Caro Hedge
210 Division
Lamar, CO 81052

The Holmesian Federation
Signe Langon
3321 NW Walnut
Corvallis, OR 97330

The Honorable Sacrifice
Bev Zuk
24 E. 13th Place
Lombard, IL 60148

How To Start A Club
Joyce Thompson
2502 N. 3rd St.
St. Joseph, MO 64505

The Human Adventure
James VanHise
10885 Angola Rd.
San Diego, CA 92126

The Human Factor
P.O. Box 887
Harlingen, TX 78550

IDIC
Leslye Lilker
Sasasher Press
61 Union Place
Lynbrook, NY 11563

Images And Dreams
P.O. Box 10
Oneonta, NY 13820
(Art and poetry)

Immortal Are The Dangers
Gateway Press
Martha Bonds
5905 Yorkwood Rd.
Baltimore, MD 21239

In A Different Reality
Marguerite Krause
4104 Webster Ave.
St. Louis Park, MN 55416

In Triplicate
Mkashef Enterprises
P.O. Box 368
Poway, CA 92064-0005

The Intergalactic Etcetera
Elena Andrews
2228 85th St.
Brooklyn, NY 11214

Interphase Calendar
IELO Book
Gayle Feyrer
Boojums Press
501 Locust St.
Kalamazoo, MI 49007

Intersect
Lisa Wahl
192 Lisbon
Buffalo, NY 14215

Interstat
Teri Meyer, Ann Crouch
13924 Jefferson Circle
Omaha, NE 68137

Interstellar Mail, Collected
160 Foster Rd.
Lake Ronkonkoma, NY 11779

Invasion Of The Klingon Empire
Arrow-Dae Booksellers
2116 E. Carson St.
Pittsburgh, PA 15203

I Survived The Con Of Wrath
Joe Baker
49 Grant St.
Fort Thomas, NY 41075

Jean Lorrah's Sarek Collection
301 S. 15th St.
Murray, KY 42091

"J" Squadron
Jeff Wilcox
Waite Hollow Rd.
Cattaraugus, NY 14719

K/S Collected
Pon Far Press
P.O. Box 1323
Ponway, CA 92064

Katra The Living Spirit
Lana Brown
P.O. Box 4188
Wanganui, New Zealand

Khan Reports
page Eileen Lewis
2611 Silverside Rd.
Wilmington, DE 19810

The Kidnapping
Elizabeth Carrie
13018 Emiline
Omaha, NE 68137

Killing Time
Keith Donovan, Nathan St.
Germaine
Ponn Far Press
Della Van Hise
10885 Angola Ave.
San Diego, CA 92126

Koyayashi Maru
Boojums Press
P.O. Box 8366
Silver Springs, MD 20907

Kraith Collected
Carol Lynn
11524 Nashville
Detroit, MI 48205

The Last Word
E.J. Briggs
91 Harman St.
Ridgewood, NY 11385

Lifestar
Shirley P. Herndon
8122 Alvin Lane
Little Rock, AR 72207

Lodestar
Gail Zehrer
889 Maple Lane
Meadville, PA 16335

Maiden Voyages
P.O. Box 12373
Florence Station
Omaha, NE 68112
(For new writers, artists)

Maine(ly) Trek
Walking Carpet Press
P.O. Box 485
Temple, ME 04984

Make-Up Guide
Dorothy Kurtz
Trent Court #410
Lindenwold, NJ 08021

Mark, Collected
Margot Klein
Heekwig 13, 5000 Koln 60
West Germany

Masiform D
Devra Langsam
627 E. 8th St.
Brooklyn, NY 11218

McCoy's Illegible Log
Debby Chapman
1771 Waverly Rd.
Holt, MI 48842

Dr. McCoy's Medical Log
Ruth Hepner
4700 Smith St.
Harrisburg, PA 17109

Menagerie
507 Locust St.
Kalamazoo, MI 49009

Minara Nova
Ruth Berman
5620 Edgewater Blvd.
Minneapolis, MN 55415

Mirror Odyssey
Dorothy Kurtz
Trent Court #410
Lindenwold, NJ 08021

N!
Gaylen Reiss
Westgate Village #421
Frazer, PA 19355

The Naked Times
Della Van Hise
10885 Angola Ave.
San Diego, CA 92126

The Neutral Zone
D/Jinn Publications
P.O. Box 654
Harrisonburg, VA 22801

Never And Always
Sue Glasgow
1525 S. Madison
Bartlesville, OK 74003

New Alliance
Guinn Berger
16271 Brandt
Romulus, MI 48174

Nexus
Marty Barquinero
EE2 Irongate Apts.
Beverly, NJ 08010

Night Of The Twin Moons
Jean Lorrah
301 S. 15th St.
Murray, KY 42071

The Ninth Quadrant
Helen Padgett
2919 Burnside
San Antonio, TX 78209

Nome
Vicki Clark
445 E. 86th St.
New York, NY 10028

Nu Ormenel, Collected
Fern Marder, Carol Walske
342 E. 53rd St. #4D
New York, NY 10022-K

Nuages
Checkmate Press
1039 E. Springs #6
Tucson, AZ 85719

Odyssey
Ingrid Cross
1100 Persons Court
Lansing, MI

One Thousand And One Trek Tales
Donna Chisolm
678 Hingham St.
Rockland, MA

One Way Mirror
Barbara Wenk, from Poison
Pen Press
627 E. 8th St.
Brooklyn, NY 11218

The Oracle Speaks
Delphi Press,
Theresa Holmes
Moulon Rouge Dr.
Romulus, MI 48174

Organian Question
Rosemary Keane
373 96th St.
Brooklyn, NY 11209

Outpost News
Rosann Nicodemo
7323 53rd Ave.
Maspeth, NY 11378

Paradise One
Michael Smith
3 William St.
Spartansburg, SC 29301

Parallax Ring
Empyrean Publications
19 Engle Street
Tenafly, NJ 07670

Pastaklan Vesla
Michelle Malkin
6649 Castor Ave.
Philadelphia, PA 19140

Peanut's Stepchildren
Cheryl Van Til,
Alberta Stout
6915 Willard SE
Grand Rapids, MI 49508

The Perfect Object
Mindy Glazer
41 W. 72nd St. #16E
New York, NY 10023

Pitchforks And Pointed Ears
Barbara Kelley
5237 W. 113th St.
Bloomington, MN 55437

Plak Tow
Bonnie Guyan
502 Dorothy Ave.
Johnstown, PA 15906

Poetry, Trek Style
Sheila Sullivan
704 Morgan
Cambell, MO 63933

Portal
2419 Greenburg Pike
Pittsburgh, PA 15221

Precessional
Laurie Huff
208 W. Crow
Eureka, IL 61530

The Price and The Prize
Gayle Feyner
1359 Mill St.
Eugene, OR 97401

Prophesy Of The Universe
Lori Paige
RFD #7,
Belknap Mountain Rd.
Laconia, NH 03246

Protocols, A Guide To Fanzines
Judith Z. Segal
15 Sheridan Dr.
Pawling, NY 12565

A Question Of Balance
Pon Farr Press
10885 Angola Rd.
San Diego, CA 92126

R & R, Yeomam Press
5456 Valles Ave.
Bronx, NY 10471

Rast 30+
Club Z
Rast, MD

Reel Images
Club Z
Star Trek, Science Fiction
Filmmakers Club
Louisiana

A Relatively Close Encounter
Anne Snell
19 Westpark, Clifton
Bristol 8, Great Britain

Relay
Ms. Janet Hunt
24 Foxhunter Dr.
Oadby, Liecester LE2 5FE,
Great Britain

The Renegades
Sara Thompson
290 Rosewae
Cortland, OH 44410

Reunion
Kim Knapp
235 Pine Ave. #Q
Carlsbad, CA 92008

Rim Of Starlight
Mat Clark
160 Foster Rd.
Lake Ronkonkoma, NY 11779

Sahaj, Collected
Leslye Lilker,
Sasashar Press
61 Union Place
Lynbrook, NY 11563

Sahndara
Marie Wolfe
RT 1, Box 109A
Greenville, TX 75401

Sahsheer
Kay Johnson, Cathy Strand
107 W. Pocahontas Lane
Kansas City, MO 64114

Sarpedion
Brend Black
1120 Stony Brook Rd.
Forest Park, GA 30050

Saurian Brandy Digest
Sylvia Stanczyk
1953 E. 18th St.
Erie, PA 16510

Security Check
Joy Baker
49 Grant St.
Ft. Thomas, KY 41075

Shadows Of
Dawn Atkins
825 NW 7th St.
Moore, OK 73160

Shatner Comet
Karen Fleming
6908 W. 1st St.
Tulsa, OK 47127

Sherlock Bones, Collected
Sharon Gumerove
3977 Sedgewick Ave.
Bronx, NY 10463

Sherlock Bones Strikes Again
Elena Andrews
2228 85th St.
Brooklyn, NY 11214

Ship To Shore
Trudy Burke
P.O. Box 12373
Florence Station
Omaha, NE 68112

Sol Plus
Jackie Bielowicz
4677 N. Boulder
Tulsa, OK 74126

Sounds Of Star Trek
Chuck, Jean Grahm
5417 Streamview Dr.
San Diego, CA 92105

Space Log
Club NL
Starfleet Base
Kyoto, Japan

Spockanalia
Devra Langsam
627 E. 8th St.
Brooklyn, NY 11218

Standard Orbit
Cheryl Shelton
13208 Herrick
Grandview, MO 64030

Starbird
Little Fragment Press
1315 Sepulveda
San Bernardino, CA 92404

Stardate
Randall Landers
Box 21224, Emory University
Atlanta, GA 30322

Star Daze
Jennie Ecklund
115 Eastern
Taft, CA 93268

Starfleet Cooking Manual
Marsha Kracht
3834 Glen Arbor #4A
Houston, TX 77025

Starfleet Operations Manual
Jim Ward
Turtle Pond Rd.
Saranac Lake, NY 12938

Stargazer
Michael Smith
3 Williams St.
Spartansburg, SC 29301

Star Trek Adventure
D.J. Wheeler, c/o Ell-Tee
740 Brockman Rd.
San Lorenz, CA 94580

Star Trek Examinations
Lorrie Marchini
RT #1 Box 51, Hamilton Rd.
Penrose, NC 28776

Star Trekkers
Cindy Bose
1935 N. Wood St.
Chicago, IL 60622

Star Trek Showcase
Sharon Emily
RR #2 Box 100
Washington, IN 47501

Starweaver
Ann Crouch
9228 "V" Plaza
Omaha, NE 68127

Stellar Gas
Della Van Hise
10885 Angola Rd.
San Diego, CA 92126

Storms
Charlene Terry-Textor
210 N. Main St. #2C
Arcanum, OH 45304

St Phile
Juanita Coulson
RT 3
Hartford City, IN 47348

Stylus
Nancy Kippax
39 Rumelia Circle
Baltimore, MD 21221

Stylus, Quarterly
Margaret DeLorenzo
6427 Hartwait St.
Baltimore, MD 21224

Sublight Readings
Caro Hedge
210 Division
Lamar, CO 81052

Sun And Shadow
Carol Ann Frisbee
518 Abdingdon St.
Arlington, VA 22204

T'Hy'La
Kathleen Resch
P.O. Box 2262 Missing St.
Santa Clara, CA 95055

T'Mera
Anne Anderson
1400 Hubbell Pl #1311
Seattle, WA 98101

T-Negative
Ruth Berman
5620 Edgewater Blvd.
Minneapolis, MN 55411

Tales Of Feldman
Mindy Glazer
88-10 34th Ave. #2C
Jackson Heights, NY 11372

Tal Shaya
Cheree Cargill
1926 Tennyson Circle
Garland, TX 75041

Tasmeen
Simone Mason, Seranis,
Danehill, Hayards Heath
South Benfleet
Essez SS7 5RF England

Tetrumbriant
P.O. Box 1065
Boston, MA 02205

The Third Verdict
Bev Zuk
24 E. 13th Place
Lombard, IL 60148

Time Warp
Isis Press
P.O. Box 1159
Brooklyn, NY 11201

**Tomorrow, For SF And
Futuristic Thought**
Timothy Beckley
303 5th Ave., Suite 1306
New York, NY 10016

To Share The Dawn
Sue Glasgow
1525 S. Madison
Bartlesville, OK 74003

Transition
Lois Welling
1518 Winston Dr.
Champaign, IL 61820

Trek Continuum
Cathi Brown
205 S. Winnebago
Lake Mills, IA 50450

Trek Force
Star Force
P.O. Box 3682
Manhattan Beach, CA 90266

Trekism
Vel Jeager
506 Canyon Dr. #M4
Oceanside, CA 92054

The Trekker Cookbook
Yeoman Press
5464 Valles Ave.
Bronx, NY 10471

Trekkers Of The Night
Cindye Bose, Trekker Press
1935 N. Woods St.
Chicago, IL 60622

Trexindex
Roberta Rogow
P.O. Box 124
Fairlawn, NJ 07410

Trojan Angel
Elysian Publications
614 3rd St.
Manchester, GA 31816

Tunisian Etcetera Press
George Perkins
1102 3rd St.
Brookings, SD 57006

UFP
Sandle Cowden
13 Glen Ave.
Port Glasgow, PA 14 5AA,
Scotland

Understanding Kraith
Judith Segal
15 Sheridan Dr.
Pawling, NY 12564

Universal
Beth Seltzer
Ridge Road
Orwigsberg, PA 17961

Universal Translator
Dr. Susan J. Bridges
200 W. 79th St., 14H
New York, NY 10024

Variations On A Theme
Sheila Clark
6 Craigsmill Cottages
Strathmartine by Dundee,
Scotland

The Vaslovic Archives
Mary Bloemker
5 Lamson St.
E. Boston, MA 02128

Vault Of Tomorrow
Marion McChesney
3429 Chestnut Ave.
Baltimore, MD 21211

Viewscreen
Victoria Mitchell
621 E. F. St.
Moscow, ID 83843

The Voice
Mrs. Rosemary Wild
Cwm Croesor Stuckton,
Fordingbridge, Hants
SP6 2HG England

Voices From The Stars
Nancy Gervals
51 S. Perl St.
Malone, NY 12953

Voyages Beyond
E. Thomson
23 Northbrook Rd.
Aldershot, Hants, GU 11

Vulcan Irregular
Vivian Bregman
P.O. Box 1701
Wayne, NJ 07470

Vulcan Kartune Book
2419 Greensburg Pike
Pittsburgh, PA 15221

Warp 10
Steven Hurst
627 Ross Drive
Pasadena, MD 21122

Warped Space
T'Kuhtian Press
5132 Jo-Don Dr.
E. Lansing, MI 48823

Web Novels
Sylvia Stanczyk
1953 E. 18th St.
Erie, PA 16501

The Weight, Collected
T'Kuhtian Press
5132 Jo-Don Dr.
E. Lansing, MI 48823

GAMES & ACCESSORIES

This section is divided by manufacturer, i.e. FASA Corp., Task Force Games and others. All additions and accessories for these games are listed in this section.

FASA Corporation has issued the Star Trek Role Playing Game. In this game, the players assume the personalities of the characters from Star Trek and react to situations as the character would.

	Price Range	
☐ **Star Trek: The Role Playing Game,** 2001 (Deluxe Limited Edition). This game contains the Star Trek Basic Set (2004) and the Star Trek III Starship Combat Game (2006) plus a set of three adventures and deck plans for the Constitution class cruiser and the Klingon D-7 battle cruiser.	40.00	50.00
☐ **Enterprise deck plans** to game 2001 (above)	10.00	15.00
☐ **Klingon deck plans** to game 2001 (above) . .	5.00	10.00
☐ **As above,** Second Edition without deck plans for Enterprise and Klingon	25.00	30.00
☐ **Star Trek: The Role Playing Game,** 2004 (Basic Set). The complete rules to role-playing are contained in three easy-to-read books outlining the Star Trek universe and how to begin adventuring.	12.00	15.00
☐ **The Klingons: A Sourcebook and Character Generation Supplement,** 2002. This add-on module for the role-playing game allows you to play the part of a Klingon. Included is a description of Klingon history and culture.	10.00	12.00
☐ **As above,** Boxed Set	15.00	25.00
☐ **The Romulans: A Sourcebook and Character Generation Supplement,** 2005. This add-on module for the role-playing game allows you to play the part of a Romulan. Included is a description of Romulan history and culture.	10.00	12.00

Price Range

☐ **Trader Captains & Merchant Princes,** 2203. This rules supplement provides all the charts and rules needed for creating traders, merchants, con-men and rogues of space. A complete system for economics in the Star Trek universe is also included. 12.00 15.00

☐ **As above,** newer, two-book version 11.00 12.00

☐ **Ship Construction Manual,** 2204. This rules supplement contains all the information and tables necessary for building your own starship. Also included is the starship combat efficiency system for rating your ships in combat. 10.00 12.00

☐ **As above,** First Edition 12.00 15.00

☐ **Star Trek III: Movie Update and Sourcebook,** 2214. This beautifully illustrated book allows players to bring their games up to the time period of the movies. Included is all the information necessary for adding the new ships and personnel to your games. 10.00 12.00

☐ **Star Trek IV Sourcebook,** 2224, updates the game to include information from Star Trek IV   10.00 12.00

☐ **Star Trek III: Starship Combat Game,** 2006. This game contains all the starship combat rules for Starship Tactics, a game of fleet actions, and Command and Control, a role-playing version of ship-to-ship combat. 10.00 15.00

☐ **Star Trek II:** Starship Combat Game, Predecessor to above game. Only released for short time 15.00 20.00

☐ **Starship Combat Game,** 2003, generic version of above two games, boxed 18.00 20.00

☐ **The Triangle,** 2007. The Triangle is a setting for a Star Trek campaign. Comes with full color map and 2 books about the Triangle area. . . 10.00 12.00

☐ **The Federation,** 2011, complete sourcebook of the United Federation of Planets 10.00 12.00

☐ **Star Fleet Intelligence Manual,** 2014, brings spies and secret operatives into the game . . 10.00 12.00

STAR TREK ADVENTURE BOOKS

Price Range

These add new scenarios to the Role Playing Game.

☐ **Witness for the Defense,** 2202	7.00	8.00
☐ **Denial of Destiny,** 2205	7.00	8.00
☐ **Termination: 1456,** 2206	7.00	8.00
☐ **Demand of Honor,** 2207	7.00	8.00
☐ **The Orion Ruse,** 2208	7.00	8.00
☐ **Margin of Profit,** 2209	7.00	8.00
☐ **The Outcasts,** 2210	7.00	8.00
☐ **A Matter Of Priorities,** 2211	7.00	8.00
☐ **A Doomsday Like Any Other,** 2212	7.00	8.00
☐ **The Mines Of Selka,** 2213	7.00	8.00
☐ **Triangle Campaign,** 2215	7.00	8.00
☐ **Graduation Exercise,** 2216	7.00	8.00
☐ **Where Has All The Glory Gone,** 2217	7.00	8.00
☐ **Return To Axanar,** 2218	7.00	8.00
☐ **Decision At Midnight,** 2219	7.00	8.00
☐ **Imbalance Of Power,** 2220	11.00	12.00
☐ **Old Soldiers Never Die/The Romulan War,** 2221	11.00	12.00
☐ **A Conflict of Interest/Klingon Intelligence Briefing,** 2222	11.00	12.00
☐ **The Dixie Gambit,** 2223	7.00	8.00
☐ **Perish By The Sword/Galaxy Exploration Command,** 2225	11.00	12.00
☐ **The Strider Incident/Regula I Deck Plans,** 2226	11.00	12.00
☐ **Deck plans to above**	6.00	7.00

SHIP RECOGNITION MANUALS

These books contain all the game statistics for the role-playing and the starship combat games. Each book contains 40 ships with a variety of variants and brief descriptions of performances and history.

☐ **The Klingons,** 2301	7.00	8.00
☐ **The Federation,** 2302	7.00	8.00
☐ **The Romulans,** 2303	7.00	8.00

PLAYING AIDS

Price Range

Playing aids are used to add to the enjoyment of your games. None of the items are required to play but each will certainly increase the appeal of your games.

☐ **Starship Combat Hex Grid,** 2801. Contains 3 22″ x 33″ starfield maps for use with 2006.	3.00	5.00
☐ **Gamemaster's Kit,** 2802. Three-panel Gamemaster's screen displaying all important tables and charts; 16-page book containing all charts and tables needed by players and gamemasters.	6.00	8.00
☐ **Tricorder/Sensors Interactive Display,** 2803. This play aid allows players to use a tricorder for scans and scientific readings. The unit is a hand-held simulated tricorder with display windows.............................	10.00	12.00

STARSHIP MINIATURES, 1/3900 SCALE, LEAD, BUBBLE PACKED

☐ **USS Enterprise (New),** 2501	4.00	5.00
☐ **USS Reliant (Cruiser),** 2502	4.00	5.00
☐ **Klingon D-7 (Battlecruiser),** 2503	4.00	5.00
☐ **Romulan Bird of Prey (Cruiser),** 2504	4.00	5.00
☐ **USS Enterprise (Old),** 2505	4.00	5.00
☐ **Regula I Space Laboratory,** 2506	4.00	5.00
☐ **USS Larson (Destroyer),** 2507	4.00	5.00
☐ **Klingon D-10 (Cruiser),** 2508	4.00	5.00
☐ **Klingon D-18 (Destroyer),** 2509	4.00	5.00
☐ **Klingon K-23 (Escort),** 2510	4.00	5.00
☐ **Gorn MA-12 (Cruiser),** 2511	4.00	5.00
☐ **Orion Blockade Runner,** 2512	4.00	5.00
☐ **Klingon L-9 (Frigate),** 2513	4.00	5.00
☐ **USS Loknar (Frigate),** 2514	4.00	5.00
☐ **Romulan Winged Defender (Cruiser),** 2515	4.00	5.00
☐ **USS Chandley (Frigate),** 2516	4.00	5.00
☐ **USS Excelsior (Battleship, ST III),** 2517	8.00	9.00

	Price Range	
☐ Klingon L-42 Bird of Prey (Frigate, ST III), 2518	4.00	5.00
☐ USS Grissom (Research Vessel, ST III), 2519	4.00	5.00
☐ Deep Space Freighter, 2520	4.00	5.00
☐ Romulan Graceful Flyer (Scout), 2521	4.00	5.00
☐ Orion Wanderer, 2522	4.00	5.00
☐ Kobayashi Maru (Freighter), 2523	4.50	5.00
☐ Romulan Gallant Wing (Cruiser), 2524	4.50	5.00
☐ Gorn BH-2 (Battleship), 2525	9.00	10.00
☐ USS Baker (Destroyer), 2526	4.50	5.00
☐ Romulan Nova (Battleship), 2527	11.00	12.00
☐ Romulan Bright One (Destroyer), 2528	4.50	5.00
☐ Klingon L-24 (Battleship), 2529	11.00	12.00
☐ Klingon D-2 (Missile Destroyer), 2530	4.50	5.00
☐ Romulan Whitewind (Cruiser), 2531	4.50	5.00
☐ USS Northampton (Frigate), 2532	4.50	5.00
☐ USS Remora (Escort), 2533	4.50	5.00
☐ USS Andor (Missile Cruiser), 2534	4.50	5.00

STAR TREK II: WRATH OF KHAN

25 mm Miniatures, lead, bubble packed.

☐ James T. Kirk, 2601	1.00	2.00
☐ 1st Officer Spock, 2602	1.00	2.00
☐ Dr. McCoy, 2603	1.00	2.00
☐ Lt. Saavik, 2604	1.00	2.00
☐ Scotty, 2605	1.00	2.00
☐ Lt. Uhura, 2606	1.00	2.00
☐ Sulu, 2607	1.00	2.00
☐ Chekov, 2608	1.00	2.00
☐ Khan, 2609	1.00	2.00
☐ David Marcus, 2610	1.00	2.00
☐ Joachim, 2611	1.00	2.00
☐ Carol Marcus, 2612	1.00	2.00
☐ Capt. Terrell, 2613	1.00	2.00
☐ Khan (Ceti Alpha V), 2614	1.00	2.00
☐ Klingon Officer, 2615	1.00	2.00
☐ Klingon Soldier 1, 2616	1.00	2.00
☐ Klingon Soldier 2, 2617	1.00	2.00

Price Range

Boxed Sets of above. Each set contains one ship and 8 crew members.

☐ **Enterprise and Crew,** 3001	10.00	20.00
☐ **Reliant and Khan's Crew,** 3002	10.00	20.00
☐ **Regula and Scientists,** 3003	10.00	20.00
☐ **Klingon D-7 and Crew,** 3004	10.00	20.00

STAR TREK MICROADVENTURE GAMES

Boxed, small games with short playing times and simple rules.

☐ **ST III The Search for Spock,** 5001	6.00	8.00
☐ **ST III Starship Duel 1,** 5002	6.00	8.00
☐ **ST III Struggle for the Throne,** 5004	6.00	8.00
☐ **ST III Starship Duel 2,** 5005	6.00	8.00

STAR FLEET BATTLES GAMES

Task Force Games has issued quite a few Star Trek related games under the heading "Star Fleet Battles." These are true war games, with combat between individual ships or whole fleets. All the items listed in this section are for use with the "Star Fleet Battles" games.

☐ **Introduction to Star Fleet Battles,** a basic introduction to the game of Star Fleet Battles. Learn to play Star Fleet Battles while actually playing this game, 3000	5.00	6.00
☐ **Star Fleet Battles** is the starting set for gaming in the Star Fleet Universe. The set includes: 108-page Volume I Commander's Rulebook, 32-page SSD and chart booklet, 216 die-cut counters and a large map, boxed set, 5001	20.00	22.00
☐ **As above,** Volume II adds new weapons, new challenges, new ships and new spacefaring races. Contains the 96-page Commander's Rulebook Volume II, a 32-page SSD booklet and 324 die-cut playing-pieces, boxed set, 5008	20.00	22.00

Star Fleet Battles Game

	Price Range	
☐ **As above,** Volume III adds a new race, new weapons, new rules and new battles. Contains a 64-page Commander's Rulebook Volume III, a 48-page booklet of SSDs and 216 new playing pieces, boxed set, 5009	**20.00**	**22.00**
☐ **Star Fleet Battles Supplement # 1: Fighters and Shuttles.** #1 adds the playing-pieces and rules needed to recreate full-scale fighter actions. Components include 216 new playing pieces and 4 SSDs, 3003	**9.00**	**10.00**
☐ **As above,** #2, X-Ships. Included in Supplement #2 are 216 counters, 32 Commander's SSDs and a rules section, 3013	**9.00**	**10.00**
☐ **As above,** #3, Fast Patrol Ships. Components include: 216 playing pieces, 16 pages of new rules and 32 new Commander's SSD sheets.	**9.00**	**10.00**

Price Range

☐ **Star Fleet Battles Reinforcements.** New and additional playing pieces, 3014 . . . .   6.00   7.00

☐ **Star Fleet Battles Rules Update 1.** Newly updated pages from Star Fleet Battles and Supplement #1, 3015 . . . .   5.00   6.00

☐ **Federation and Empire** brings you the Galactic War that created the battles from Star Fleet Battles. A larger scale game, includes two large maps, 1080 playing pieces, 8 charts and a rules and scenario booklet, 5006 . . . .   35.00 40.00

☐ **Federation and Empire Fleet Pack** includes 432 more ships to add to the above game, 3201 . . . .   14.00 15.00

STAR FLEET BATTLE CAPTAIN'S LOGS

Each issue features a story, over 20 scenarios and new rules for playing Star Fleet Battles.

☐ **#1,** 3004 . . . .   5.00   6.00
☐ **#2,** 3008 . . . .   5.00   6.00
☐ **#3,** 3010 . . . .   5.00   6.00
☐ **#4,** 3012 . . . .   5.00   6.00

STAR FLEET BATTLE COMMANDER'S SSD BOOKS

Each of the Commander's SSD books contains forty-eight SSDs per book.

☐ **Book #1,** Races covered: Federation, Andromedan, Orions and Kzintis; Stock Number 3005 . . . .   5.00   6.00

☐ **Book #2,** Races covered: Klingon, Lyran, Hydran and Wyn; Stock Number 3006 . . . .   5.00   6.00

☐ **Book #3,** Races covered: Romulan, Tholian and Gorn; Stock Number 3007 . . . .   5.00   6.00

☐ **Book #4,** Items covered: Tugs, Star-bases, Battle Stations and Freighters; Stock Number 3009 . . . .   5.00   6.00

Price Range

☐ **Book #5,** Items covered: Q-ships, independent booms and saucers, and a selection of special and variant ships; Stock Number 3016 ..   5.00   6.00

☐ **Book #6,** Covers police ships, light tugs, survey cruisers and space control ships; Stock Number 3018 ....   5.00   6.00

☐ **Book #7,** More ships for Tholians, Gorns, Federation, Kzintis and Hydrans; Stock Number: 3020 ....   5.00   6.00

☐ **Book #8,** More ships for Klingons, Lyrans, Orions and Romulans; Stock Number: 3021. ...   5.00   6.00

☐ **Book #9,** New Commander's SSDs for all races, including 26 completely new ships. Stock Number: 3023 ....   5.00   6.00

STARLINE 2200 MINIATURES

1/3900 scale plastic or lead miniatures

☐ **Starline 2200 Hex Sheets—**4 18″ x 24″ maps, 7000 ....   4.95

THE FEDERATION

☐ **Federation Dreadnought,** 7010 ....   4.00
☐ **Federation Heavy Cruiser,** 7011 ....   4.00

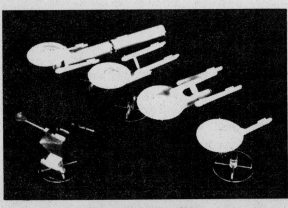

Miniature Gaming Ships

	Price Range
☐ **Federation New Light Cruiser,** 7012	4.00
☐ **Federation Light Cruiser,** 7013	4.00
☐ **Federation Destroyer,** 7014	3.50
☐ **Federation Scout,** 7015	3.50
☐ **Federation Tug,** 7016	4.50
☐ **Federation Frigate (2),** 7017	5.00
☐ **Federation Carrier,** 7020	6.00
☐ **Federation Starbase,** 7025	8.00

THE KLINGONS

☐ **Klingon B-10 Battleship,** 7040	8.00
☐ **Klingon C-8 Dreadnought,** 7042	6.00
☐ **Klingon D-7 Battlecruiser,** 7043	4.00
☐ **Klingon D-5 Cruiser,** 7044	4.00
☐ **Klingon F-5 Frigate (2),** 7046	4.00
☐ **Klingon Tug (Carrier),** 7051	6.00
☐ **Klingon PFs (6),** 7053	4.00

THE ROMULANS

☐ **Romuian Condor,** 7060	6.00
☐ **Romulan Warbird (2),** 7064	4.00
☐ **Romulan Sparrowhawk,** 7071	4.00
☐ **Romulan Skyhawk and Seahawk,** 7073	5.00

THE GORNS

☐ **Gorn Dreadnought,** 7080	6.00
☐ **Gorn Heavy Cruiser,** 7081	4.00
☐ **Gorn Light Cruiser,** 7082	4.00
☐ **Gorn Destroyer (2),** 7084	5.00

THE KZINTIS

☐ **Kzinti Space Control Ship,** 7100	6.00
☐ **Kzinti Carrier,** 7101	4.50
☐ **Kzinti Escort Carrier,** 7103	4.00
☐ **Kzinti Strike Cruiser,** 7104	4.50

	Price Range
☐ **Kzinti Frigate (2),** 7107	5.00
☐ **Kzinti Tug,** 7108	5.50
☐ **Kzinti PFs (6),** 7110	4.00

THE LYRANS

☐ **Lyran Lion Dreadnought,** 7120	5.50
☐ **Lyran Cruiser,** 7122	4.00
☐ **Lyran War Cruiser,** 7123	4.00
☐ **Lyran Destroyer (2),** 7124	5.00
☐ **Lyran PFs (6),** 7126	4.00

THE HYDRANS

☐ **Hydran Paladin DN,** 7140	5.50
☐ **Hydran Ranger,** 7141	4.00
☐ **Hydran Horseman,** 7142	4.00
☐ **Hydran Lancer (2),** 7143	5.00
☐ **Hydran Hunter/Scout (2),** 7144	4.00
☐ **Hydran PFs (6),** 7147	4.00

THE THOLIANS

☐ **Tholian Dreadnought,** 7160	4.00
☐ **Tholian Cruiser (2),** 7161	5.00
☐ **Tholian Patrol Cruiser (2),** 7164	4.00
☐ **Neo-Tholian Dreadnought,** 7172	4.00
☐ **Neo-Tholian Cruiser (2),** 7174	5.00

THE ORIONS

☐ **Orion Heavy Cruiser,** 7181	4.00
☐ **Orion Salvage Cruiser,** 7182	4.00
☐ **Orion Raider (2),** 7183	4.00
☐ **Orion Slaver (2),** 7184	5.00

THE ANDROMEDANS

☐ **Andromedan Intruder,** 7221	6.00
☐ **Andromedan Satellite Ships (3),** 7222	5.50

	Price Range
☐ **Andromedan Conquistador and Python,** 7223	5.00

THE INTERSTELLAR CONCORDIUM

	Price Range
☐ **ISC Dreadnought,** 7250	6.00
☐ **ISC Star Cruiser,** 7252	4.50
☐ **ISC Destroyer and Frigate,** 7256	5.00

ALL RACES

☐ **Small Freighter (2),** 7200		4.50
☐ **Battle Station,** 7211		4.00
☐ **Starline 2220 Starships,** (Boxed Set) includes one each of the Federation Heavy Cruiser, Klingon D-7 Battlecruiser, Klingon F-5 Frigate, Gorn Destroyer and Romulan Warbird, 7300	10.00	13.00

OTHER GAMES

☐ **Arcade Game,** Sega, Star Trek: The Motion Picture, standing or sitting versions, commercial	800.00	2500.00
☐ **As above,** Home version for Atari	15.00	25.00
☐ **Crossword Puzzle,** Running Press, "Incredible Interplastic Star Trek Crossword Puzzle"	6.00	10.00
☐ **Enterprise IV Encounter, The.** Boxed board game, West End Games, 1985	16.00	18.00
☐ **Photon Balls,** like a dart board game, contains three balls and a board with pictures of famous space ships	10.00	15.00
☐ **Pinball Game,** Azrak-Hamway, TV show, Kirk or Spock	15.00	25.00
☐ **Pinball Game,** Bally, STTMP, electronic, commercial, 1979	200.00	500.00
☐ **Playing Cards,** Aviva Enterprises, Star Trek: The Motion Picture, standard size deck with a drawing of the Enterprise on back (drawing based on early promotional poster for the		

Price Range

movie), packed in a blister pack, back card-
boad features the "rainbow" painting, stock
number 849 ....   15.00   20.00

☐ **Playing Cards,** ST II, Wrath of Khan, 1982,
movie players, standard deck, different picture
on face of each card, ST II logo on back. First
printing—"II" was left off of logo 10.00   15.00

☐ **Second Printing** 5.00   10.00

☐ **Star Fleet Battle Manual,** Gamescience, starship combat game, booklet 10.00   12.00

☐ **As above,** deluxe boxed version, includes 8
plastic starships 25.00   27.00

☐ **Star Fleet Ships,** plastic cruiser/stand, 1/3788
scale models, snap together, Gamescience,
No. 10504 ....   2.50   3.00

☐ **As above, Clear Plastic Cruiser/Stand,** No.
10504-C 2.50   3.00

☐ **As above, Blue-glow Plastic Cruiser,** No.
10504-B 2.50   3.00

☐ **As above, Green-glow Plastic Cruiser,** No.
10504-G 2.50   3.00

☐ **As above, Plastic Destroyer,** No. 10505 ...   2.50   3.00

☐ **As above, Clear Destroyer,** No. 10505-C ...   2.50   3.00

☐ **As above, Blue-glow Destroyer,** No. 10505-B   2.50   3.00

☐ **As above, Green-glow Destroyer,** No. 10505-
G 2.50   3.00

☐ **As above, Plastic Scout,** No. 10506 ....   2.50   3.00

☐ **As above, Clear Scout,** No. 10506-C 2.50   3.00

☐ **As above, Blue-glow Scout,** No. 10506-B ..   2.50   3.00

☐ **As above, Green-glow Scout,** No. 10506-G   2.50   3.00

☐ **As above, Plastic Dreadnought,** No. 10507   3.00   4.00

☐ **As above, Clear Dreadnought,** No. 10507-C   3.00   4.00

☐ **As above, Blue-glow Dreadnought,** No.
10507-B 3.00   4.00

☐ **As above, Green-glow Dreadnought,** No.
10507-G 3.00   4.00

☐ **As above, Plastic Tug,** No. 10508 ....   3.50   4.00

☐ **As above, Clear Tug,** No. 10508-C 3.50   4.00

	Price Range	
☐ **As above, Blue-glow Tug,** No. 10508-C	3.50	4.00
☐ **As above, Green-glow Tug,** No. 10508-G ..	3.50	4.00
☐ **Star Flite,** by Lance Micklus, Adventure International, computer game, tape will fit variety of computers, formerly titled Star Trek 3.5, 1981	15.00	30.00
☐ **Star Trek Game, The,** Hasbro, based on the television series, 1974	6.00	10.00
☐ **Star Trek Game, The,** Ideal, first game based on the television series, 1966	15.00	25.00
☐ **Star Trek Game, The,** Milton-Bradley, based on STTMP, 1979	6.00	10.00
☐ **Star Trek: The Adventure Game,** boxed board game, West End Games, 1985	16.00	18.00
☐ **Star Trek: The Enterprise 4 Encounter,** boxed board game, West End Games, 1985	16.00	18.00
☐ **Star Trek: Three Solitaire Games,** boxed board game, West End Games, 1985	16.00	18.00
☐ **Star Trek Trivia Game,** compatible with "Trivial Pursuit," over 1,000 questions and answers, Western Publishing	15.00	20.00
☐ **As above,** cards only, smaller box, Western Publishing	10.00	15.00

GREETING CARDS

CALIFORNIA DREAMERS

Pictures from TV series on 5″ x 7″ color cover, 1985.

	Price Range	
☐ **Chekov screaming,** "Inhuman Cossacks! Pigs! They've destroyed everything. You'll never be 29 again. Happy Birthday."	1.00	2.00
☐ **Spock giving Vulcan salute,** "You were born on this day. It is therefore quite logical to wish you a Happy Birthday ... Live Long and Prosper."	1.00	2.00

Price Range

☐ **Kirk and Spock,** "Fire all phasers . . . Fire all photon torpedos . . . What the heck. It's your Birthday!" **1.00**   **2.00**

☐ **Spock wearing visor,** "Just because one is logical . . . does not mean one cannot be cool. You're cool. Happy Birthday." **1.00**   **2.00**

☐ **McCoy checking instrument,** "I've run every test. Checked every medical reference in the galaxy, and damn it. I can't find a cure for what you've got . . . Old Age . . . Happy Birthday."   **1.00**   **2.00**

☐ **Scotty,** "Three dilithium crystals. A tablespoon of kironide, a pinch of antimatter, and just a dash of phaser . . . I'm going to make you a Birthday cake that will light up the universe . . . Happy Birthday." **1.00**   **2.00**

☐ **Spock,** "Readings indicate an unparalleled cosmic phenomena occurred on this day. It was in a time so ancient, the year cannot be ascertained by ship's computers . . . I guess we'll just have to look at the cake and count all those candles! Happy Birthday." **1.00**   **2.00**

☐ **Kirk talking into communicator,** "The landing party is expendable. The ship is not. If we're not back by 0500, contact Star Fleet Command, get the Enterprise out of here, and whatever you do . . . Have a good time on your Birthday!"   **1.00**   **2.00**

☐ **McCoy,** (injured) "Listen to me. I'm a doctor. I know . . . Birthdays are hell!!" **1.00**   **2.00**

☐ **Spock looking at bridge instruments,** "History banks indicate that inhabitants of 20th-century earth would oftentimes undergo a strange suicidallike ritual on many of their post-30th birthdays . . . Death by Chocolate. Happy Birthday." **1.00**   **2.00**

☐ **Spock with harp,** "I fail to understand the inexplicable human need to so primitively celebrate the anniversary of one's birth. Nevertheless, I offer you the words of Surak, the most revered

	Price Range	

of all Vulcan philosophers. 'Krut Toba Grig—Toba Grig.' If you party, party BIG!! Happy Birthday." **1.00 2.00**

☐ **Spock in environment suit,** "The heat here is extreme. Far beyond normal ranges ... How many candles were on that cake, anyway? Happy Birthday." **1.00 2.00**

☐ **Spock holding cat,** "There are 3 billion worlds in the known universe, with a combined population of approximately 6,307,000,000,000 composed of carbon- and noncarbon-based life forms ... But there's only 1 you. Happy Birthday." **1.00 2.00**

☐ **Kirk as Romulan talking into communicator,** "This is Captain James T. Kirk of the Starship Enterprise. Our mission is a peaceful one. We mean no harm ... Sure the check's in the mail and you're 29. Happy Birthday." **1.00 2.00**

☐ **Spock seated,** "It is not logical. It makes no sense ... It must be Love! **1.00 2.00**

☐ **Spock smiling,** "You make me smile!" **1.00 2.00**

☐ **Enterprise,** "Space is not the final frontier ... You are!" **1.00 2.00**

☐ **Kirk, McCoy, and Uhura,** "Phasers charged and ready. Photon torpedos fully armed ... Here comes Monday!" **1.00 2.00**

☐ **Planet on bridge screen,** "To boldly go where no man has gone before ... or woman either. Congratulations." **1.00 2.00**

☐ **Gorn attacking Kirk,** "Beam me up Scotty ... It's been one of those days!" **1.00 2.00**

☐ **Kirk with providers from Gamesters of Triskelion,** "Who am I? Where am I? Why do I have on these strange clothes ... Why do I have such strange friends?" **1.00 2.00**

☐ **Kirk, Spock, and McCoy from Piece of the Action,** "You've got to dress for success!" .. **1.00 2.00**

Price Range

☐ **Kirk with bow and arrow,** "I was going to shoot you with a phaser . . . But it seemed so unromantic." 1.00   2.00

☐ **Kirk with arms folded,** "There's an amusing little custom we have on earth . . . Report to my quarters and I'll explain!" 1.00   2.00

☐ **Kirk looking disgusted,** "Sometimes I just want to say to hell with Star Fleet, to hell with regulations and responsibility, to hell with everything . . . Except you!" 1.00   2.00

☐ **Kirk and Spock in force field,** "Time is a dimension, like height, width or depth, therefore . . . We're getting shorter, fatter, denser and older! Happy Birthday!" 1.00   2.00

☐ **Spock,** "Forgive me if I'm lengthy, however, mathematics is an extremely precise science . . . You're a 9.99999999999999." 1.00   2.00

☐ **Smiling group,** "A group of us got together to do something special for your birthday . . . We're having you sent into space. Happy Birthday." 1.00   2.00

☐ **Kirk, Spock, and McCoy,** (in bushes) "Analysis concludes that this is both the correct time and correct place . . . Throw down the blanket and let's party. Happy Birthday." 1.00   2.00

☐ **Kirk and Spock,** "You are correct, Captain, I see them. On our right as well as our left . . . Gray hair. Happy Birthday." 1.00   2.00

☐ **Kirk,** "The universe is a big place . . . How did two great people like us ever find each other?"   1.00   2.00

☐ **Spock,** "It is one of the most painful of all biological phenomena . . . I've got you under my skin." 1.00   2.00

☐ **Kirk and Chekov on bridge,** "Damage control reports we've taken a direct hit. Power out on decks 1,2 and 3. Life-support systems functioning on auxiliary power . . . Has anybody got an aspirin? Get well soon." 1.00   2.00

Price Range

☐ **Kirk in pain,** "This syndrome is like that of the madness associated with severe cases of rigellian fever. Actually, it's something quite different . . . Love." 1.00   2.00

☐ **Spock,** "Regrettably, the laws of gravity are absolute . . . Birthdays are a drag. Happy Birthday." 1.00   2.00

HALLMARK

☐ **Cartoon of Kirk, Spock, and McCoy as birds,** "Your mission, Graduate, is to boldly go where no man has gone before . . . Bet you're proud as a peacock." 1.00   2.00

RANDOM HOUSE

☐ **McCoy and Kirk,** caption "Happy Birthday from one big shot . . . ," inside caption ". . . to another." This includes a 3-piece punch-out blue phaser, 1976 . . . .   2.00   3.00

☐ **Kirk with open communicator,** inside caption "Let's Communicate." This includes a 2-piece punch-out blue communicator, 1976 . . . .   2.00   3.00

☐ **U.S.S. Enterprise over a planet,** caption "The world's a better place because of you." 1976   2.00   3.00

☐ **U.S.S. Enterprise entering orbit around an orange planet** (rear view), caption "I'm sending you something from outer space. . . ." This includes a 4-piece punch-out of the U.S.S. Enterprise, 1976 . . . .   2.00   3.00

☐ **Lt. Uhura,** caption "I hear it's your Birthday," inside caption "Open all hailing frequencies!," 1976 . . . .   2.00   3.00

☐ **Kirk holding a rose,** caption "The Captain and I both wish you a very happy birthday," 1976   2.00   3.00

Price Range

☐ **Spock putting hand on a red door** (from the episode "A Taste of Armageddon"), inside caption "Let's keep in touch!," 1976 . . . . 2.00 3.00

☐ **Kirk,** caption "This is your Captain speaking . . .," inside caption ". . . Have a far-out Birthday!," 1976 . . . . 2.00 3.00

☐ **Spock in dress uniform,** caption "It is illogical not to wish a Happy Birthday to someone so charming. . . . ," 1976 . . . . 2.00 3.00

☐ **Spock in yellow triangle,** caption "Know what I like about you (in orange circle)," 1976 . . . . 2.00 3.00

☐ **Kirk, Spock, Scott, Uhura and McCoy** in five individual squares, caption "Happy Birthday to a great human being!," 1976 . . . . 2.00 3.00

☐ **Spock inside a yellow circle,** inside an orange circle, inside a pink circle, caption "Sorry I blew it . . . ," 1976 . . . . 2.00 3.00

☐ **Spock giving 'Live Long and Prosper' sign** and has an eye shield, caption "Having a Birthday?," 1976 . . . . 2.00 3.00

☐ **Kirk resting head on arm** on a small viewer inside 2 blue circles on a purple background (open card) COURAGE! 1976 . . . . 2.00 3.00

☐ **U.S.S. Enterprise orbiting an orange planet,** caption "One of the nicest earthlings in the universe . . . (inside caption) . . . just opened this card! Happy Birthday," 1976 . . . . 2.00 3.00

☐ **Kirk,** caption "Star light star bright first star I see tonight I wished on a star for your birthday," 1976 . . . . 2.00 3.00

☐ **Kirk on the front with medals** and caption "Congratulations," 1976 . . . . 2.00 3.00

☐ **Kirk standing on a planet looking towards earth** with caption "There's so Much Space Between Us . . . ," 1976 . . . . 2.00 3.00

☐ **McCoy and Kirk** on the front with caption "Don't Worry—You'll Feel Better Soon," 1976 2.00 3.00

	Price Range	
☐ **McCoy, Scott, Chekov and Uhura** on front with caption "Happy Birthday," 1976	2.00	3.00
☐ **Scott, Spock, Kirk, McCoy, Uhura and Chekov** on front with inside caption "Happy Birthday From The Whole Spaced Out Crew," 1976	2.00	3.00
☐ **Spock listening to headset,** captioned "I must be hard of hearing," 1974	2.00	3.00
☐ **Uhura and Kirk on bridge** with caption "Off Course," inside caption "Hope You're Back on The Right Trek Soon," 1976	2.00	3.00
☐ **U.S.S. Enterprise** on the front with caption "For Your Birthday I'd Like To Take You on a Trip to Venus," 1976	2.00	3.00

STRAND ENTERPRISES

	Price Range	
☐ **All occasion notecards,** Leonard Nimoy for Actors and Other Animals, 1979	2.00	3.00

HOUSEHOLD WARES

	Price Range	
☐ **Bandages,** plastic, adhesive, silver, pink and blue box with etching of Dr. McCoy, Mr. Spock and the Enterprise, 30 assorted sizes, J. Adams Industries, 1979	2.00	3.00
☐ **Bank,** approx. 12″, plastic, Kirk	30.00	50.00
☐ **Bank,** approx. 12″, plastic, Spock	30.00	50.00
☐ **Beach Towel,** Enterprise design, 1976	25.00	30.00
☐ **Beach Towel,** Spock design, 1976	15.00	25.00
☐ **Beach Towel,** Kirk and Spock	15.00	25.00
☐ **Bowl,** plastic, cereal, Star Trek: The Motion Picture, Deka, 1979	5.00	8.00
☐ **Bowl,** plastic, soup, Star Trek: The Motion Picture, Deka, 1979	5.00	8.00
☐ **Bulletin Board,** Whiting, die-cut board and four pens, 1979	5.00	10.00

Price Range

☐ **Cake Decorator,** Tuttle, TV show, with scenes on the Enterprise, 1976 .... 5.00 10.00

☐ **Chair,** beanbag, Star Trek: The Motion Picture, group drawing, assorted colors 25.00 50.00

☐ **Chair,** director's, white metal with blue cloth, Star Trek IV logo on backrest, Official Star Trek Fan Club, 1986 .... 45.00 55.00

☐ **Chair,** inflatable, Star Trek: The Motion Picture, Spock, 1979 .... 15.00 25.00

☐ **Clock,** digital travel alarm with TV command symbol in upper left corner, Lincoln Enterprises. 25.00 30.00

☐ **Clock,** picture of Kirk, Spock and McCoy from TV series on face, no date or manufacturer, probably unlicensed 20.00 30.00

☐ **Clock,** white wall clock with red 20th Anniversary logo on face. Official Star trek Fan Club, 1986 .... 25.00 30.00

☐ **Comb and Brush Set,** Oval brush with color transfer, 6″ x 3″, blue with clear plastic box. Gabil, 1977 .... 15.00 25.00

☐ **First Aid Kit,** Aviva Enterprises, pictures scenes from the motion picture, adhesive bandages and tape 8.00 15.00

☐ **Flashlight,** Azrak-Hamway, TV show, small phaser shaped, battery operated, 1976 ..... 3.00 6.00

☐ **Freezicles,** molds and concentrate, three kinds, busts of Kirk, Spock and McCoy 20.00 30.00

☐ **Glasses,** Coca-Cola, set of three with pictures on front and description on the back: one with Kirk, Spock and McCoy, second one with Decker and Ilia and third one with The Enterprise. Coca-Cola never found a franchise to distribute these except a few stores, height 5½″, 1979, rare 25.00 30.00

Price Range

☐ **Glasses,** Dr. Pepper, set of four drinking glasses with pictures on front and paragraphs on back describing picture: Captain James T. Kirk, Dr. Leonard McCoy, Mr. Spock, and the U.S.S. Enterprise, height 6¼″, 1976 . . . .   40.00   60.00

☐ **As above,** Dr. Pepper, set of four, same glass style and subject matter as above, different art-work and date (1978), less common than the first set 50.00   75.00

☐ **Glasses,** Taco Bell, four glasses based on Star Trek III: "Spock Lives," "Enterprise Destroyed," "Lord Kruge," "Fal-tor-pan," 1984, set 10.00   15.00

☐ **Lunch Box,** Aladdin, TV show, rectangular metal, 1978 . . . .   25.00   50.00

☐ **Lunch Pail,** King-Seeley Thermos Co., from the motion picture, shows Kirk on one side, Spock and McCoy on the other, thermos captioned "Star Trek," 1979 . . . .   10.00   25.00

☐ **Lunch Pail,** Thermos, Enterprise on the side with scenes from the television show "Aladdin-Hump Backed," 1968 . . . .   75.00   150.00

☐ **Matches,** D. D. Bean and Sons, California, Star Trek: The Motion Picture 2.00   4.00

Glasses, Dr. Pepper, set of four, animated

Price Range

☐ **Matches,** D.D. Bean and Sons, Star Trek II: The Wrath of Khan, 1982, white with red print of movie logo on front and cap offer on back .. 1.00 2.00

☐ **Mirror,** Kirk and Spock, or Spock, 2 sizes, 1977 20.00 50.00

☐ **Mug,** plastic, Star Trek: The Motion Picture, Deka, 1979 .... 2.00 5.00

☐ **Mug,** porcelain, 20th Anniversary and Fan Club logos, Official Star Trek Fan Club, 1986 ..... 8.00 12.00

☐ **Mug And Bowl,** Deka, 10 oz. mug and 20 oz. bowl with pictures of major characters and starship, 1975 .... 10.00 25.00

☐ **Mugs,** Image Products, Wrath of Khan, plastic photo mugs, four different, 1982, each 5.00 10.00

☐ **Needlepoint Kit,** Arista Designs, design imprinted on #10 mesh canvas, black and white yarn portrait of Spock, captioned "Live Long and Prosper," 14″ x 18″, 1980 .... 30.00 40.00

☐ **Needlepoint Kit,** Arista Designs, design imprinted on #10 mesh canvas, Captain Kirk on white background, 14″ x 18″, 1982 .... 30.00 40.00

☐ **Paper Products,** plates, cups, tablecloth, beverage and dinner napkins, white background with Kirk, Spock, Dr. McCoy and Enterprise printed in red, white and blue, Tuttlecraft, 1976, set 15.00 30.00

☐ **Spoons,** collectors' spoons, Kirk and Spock, 4¼″, per pair, 1974 .... 15.00 35.00

☐ **String Art Kit,** TV, 1976, open door 20.00 30.00

☐ **Throw rugs,** fur, 4 different, crew action collage, crew with space scene and Enterprise 20.00 40.00

☐ **Tote bags,** Star Trek: The Motion Picture, Kirk, Spock, or the Enterprise, Aviva, 1979 .... 15.00 25.00

☐ **Tray,** Enterprise, Inc., metal, lap tray with legs, picture of Mr. Spock, length 17½″, 1979 .... 5.00 15.00

☐ **Tumbler,** plastic, Star Trek: The Motion Picture, Deka, 1979 .... 1.00 4.00

Price Range

☐ **Waste Basket,** Star Trek: The Motion Picture, front features the standard motion picture "rainbow" painting, back shows standard photograph of the Enterprise surrounded by six stills of ship's space station, oval, 13″ high, Chein Industries, Inc. 10.00   20.00

☐ **Waste Paper Basket,** black, pictures of the Enterprise and Star Trek characters, metal 20.00   40.00

LINENS

☐ **Draperies,** featuring scenes from the motion picture, various sizes 12.00   20.00

☐ **Drapes,** Pacific Mills, different scenes of the Enterprise 10.00   20.00

☐ **Pillow Case,** Pacific Mills, different scenes of the Enterprise 5.00   10.00

☐ **Sheets,** Cannon Industries, set of twins featuring scenes from The Motion Picture 12.00   20.00

☐ **Sheets,** Pacific Mills, different scenes of the Enterprise 15.00   20.00

☐ **Sleeping Bag,** Alp Industries, action scenes of TV show, says "Star Trek," 1976 .... 30.00   50.00

☐ **Sleeping Bag,** pictures the Enterprise with action poses of Kirk and Spock 25.00   35.00

☐ **Table Cloth,** Tuttle, TV show, with scenes on the Enterprise, 1976 .... 5.00   10.00

LIQUOR DECANTERS

☐ **Dickel Anniversary Special,** approximately 2 feet tall, given only to employees of Distillery, 1 gal. Very rare 200.00   300.00

☐ **Gold** (Special Edition) 2.00   3.00

☐ **Saurian Brandy Bottle,** George Dickel commemorative, used on television show as brandy bottle, curved neck, real leather base and strap.

Saurian Brandy Bottle, Dickel Distilleries

	Price Range	
☐ **Nipper size**	15.00	25.00
☐ **Fifth size**	40.00	55.00
☐ **Quart size**	40.00	85.00
☐ **Spock Liquor Decanter,** by Granadier, 10″ x 20″, fully printed bust of Spock from Star Trek: The Motion Picture, contained cielo liqueur, 1979.		
Note: A hoard of these surfaced in California in 1984. Price is lowered until supply is used up.		
☐ **Without box**	15.00	25.00
☐ **With box**	20.00	30.00
☐ **Full**	50.00	100.00

JEWELRY

	Price Range	
☐ **Belt Buckle,** black with painting, embossed Enterprise and lettering "Star Trek," blue background	6.00	10.00
☐ **As above,** black with painting, lettering "Star Trek Lives," "U.S.S. Enterprise," embossed picture of Enterprise in center	6.00	10.00
☐ **As above,** Command Insignia, round, flat, gold plate, 2½", Lincoln Enterprises	5.00	8.00
☐ **As above,** Indiana Metal Craft, circular, embossed Enterprise and Saturn, painted red, white, and blue, introduction to TV series impressed on back	6.00	10.00
☐ **As above,** Enterprise orbiting planet, oval, 1976, Lee Belts	6.00	10.00
☐ **As above,** TV show, metal, Kirk and Spock, the Enterprise, or Spock alone, Lee Belts, 1976	6.00	10.00
☐ **As above,** Kirk and Spock looking to the left and the Enterprise and "Star Trek" are at the top, bronze, Lincoln Enterprises, not dated, 2" x 3"	10.00	12.00
☐ **As above,** Mr. Spock, round brass, some with enamel trim, 2", Lee Belts, 1976	4.00	6.00
☐ **As above,** rectangular, brass, some with enamel trim, Lee Belts, 1979	4.00	6.00
☐ **As above,** roughly rectangular, 2", brass, some with enamel trim	4.00	6.00
☐ **As above,** oval-shaped with four flat corners, Kirk and Spock in center with "Star Trek" on top, brass, Tiffany Studio	10.00	12.00
☐ **As above,** "Star Trek, The Final Frontier," gold or brass trim, Lincoln Enterprises, 1985	10.00	12.00
☐ **As above,** "Star Trek III: The Search for Spock" with a picture of the Enterprise, limited edition, number on back and synopsis of story, Lincoln Enterprises, 1984	20.00	25.00

	Price Range	
☐ **As above,** 20th Anniversary U.S.S. Enterprise, 24K gold-plated silver, numbered series, Lincoln Enterprises, 1983	25.00	40.00
☐ **As above,** U.S.S. Enterprise commemorative, sterling silver with gold trim, Lincoln Enterprises	175.00	200.00
☐ **As above,** same as above, bronze with gold trim	25.00	30.00
☐ **As above,** uniform buckle, Star Trek II–IV, authentic reproduction, gold plate or bronze finish, Lincoln Enterprises	15.00	20.00
☐ **As above,** oblong-shaped, embossing, relief of Kirk and Spock in center circle, silver finish	6.00	10.00
☐ **Celestial Pendant,** depicts scene from "The Menagerie," gold 24K filigree, inscribed "Where No Man Has Gone Before," Lincoln Enterprises	6.00	8.00
☐ **Command Circle Necklace,** from Star Trek: The Motion Picture, painted, Lincoln Enterprises		
Large necklace	5.00	8.00
Small necklace	4.00	6.00
☐ **Command Circle Pin,** same as above		
Large pin	5.00	8.00
Small pin	4.00	6.00
☐ **As above,** brushed brass, Don Post Studios	10.00	15.00
☐ **Command Insignia Charm,** with 18″ gold-plated chain, Lincoln Enterprises	4.00	6.00
☐ **As above,** sterling silver	7.00	10.00
☐ **Command Insignia Earrings,** post, dangling, or clip-on, Lincoln Enterprises	8.00	10.00
☐ **As above,** sterling silver	12.00	16.00
☐ **Command Insignia Pin,** 22K gold plated, Lincoln Enterprises	4.00	6.00
☐ **Command Insignia Ring,** adjustable, Lincoln Enterprises		
22K gold plated	6.00	8.00
Sterling silver	7.00	10.00

Price Range

☐ **Earrings,** miniature models of the Enterprise, pierced or screw-on, gold or silver 7.00   10.00

☐ **Enterprise Charm,** 1¾", replica of TV Enterprise, soft unplated metal, Goodtime Jewelry   4.00   6.00

☐ **As above,** three dimensions, gold plated, 1¾", replica of movie Enterprise, Lincoln Enterprises   6.00   8.00

☐ **As above,** gold or silver plated, 1¾", replica of TV Enterprise, Star Trek Galore 6.00   8.00

☐ **As above,** gold or silver plated, ½", replica of TV Enterprise, Star Trek Galore 3.00   5.00

☐ **Enterprise Circle,** replica of ship whirling over planet, gold filigree, on 18" chain, Lincoln Enterprises 6.00   8.00

☐ **Federation Whistle,** gold plated on chain, Lincoln Enterprises 2.00   3.00

☐ **Identification Bracelet,** from Star Trek: The Motion Picture, General Mills premium, gold or silver, children's 2.00   3.00

☐ **IDIC Earrings,** Infinite Diversity, Infinite Combinations, based on the pendant worn by Mr. Spock, small size, closed wire, posts or screw-on 8.00   10.00

☐ **IDIC Necklace,** Infinite Diversity, Infinite Combinations, based on pendant worn by Mr. Spock, assorted sizes, circular shape with triangle and jewel

Small 4.00   6.00

Medium 6.00   8.00

Large 8.00   10.00

☐ **IDIC Ring,** Infinite Diversity, Infinite Combinations, based on pendant worn by Mr. Spock, circular shape with triangle and jewel on gold band 4.00   6.00

☐ **Key Chain,** large, clear, square-shaped slab with two-sided pictures, the Enterprise with an oval blue background, Aviva Enterprises, 1½" x 1½" 2.00   3.00

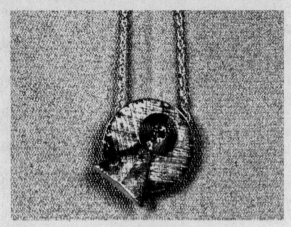

IDIC Pendant

	Price Range	

☐ **As above,** large, clear, square-shaped slab with two-sided picture, Kirk and Spock with Enterprise, large red and lavender planets, black background, Aviva Enterprises, 1½″ x 1½″ — 2.00 / 3.00

☐ **As above,** large, clear, square-shaped slab with two-sided picture of Spock, "Live Long and Prosper," printed in semicircle, red, black and lavender, Aviva Enterprises, 1½″ x 1½″ — 2.00 / 3.00

☐ **As above,** large, clear, square-shaped slab with two-sided picture, Mr. Spock bust with his uniform insignia, white and gray, Aviva Enterprises, 1½″ x 1½″ .... — 2.00 / 3.00

☐ **As above,** large, clear, square-shaped slab with two-sided picture, Spock with arms behind his back, "Star Trek: The Motion Picture" printed up the side, Aviva Enterprises, 1½″ x 1½″ .... — 2.00 / 3.00

☐ **As above,** large, clear, square-shaped slab with two-sided picture, Mr. Spock giving Vulcan salute, circular black background, Aviva Enterprises, 1½″ x 1½″ .... — 2.00 / 3.00

☐ **As above,** features the Enterprise, all brass, metal casted .... — 6.00 / 8.00

	Price Range	
☐ **Key Chain Viewer,** various Star Trek TV film clips, Lincoln Enterprises	2.00	3.00
☐ **Mount Seleya Symbol Necklace,** Lincoln Enterprises, 1985	6.00	8.00
☐ **Necklace,** orbiting Enterprise on medallion, Goodtimes Jewelry	4.00	6.00
☐ **As above,** Spock or Kirk and Spock on TV insignia, pewter, Goodtimes Jewelry, poor quality	4.00	6.00
☐ **As above,** lightweight, gold plated, Spock on a chain, American Miss Co.	3.00	5.00
☐ **Pendant,** phaser, gold or silver, flat on back side	3.00	5.00
☐ **As above,** Vulcan salute, gold, Star Trek Galore	3.00	5.00
☐ **As above,** Vulcan salute, plain gold	3.00	4.00
☐ **As above,** Vulcan salute, flat gold or silver, Star Trek Galore	3.00	4.00
☐ **Pins, Brass,** Aviva		
Enterprise	2.00	3.00
Spock	2.00	3.00
Star Trek: The Motion Picture	2.00	3.00
Uniform pin	2.00	3.00
Vulcan salute	2.00	3.00
☐ **Pins, Cloisonne,** Lincoln Enterprises, 1986		
Enterprise cutout	5.00	6.00
Enterprise and Statue of Liberty	5.00	6.00
Klingon Bird of Prey cutout	5.00	6.00
Peace in Our Galaxy (IDIC)	5.00	6.00
Star Trek, Gateway to a New Beginning ..	5.00	6.00
Star Trek, The Final Frontier	5.00	6.00
Star Trek: The Motion Picture, movie poster design	5.00	6.00
Star Trek: The Search For Spock, commemorative	5.00	6.00
As above, movie poster design	5.00	6.00
Twentieth Anniversary pin	5.00	6.00

	Price	Range
United Federation of Planets symbol	5.00	6.00
☐ **Pins, Cloisonne,** Hollywood Commemorative Pin Co., colorful, high quality, military clutch-back		
Enterprise, cutout, 1985	6.00	7.00
Enterprise and Logo, on blue background, 1985	6.00	7.00
As above, on red background, 1985	6.00	7.00
As above, on red background (small), 1985	6.00	7.00
Insignia Cutout: Movie, small, blue, burgundy, green, orange, red, white, or yellow, 1985 ...	6.00	7.00
As above, large, 1986	8.00	9.00
☐ **Insignia Cutout: TV,** 1986		
Command, black, white, red or blue	6.00	7.00
Science	6.00	7.00
Engineering	6.00	7.00
☐ **Insignia and Logo,** 1985		
Blue background	6.00	7.00
White background	6.00	7.00
☐ **Klingon Admiral,** 1985	6.00	7.00
☐ **Klingon Captain,** 1985	6.00	7.00
☐ **Klingon Symbol,** 1986	8.00	9.00
☐ **Live Long and Prosper,** words and Vulcan sa-lute on blue background, 1985	8.00	9.00
☐ **Rank Insignias,** 1986		
Admiral	6.00	7.00
Captain	8.00	9.00
Commodore	8.00	9.00
Fleet Admiral	8.00	9.00
☐ **Romulan Symbol,** 1985	6.00	7.00
☐ **Spock,** cutout, 1986	6.00	7.00
☐ **Starfleet Division Insignias**		
Colonial Operations, 1986	8.00	9.00
Communications, 1986	8.00	9.00
Engineering, 1986	8.00	9.00
Headquarters, 1986	8.00	9.00
Intelligence, 1986	8.00	9.00
Marines, 1985	8.00	9.00

	Price Range	
Material, 1985	8.00	9.00
Merchant Marines, 1986	8.00	9.00
Military, 1985	8.00	9.00
☐ **UFP Symbol,** large cutout, 1985	8.00	9.00
As above, small cutout, 1985	8.00	9.00
☐ **Twentieth Anniversary Pin,** early logo, white and blue, blue and yellow, red, white, and blue, 1986	6.00	7.00
As above, special logo, 1986	10.00	12.00
As above, "To Boldly Go ... ," 1986	8.00	10.00
As above, "WOW Pin", 1986	8.00	10.00
☐ **Pins, Enamel,** Aviva		
Kirk	3.00	4.00
McCoy	3.00	4.00
☐ **Rank pins,** from Star Trek II–IV		
Admiral, metal, gold with black or silver	8.00	12.00
As above, fiberglass	2.00	3.00
Captain, metal, gold and silver	8.00	12.00

Jewelry for Costumes

	Price Range	
As above, fiberglass	2.00	3.00
Commodore, metal, gold and silver, two different designs	8.00	12.00
Commander, metal, gold and silver	8.00	12.00
As above, fiberglass	2.00	3.00
Fleet Admiral, metal, gold and silver	4.00	7.00
As above, fiberglass	2.00	3.00
Lt. Commander, metal, gold and silver, two designs	8.00	12.00
Service pins, circles plus bars, Star Trek III, metal	1.00	2.00
Shoulder strap clasp, Star Trek III, metal ..	2.00	3.00
☐ **Spock**	3.00	4.00
☐ **Uniform Patch Design**	4.00	5.00
☐ **Sparkle Necklace,** pendant, circular, black background with silver outline of the Enterprise, rests on gold or silver beveled frame ..	3.00	4.00
☐ **As above,** pendant, circular, black background with silver outline of the United Federation of Planets emblem, rests on silver beveled frame	3.00	4.00
☐ **Tie Clasp,** circular shape with Vulcan salute, gold with hand and lettering in black, Aviva Enterprises	3.00	4.00
☐ **As above,** circular with Mr. Spock, printing "Live Long and Prosper," gold and black, Aviva Enterprises	3.00	4.00
☐ **As above,** outline of the Enterprise, gold with black outlines, Aviva Enterprises	3.00	4.00
☐ **As above,** uniform insignia from the TV series, gold	3.00	4.00
☐ **Try Trekking Pendant,** quartz crystal, changes color with your mood, Lincoln Enterprises ...	4.00	5.00
☐ **Uniform Insignia,** Command, Science or Engineering from TV series, gold or silver with black, inlaid, as pendant, tie clasp, or earrings	3.00	4.00
☐ **As above,** from Star Trek II, oblong and triangular shape overlap, bronze finish, Don Post, 1982	4.00	6.00

Price Range

☐ **United Federation of Planets Emblem Tie Clasp,** circular, blue, black and silver, same emblem as appears on Starfleet Technical Manual, Janus head with star map in the middle   3.00   4.00

☐ **United Federation of Planets Emblem Pendant,** same as above 3.00   4.00

☐ **United Federation of Planets Security Badge,** from Star Trek IV: The Voyage Home, hinged, two-piece, Lincoln Enterprises 12.00   18.00

☐ **Uniform Insignia,** Star Trek II–IV, similar to Don Post version but gold plated, painted detail, two sizes, Lincoln Enterprises

    Large 8.00   15.00

    Small 6.00   8.00

☐ **Vulcan Hand of Peace,** gold-plated chain, 18″, Lincoln Enterprises 4.00   6.00

☐ **Watch,** picture of the Enterprise and the words "Star Trek" on the face, men's or ladies', Lincoln Enterprises 25.00   30.00

☐ **As above,** pictures Kirk, Spock, and McCoy from TV series, men's or ladies' styles, no date or manufacturer, probably unlicensed 10.00   20.00

☐ **As above,** pocket watch, same as above 10.00   20.00

☐ **As above,** L.E.D. game watch, Collins Industrial, 1982 ....   10.00   20.00

☐ **As above,** Mr. Spock with a rotating "Enterprise" secondhand, chrome case 20.00   25.00

☐ **As above,** Mr. Spock appears on the dial from Star Trek: The Motion Picture, Bradley Time Co., 1979 ....   20.00   25.00

☐ **As above,** Spock and Enterprise in relief on band, digital, 20th Anniversary packaging, Lewco, 1986 ....   9.00   12.00

☐ **Where No Man Has Gone Before Necklace,** Lincoln Enterprises 5.00   7.00

MAGAZINES

Price Range

☐ **All About Star Trek Fan Clubs,** Ego Enterprises, New York, NY, series of five fanzines with complete membership information plus biographies, portraits, episodes and conventions, first published, Dec. 1976.

☐ #1	8.00	12.00
☐ #2–6	4.00	8.00

☐ **American Cinematographer,** ASC Holding Corp., Hollywood, California, Vol. 61, No. 2, Feb. 1980, issue devoted to a look behind the scenes of "Star Trek: The Motion Picture" .. 15.00 25.00

☐ **Vol. 63, No. 10,** Oct. 1982, "Special Effects For Star Trek II" 4.00 8.00

☐ **Vol. 65, No. 8,** issue on Star trek III 5.00 6.00

☐ **Vol 67, No. 12,** cover and article on Star Trek IV 5.00 6.00

☐ **Bananas #33,** Kirk and Spock on cover, preview of Star Trek I, 1979 .... 4.00 6.00

☐ **Best of Starlog #1** 3.00 4.00

☐ **Best of Starlog #2** 3.00 4.00

☐ **Best of Starlog #3,** Spock on cover. 3.00 4.00

☐ **Biography Of Majel Barrett,** Lincoln Enterprises, star who played Nurse Chapel, pamphlet .... .50 .75

☐ **Biography Of James Doohan,** Lincoln Enterprises, star who played in "Star Trek," pamphlet .... .50 .75

☐ **Biography Of Deforest Kelley,** Lincoln Enterprises, star who played Dr. McCoy, pamphlet .50 .75

☐ **Biography Of Walter Koenig,** Lincoln Enterprises, star who played Chekov, pamphlet ... .50 .75

☐ **Biography Of Nichelle Nichols,** Lincoln Enterprises, star who played Uhura, pamphlet .... .50 .75

☐ **Biography Of Leonard Nimoy,** Lincoln Enterprises, star who played Mr. Spock, pamphlet .50 .75

	Price Range	
☐ **Biography Of Gene Roddenberry,** Lincoln Enterprises, creator and executive producer of Star Trek, pamphlet	.50	.75
☐ **Biography Of William Shatner,** Lincoln Enterprises, star who played Captain Kirk, pamphlet	.50	.75
☐ **Biography Of George Takei,** Lincoln Enterprises, star who played Sulu, pamphlet	.50	.75
☐ **Byte,** The Small Systems Journal Computer magazine, #7, Vol. 9, July 1984, cover shows a sophisticated computer system with Mr. Spock appearing on the screen	3.00	4.00
☐ **Castle Of Frankenstein** #11, 1967, Star Trek issue, Spock on cover	12.00	20.00
Cinefantasque, F.S. Clark Publishers, the magazine with a "Sense of Wonder,"		
☐ **Vol. 12,** No. 5 and 6, July/August 1982, "Star Trek II" and "The Revenge of The Jedi"	10.00	12.00

Cinefantasque, Star Trek II Issue

	Price Range	

☐ **Vol. 17, No. 2,** cover and article on Star Trek's
20th Anniversary **5.00**   **6.00**
Cinefex, a journal of cinematic illusions, Dan
Shay Publishing, Riverside, California

☐ **Number 1,** March 1980, "Into V'ger Mau with
Douglas Truniball," director of special effects
of Star Trek, beautiful color illustrations **10.00**   **15.00**

☐ **Number 2,** August 1980, "Star Trekking at Apo-
gee" **8.00**   **10.00**

☐ **Number 18,** "Last Voyage of Starship Enter-
prise" **5.00**   **6.00**

☐ **Number 29,** "Humpback to the future," 1987   **5.00**   **6.00**

☐ **The Electric Company,** Dec. 1979/Jan. 1980
"The Outer Space Creatures of Star Trek,
What Are They Like?" cover and article **2.00**   **5.00**

Enterprise, HJS Publications, a magazine totally dedicated to Star
Trek, bi-monthly publication.

☐ **Number 1,** April 1984 . . . .   **5.00**   **6.00**
☐ **Number 2,** June 1984 . . . .   **4.00**   **5.00**
☐ **Number 3** **4.00**   **5.00**
☐ **Numbers 4–13** **3.00**   **4.00**
☐ **Enterprise Spotlight 2,** memory book, New
Media Publishing **4.00**   **5.00**

Enterprise Incident, Star Trek Federation of Fans, Coral Gables,
Florida. A prozine for Star Trek fans, slick paper and color covers.

☐ **Issue 1** **20.00**   **30.00**
☐ **Issue 2** **15.00**   **20.00**
☐ **Issue 3** **15.00**   **20.00**
☐ **Issues 4–6** **10.00**   **15.00**
☐ **Issues 7–8** **8.00**   **12.00**
   As above, issued by New Media Publishing,
   mass produced, lower production values
☐ **Issue 9** **5.00**   **8.00**
☐ **Issues 10–12** **4.00**   **6.00**
☐ **Issues 13–17** **3.00**   **4.00**
☐ **Issues 18–27** **2.00**   **3.00**
☐ **Issues 28 up,** Name changes to SF Movieland   **2.00**   **3.00**

	Price Range	
☐ **Summer Special,** between issues 12 & 13 ..	3.00	4.00
☐ **Collectors Edition #1,** Reprints #1 & 2	6.00	8.00
☐ **Collectors Edition #2,** Reprints #3 & 4	5.00	6.00
☐ **Collectors Edition #3,** Reprints #5	4.00	5.00
☐ **Collectors Edition #4,** Reprints #6	4.00	5.00
☐ **Collectors Edition #5,** Reprints #7	4.00	5.00
☐ **Collectors Edition #6,** Reprints #8	4.00	5.00
☐ **Enterprise Incidents,** Spotlight on Leonard Nimoy	4.00	5.00
☐ **As above,** Spotlight on Interview of Star Trek personalities	4.00	5.00
☐ **As above,** Spotlight on the Technical Side ..	5.00	6.00
☐ **As above,** Spotlight on William Shatner	4.00	5.00
☐ **Famous Monsters No. 187,** Star Trek III cover and article	4.00	6.00
Fantastic Films, the magazine of fantasy and science fiction in the cinema, Blake Publishing Company, Chicago, IL.		
☐ **Vol. 1, No. 3,** August 1973, Star Trek: "Interview with Susan Sackett"	3.00	6.00
☐ **Vol. 1, No. 5,** Dec. 1978, "Spock Speaks," with cover photo of Leonard Nimoy	3.00	6.00
☐ **Vol. 2, No. 4,** Sept. 1979, Star Trek: The Motion Picture "Robert Wise: A Comprehensive Interview"	3.00	6.00
☐ **Vol. 2, No. 8,** Feb. 1980, "Designing Star Trek," "Star Trek: The Costumes"	3.00	6.00
☐ **Vol. 2, No. 9,** March 1980, "Star Trek: The Costumes" part two of designer Bob Fletcher's interview	3.00	6.00
☐ **Vol. 7, No. 3,** May 1984, Star Trek III	3.00	4.00
☐ **Vol. 7, No. 4,** July 1984, Star Trek III	3.00	4.00
☐ **Vol. 7, No. 5,** September 1984, James Doohan Interview	3.00	4.00
☐ **Fantasy Enterprises,** New Media Publishing, 1985	4.00	5.00
Future, the magazine of Science Adventure, Future Magazine, Inc., New York.		

	Price Range	
☐ **No. 4,** August 1978, preview of "Star Trek: The Movie"	2.00	4.00
☐ **No. 14,** November 1979, "Re-designing Star Trek"	2.00	4.00
☐ **No. 15,** December 1979, "Star Trek's New Faces"....................................	2.00	4.00
☐ **No. 16,** February 1980, "Star Trek Takes Off"	2.00	4.00
☐ **No. 17,** March 1980, "Designing The 23rd Century"	2.00	4.00
☐ **Hollywood Studio Magazine,** D. Denny Publisher, Vol. 12, No. 5, June 1978, "New 15 Million Star Trek Movie"	5.00	7.00
☐ **Journal of Popular Film and Television,** Vol 12, No. 2, Summer 1984, Spock cover	2.00	3.00
☐ **Mad Magazine #186,** October 1976, "The Star Trek Musical"	5.00	6.00
☐ **Mad #251,** satire on Star Trek III, Dec 1984	4.00	6.00
Mediascene Preview, the magazine of Tomorrow's Entertainment, Supergraphics, Reading, Pennsylvania.		
☐ **Number 6,** Feb. 1980, "Star Trek: The Motion Picture"—the Enterprise encounters a most powerful obstacle, its own reputation	6.00	10.00
☐ **Vol. 1, No. 31,** Dec./Jan. 1978, backstage on the Star Trek set	4.00	6.00
☐ **Media Spotlight,** J. Schuster Publishers, issue 1, Summer, 1975, issue devoted to Star Trek, the television show, star biographies and commentaries	8.00	10.00
☐ **Issue 2,** Fall, 1976, "Star Trek Lives Again"—another issue on the television show with a photo article on Mr. Spock	6.00	8.00
☐ **Issue 3,** March, 1977, "The Roddenberry Tapes," "The Spirit of Star Trek"	6.00	8.00
☐ **Issue 4,** May, 1977, Spock on the cover plus articles on "Fandom, Nichelle Nichols" and robots	6.00	8.00

	Price Range	
☐ **Megastars Poster Magazine,** magazine contains information on Star Trek III and a large Spock poster.	3.00	5.00
☐ **Monsters Of The Movie,** Magazine Management, Inc., Vol. No. 9, Summer, 1975, "An Interview with Leonard Nimoy"	5.00	7.00
☐ **Newsweek,** Dec. 22, 1986, Spock cover and Star Trek IV article	2.00	3.00
☐ **Official Star Trek II Movie Magazine,** printed by Starlog	3.00	5.00
☐ **Parade Magazine,** Dec. 10, 1978, Star Trek: The Motion Picture, issue with color cover . .	5.00	8.00
Questar, The New Magazine of Science Fiction and Fantasy, William Wilson Publishing, Jefferson, Pennsylvania.		
☐ **No. 5,** Nov. 1979, Questar preview "An Advance Look at the Crew of the New Enterprise"	5.00	7.00
☐ **Science And Fantasy Film Classics,** R. Fenton Publisher, No. 3, July, 1978, features Star Trek: the computers, technology, characters	4.00	8.00
Sci-Fi Monthly, Sportscene Publishers Ltd., a British publication in poster format, high quality color photography		
☐ **Issue 1,** date unknown, The Star Trek story, Spock's boyhood	4.00	6.00
☐ **Issue 2,** more in the story of Spock's life, The Enterprise Blueprints, an interview with Spock's creator	4.00	6.00
☐ **Issue 3,** Star Trek's evil empires—Klingons and Romulons	4.00	6.00
☐ **Issue 4,** Enterprise Bridge Blueprints	4.00	6.00
☐ **Issue 6,** Star Trek Alien Poster, Enterprise crew, Part 2	4.00	6.00
Star Burst, Science Fantasy in television, cinema, and comics, Starburst Magazines Ltd., London, a British publication, similar to Starlog, first published in 1978.		

	Price Range	
☐ **Vol. 1, No. 1,** "The Writers of Star Trek," "Star Wars Buccaneers of Space," "The Making of Star Wars"	3.00	5.00
☐ **Vol. 1, No. 10,** June 1979, "The Star Trek Interviews: Part 1"	7.00	9.00
☐ **Vol. 1, Number 11,** July 1979, "The Star Trek Interviews: Part 2"	5.00	7.00
☐ **Vol. 2, No. 5,** a preview of "Star Trek: The Motion Picture"	4.00	6.00
☐ **Vol. 2, No. 7,** a review of "Star Trek: The Motion Picture"	4.00	6.00
☐ **Vol. 5, No. 1,** Star Trek interview with the producer, Star Wars Double Bill, Star Trek II ...	4.00	6.00
Stardate, primarily a gaming magazine, some issues were devoted to the Star Trek role playing game.		
☐ **No. 1,** 1984	5.00	6.00
☐ **No. 2,** 1984	3.00	5.00
☐ **Vol. 3, No. 1,** 1987	3.00	4.00
☐ **Starfleet Communique,** Starfleet Publications, booklet devoted to fan commentary and analysis, published quarterly	7.00	11.00
Starlog, the magazine of the future, O'Quinn Studios, Inc., New York, NY, features regular columns about Star Trek and its fandom, issues with cover stories and special features have added collector value.		
☐ **No. 1,** Star Trek Episode	10.00	20.00
☐ **No. 2,** interview with Roddenberry	5.50	7.50
☐ **No. 3,** convention news	6.00	8.00
☐ **No. 9,** interview with Shatner	10.00	15.00
☐ **No. 14,** Star Trek Spock	4.00	7.00
☐ **No. 24,** 3rd Anniversary, Shatner and Nimoy	6.00	8.00
☐ **No. 25,** Star Trek: The Motion Picture	3.75	5.25
☐ **No. 30,** Star Trek Movie preview, Chekov's Enterprise	3.75	5.25

	Price Range	
☐ **No. 83,** June 1984, Star Trek III, the new Mr. Saavik, Ann Crispin's Trek novel, poster of alien	3.00	4.00
☐ **Starlog Poster Magazine,** Volume 2, 1984, contains ten 16" x 21" color posters, includes poster of Enterprise in Mutara Nebula with Reliant in background.	3.00	4.00
☐ **Starship Design,** 1984, Starstation Aurora. Done as technical magazine of the future ...	9.00	12.00
☐ **Star Trek III: The Search for Spock,** 1984, Starlog, Official Movie magazine, Final Voyage of the Starship Enterprise, making of the movie, Nimoy Directs, Shatner Stars, Kirk risks everything for his Vulcan friend	3.00	4.00
☐ **Star Trek III: The Search for Spock Poster Magazine,** Starlog, 1984, contains ten color posters from the movie	3.00	4.00
☐ **Star Trek IV: The Voyage Home Movie Magazine,** Starlog, 1986	3.00	4.00
☐ **Star Trek IV: The Voyage Home Poster Magazine,** contains 10 posters, Starlog, 1986 ...	3.00	4.00
☐ **Star Trek, The Official Fan CLub Magazine,** slick, 5" x 7", ...	2.50	5.00
☐ **Super Visual,** magazine and complete visual guide of Star Trek, Vol. 1–3, a Japanese publication of high quality color styles of different television stories	25.00	50.00
Trek, the magazine for Star Trek Fans, G.B. Love and W. Irwing, Houston, Texas, a fanzine turned prozine, dedicated to Star Trek information—about the show and the gaining momentum of the fans, published from 1974–81, a series of 19.		
☐ **No. 1,** negatives were destroyed, potentially very valuable	40.00	50.00
☐ **No. 2–3**	10.00	15.00
☐ **No. 4,** rare	20.00	25.00

Trek Magazine

	Price Range	
☐ **No. 5–19**	8.00	15.00
☐ **Special Issue #1,** Feb. 1977	8.00	12.00
☐ **Special Issue #2,** Nov. 1978	8.00	12.00
T.V. Guide, issues with cover stories have higher collectible value.		
☐ **March 4, 1967,** Star Trek cover	25.00	30.00
☐ **July 15, 1967,** Nichelle Nichols	7.50	10.00
☐ **November 18, 1967,** Star Trek cover	25.00	30.00
☐ **June 22, 1968,** William Shatner	7.50	10.00
☐ **August 24, 1968,** Star Trek cover	20.00	25.00
☐ **October 14, 1976,** Star Trek article	7.50	10.00
☐ **March 25, 1972,** Trek Conventions	15.00	20.00
☐ **UFO Report,** August 1978, "Beaming Aboard The Star Trek Movie," Enterprise shown on cover	2.00	3.00

Price Range

☐ **Videogaming,** June 1983, article on computer of Star Trek, Spock on cover, magazine title now out of print. 5.00 7.00

MEDALLIONS

Price Range

☐ **Commemorative Coin,** Lincoln Enterprises, commemorates Star Trek's 10th anniversary, silver, dollar size, three-dimensional bas relief, sculpture of Kirk, Spock, McCoy and Scotty on one side, the Enterprise orbiting a planet on the other 6.00 8.00

Medallion, Hanover mint, obverse (heads) and reverse

	Price Range	
☐ **Star Trek Medallion,** Hanover Mint, original was roughly the size of a half dollar. First Series has detachable rim, produced in bronze, Kirk and Spock on front with alien landscape captioned. Originals can be identified by number stamp, fine detailing, sharp lettering	50.00	100.00
☐ **As above, Silver** with edge numbers and marked	200.00	500.00
☐ **As above, Gold Plated**	150.00	200.00
☐ **Second Series,** clean strike but no serial number on the rim, bronze, small hoard turned up in New York in 1984	25.00	50.00
☐ **Third Series,** featured a hole for the chain cast as an integral part of the coin, numbered series	20.00	40.00
☐ **Star Trek III,** "Star Trek III: The Search for Spock," picture of Kirk and Spock on front, back says "Of all the souls I have encountered, his was the most human," with the Enterprise and planet, gold tone with chain. Lincoln Ent.	13.00	15.00
☐ **20th Anniversary,** 1966–86 and Enterprise on one side, Kirk and Spock in ST uniform on other, bronze or pewter, Lincoln Enterprises	20.00	25.00
☐ **Vulcan Nickel,** Huckleberry Designs, large wooden nickel, picture of Spock on the face, legends "In Spock We Trust" and "Leonard Nimoy Wouldn't Lie" on obverse, issued in 1972	3.00	5.00
☐ **Same as above,** 1975 issue	2.00	3.00

MODEL KITS

Models in general are excellent collectibles but only in original condition. An assembled model, even a rare one, is virtually worthless. AMT, the original manufacturer of Star Trek models in this country, is no longer in business. ERTL, however, has used AMT's original molds to reissue some of the original models. These kits are still in production, as indicated by their prices in this section.

	Price Range	
☐ **Enterprise,** A.M.T. Corp., S.T.T.M.P., large box, lighted unit	60.00	75.00
☐ **Second Series,** ERTL reissue, no light	20.00	25.00
☐ **As above,** Star Trek III packaging	15.00	20.00
☐ **As above,** Star Trek IV packaging	12.00	13.00
☐ **Enterprise,** distributed in England, says "As seen on BBC TV," No. 921, Aurora Plastics	20.00	30.00
☐ **Enterprise,** first series, large box vertical or horizontal on cover, includes lighting, says "As seen on NBC TV"	100.00	200.00
☐ **Second Series,** large box, from TV show, horizontal design, no lights	75.00	125.00
☐ **Third Series,** A.M.T. Corp., small box, from TV show, no lights, shows other A.M.T. Corp. kits on side of box	20.00	40.00
☐ **Fourth Series,** A.M.T. Corp., ERTL reissue, white information panel on side	6.00	8.00
☐ **Enterprise,** made for foreign distribution only, Mego, 1980	50.00	75.00
☐ **Enterprise,** Star Trek: The Motion Picture, electronic, South Bend, 1979	75.00	100.00
☐ **Enterprise Model Kit,** M. Shokal and Company, Tokyo, Japanese distributor version with propeller	25.00	50.00
☐ **Exploration Set,** A.M.T., features undersized communicator, tricorder and Type II phaser, very rare.		
☐ **Large Box,** First Edition	100.00	150.00
☐ **Small Box,** Second Edition	50.00	75.00
☐ **Flying Model Rocket,** Klingon and Enterprise, actual flying rockets by Estes, 15″ x 17″, parachute recovery systems	12.00	15.00
☐ **Galileo Shuttlecraft, AMT**		
☐ **Large Box**	100.00	150.00
☐ **Small Box**	75.00	100.00
☐ **K-7,** Space Station, A.M.T., glue together	50.00	75.00

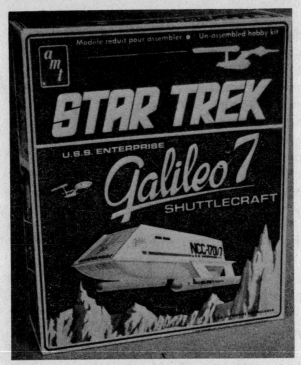

Model Kit, Galileo 7, second series, AMT

	Price Range	
☐ **Katanga Class Klingon Ship,** S.T.T.M.P., large box	25.00	40.00
☐ **1984 ERTL Reissue**	7.00	9.00
☐ **Klingon,** A.M.T., first edition has illuminated portholes, in a larger box, 14¼″ x 10″, later editions were not illuminated and were in an 8½″ x 10″ box, 1976.		
☐ **First Edition**	100.00	200.00
☐ **Second Edition,** large box, no lights	75.00	125.00
☐ **Third Edition,** smaller box	50.00	75.00
☐ **Klingon,** approx. 8″, made for foreign distribution only, Mego, 1980	50.00	75.00
☐ **Model Of The Romulan Bird Of Prey,** A.M.T. Corp., snap-together pieces, plastic, licensed and last produced 1977	75.00	100.00

	Price Range	
☐ **Mr. Spock,** model kit, A.M.T. Corp., action posed, extraterrestrial base, from the motion picture, 1979	10.00	15.00
☐ **Mr. Spock,** from the TV series, "Phasering a Serpent," make-to-scale pieces snap together, licensed, last produced 1977, AMT Corp., large box	25.00	50.00
☐ **Same as above,** small box	15.00	25.00
☐ **Mr. Spock,** model kit, Aurora Plastics, Ltd., distributed in England, featured a diorama and three-headed monster, number 922, in box ..	15.00	25.00
☐ **Space Ship Set,** A.M.T., includes Enterprise, Klingon and Romulan ships, snap-together, requires no glue, all in one box, 1976	25.00	40.00
☐ **Second Edition,** ERTL reissue	6.00	8.00
☐ **U.S.S. Enterprise Command Bridge,** A.M.T. Corp., glue-together, figures of Kirk, Spock and Sulu, diameter 12″, 1975	30.00	50.00
☐ **Vulcan Shuttle,** A.M.T. Corp., model kit, from the motion picture	20.00	30.00
☐ **1984 ERTL Reissue**	6.00	8.00
☐ **Vulcan Shuttle,** approx. 8″, made for foreign distribution only, Mego, 1980.	40.00	60.00

PATCHES

All patches in this section are embroidered unless otherwise indicated. The values listed for these patches reflect current sale prices. Most are still in production and will remain so. Future appreciation of values is not likely since these patches will probably remain in production.

	Price Range	
☐ **Alpha Centauri Symbol,** gold & purple, from Tech Manual	2.00	4.00
☐ **Commendation Ribbons,** set of 19 from TV show; small triangular patches from TV show.	10.00	15.00

Assorted Star Trek Patches, different manufacturers

	Price Range	
☐ **Dreadnought,** blue & yellow, NCC-1707	2.00	4.00
☐ **Enterprise,** black background, Lincoln Ent. . .	2.00	4.00
☐ **Enterprise,** black background with white silhouette captioned "Star Trek"	2.00	4.00
☐ **Enterprise,** dark blue background, cut-out . . .	1.50	3.00
☐ **Enterprise orbiting planet,** 6-color, fan shaped, 4½", Star Trek Welcommittee	1.00	3.00
☐ **As above,** with name and number, oval, 4", white or black background, Star Trek Welcommittee	1.00	3.00
☐ **Federation,** word with Enterprise, 3", Star Trek Welcommittee	1.00	3.00
☐ **Figure Patch,** cutout of Kirk	1.50	2.50
☐ **As above,** Spock	1.50	2.50
☐ **As above,** McCoy	1.50	2.50
☐ **As above,** Uhura	1.50	2.50

	Price Range	

☐ **Galileo,** word, number and picture, 2″, Star Trek Welcommittee 1.00 3.00

☐ **IDIC Symbol,** says "Peace in Our Galaxy," Lincoln Enterprises 2.00 4.00

☐ **Insignia Patch from TV,** Command, black star with gold background 1.50 2.50

☐ **As above,** science, black circle with football-shaped symbol inside 1.50 2.50

☐ **As above,** engineering, black curved symbol 1.50 2.50

☐ **As above,** nursing, red cross on gold background 1.50 2.50

☐ **As above,** pi symbol on gold background 1.50 2.50

☐ **As above,** gamma symbol on gold background 1.50 2.50

☐ **Insignia Patch,** from *Star Trek: The Motion Picture,* Command, black star with white background 1.50 2.50

☐ **As above,** science, orange background 1.50 2.50

☐ **As above,** engineering, red background 1.50 2.50

☐ **As above,** medical, green background 1.50 2.50

☐ **As above,** operations, yellow background ... 1.50 2.50

☐ **As above,** security, silver background 1.50 2.50

☐ **Keep on Trekkin',** rectangular, red backgroud, 3½″, Star Trek Welcommittee 1.00 3.00

☐ **Klingon,** word with picture of Klingon Cruiser, 3″, Star Trek Welcommittee 1.00 3.00

☐ **Klingon Ship,** black background, Lincoln Ent. 2.00 4.00

☐ **Live Long and Prosper,** Thinking Cap Co. .. 2.00 5.00

☐ **Live Long and Prosper,** words with Vulcan salute, hand, 4″, Star Trek Welcommittee 1.00 3.00

☐ **Mascot Patch,** shows tribbles 2.00 3.00

☐ **Medical Caduceus,** green, Lincoln Ent 2.00 3.00

☐ **Phaser Patch** 1.50 2.50

☐ **Photo Patch,** from *Star Trek: The Motion Picture,* Aviva Ent., with Spock, Kirk and McCoy 3.00 5.00

☐ **As above,** with Kirk in full dress uniform 3.00 5.00

☐ **As above,** with worried Admiral Kirk 3.00 5.00

☐ **As above,** with Spock and Kirk 3.00 5.00

☐ **As above,** with Spock in white 3.00 5.00

	Price Range	
☐ **Romulan,** word with picture of Romulan Bird of Prey, 3″, Star Trek Welcommittee	1.00	3.00
☐ **Space Station K-7,** words and picture, 3″, Star Trek Welcommittee	1.00	3.00
☐ **Spock,** with "Live Long and Prosper," square	2.00	4.00
☐ **Spock Lives,** 3″, Thinking Cap Co.	2.00	5.00
☐ **61 Cygni Symbol,** planetary system, copper bird from Tech Manual	2.00	4.00
☐ **Star Trek III Commemorative Patch,** embroidered, Lincoln Enterprises	6.00	8.00
☐ **Star Trek 20th Anniversary Patch,** embroidered, Lincoln Enterprises	6.00	8.00
☐ **United Federation of Planets,** silver and red banner	2.00	3.00
☐ **As above,** silver & black banner	2.00	3.00
☐ **As above,** silver & blue circle, 4″	4.00	6.00
☐ **As above,** silver & blue, 3″, Thinking Cap Co.	2.00	5.00
☐ **USS Enterprise,** light blue background, dark blue border, lettering in orange, silver ship . .	2.00	4.00
☐ **As above,** yellow background, light blue border, lettering in orange, silver & grey ship . . .	2.00	4.00
☐ **As above,** insignia in red, 3″, Thinking Cap Co.	2.00	5.00
☐ **As above,** words on yellow felt background.	1.50	2.50
☐ **Zap,** word with Enterprise firing phasers, rectangle, 4-color, 3½″, Star Trek Welcommittee	1.00	3.00

POSTCARDS

CALIFORNIA DREAMERS

From Star Trek TV series, in color.

	Price Range	
☐ **Enterprise,** "To seek strange new worlds . . . like you!"	.50	.75

	Price Range	
☐ **Kirk,** "Screens up full, magnification 10"	.50	.75
☐ **Kirk speaking into communicator,** "Lock me in and beam me up, baby, I'm yours"	.50	.75
☐ **Kirk with aliens at party,** "...Call me. We'll have lunch!"	.50	.75
☐ **Spock,** "Bizarre ... but I like it"	.50	.75
☐ **Spock,** touching wall	.50	.75
☐ **Spock wearing instrument on head,** "... Batteries may fail, but rock and roll will never die!"	.50	.75
☐ **Sulu,** "Control systems out, navigation out. Directional systems out... I'm so confused" ...	.50	.75

LINCOLN ENTERPRISES—ST-TV, COLOR

☐ **Chekov**	.50	1.00
☐ **Kirk**	.50	1.00
☐ **McCoy**	.50	1.00
☐ **Scotty**	.50	1.00
☐ **Spock**	.50	1.00
☐ **Sulu**	.50	1.00
☐ **Uhura**	.50	1.00
☐ **Complete Set**	3.00	4.00

LINCOLN ENTERPRISES—STTMP, COLOR

☐ **Chapel**	.50	1.00
☐ **Chekov**	.50	1.00
☐ **Decker**	.50	1.00
☐ **Enterprise**	.50	1.00
☐ **Ilia**	.50	1.00
☐ **Kirk**	.50	1.00
☐ **McCoy**	.50	1.00
☐ **Rand**	.50	1.00
☐ **Scotty**	.50	1.00
☐ **Spock**	.50	1.00
☐ **Sulu**	.50	1.00
☐ **Uhura**	.50	1.00
☐ **Complete set**	4.00	5.00

LINCOLN ENTERPRISES—ST III, COLOR

	Price Range	
☐ Chekov	.50	1.00
☐ Kirk	.50	1.00
☐ McCoy	.50	1.00
☐ Saavik	.50	1.00
☐ Sarek	.50	1.00
☐ Scotty	.50	1.00
☐ Spock	.50	1.00
☐ Sulu	.50	1.00
☐ Tilar	.50	1.00
☐ Uhura	.50	1.00
☐ Complete Set	4.00	5.00
☐ Movieland Wax Museum, Star Trek exhibit (California) published by Impact, 32148, 1979	.50	1.00
☐ Set UFP Banner, says Star Fleet Headquarters Tactical Center, 8 per set, assorted colors, T-K Graphics	1.00	2.00
☐ Set UFP Emblem, says Star Fleet Headquarters, Official mail, 8 per set, assorted colors, T-K Graphics	1.00	2.00
☐ Star Trek Postcard Book, G. Cerani, 48 color postcards, action and portrait photos plus an index of the TV series, softcover, Prime Press, 1977	10.00	15.00
☐ Star Trek II: Wrath of Khan, Fantasy Trading Company, set of 30 (see Trading Cards)		
☐ Set Star Trek III: The Search for Spock Postcard Book, 22 full color postcards with scenes from the third Star Trek movie. Simon and Schuster Inc., 1984	6.00	8.00
☐ USS Enterprise Model, from the National Air and Space Museum in Washington, D.C. Full color photograph of model with a spiral galaxy in the light blue background.	1.00	2.00

POSTER BOOKS

	Price Range	
☐ **Star Trek: The Motion Picture Magazine** Poster	5.00	8.00
☐ **Voyage One,** close-up of the Starship Enterprise with articles on the evolution of Spock, a city in space	10.00	18.00
☐ **Voyage Two,** Kirk, McCoy and Spock on giant poster plus articles about special effects, the interrelationships of the crew	6.00	8.00
☐ **Voyage Three,** Spock on the bridge, blooper photos, The Trouble with Tribbles, "I'm a doctor not a mechanic"	6.00	8.00
☐ **Voyage Four,** Kirk and the Klingon on poster, The Super Aliens Of Star Trek, A Journey To Babel	6.00	8.00
☐ **Voyage Five,** Spock with weapon, Inside a Vulcan Mind, Planet Vulcan Revisited	6.00	8.00
☐ **Voyage Six,** The Enterprise's laser on poster, Amok Time, The Art Of Star Trek	6.00	8.00
☐ **Voyage Seven,** Kirk with glass toasting, For The Love Of Jim, The Enemy Within	6.00	8.00
☐ **Voyage Eight,** Dr. McCoy on poster, interview with McCoy and his medical miracles	6.00	8.00
☐ **Voyage Nine,** Lt. Uhura on poster, Assignment Earth, The Music Of Star Trek	6.00	8.00
☐ **Voyage Ten,** the Klingons on poster, a pictorial inspection of Star Trek miniatures	6.00	8.00
☐ **Voyage 11,** Spock The Navigator, an exclusive interview with Leonard Nimoy, The Enterprise Incident	6.00	8.00
☐ **Voyage 12,** Yeoman Rand, articles on the Heroines Of Star Trek, The Paradise Syndrome	8.00	14.00
☐ **Voyage 13,** Scotty and Uhura on poster, plus an interview with Montgomery Scott	10.00	15.00
☐ **Voyage 14,** articles on the history of the Federation, tri-dimensional chess	15.00	20.00

	Price Range	
☐ **Voyage 15,** Kirk and Sulu on poster, The Non-Humanoid Aliens, The Conscience Of The King	10.00	15.00
☐ **Voyage 16,** Kirk and the crew on the bridge on the poster, articles on the Space Seed and the costumes of Star Trek	10.00	15.00
☐ **Voyage 17,** last one	15.00	20.00
☐ **Wrath of Khan Poster Book,** British edition, available but difficult to find	5.00	7.00

POSTERS

The posters in this section are divided chronologically by TV show and movie. Values are for unfolded posters except for theatre posters (27″ x 42″). Values for rolled theatre posters are about 25% higher.

THE TELEVISION SERIES

	Price Range	
☐ **#3390,** Dargis Associates, "Captain Kirk," shows Kirk in command chair with bridge in background, 1976	3.00	5.00
☐ **#3391,** Dargis Associates, "Mister Spock," shows Spock holding phaser with shuttlecraft in background, 1976	3.00	5.00
☐ **Black Light Poster Of The Enterprise,** Dynamic Publishing Company, flocked, 19″ x 28″	3.00	5.00
☐ **Black Light Poster Of Kirk,** Dynamic Publishing Company, flocked and colorful, 19″ x 28″	3.00	5.00
☐ **Black Light Poster Of Spock,** Dynamic Publishing Company, flocked and colorful, 19″ x 28″	3.00	5.00
☐ **The Enterprise,** chrome mylar, cutaway illustration, detailed interior view	10.00	30.00
☐ **Spock,** Huckleberry Designs, from original art by M. Beard, entitled "Spock in Pain," 29″ x 23″	5.00	8.00

Spock Black Light Poster

	Price Range	
☐ **Collage,** Langley Associates, features all the characters and scenes from the episodes, 20″ x 24″	**3.00**	**5.00**
☐ **Captain Kirk,** Langley Associates, life-size portrait, ready to beam down, height 6′	**5.00**	**8.00**
☐ **Crew,** Langley Associates, about to beam down, 20″ x 24″	**3.00**	**5.00**
☐ **Crew,** Langley Associates, portrait on bridge, 20″ x 24″	**3.00**	**5.00**
☐ **Enterprise,** Langley Associates, dogfighting with enemy ships, 20″ x 24″	**3.00**	**5.00**
☐ **Enterprise,** Langley Associates, firing on enemy ship, 20″ x 24″	**3.00**	**5.00**
☐ **Enterprise,** Langley Associates, firing phasers, 2′ x 3′	**3.00**	**5.00**

	Price Range	
☐ **Enterprise,** Langley Associates, top view with whole crew around, 20″ x 24″	3.00	5.00
☐ **Kirk,** as a Romulan, 17″ x 22″, Lincoln Enterprises	4.00	5.00
☐ **Kirk collage,** 2′ x 3′, Lincoln Enterprises	5.00	6.00
☐ **Rigel Castle from Menagerie,** Langley Associates	3.00	5.00
☐ **Spock Collage,** 2′ x 3′, Lincoln Enterprises ..	5.00	6.00
☐ **Spock Mindmelding with Nixon,** 17″ x 22″, Lincoln Enterprises	4.00	5.00
☐ **Spock,** Langley Associates, life-size figure with phaser on transporter about to beam down, height 6′	5.00	8.00
☐ **Spock And Kirk,** Langley Associates, artist's rendering with Enterprise in the background, 20″ x 24″	3.00	5.00
☐ **Spock And Kirk,** Langley Associates, high quality laser portrait, 20″ x 24″	3.00	5.00
☐ **Computer Printout,** Lincoln Enterprises, The U.S.S. Enterprise, intricately detailed, 28″ x 12″	2.00	3.00
☐ **Star Trek TV Poster,** featuring artwork with Enterprise passing between two planets, 30″ x 22″, Scholastic Books, 1978, rare.	8.00	12.00
☐ **Star Trek,** Steranko, collage print of television show	5.00	8.00
☐ **Star Trek Galore,** Captain Kirk with Lirpa (19″ x 23″)	3.00	4.00
☐ **Star Trek Galore,** the Klingon recruiting poster	5.00	6.00
☐ **Star Trek Galore,** pictures the Babel party (19″ x 23″)	3.00	4.00
☐ **Star Trek Galore,** pictures the crew of the Enterprise on the bridge	3.00	4.00
☐ **Star Trek Galore,** pictures the Enterprise firing phasers	3.00	4.00
☐ **Star Trek Galore,** pictures the Klingon landing party, the Enterprise's arch enemies (19″ x 33″)	3.00	4.00

	Price	Range
☐ **Kirk,** Star Trek Galore	3.00	4.00
☐ **Spock,** with Vulcan harp, Star Trek Galore ...	4.00	6.00
☐ **Star Trek Galore,** "The United Federation of Planets Wants You," recruiting poster	5.00	6.00
☐ **Planetscape,** A Taste of Armageddon, Star Trek Galore, 19″ x 23″	3.00	4.00
☐ **Star Trek TV B/W artwork poster,** featuring Kirk, Spock, Uhura, and Sulu, 19″ x 28″.	2.00	3.00
☐ **Star Trek TV B/W artwork poster,** featuring crew and Enterprise, 19″ x 28″.............	2.00	3.00
☐ **Starfleet Fantasy Poster,** a fantasy collage based on television episode, "The Enterprise Incidents," 22″ x 30″	4.00	6.00

STAR TREK: THE MOTION PICTURE

	Price	Range
☐ **Billboard Poster,** Star Trek: The Motion Picture, logo says "The new adventure is about to begin," 8′ x 19′	50.00	100.00
☐ **Giant Movie Poster,** all the new faces with the Enterprise overhead, also the inside scoop about the production on the back	6.00	10.00
☐ **Group Shot From Star Trek: The Motion Picture,** Lincoln Enterprises	5.00	6.00
☐ **Group With The Enterprise,** "The human adventure is just beginning," Lincoln Enterprises	4.00	5.00
☐ **Kirk,** Lincoln Enterprises	4.00	5.00
☐ **Kirk, Spock and Enterprise,** Lincoln Enterprises	5.00	6.00
☐ **Klingon From Movie and Ronald Reagan in Star Trek: The Motion Picture Starfleet Uniform,** Lincoln Enterprises	4.00	5.00
☐ **Movie Poster,** Star Trek: The Motion Picture, shows cutaway illustration of the Enterprise's interior decks, 1979, 22″ x 48″, Superior Poster Sales Corp. of America	10.00	12.00

	Price Range	
☐ **Smaller Promotional Version** (Coca-Cola), with drawing of crew in lower right corner, 11″ x 23″	5.00	10.00
☐ **Movie Poster Of The Enterprise,** Paramount Pictures, captioned "The 23rd Century Now, Star Trek: The Motion Picture," full cast and credits, 1979	15.00	25.00
☐ **Poster,** Star Trek: The Motion Picture, chrome mylar, mirror finish, shows Enterprise looming overhead in deep space, 22″ x 29″	6.00	10.00
☐ **Poster,** Star Trek: The Motion Picture written at the bottom, full cast, Enterprise in space dock, 34″ x 22″	10.00	15.00
☐ **Proctor And Gamble Premium Poster,** series of three, No. 1 features the Enterprise and other vehicles; No. 2 Spock and Kirk back to back with starburst behind; No. 3 the Enterprise crew with Enterprise overhead, for set	10.00	15.00
☐ **Star Trek: The Motion Picture,** "There is no comparison," known as the rainbow poster, picturing Spock, Kirk, and Ilia in the rays of the Enterprise, 1979, large size, 27″ x 42″	15.00	25.00
☐ **As above,** small size, 18″ x 24″	5.00	6.00
☐ **Foreign Editions Of The Rainbow Poster,** German	15.00	20.00

Poster, Enterprise cutaway, small promotional version done for Coca-Cola

	Price Range	
☐ **As above,** Italian	15.00	20.00
☐ **As above,** Japanese	15.00	20.00
☐ **As above,** French	15.00	20.00
☐ **As above,** Mexican	15.00	20.00
☐ **Star Trek: The Motion Picture, 2′ x 3′,** poster of the new Enterprise, Lincoln Enterprises ...	6.00	7.00
☐ **Star Trek: The Motion Picture, 17″ x 22″,** close-up of Admiral Kirk, Lincoln Enterprises	4.00	5.00
☐ **Star Trek: The Motion Picture, Coca-Cola, 18″ x 24″,** promo poster with Kirk and crew over bridge scene and Enterprise looming overhead	4.00	5.00
☐ **Star Trek: The Motion Picture, 17″ x 22″,** two sides of Spock captioned "Kolinar," Lincoln Enterprises	4.00	5.00
☐ **Star Trek: The Motion Picture, 22″ x 34″,** poster, with Enterprise looming over planet with Vulcan Shuttle coming up from bottom, "Star Trek" at top of poster and major characters pictured at bottom	10.00	15.00
☐ **Star Trek: The Motion Picture, 17″ x 22″,** Kirk and Spock artwork poster, Lincoln Enterprises	4.00	6.00
☐ **Two-Sided Poster,** Star Trek: The Motion Picture, Sales Corp. of America, one side printed, other lithographed, three-dimensional, comes with glasses, 22″ x 24″	6.00	10.00

STAR TREK II: THE WRATH OF KHAN

☐ **Admiral Kirk, 2′ x 3′,** Star Trek close-up, Lincoln Enterprises	6.00	7.00
☐ **Advertising Poster,** for the original soundtrack album, Enterprise with starburst in orbit around planet with rings, used in theatres, one sheet poster, 27″ x 41″, advance	15.00	25.00
☐ **As above,** style A	10.00	15.00
☐ **As above,** logo in silver	10.00	15.00

	Price Range	
☐ **Star Trek II Collage 1–Sheet**	15.00	25.00
☐ **Small Promotional Version**	4.00	5.00
☐ **Captain Spock, 17″ x 22″,** Star Trek II close-up, Lincoln Enterprises	4.00	5.00
☐ **Khan with Gonzo the Muppet, 17″ x 22″,** Lincoln Enterprises	4.00	5.00
☐ **McCoy with Medical Instrument, 17″ x 22″,** Star Trek II poster, Lincoln Enterprises	4.00	5.00
☐ **Spock Giving Vulcan Salute,** behind Enterprise and planet, 17″ x 22″, Lincoln Enterprises	4.00	5.00
☐ **Spock is dead?** Star Trek II poster, Lincoln Enterprises	6.00	7.00
☐ **Star Trek II, 22″ x 30″,** done for fanzine cover, collage poster artwork by Sat Nam Kaur, 1982	4.00	5.00
☐ **Star Trek II Picture Montage, 2′ x 3′,** Lincoln Enterprises	5.00	6.00
☐ **Star Trek II, The Wrath Of Khan,** pictures Kirk, McCoy, Spock, and Khan around the Enterprise, Sales Corp. of America	3.00	4.00
☐ **Star Trek II,** Wrath of Khan logo in full color, Sales Corp. of America	3.00	4.00

STAR TREK III: SEARCH FOR SPOCK

☐ **Bird of Prey and logo,** Lever Bros.	4.00	10.00
☐ **Enterprise and logo,** Lever Bros.	4.00	10.00
☐ **Group,** Lever Bros.	4.00	10.00
☐ **Kirk and Kruge,** Lever Bros.	4.00	10.00
☐ **Star Trek III: The Search for Spock,** one sheet outline of Spock, 27″ x 41″	10.00	15.00
☐ **One Sheet Art,** Lincoln Enterprises	4.00	6.00
☐ **Smaller Promotional Version,** one sheet art	5.00	7.00
☐ **Star Trek III Montage,** one sheet used for foreign releases (same art was used for ads in U.S.A.)	20.00	30.00
☐ **Star Trek III Montage,** similar to foreign one-sheet design, in brilliant color, 22″ x 28″	4.00	5.00

STAR TREK IV: THE VOYAGE HOME

Price Range

☐ **Enterprise Cutaway,** reprint, same poster done during Star Trek: The Motion Picture with Star Trek IV header and in smaller size, 24″ x 36″, Minds Eye Press 10.00 15.00

☐ **One-Sheet Art,** Lincoln Enterprises, 24″ x 36″ 6.00 8.00

☐ **As above,** NMR, Canadian, 22″ x 36″ 3.00 5.00

☐ **Star Trek IV Montage,** new Enterprise with small inset pictures, 23″ x 35″, One Stop Poster Co. 3.00 5.00

☐ **Star Trek IV: The Voyage Home,** advance teaser one-sheet, 27″ x 41″, words with San Francisco pictured in corner 20.00 40.00

☐ **Smaller Promotional Version,** of advance art, 13½″ x 20″ 1.00 4.00

☐ **As above,** one sheet, 27″ x 41″, shows Bird of Prey flying over San Francisco 15.00 20.00

☐ **Star Trek IV Whale Poster,** 18″ x 28″, Lincoln Enterprises 5.00 7.00

☐ **Twentieth Anniversary Commemoratives**

☐ **Personalities Inc.,** artword, characters in TV costumes at top, New Enterprise at bottom, 23″ x 34″ 28.00 32.00

☐ **Verkerke,** photo, Kirk, Spock, McCoy, and Uhura, 23″ x 36″ 5.00 7.00

PROMOTIONAL ITEMS

STUDIO

Price Range

☐ **Advance Brochure, "Star Trek, The Next Generation,"** metal folder with etched title and "Captain's Log" on cover, includes spiral-bound booklet of demographics and 20-year anniversary T-shirt. Boxed 100.00 200.00

	Price Range	
☐ **Advance Brochure: Star Trek TV series,** 1966–67 season, 12 pages. Very rare.	100.00	200.00
☐ **Brochure,** Paramount Pictures, four pages, The Wrath of Khan, photos from the movie . .	2.00	3.00
☐ **Brochure,** Star Trek II, The Wrath of Khan, Paramount Pictures, lists the cast, credits, special effects crew	2.00	3.00
☐ **Cardboard Dump,** for books, several different titles	10.00	20.00
☐ **As above,** for video-cassettes	10.00	20.00
☐ **Flyer,** Star Trek II, color photos	2.00	3.00
☐ **As above,** Star Trek IV, blue and silver cover, color scenes from movie inside	2.00	3.00
☐ **As above,** Star Trek IV, silver cover, "Coming This Christmas," Photos inside	2.00	3.00
☐ **Lobby Cards,** Star Trek: The Motion Picture, 11" x 14", each	5.00	7.00
☐ **As above,** set of 8	30.00	35.00
☐ **As above,** 8" x 10" still set, in color	20.00	25.00
☐ **Lobby Cards,** Star Trek: Wrath of Khan, 11" x 14"	5.00	7.00
☐ **As above,** set of 8	30.00	35.00
☐ **As above,** 8" x 10" still set	20.00	25.00
☐ **Star Trek III,** 11" x 14", each	5.00	7.00
☐ **As above,** set of eight	30.00	35.00
☐ **As above,** set of eight, 8" x 10"	20.00	25.00
☐ **Movie Stand Up,** Star Trek: The Motion Picture, with lights, large 5' x 6'	90.00	250.00
☐ **Newsletter,** Star Trek: The Motion Picture, Paramount Pictures, four-page promotional piece about the first movie, articles about two new major characters, Stephen Collins and Persis Khambatta, summer 1979	1.00	2.00
☐ **Newsletter,** Star Trek: The Motion Picture, second issue, Paramount Pictures, four-page promotional piece about the first movie, reproduction of the Rainbow poster, articles on special effects and costuming, autumn 1979	1.00	2.00

	Price Range	
☐ **Paramount 1979 Preview Book,** full-color picture of Star Trek: The Motion Picture, 11″ x 14″	**15.00**	**20.00**
☐ **Press Book,** features background stories, cast biographies, episode synopses, Archival Marketing Associates, August 1983	**8.00**	**10.00**
☐ **Press Book,** Star Trek: The Motion Picture, contains promotional material, especially ad mats which local theatres will cut up to create their ads	**8.00**	**10.00**
☐ **Press Book** ST III	**8.00**	**10.00**
☐ **Press Kit,** promotional packet from the Film Studio, contains 8–12 black and white photographs, 8″ x 10″, synopsis of the script, biographies of the actors, and production notes. Highly desirable collectible, not available to the public, they are produced in limited numbers and often feature highly colorful and elaborate covers. Star Trek: The Motion Picture, promotional packages.		
☐ **Standard Press Kit**	**35.00**	**50.00**
☐ **Giant,** included novel, velcro closures	**100.00**	**150.00**
☐ **Press Kit,** The Wrath of Khan, extremely rare, approximately two dozen sets were auctioned at Stanford, CT premiere, signed by Leonard Nimoy.		
☐ **Unsigned**	**40.00**	**50.00**
☐ **Signed**	**75.00**	**100.00**
☐ **Program,** Star Trek: The Motion Picture, sold in the theatres, list of cast and crew, biographies of the stars, an article on the aliens, production notes, with color reproductions	**5.00**	**10.00**
☐ **Program Book,** Star Trek II—The Wrath of Khan	**4.00**	**6.00**
☐ **Program Book,** Star Trek III—The Search for Spock	**4.00**	**6.00**
☐ **Promotional Flyer,** shows Spock without pointed ears, ears air brushed out by artists while NBC tried to suppress the pointed ears	**125.00**	**130.00**

Price Range

☐ **Promotional Flyer,** Star Trek: The Motion Picture, newsletter, four pages, 8½" x 11" 2.00   5.00

☐ **Second Season Publicity Folder,** for TV series, sent to NBC affiliates. Rare 50.00   100.00

☐ **Star Trek Mail Call,** 20-page booklet of letters from series viewers produced by NBC for network affiliates, 1967 ....   50.00   100.00

☐ **Star Trek Syndication Package,** slick color folder with pamphlets showing demographics intended to induce stations to carry Star Trek in syndication. 10.00   25.00

Note: For commercial promotional items, see individual categories, Posters, Glasses, etc. Definition of a *promotional—commercial* item is one relating to Star Trek, also bearing a product or organizational trade name (Coca-Cola, Burger King, Topps Chewing Gum, etc.). Such items were either given away free with purchase of the brand-name product, or offered in a special promotion at a discount rate, often involving coupons or proofs-of-purchase.

PUZZLES

Price Range

☐ **Aviva Enterprises Inc.,** Enterprise, 551 pieces, photos from the first movie, 18" x 24", 1979 ....   6.00   10.00

☐ **Aviva Enterprises Inc.,** Mr. Spock, 551 pieces, photos from the first movie, 18" x 24", 1979   6.00   10.00

☐ **Crossword,** Incredible Intergalactic Star Trek Crossword Puzzle, Running Press, Enterprise as base, in paper envelope with pictures of Kirk and Spock, 1976 ....   5.00   10.00

☐ **Enterprise Cutaway Puzzle,** Star Trek IV, Mind's Eye Press, 1986, 18" x 24", 551 pieces   15.00   18.00

☐ **H.G. Toys Inc.,** 150 pieces, series II, cartoons, "The Alien," 14" x 10" 5.00   10.00

	Price Range	
☐ **H.G. Toys, Inc.,** #495-02, cartoon drawing, "Battle on the Planet Klingon," 150 pieces, 10" x 14", 1974	5.00	10.00
☐ **H.G. Toys, Inc.,** #495-03, cartoon drawing, "Battle on the Planet Romulan," 150 pieces, 10" x 14", 1974	5.00	10.00
☐ **H.G. Toys, Inc.,** #495-04, 10" x 14", 150 pieces, cylindrical container, "Beaming Down," cartoon drawing, 1974	5.00	10.00
☐ **H.G. Toys Inc.,** 150 pieces, series II, cartoon drawing, "Captain Kirk," Mr. Spock and Dr. McCoy, 14" x 10"	5.00	10.00
☐ **H.G. Toys Inc.,** 150 pieces, series II, cartoons, "Force Field Capture," 14" x 10"	5.00	10.00
☐ **Jigsaw,** cartoon-style, frame tray puzzle, Merigold Press, four to a set, Kirk and Spock with the Enterprise in the background, 1978	3.00	5.00
☐ **Jigsaw,** cartoon-style, frame tray puzzle, Merigold Press, four to a set, picture of Kirk and Spock in foreground with the bridge in the background, 1978	3.00	5.00
☐ **Jigsaw,** cartoon-style, frame tray puzzle, Merigold Press, four to a set, Kirk in outer space suit, 1978	3.00	5.00
☐ **Jigsaw,** cartoon-style, frame tray puzzle, Merigold Press, four to a set, the transporter, 1978	3.00	5.00
☐ **Larami Corp.,** Star Trek: The Motion Picture, 15 pieces, 1979	3.00	4.00
☐ **Milton Bradley,** jigsaw, "Star Trek Faces of the Future," 250 pieces	5.00	10.00
☐ **As above,** jigsaw, "Star Trek Sick Bay," 250 pieces	5.00	10.00
☐ **As above,** jigsaw, "Star Trek, U.S.S. Enterprise," 250 pieces	5.00	10.00
☐ **150 pieces,** three to a series, photos from the TV series, jigsaw, movie	10.00	12.00
☐ **Whitman,** 200 pieces, cartoon pictures, set of four, 14" x 18", 1978	10.00	12.00

Jigsaw Puzzle, Whitman

RECORDS AND TAPES

For convenience, records are divided into the following categories: dramatic readings by Star Trek personalities, records about Star Trek, songs performed by Star Trek personalities, soundtracks and themes, and Star Trek stories.

DRAMATIC READINGS BY STAR TREK PERSONALITIES

	Price	Range
☐ **Captain of the Starship,** Canadian pressing of *William Shatner—Live!,* 2 12-inch LP album, Imperial Music, #9400	9.00	15.00
☐ **Captain of the Starship,** another Canadian pressing of *William Shatner—Live!,* 2 12-inch LP album, K-TEL Record, #9400	9.00	15.00

Price Range

☐ **The Green Hills of Earth and Gentlemen, Be Seated,** by Robert A. Heinlein, read by Leonard Nimoy, 12-inch LP album, Caedmon Records, #TC 1526 ....   9.00   15.00

☐ **Halley's Comet: Once in a Lifetime,** narrated by Leonard Nimoy with original space music and sound effects by Geodesium. Notes by Dr. William Gutsch, Chairman of American Museum, Hayden Planetarium, audio cassette, Caedmon Cassette, #S 1788, 1986 ....   9.00   12.00

☐ **The Illustrated Man,** by Ray Bradbury, read by Leonard Nimoy, 12-inch LP album, Caedmon Records, #TC 1479 ....   9.00   15.00

☐ **Inside Star Trek,** recorded by Gene Roddenberry, and features William Shatner, Isaac Asimov, Mark Lenard, De Forest Kelley. Discussion of the origin of the series, the personalities involved, and other insider's information. Selected musical themes, Columbia Records, #34279 ....   9.00   15.00

☐ **The Martian Chronicles,** by Ray Bradbury, read by Leonard Nimoy, 12-inch LP album, Caedmon Records, #TC 1466 ....   9.00   15.00

☐ **Mimsy Were the Borogoves,** by Henry Kuttner, read by William Shatner, 12-inch LP album, Caedmon Records, #TC 1509 ....   12.00   20.00

☐ **The Mysterious Golem,** Leonard Nimoy narrates the story of the *Mysterious Golem,* which, in Jewish folklore, is an artificially created human being endowed with life by supernatural means, 12-inch LP album, JRT Records 9.00   15.00

☐ **The Psychohistorians,** from *Foundation,* by Isaac Asimov, read by William Shatner, 12-inch LP album, Caedmon Records, #TC 1508 ...   9.00   15.00

☐ **Starfleet Beat, Phasers on Stun,** special Star Trek 20th Anniversary record, 12-inch LP album, Penguin Records 10.00   12.00

Price Range

☐ **The Star Trek Philosophy and Star Trek Theme,** performed by Gene Roddenberry and The Inside Star Trek Orchestra. From the *Inside Star Trek* album, 7-inch 45 rpm, Columbia Records, #3-10448 ....   3.00   7.00

☐ **Star Trek Tapes,** a compilation of official press recordings featuring the cast of Star Trek television show, Jack M. Sell, Producer 8.00   15.00

☐ **Tape Cassettes, Inter Audio Associates,** parody of *Star Trek, Sterling Bronsan: Space Engineer.* A series of four tapes started in 1973 as a lampoon for a college radio station, featuring James T. Clerk and Science Officer Spook, volumes I–IV 10.00   20.00

☐ **The Transformed Man,** performed by William Shatner. Captain Kirk reads six selections with chorus and instrumental background, 12-inch LP album, Decca Records, #DL 75043 .....   30.00   60.00

☐ **The Transformed Man and How Insensitive,** from the album, *The Transformed Man,* read by William Shatner, 7-inch 45 rpm, Decca Records, #32399 ....   7.50   10.00

☐ **Trek Bloopers,** compiled from unedited sound tapes of six "Third Season" episodes of *Star Trek.* Unusual record. Features audio bloopers made by original casts, 12-inch LP album, Blue Pear Records, #1 ....   7.00   15.00

☐ **Voice Tracks, U.S. Marine Corps Toys for Tots,** readings by Leonard Nimoy, Clarence Williams III, Charlton Heston, Phyllis Diller, John Wayne, Jimmy Stewart, Jack Webb, Jimmy Durante. Introduction by Efrem Zimbalist, Jr. Music played by U. S. Marine Band. Edward Mulhare, Natalie Wood, Col. Frank Borman, 7-inch 33⅓ rpm, Warner Bros.—Sevent Arts Records, #PRO 381 ....   10.00   20.00

Price Range

☐ **The Voyage of Star Trek,** coming attractions—60-minute radio special, from *The Source,* NBC Radio's Young Adult Network. Promotional copy—not for sale. Discusses *Star Trek* from television years to *Star Trek The Wrath of Khan,* 12-inch LP album, 1982 . . . . .   **15.00**   **20.00**

☐ **The War of the Worlds,** by H. G. Wells, read by Leonard Nimoy, 12-inch LP album, Caedmon Records, #TC 1520 . . . .   **9.00**   **15.00**

☐ **William Shatner—Live!,** two-record LP album, dramatic narratives recited with musical background. William Shatner's college tour, Lemli Records, #9400 . . . .   **7.95**   **15.00**

SONGS PERFORMED BY STAR TREK PERSONALITIES

☐ **Beyond Antares and Uhura's Theme,** sung by Nichelle Nichols, 7-inch 45 rpm, R-Way Records, #RW-1001 . . . .   **3.00**   **5.00**

☐ **Consilium and Here We Go 'Round Again,** sung by Leonard Nimoy from the album *The Way I Feel,* 7-inch 45 rpm, Dot Records, #45-17175 . . . .   **5.00**   **10.00**

☐ **Dark Side of the Moon,** sung by Nichelle Nichols, two 7-inch records, 45 rpm, four songs. EP album jacket opens out to a poster, Americana Records, EP-1 . . . .   **5.00**   **10.00**

☐ **Disco Trekin' and Star Child,** sung by Grace Lee Whitney (Yeoman Rand from Star Trek) and Star, 7-inch 45 rpm, GLW Star Enterprises   **3.00**   **7.00**

☐ **Down to Earth,** sung by Nichelle Nichols, eight popular songs sung by Lt. Uhura, 12-inch LP album, Epic Records, #BNZ 6351 . . . .   **15.00**   **25.00**

☐ **Leonard Nimoy Presents Mr. Spock's Music From Outer Space,** Leonard Nimoy sings and recites 11 songs, 12-inch LP album, Dot Records, #DLP 25794 . . . .   **25.00**   **50.00**

Price Range

- ☐ **Same as above,** British version, diffusion, 1973, #25156 .... | 25.00 | 50.00
- ☐ **The New World of Leonard Nimoy,** Leonard Nimoy sings eight popular songs, 12-inch LP album, Dot Records, #DLP 25966 .... | 25.00 | 40.00
- ☐ **Outer Space/Inner Mind,** two-record album contains all of *Leonard Nimoy Presents Mr. Spock's Music From Outer Space,* and cuts from *The Two Sides of Leonard Nimoy, The Touch of Leonard Nimoy, The Way I Feel,* and *The New World of Leonard Nimoy,* 2 12-inch LP album, Paramount Records Famous Twin-sets PAS, 2–1030 .... | 15.00 | 25.00

Record, "Mr. Spock's Music From Outer Space," Dot Records

Price Range

☐ **Please Don't Try to Change My Mind and I'd Love Making Love to You,** sung by Leonard Nimoy, from the album, *The Way I Feel,* 7-inch 45 rpm, Dot Records, #45-17125 .... 5.00 10.00

☐ **Space Odyssey,** nine cuts from Leonard Nimoy's five Dot Records albums, Pickwick/33 Records, #SPC 3199 .... 15.00 25.00

☐ **The Sun Will Rise and Time to Get it Together,** sung by Leonard Nimoy from the album *The New World of Leonard Nimoy,* 7-inch 45 rpm, Dot Records, #45-17330 ..... 5.00 10.00

☐ **Take A Star Trip,** 45 rpm by Grace Lee Whitney 2.00 5.00

☐ **The Touch of Leonard Nimoy,** Leonard Nimoy sings 11 songs, Dot Records, #DLP 25910 .... 25.00 40.00

☐ **Two Sides of Leonard Nimoy,** Leonard Nimoy sings and recites 13 songs, 12-inch LP album, Dot Records, #DLP 25835 .... 25.00 50.00

☐ **Uhura Sings,** 9 songs by Nichelle Nichols, AR-WAY Productions, Album or cassette, 1986 10.00 12.00

☐ **Visit to a Sad Planet and Star Trek Theme,** sung by Leonard Nimoy from the album *Leonard Nimoy Presents Mr. Spock's Music From Outer Space,* 7-inch 45 rpm, Dot Records, #17038, 1967 .... 5.00 10.00

☐ **As above,** cassette 5.00 10.00

☐ **The Way I Feel,** 12 songs sung and narrated by Leonard Nimoy, 12-inch LP album, Dot Records, #DLP 25883 .... 20.00 35.00

☐ **As above,** Reel to Reel 15.00 20.00

SOUNDTRACKS AND THEMES

☐ **The Cage and Where No Man Has Gone Before,** original television soundtrack. Music composed and conducted by Alexander Courage, 12-inch LP album, GNP Crescendo Records, #GNPS 8006 .... 9.00 12.00

	Price Range	
☐ **Also available on cassette and compact disc**	**19.95**	**—**
☐ **Charlie X, The Corbomite Maneuver, Mudd's Women, and The Doomsday Machine.** Newly recorded from selected episodes of the Paramount Pictures Corporation Television series by the Royal Philharmonic Orchestra, conducted by Fred Steiner, 12-inch LP album or cassette, Varese Sarabande Records, #704.270–Digital	**10.00**	**12.00**
☐ **As above,** compact disc	**18.00**	**22.00**
☐ **Children's TV Themes** by Cy Payne and His Orchestra, contains theme from *Star Trek TV,* 12-inch LP album, Contour Records, #2870–185 (English)	**15.00**	**20.00**
☐ **Classic Space Themes,** by The Birchwood Pops Orchestra, includes main theme from *Star Trek: The Motion Picture,* 12-inch LP album, Pickwick Records, #SPC-3772, stereo	**9.00**	**11.00**
☐ **Close Encounters,** performed by Gene Page and His Orchestra, contains theme from *Star Trek,* 12-inch LP album, Arista Records, #AB–4174	**9.00**	**12.00**
☐ **The Colors of Love and Only Stars Can Last,** fan-produced album with original words and music, 12-inch LP album, Omicron Ceti Three	**15.00**	**20.00**
☐ **Conquistador,** performed by Maynard Ferguson and His Orchestra, contains theme from *Star Trek TV,* 12-inch LP album, trumpet solo by Maynard Ferguson, flute solo by Bobby Militello, 1977, Columbia Records, #PC-34457	**10.00**	**12.00**
☐ **Dementia Royale,** compiled by Dr. Demento, contains *Star Trek,* a parody of *Star Trek* by Bobby Pickett and Peter Ferrara, 12-inch LP album, Rhino Records, #RNLP 010	**8.00**	**12.00**
☐ **Dyn-O-Mite Guita,** performed by Billy Strange, contains theme from *Star Trek,* 12-inch LP album, GNP Crescendo Record, #LP 2094	**8.00**	**9.00**

Price Range

☐ **Fifty Popular TV Themes,** performed by The Bruce Baxter Orchestra, contains main theme from *Star Trek TV,* 2 12-inch LP album, Pickwick Records, #50 DA 315 .... 15.00 20.00

☐ **Genesis Project,** two-record album containing new expanded versions *not* in the original soundtracks of *Star Trek II: The Wrath of Khan* and *Star Trek III: The Search of Spock.* Composed and performed by Craig Huxley, 2 12-inch LP album, Sonic Atmo Spheres, #101, also available on cassette 12.00 15.00

☐ **The Hustle,** performed by Van McCoy and His Orchestra, contains theme from *Star Trek TV,* 12-inch LP album, 1976 H & L Records, #HL69016 698 stereo 8.00 9.00

☐ **I, Mudd, The Enemy Within, Spectre of the Gun, and Conscience of the King.** Newly recorded *Star Trek, volume II.* Symphonic suites arranged from the original television scores, recorded by the Royal Philharmonic Orchestra, conducted by Tony Bremner, 12-inch LP album, Label X Record, #LXDR 704 (stereo–digital), also available on cassette 10.00 12.00

☐ **Is There in Truth No Beauty? and Paradise Syndrome,** newly recorded *Star Trek Volume I.* Symphonic suites arranged from original television scores, recorded by the Royal Philharmonic Orchestra, conducted by Tony Bremner, 12-inch LP album, Label X Record, #LXDR 703, (stereo–digital), also available on cassette 10.00 12.00

☐ **Love Theme From Star Trek: The Motion Picture (A Star Beyond Time),** sung by Shaun Cassidy, 7-inch 45 rpm, Warner Bros. Records, #WBS 49154 (not for sale—promotional record) 5.00 10.00

Price Range

☐ **Main Theme From Star Trek: The Motion Picture,** arranged and conducted by Bob James, 7-inch 45 rpm, Tappan Zee (Columbia) Records, #1-11171 . . . .   4.00   6.00

☐ **Main Theme From Star Trek: The Motion Picture,** from *Music From the Original Soundtrack—Star Trek: The Motion Picture,* composed and conducted by Jerry Goldsmith, 7-inch 45 rpm, Columbia Records, #1-11212   2.00   5.00

☐ **Masterpiece,** performed by Charles Randolph Grean Sounde, contains theme from *Star Trek TV,* 12-inch LP album, Ranwood Records, #5-8105 . . . .   10.00   12.00

☐ **Mirror, Mirror, By Any Other Name,** Vol. II, symphonic suites from the original TV scores, 1986, Varise Sarabande, #704-3001, also on cassette 10.00   12.00

☐ **Music From Return of the Jedi and Other Space Hits,** performed by The Odyssey Orchestra, includes main theme from *Star Trek TV* by Alexander Courage, 12-inch LP album, Sine Qua Non Records, #SQN 79065-1, stereo 10.00   12.00

☐ **Music From Star Trek and the Black Hole,** Disco Music performed by Meco Monardo, Casablanca Record, #NBLP 7196 . . . .   8.00   10.00

☐ **Music From the Original Soundtrack—Star Trek: The Motion Picture,** music by Jerry Goldsmith, 12-inch LP album, CBS/SONY Record, #25AP, 1752, Japanese Pressing . .   15.00   18.00

☐ **Nadia's Theme,** performed by Lawrence Welk and His Orchestra, contains theme from *Star Trek TV,* Ranwood Records, #(S)8165 . . . . .   10.00   15.00

☐ **1984—A Space Odyssey,** performed by John Williams and The Boston Pops Orchestra, includes main theme from *Star Trek TV* and main

	Price Range	

theme from *Star Trek: The Motion Picture,* 12-inch LP album, J & B Records, stereo, #JB-177 .... 9.00 11.00

☐ **Out of This World,** performed by John Williams and The Boston Pops Orchestra, includes main theme from *Star Trek TV* and main title from *Star Trek: The Motion Picture,* Philips Digital Recording, #411-185-1 .... 10.00 12.00

☐ **Spaced Out Disco Fever,** contains main theme from *Star Trek TV,* 12-inch LP album, Wonderland Records, stereo, #WLP 315 ... 6.00 8.00

☐ **Spectacular Space Hits,** performed by The Odyssey Orchestra, contains theme from *Star Trek TV* 12-inch LP album, Sine Qua Non Records, stereo, SQN 7808 .... 10.00 12.00

☐ **Starship,** Frank Argus, 45 rpm, fan-produced, 1984 .... 2.00 5.00

☐ **Star Tracks,** performed by The Cincinnati Pops Orchestra, conducted by Erich Kunzel, contains main theme from *Star Trek TV,* Telarc Digital Records, stereo, #DG-10094 .... 12.00 15.00

☐ **Star Trek: The Motion Picture,** 7-inch 45 rpm, Capitol Expositions Record, 1981 .... 3.00 5.00

☐ **Star Trek: The Motion Picture,** music from the original soundtrack, composed and conducted by Jerry Goldsmith, digital recording, Columbia Records, #AL 36334, also available on cassette 10.00 15.00

☐ **Star Trek—Main Theme From The Motion Picture,** contains *A Star Beyond Time* (Love Theme from *Star Trek: The Motion Picture)* and *Star Trek TV* theme, performed by The Now Sound Orchestra, 12-inch LP album, Synthetic Plastics Record, #6001 .... 10.00 12.00

☐ **Star Trek—21 Space Hits,** contains theme from *Star Trek TV,* 12-inch LP album, Music World, #EMS-1003 (Music World, Ltd., New Zealand) 12.00 16.00

Price Range

☐ **Star Trek II: The Wrath of Khan,** original motion picture soundtrack, composed and conducted by James Horner, 12-inch LP album, Atlantic Records, #P-11301, Japanese Pressing   **15.00**   **18.00**

☐ **Star Trek III: The Search for Spock, The Audio Movie Kit,** kit contains transcripts of "The Movie for Radio" and "Behind the Scenes" narrative regarding the story of the movie. Two audio cassette tapes cover the same material, 2 audio cassette tapes and a script in folder, Riches/Rubinstein and Radio, Inc. **25.00**   **40.00**

☐ **Star Trek III: The Search For Spock,** original motion picture soundtrack, music composed and conducted by James Horner, 2 12-inch LP album, Capitol-EMI Record, #SKBK 12360, stereo, 1984, also available on cassette **12.00**   **14.00**

☐ **Star Trek IV, the Voyage Home,** soundtrack from the movie **10.00**   **12.00**

☐ **Star Wars,** performed by Ferrante and Teicher, contains theme from *Star Trek TV,* 12-inch LP album, United Artists Record, #UA-LA855-G, 1978 . . . .   **12.00**   **15.00**

☐ **Themes From E. T. and More,** arranged and conducted by Walter Murphy, contains main theme from *Star Trek TV,* 12-inch LP album, MCA Records, #MCA-6114 . . . .   **8.00**   **10.00**

☐ **Theme From Star Trek TV,** from the album *Masterpiece,* by The Charles Randolph Grean Sounde, 7-inch 45 rpm, Ranwood Records, #R-1044 . . . .   **3.00**   **5.00**

☐ **Theme From Star Trek (TV), Greatest Science Fiction Hits,** performed by Neil Norman and His Cosmic Orchestra, 12-inch LP album, GNP Crescendo Record #GNPS-2128, 1979, also available on cassette **9.00**   **11.00**

Price Range

☐ **Theme From Star Trek,** performed by Tristar Orchestra and Chorus, produced by John Townsley, 7-inch 45 rpm, Tristar Records, #T-101 .... 3.00   7.00

☐ **Theme From Star Trek,** performed by The Jeff Wayne Space Shuttle, Wonderland Records, #WLP 301 .... 7.00   9.00

☐ **Theme From Star Trek,** by Warp Nine, fan-produced electronically synthesized space music. Record was sold to make money to get *Star Trek* back on television, 7-inch 45 rpm, Privilege Records 5.00   10.00

☐ **Theme From Star Trek,** performed by Ferrante and Teicher, 7-inch 45 rpm, United Artists Record #UA-S1173-Y from the album *Star Wars,* United Artists UA-LA-855-6, 1978 ..... 3.00   4.00

☐ **Theme From Star Trek,** performed by Meco Monardo from the album *Music From Star Trek and the Black Hole,* 7-inch 45 rpm, Casablanca Record, #NB2239DJ 2.00   5.00

☐ **Theme from Star Trek,** performed by Gene Page and His Orchestra, from the album *Close Encounters* ARI (S) 4174, 7-inch 45 rpm, Arista Record #ARI-0322 .... 4.00   5.00

☐ **Theme From Star Trek,** performed by Billy Strange, from the album, *Dyn-O-Mite Guitar,* 7-inch 45 rpm, GNP Crescendo Record, #GNP 800 .... 2.00   4.00

☐ **Theme From Star Trek: The Motion Picture,** on *Greatest Science Fiction Hits II,* performed by Neil Norman and His Cosmic Orchestra, 12-inch LP album, GNP Crescendo Records, #GNPS 2133, 1980, also available on cassette 9.00   12.00

Price Range

☐ **Theme From Star Trek II: The Wrath of Khan,** performed by James Horner and Orchestra, from the original soundtrack—*Star Trek II: The Wrath of Khan,* 7-inch 45 rpm, Atlantic Records, #4057, 1982 ....   2.00   5.00

☐ **Theme From Star Trek III,** by James Horner, from the original soundtrack *Star Trek III, The Search for Spock,* 7-inch 45 rpm, Capitol Records, #P-B-5365 ....   2.00   5.00

☐ **The Theme Scene,** performed by Henry Mancini and His Orchestra, contains theme from *Star Trek TV,* 12-inch LP album, Victor Records, #AQLI-3052 ....   9.00   11.00

☐ **TV Themes,** performed by The Ventures, contains theme from *Star Trek TV,* 12-inch LP album, United Artists Records, #US-LA 717-G   9.00   12.00

☐ **Very Together,** performed by Deodata, contains main theme from *Star Trek TV,* 12-inch LP album, MCA Records, #S-2219, 1976 ...   10.00   12.00

STAR TREK STORIES

☐ **Star Trek: The Motion Picture,** a read-along adventure record with 24-page color illustrated book, 7-inch 33⅓ rpm, Buena Vista Record, #461, also available on cassette, Buena Vista Records, #161-DC 2.00   7.00

☐ **Star Trek II: The Wrath of Khan,** a read-along adventure record with 24-page full color illustrated book, 7-inch 33⅓ rpm, Buena Vista Record, #462, also available on cassette, Buena Vista Records, #162-DC 2.00   7.00

☐ **Star Trek III: The Search for Spock,** a read-along adventure record with 24-page full-color illustrated book, 7-inch 33⅓ rpm, Buena Vista Record, #463, also available on cassette, Buena Vista Records, #163-DC 2.00   7.00

Price Range

☐ **Star Trek,** book and record set, contains adventure story *Passage to Moauv,* 7-inch 45 rpm record and 20-page illustrated book [two different covers—one, a color photo of Spock, Kirk, and The Enterprise, the other (an earlier edition), a drawing of Kirk and Spock and a strange animal], Power Records #PR-25 ...   2.00   5.00

☐ **Star Trek,** book and record set, contains adventure story, *The Crier In Emptiness,* 7-inch 45 rpm record and 20-page full-color illustrated book [two different covers—one, a color photo of Kirk, Spock and McCoy, the other (an earlier edition), a drawing of Kirk, Spock and Uhura], Peter Pan Records, #26 ....   2.00   5.00

☐ **Star Trek,** book and record set, contains adventure story, *Dinosaur Planet,* 7-inch 45 rpm record and 20-page full-color illustrated book, Peter Pan Records, #PR–45 ....   2.00   5.00

☐ **Star Trek,** book and record set, contains adventure story, *The Robot Masters,* 7-inch 45 rpm record and 20-page full-color illustrated book, Peter Pan Records, #PR–46 ....   2.00   5.00

☐ **Star Trek,** book and record set, contains two adventure stories, *A Mirror For Futility* and *The Time Stealer,* 12-inch LP album and 16-page full-color comic book, Power Records, #BR 513. (These two adventure stories are also recorded on Peter Pan Records, #8168) 4.00   8.00

☐ **Star Trek,** book and record set, contains two adventure stories, *The Crier in Emptiness* and *Passage to Moauv,* 12-inch LP album and 16-page full-color comic book, Peter Pan Records, #BR 522. (These two adventure stories are also recorded on Power Records, #8158) ..   5.00   10.00

Price Range

☐ **Star Trek,** five incredible all-new action adventures, *The Time Stealer, In Vino Veritas, To Starve a Fleaver, Dinosaur Planet,* and *Passage to Moauv,* 12-inch LP album, Peter Pan Records, #1110 .... 5.00 10.00

☐ **Star Trek,** original stories for children, inspired by *Star Trek—In Vino Veritas,* 7-inch 45 rpm, Power Records, #F–1298 .... 2.00 5.00

☐ **Star Trek,** original stories for children, inspired by *Star Trek—The Human Factor,* 7-inch 45 rpm, Peter Pan Records, #1516 .... 2.00 5.00

☐ **Star Trek,** original stories for children, inspired by *Star Trek—The Time Stealer,* 7-inch 45 rpm, Power Records, #2305 .... 2.00 5.00

☐ **Star Trek,** original stories for children, inspired by *Star Trek—To Starve a Fleaver,* 7-inch 45 rpm, Power Records, #2307 .... 2.00 5.00

☐ **Star Trek,** three exciting new complete stories, *Passage to Moauv, In Vino Veritas,* and *The Crier in Emptiness,* 12-inch LP album, Power Records, #8158. (These stories are also recorded on Peter Pan Records, #BR 522) ... 5.00 10.00

☐ **Star Trek,** four exciting all-new action adventure stories, *The Time Stealer, To Starve a Fleaver, The Logistics of Stampede,* and *A Mirror of Futility,* 12-inch LP album, Power Records, #8168. (This album appears in two different jackets) 5.00 10.00

☐ **Star Trek,** four exciting all-new action adventure stories, *The Man Who Trained Meteors, The Robot Masters, Dinosaur Planet,* and *The Human Factor,* 12-inch LP album, Peter Pan Records, #8236 .... 5.00 10.00

SCRIPTS

Scripts are one of the most popular items among collectors and one of the hardest to authenticate. Unless you have positive proof to the contrary, you should assume the script is a copy, not an original. All scripts these days, including the ones the actors use, are photocopies of older scripts. Different color pages can be a clue, though by no means conclusive. People using scripts on the set often write notes in the margin and of course an autograph adds to the value even if the script is a copy. Assuming it is a copy, a reasonable price for a TV script would be $10.00 to $20.00 with any of the movies at $20.00 to $30.00. If you are sure the script is original, $50.00 to $200.00 would be reasonable depending on which episode or movie.

SCHOOL AND OFFICE SUPPLIES

	Price Range	
☐ **Book Cover,** Star Fleet Headquarters Tactical Operations Center, silk-screened vinyl, 5″ x 7½″, T-K Graphics	3.00	4.00
☐ **As above,** 6″ x 9½″, T-K Graphics	4.00	5.00
☐ **Book Cover,** United Federation Of Planets Diplomatic Service, with Janus head emblem, soft vinyl silk screened, 5″ x 7½″, T-K Graphics	3.00	4.00
☐ **As above,** 6½″ x 9½″, T-K Graphics	4.00	5.00
☐ **Book Cover,** Vulcan Science Academy, silk-screened vinyl, 5″ x 7½″, T-K Graphics	3.00	4.00
☐ **As above,** 6½″ x 9½″, T-K Graphics	4.00	5.00
☐ **Business Cards,** April Publications, set 1, Captain James T. Kirk, Leonard McCoy, M.D., Spock, Montgomery Scott, Lt. Uhura, Gary Seven, Cyrano Jones, Kang, Harcourt Fenton Mudd and Bela Oxmyx. All are plastic coated with raised lettering and come in assorted colors, set	2.00	4.00
☐ **Business Cards,** April Publications, set 2, Lt. Sulu, Pavel Chekov, Christine Chapel, RN, Janice Rand, Landru, Captain Koloth, Edith Keeler,		

Price Range

Sarek of Vulcan, T'Pring and Korob and Sylvia. All are plastic coated with raised lettering and come in assorted colors, set 2.00   4.00

☐ **Checkbook Cover,** Star Fleet Academy, silk-screened vinyl, 6½" x 3½", T-K Graphics . . .   3.00   4.00

☐ **Checkbook Cover,** United Federation Of Planets Diplomatic Service, silk-screened vinyl, 6½" x 3½", T-K Graphics 3.00   4.00

☐ **Checkbook Cover,** U.S.S. Enterprise, silk-screened vinyl, 6½" x 3½", T-K Graphics . . .   3.00   4.00

☐ **Date Book,** The Official U.S.S. Enterprise Officer's Date Book, 1980, Pocket Books, Star Trek: The Motion Picture, each week illustrated with photographs, Pocket Books, September, 1979 . . . .   10.00   15.00

☐ **Envelopes,** Lincoln Enterprises, shows Enterprise with a starry blue background, 15 . . . . .   1.00   2.00

☐ **Erasers,** from "The Search for Spock," includes Enterprise, Excelsior, Spock, Kirk, Kruge, Scotty, McCoy, Diener Industries, pencil top, 1983, set of seven 4.00   8.00

☐ **Labels,** Lincoln Enterprises, TV, 60 different sayings on mylar 4.00   6.00

☐ **Memo Holder,** Tal Rad, TV show, pictures Enterprise, 1975 . . . .   5.00   10.00

☐ **Memo Pads,** Lincoln Enterprises, miniature versions of the official stationery used in the Star Trek offices 50   1.00

☐ **Pencils,** Lincoln Enterprises, starry blue with gold lettering which reads "Star Trek Lives," six 1.00   1.50

☐ **Pencils,** "Starfleet Academy," 7 7/16" long, yellow wood with gold lettering, set of 10 . . .   3.00   4.00

☐ **Pen,** Bic stick pen, "U.S.S. Enterprise Starfleet Property," dark blue 1.00   2.00

☐ **Pen,** pictures the Enterprise from the space museum in Washington 1.00   3.00

	Price Range	
☐ **Pen,** retractable, "James T. Kirk, Admiral, Starfleet Command," sky blue barrel with black lettering	1.00	2.00
☐ **Pen,** retractable, "Mr. Spock, First Officer, U.S.S. Enterprise," red barrel with silver lettering	1.00	2.00
☐ **Portfolio,** Star Fleet Academy, 10½" x 16", zippered top, vinyl, T-K Graphics	6.00	8.00
☐ **As above,** Star Fleet Headquarters Tactical Operations Center	6.00	8.00
☐ **UFP Diplomatic Corp.**	6.00	8.00
☐ **Rubber Stamps,** self inking stamp pads, feature Spock, the Vulcan hand salute, Kirk, and the Enterprise, Aviva Enterprises	3.00	5.00
☐ **Starfleet Memo Pads,** white bond with Federation blue ink, 20 sheets, 5½" x 8½"	1.00	1.50
☐ **Stationery,** Lincoln Enterprises, shows Enterprise with a starry blue background, 15 sheets, 8½" x 11"	1.00	1.75
☐ **Stationery,** "Station Keeping," features two star ships against a starry background, 25 sheets, 8½" x 11"	2.50	3.50
☐ **Stationery Pad,** fan-produced, collage of major characters and the Enterprise, light grey, looks like a sketch, 8½" x 9¼"	1.00	2.00

SHEET MUSIC

	Price Range	
☐ **A Visit to a Small Planet,** *Star Trek TV,* Caterpillar Music, 1979	3.00	5.00
☐ **You Are Not Alone,** *Star Trek TV,* Petunia Music Co., 1967	5.00	7.00
☐ **Caterpillar Music Co., 1979**	3.00	5.00
☐ **Star Trek Theme,** *Star Trek TV,* Bruin Music Co., 1966	5.00	7.00

	Price Range	
☐ **Main Theme From Star Trek II, The Wrath of Khan,** music by James Horner, Famous Music Corp., 1982, published by Columbia Pictures Corporation	2.00	5.00
☐ **Main Theme From Star Trek III, The Search For Spock,** music by James Horner, Famous Music Corp., 1984, published by Columbia Pictures Corporation	2.50	5.00
☐ **Star Trek, The Musical Themes,** by Jerry Goldsmith, contains *Main Theme, Love Theme,* and *TV Theme* by Alexander Courage and Gene Roddenberry. Also contains color photos and black and white stills, 16 pages, bound book	4.95	8.00
☐ **Elaine Sevin's Space Notes,** *Play and Color, Enterprise Edition for Trekkers,* contains *The Human Adventure is Just Beginning* from *Star Trek: The Motion Picture,* and *Love Theme—A Star Beyond Time.* Big Notes and Lyrics. (This is a coloring book for kids.)	3.95	5.00

Columbia Pictures Corporation has published the following Sheet Music from *Star Trek:*

	Price Range	
☐ **Main Theme From Star Trek, TV**	2.95	5.00
☐ **Main Theme From Star Trek: The Motion Picture**	2.95	5.00
☐ **Main Theme From Star Trek II, The Wrath of Khan**	2.95	5.00
☐ **Main Theme From Star Trek III, In Search of Spock**	2.95	5.00

STILLS, SLIDES & PHOTOGRAPHS

There is a great deal of confusion about these items among collectors. To start with, many collectors do not realize the difference between lithographs and photographs. A photograph is a film process. A lithograph is a printing process. Lithographs are much cheaper to produce than photographs and are practical only in large quantities.

Where it concerns films, all one needs to do to make slides is have a print of the film and a pair of scissors. Another slide or a photograph can be made easily from any frame of the film. For this reason there are as many possible photographs and slides from a film as there are frames in that film. All of the "stills" in this section (including lobby cards) are therefore lithographs. Fair prices for slides range from about $.25 to $1.50 for mounted slides, less for unmounted film clips. Photographs should sell for $1.50 to $3.00 for black and white photographs, $4.00 to $6.00 for color.

	Price Range	
☐ **Fantasy House,** set of six 4″ x 6″ mini-posters, Kirk, Sulu, Kirk and Chekov, McCoy, Spock and Spock close-up	2.00	5.00
☐ **Langley Associates,** Enterprise, surrounded by alien ships, color reproductions, 8″ x 10″	1.00	2.00
☐ **Langley Associates,** Chekov, portrait reproduction, 8″ x 10″	1.00	2.00
☐ **Langley Associates,** Kirk, Spock, McCoy and Scotty at conference table, color reproductions, 8″ x 10″	1.00	2.00
☐ **Langley Associates,** The Crew, in mid-beam, color reproductions, 8″ x 10″	1.00	2.00
☐ **Langley Associates,** The Crew, on a Bare Planet, 8″ x 10″	1.00	2.00
☐ **Langley Associates,** The Crew, portrait on bridge, color reproductions, 8″ x 10″	1.00	2.00
☐ **Langley Associates,** Dr. McCoy, close-up portrait, color reproductions, 8″ x 10″	1.00	2.00
☐ **Langley Associates,** The Enterprise, captioned "Star Trek," color reproductions, 8″ x 10″	1.00	2.00
☐ **Langley Associates,** Enterprise, firing phasers, color reproductions, 8″ x 10″	1.00	2.00
☐ **Langley Associates,** The Enterprise, following another Federation Ship, color reproductions, 8″ x 10″	1.00	2.00
☐ **Langley Associates,** The Enterprise, in Starburst, color reproductions, 8″ x 10″	1.00	2.00

	Price Range	
☐ **Langley Associates,** Kirk, cocked head, looking flirtatious, color reproductions, 8″ x 10″ ..	1.00	2.00
☐ **Langley Associates,** Kirk, head shot of the captain, color reproductions, 8″ x 10″	1.00	2.00
☐ **Langley Associates,** Kirk, looking seductive, color reproductions, 8″ x 10″	1.00	2.00
☐ **Langley Associates,** Kirk, surrounded by Tribbles, color reproductions, 8″ x 10″	1.00	2.00
☐ **Langley Associates,** Kirk, three-quarter shot in dress uniform, color reproductions, 8″ x 10″	1.00	2.00
☐ **Langley Associates,** Kirk, using communicators, color reproductions, 8″ x 10″	1.00	2.00
☐ **Langley Associates,** Lt. Uhura, color portrait, 8″ x 10″	1.00	2.00
☐ **Langley Associates,** Mr. Scott, in dress uniform, looking tense, color reproductions, 8″ x 10″	1.00	2.00
☐ **Langley Associates,** Spock, close-up with beard, color reproductions, 8″ x 10″	1.00	2.00
☐ **Langley Associates,** Spock, color portrait, 8″ x 10″	1.00	2.00
☐ **Langley Associates,** Spock, giving Vulcan hand signal, color reproductions, 8″ x 10″ ...	1.00	2.00
☐ **Langley Associates,** rare smile, color reproductions, 8″ x 10″	1.00	2.00
☐ **Langley Associates,** Spock and Kirk, seen through hole in cavern, color reproductions, 8″ x 10″	1.00	2.00
☐ **Langley Associates,** Sulu, on the bridge, color reproductions, 8″ x 10″	1.00	2.00
☐ **Lincoln Enterprises,** art prints by Doug Little, color, Star Trek: The Motion Picture, 11″ x 14″:		
☐ **Chapel**	1.00	3.00
☐ **Chekov**	1.00	3.00
☐ **Decker**	1.00	3.00
☐ **Ilia**	1.00	3.00
☐ **Klingon**	1.00	3.00
☐ **McCoy**	1.00	3.00

	Price Range	
☐ **Saavik**	1.00	3.00
☐ **Scotty**	1.00	3.00
☐ **Spock**	1.00	3.00
☐ **Sulu**	1.00	3.00
☐ **Uhura**	1.00	3.00

☐ **Lincoln Enterprises,** art prints by Probeget, color, *Star Trek* television show, 8" x 11":

☐ **Chapel**	.50	1.00
☐ **Chekov**	.50	1.00
☐ **Enterprise**	.50	1.00
☐ **Kirk**	.50	1.00
☐ **McCoy**	.50	1.00
☐ **Scotty**	.50	1.00
☐ **Spock**	.50	1.00
☐ **Sulu**	.50	1.00
☐ **Uhura**	.50	1.00

☐ **Lincoln Enterprises,** Evolution of the Enterprise, starship in different phases of conception, color 11"x17", 12 different pictures per set 4.00 6.00

☐ **Lincoln Enterprises,** wallet pictures, color, 2" x 3", 15 per set

☐ **Costumes #1,** per set	1.00	3.00
☐ **Costumes #2,** per set	1.00	3.00
☐ **Kirk,** per set	1.00	3.00
☐ **Make up and Aliens,** per set	1.00	3.00
☐ **Scenes from Star Trek: The Motion Picture,** per set	1.00	3.00
☐ **Scenes from Star Trek: The Motion Picture,** action, per set	1.00	3.00
☐ **Spock,** per set	1.00	3.00
☐ **Stars and groups (STTMP),** per set	1.00	3.00
☐ **Star Trek: The Wrath of Kahn #1,** per set	1.00	3.00
☐ **Star Trek: The Wrath of Kahn #2,** per set	1.00	3.00
☐ **Star Trek: The Wrath of Spock #3,** per set	1.00	3.00
☐ **Star Trek: The Wrath of Kahn #4,** per set	1.00	3.00
☐ **Star Trek television series #1,** per set	1.00	3.00
☐ **Star Trek television series #2,** per set	1.00	3.00

	Price Range	
☐ **Star Trek television series #3,** per set	1.00	3.00
☐ **Star Trek: The Search for Spock #1,** per set	1.00	3.00
☐ **Star Trek: The Search for Spock #2,** per set	1.00	3.00
☐ **Star Trek: The Search for Spock #3,** per set	1.00	3.00
☐ **Star Trek: The Search for Spock #4,** per set	1.00	3.00
☐ **Lincoln Enterprises,** weapons and field equipment, color, 12 different pictures per set	3.00	5.00
☐ **LOBBIE CARDS,** set of 8, color, 11″ x 13″ cards made for theatre display.		
☐ **Star Trek: The Motion Picture,** per set	40.00	60.00
☐ **Star Trek: The Wrath of Kahn,** per set	30.00	50.00
☐ **Star Trek: The Search for Spock,** per set ..	20.00	40.00
☐ **LOBBIE STILLS,** set of 8, color, 8″ x 10″ cards made for theatre display, usually the same scenes as the larger cards.		
☐ **Star Trek: The Motion Picture,** per set	30.00	50.00
☐ **Star Trek: The Wrath of Kahn,** per set	20.00	40.00
☐ **Star Trek: The Search for Spock,** per set ..	10.00	30.00
☐ **Print of U.S. Space Shuttle Enterprise,** with the Starship Enterprise in background, "To Go Places and Do Things That Have Never Been Done Before ..., " 8″ x 10″	1.00	2.00
☐ **Star Trek Episode Cards,** manufactured by an individual dealer, large picture with 3 smaller insets on each card, color, 7½″ x 8½″, 1978.		
☐ **All Our Yesterdays**	2.00	4.00
☐ **Amok Time**	2.00	4.00
☐ **Bloopers**	2.00	4.00
☐ **The Cage**	2.00	4.00
☐ **City on the Edge of Forever**	2.00	4.00
☐ **Doomsday Machine**	2.00	4.00
☐ **Journey to Babel**	2.00	4.00
☐ **Mirror, Mirror**	2.00	4.00
☐ **Paradise Syndrome**	2.00	4.00
☐ **Patterns of Force**	2.00	4.00
☐ **Star Trek**	2.00	4.00
☐ **Tholian Web**	2.00	4.00

	Price Range	
☐ **Trouble With Tribbles**	2.00	4.00
☐ **What Are Little Girls Made Of?**	2.00	4.00
☐ **Where No Man Has Gone Before**	2.00	4.00
☐ **Star Trek Galore,** Alien Ship, firing lasers, color reproduction, 8″ x 10″	1.00	2.00
☐ **Star Trek Galore,** The Bridge, Chekov and Sulu in forefront, color reproduction, 8″ x 10″	1.00	2.00
☐ **Star Trek Galore,** The Bridge, Kirk, Spock, Uhura, and Mr. Chekov, color reproduction, 8″ x 10″	1.00	2.00
☐ **Star Trek Galore,** Captain Pike, early episode with Jeffrey Hunter, color reproduction, 8″ x 10″	1.00	2.00
☐ **Star Trek Galore,** Chekov and Sulu, on the bridge of the Enterprise, color reproduction, 8″ x 10″	1.00	2.00
☐ **Star Trek Galore,** Chekov, portrait, color reproduction, 8″ x 10″	1.00	2.00
☐ **Star Trek Galore,** The Crew, minus Captain Kirk and the suspense is high, color reproduction, 8″ x 10″	1.00	2.00
☐ **Star Trek Galore,** The Crew, on the bridge of the Enterprise, color reproduction, 8″ x 10″	1.00	2.00
☐ **Star Trek Galore,** The Crew, portrait on bridge, color reproduction, 8″ x 10″	1.00	2.00
☐ **Star Trek Galore,** The Crew, portrait type, color reproduction, 8″ x 10″	1.00	2.00
☐ **Star Trek Galore,** The Crew, suspense on the bridge, color reproduction, 8″ x 10″	1.00	2.00
☐ **Star Trek Galore,** Dr. McCoy, Captain Kirk and Mr. Spock, color reproduction, 8″ x 10″	1.00	2.00
☐ **Star Trek Galore,** The Enterprise, firing phasers, color reproduction, 8″ x 10″	1.00	2.00
☐ **Star Trek Galore,** The Enterprise, looming overhead, color reproduction, 8″ x 10″	1.00	2.00
☐ **Star Trek Galore,** The Enterprise, surrounded by alien ships, color reproduction, 8″ x 10″ ..	1.00	2.00

Price Range

☐ **Star Trek Galore,** The Galileo, zooming through space, color reproduction, 8″ x 10″ — 1.00 — 2.00

☐ **Star Trek Galore,** Kirk, drowning in Tribbles, color reproduction, 8″ x 10″ . . . . — 1.00 — 2.00

☐ **Star Trek Galore,** Kirk and Mr. Spock, shooting lasers at The Horta, color reproduction, 8″ x 10″ . . . . — 1.00 — 2.00

☐ **Star Trek Galore,** Kirk, looking debonair, color reproduction, 8″ x 10″ . . . . — 1.00 — 2.00

☐ **Star Trek Galore,** Kirk, with Federation Flag, color reproduction, 8″ x 10″ . . . . — 1.00 — 2.00

☐ **Star Trek Galore,** Mr. Scott, looking worried, color reproduction, 8″ x 10″ . . . . — 1.00 — 2.00

☐ **Star Trek Galore,** Scott, on the bridge of The Enterprise, color reproduction, 8″ x 10″ . . . . . — 1.00 — 2.00

☐ **Star Trek Galore,** Spock, aiming phaser, color reproduction, 8″ x 10″ . . . . — 1.00 — 2.00

☐ **Star Trek Galore,** Spock, giving Vulcan hand signal, color reproduction, 8″ x 10″ . . . . — 1.00 — 2.00

☐ **Star Trek Galore,** Spock, making a point, 8″ x 10″ . . . . — 1.00 — 2.00

☐ **Star Trek Galore,** Mr. Spock, a rare display of emotion, color reproduction, 8″ x 10″ . . . . — 1.00 — 2.00

☐ **Star Trek Galore,** Spock, with beard, color reproduction, 8″ x 10″ . . . . — 1.00 — 2.00

☐ **Star Trek Galore,** Spock, with child Vulcan, color reproduction, 8″ x 10″ . . . . — 1.00 — 2.00

☐ **Star Trek Galore,** Mr. Spock, with harp, color reproduction, 8″ x 10″ . . . . — 1.00 — 2.00

☐ **Star Trek Galore,** Spock, with three-dimensional chess game, color reproduction, 8″ x 10″ . . . . — 1.00 — 2.00

☐ **Star Trek Galore,** Sulu, portrait, color reproduction, 8″ x 10″ . . . . — 1.00 — 2.00

☐ **Star Trek Galore,** The Transporter Room, Kirk, McCoy, Uhura and Scotty beaming, color reproduction, 8″ x 10″ . . . . — 1.00 — 2.00

	Price Range	
☐ **Star Trek Galore,** The Tribbles, Captain Kirk looking dismayed, color reproduction, 8″ x 10″	1.00	2.00
☐ **Star Trek Galore,** Uhura and Chekov, smiling on the bridge, color reproduction, 8″ x 10″ ..	1.00	2.00

TOYS

	Price Range	
☐ **Action Fleet,** Star Trek: The Motion Picture, cardboard mobile of various ships, candy promotional	20.00	30.00
☐ **Astrotank,** TV show, box pictures Enterprise, includes several figures, Remco, 1967	50.00	100.00
☐ **Balloon,** Star Trek: The Motion Picture, red or blue	1.00	2.00
☐ **Binoculars,** Larami Corporation, Mr. Spock on package, glasses say "Star Trek"	10.00	15.00
☐ **Binoculars,** Larami Corporation, TV show, plastic with "Star Trek" written on	15.00	20.00
☐ **Bird of Prey,** die-cast metal from Star Trek II, approx. 4″, comes with stand, ERTL, 1984 ..	2.00	5.00
☐ **Bop Bag,** Spock, came in box, Azrak-Hamway, 1975	15.00	25.00
☐ **Bridge,** Star Trek: The Motion Picture, scaled for 3¼″ dolls, docking port, chairs and control panel, Mego Corporation	50.00	75.00
☐ **Bridge,** Mego Corporation, for 8″ dolls, vinyl-covered cardboard, captain's chair included	65.00	85.00
☐ **Cartoons Capers,** made in France for British market, battery-powered light box overlays and colored PGNS, Wiggins Teape, 1978	25.00	30.00
☐ **Colorform Adventure Set,** plastic stick-ons, 1975	15.00	25.00
☐ **Star Trek Color 'N Recolor Game Cloth,** seven fun games to play, plastic wipe-off game cloth is reusable, 40″ x 36″, by Avalon	5.00	10.00

Price Range

☐ **Command Communications Console,** features: multi-color phaser light screen, telescoping antenna, Morse code indicator (sends and receives Morse code signal), Star Trek twin warp sound, transmits voice and sound, working condition **40.00 60.00**

☐ **Communicators,** 1976, Mego, flip-up, electronic, sold in pairs, maximum range 1200 feet, features flip-up cover and sound effects generator **100.00 150.00**

☐ **Enterprise,** die-cast, ERTL, 4½", white with decal, 1984, Star Trek III **2.00 5.00**

☐ **Enterprise,** die-cast metal, white with decal, Corgi, made in England, 1982 . . . . **2.00 5.00**

☐ **Enterprise,** Star Trek: The Motion Picture, 12" long, made for foreign market. Mego, 1980 . . **125.00 175.00**

☐ **Figurine Painting Kit,** Milton Bradley, Kirk or Spock, 1979 . . . . **10.00 20.00**

☐ **Frisbee,** blue with black lettering, black line drawing of Enterprise **5.00 10.00**

☐ **Frisbee,** Remco, TV show, Enterprise, 1967 **25.00 50.00**

☐ **Happy Meals,** featuring two versions of Spock, Klingon, bridge, space suit, transporter, highly colorful cardboard food carrying carton, McDonald's premium includes games and colorful illustrations, set of 6 . . . . **6.00 10.00**

☐ **Helmet,** Enco Industries, a similar version of the same thing by Remco, flashing light and sound, 1976 . . . . **40.00 75.00**

☐ **Kite,** TV show, Hi-Flier, Enterprise pictured, 1975 . . . . **10.00 20.00**

☐ **Kite,** Aviva, Spock pictured, assorted colors, 1979 . . . . **10.00 15.00**

☐ **Kite,** Enterprise, Coast soap promotional advertisement **10.00 15.00**

☐ **Kite,** promotion, pictures Enterprise, Lever Bros., 1984 . . . . **10.00 15.00**

	Price Range	
☐ **Klingon,** Meccano, TV Klingon, accurate reproduction fires plastic discs, metal and plastic, blue, Dinky	50.00	60.00
☐ **Klingon,** die-cast, blue with decal, Corgi, made in England, 1982	2.00	5.00
☐ **Klingon Bird Of Prey,** die-cast, ERTL, 2½", light blue with decals, 1984, Star Trek III	2.00	5.00
☐ **Klingon Ship,** Star Trek: The Motion Picture, approx 8" long, made for foreign market	100.00	150.00
☐ **Magic Putty,** transfers image to any surface, grey egg, by Larami Corporation, 1979	1.00	3.00
☐ **Metal Detector,** Star Trek metal detection probe, working red and white box 24" x 10", decal on toy reads "Property of U.S.S. Enterprise," Jetco, 1976	75.00	150.00
☐ **Mission To Gamma V,** Mego Corporation, landscape action set for dolls, has acto-glove, a man-eating plant, four aliens, an idol with moving jaw and secret trap door, 1976	150.00	250.00
☐ **Star Trek Mix 'N Mold Plaster Casting Sets,** features Kirk, Spock or McCoy	15.00	30.00
☐ **Paint By Numbers,** one 16" x 12" canvas featuring Spock and Kirk, Hasbro, 1974	15.00	30.00
☐ **Pen And Poster Kit,** Open Door Enterprises, four line posters, ten felt-tip pens, 1976	10.00	25.00
☐ **Pen and Poster Kit,** Star Trek: The Motion Picture, 14" x 20" posters and 5 pens, Aviva, 1979	10.00	15.00
☐ **Phaser,** came in Star Trek box, Daisy	10.00	20.00
☐ **Phaser,** Remco, electronic space sound and light beam, contains Project-A-Light target, three discs, uses 9-V and AA batteries, 1977	20.00	40.00
☐ **Phaser Battle Game,** Mego Corporation, Klingon and Romulan ships appear on telescreen, LED scoring device, battle sounds, adjustable speed controls, standard current, or six "C" batteries	100.00	350.00
☐ **Phaser Guns,** Mego Corporation, 1976, features a gun with electronic phaser	40.00	60.00

Price Range

☐ **Phaser Set,** in Star Trek: The Motion Picture, fires infared beam which could disarm other phaser 75.00 150.00

☐ **Pin Ball Game,** Star Trek, choice of Kirk or Spock face on game field, packaged in colorful box, rare, 1' 15.00 25.00

☐ **Pocket Flix,** Ideal, hand-held movie viewer, with cartridge, shows scenes from "By Any Other Name" television episode, battery operated, 1978 .... 20.00 40.00

Note: Prop quality items are one of the most popular collectibles. Each piece must be handcrafted, at least in part and consequently there are never enough to satisfy demand.

☐ **Prop Reproduction, TV Phaser I,** hand phaser, these vary greatly in quality, solid-cast plastic and vac-form plastic varieties as well as kits, fan produced, various manufacturers ... 20.00 40.00

☐ **Prop Reproduction, TV Phaser II,** pistol phaser, vary in quality, cast-plastic and metal varieties, some kits, in non-working and light and sound varieties; working ones use simple electronics and should not be greatly more expensive; fan produced, various manufacturers 90.00 200.00

☐ **Prop Reproduction, TV Communicators,** vary in quality, solid plastic or vacu-form with metal grid, some kits, a few with flashing lights, sound, fan produced, various manufacturers 40.00 100.00

☐ **Prop Reproduction, Tricorder Kit,** a few prototypes only, fan produced 75.00 200.00

☐ **Sky Diver,** Kirk or Spock with parachute, Azrak-Hanway 4.00 10.00

☐ **Soft Kirk Doll,** Knickerbocker, rubber molded head, cloth body, velcro hands, 12″ 15.00 25.00

☐ **Soft Spock Doll,** Knickerbocker, rubber soft molded head, cloth body, velcro hands for posing placement, 12″ 15.00 25.00

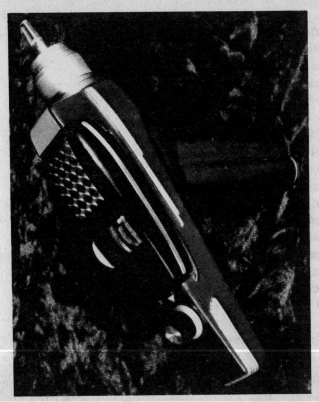

Prop Reproduction TV Phaser II, fan-produced

	Price Range	
☐ **Star Trek Tracer Gun,** with jet disks, NBC Productions, original	5.00	10.00
☐ **Star Trek III Pen and Poster Kit,** 3-D pen poster kit	3.00	5.00
☐ **As above,** later versions	4.00	6.00
☐ **Star Trekulator, The,** Mego Corporation, adds, subtracts, divides and multiplies, takes square roots and percentages, flashing console screen lights up with pictures of the Star Trek crew, L.E.D. screen, uses four "AA" batteries, not included	75.00	100.00

	Price Range	
☐ **String Art Kit,** Open Door Enterprises, features the Enterprise firing phasers at two Romulan ships	20.00	30.00
☐ **Telescreen, Mego,** TV show, target game with sound and light, approximately 14″ x 10″, 1977	60.00	100.00
☐ **Toy Movie Viewer,** from the television show, two films included, 1967	5.00	10.00
☐ **Tribble,** fan produced fur balls, assorted sizes and colors; some squeak. Mego claims it produced Tribbles in boxes; none are known to exist	3.00	6.00
☐ **Tricorder,** Mego Corporation, toy cassette player, features flip-open top, play back and record, factory sealed unit will come with a tape, a portion of the episode "The Menagerie"	75.00	100.00
☐ **Twin Gift Set,** one metal and plastic Enterprise and Klingon ships, ships fire photo "disks," box has cut-out communicatory and alien landscapes, rare, Dinky	100.00	125.00

Tricorder, from Mego

Dinky Die-Cast Ships

	Price Range	
☐ **U.S.S. Enterprise,** Dinky, with decals, die-cast metal, white, 4″	7.00	12.00
☐ **U.S.S. Excelsior,** die-cast metal from Star Trek III, approx., 4″, white, comes with stand, from ERTL, 1984	2.00	5.00
☐ **U.S.S. Enterprise,** Meccano (Dinky) television Enterprise, metal and plastic, fires plastic proton torpedo, plastic discs, boxed, 10⅛″ x 5⅜″, no longer manufactured, open bay doors act as stand and include shuttle craft	50.00	75.00
☐ **U.S.S. Enterprise,** Remco, controlled space flight, double lever helm, operates in forward, reverse, fast, slow and hover, picks up and delivers objects, uses three dimensions, batteries, 1977	75.00	150.00
☐ **Utility Belt,** Remco, contains all necessary tools and weapons, complete with disc shooter, phaser, eight discs, tricorder and communicator, adjustable sizes, 1977	40.00	50.00
☐ **View Master,** series of three reels from "Mr. Spock's Time Trek," in three dimension, 1978	5.00	10.00
☐ **View Master,** series of three reels from "The Omega Glory," in three dimension, 1968	5.00	10.00

	Price Range	
☐ **View Master,** series of three reels about Star Trek: The Motion Picture, in three dimension	5.00	10.00
☐ **View Master,** series of three reels from Star Trek II: The Wrath of Khan	5.00	10.00
☐ **Vulcan Shuttle,** Star Trek: The Motion Picture, approx. 8″ long, detachable sled, made for foreign market, Mego, 1980	100.00	150.00
☐ **Water Gun,** Azrak-Hanway Co., Star Trek U.S.S. Enterprise, white, plastic, rare, 1976 ..	15.00	25.00
☐ **Water Pistols,** reproduction of the phaser used in Star Trek: The Motion Picture	6.00	5.00
☐ **Wrist Communicators,** Mego Corporation, energy pack straps to arm, walkie talkie to wrist, two to a set, uses two 9-V batteries, 1981 ..	50.00	75.00
☐ **Yo Yo,** from Star Trek: The Motion Picture, blue sparkly plastic with the Enterprise logo	3.00	5.00

TRADING CARDS

This section is divided into three parts: gum cards (American), collector's cards, and promotional and foreign cards. Each section is divided chronologically by TV and then movie. Values given are for excellent to mint cards. These cards have no creases or rounded edges. Defects like these mentioned can lower the value of the cards by 50%–75%. The values for individual cards will often be higher than the average price per card of a complete set. This is because of the time involved in stocking single cards for collectors.

AMERICAN GUM CARDS, STAR TREK TV SHOW

	Price Range	
☐ **Leaf Photo Cards,** Star Trek, 72 card set, withdrawn from the market because of contractual disputes, black and white photos from the television series, captions in black panels below picture, story on back, 1967, 2 3/8″ x 3 7/16″		
☐ **Set**	600.00	800.00
☐ **1 No Time For Escape**	8.00	12.00

CAPTAIN'S STATUE

PAIN OF VICTORY

Trading Cards, 1967, leaf, black and white

	Price	Range
☐ 2 Attempted Mutiny	8.00	12.00
☐ 3 A Grup Appears	8.00	12.00
☐ 4 Come In, Captain Kirk	8.00	12.00
☐ 5 Murasaki Mischief	8.00	12.00

	Price Range	
☐ 6 Beam Down To Dawn	8.00	12.00
☐ 7 Beside Himself	8.00	12.00
☐ 8 Back Through Time	8.00	12.00
☐ 9 Horta Emerging	8.00	12.00
☐ 10 Spock's Box	8.00	12.00
☐ 11 Spock In Command	8.00	12.00
☐ 12 Spock In Command	8.00	12.00
☐ 13 Befuddled Bones	8.00	12.00
☐ 14 Prepare To Fire Phasers	8.00	12.00
☐ 15 Command Decision	8.00	12.00
☐ 16 Kirk Battles A Gorn	8.00	12.00
☐ 17 Phaser Daser	8.00	12.00
☐ 18 Space Race	8.00	12.00
☐ 19 Fight Fire With Fire	8.00	12.00
☐ 20 Captain's Bluff	8.00	12.00
☐ 21 Underground Pursuit	8.00	12.00
☐ 22 The Bird	8.00	12.00
☐ 23 Teeny Bopper	8.00	12.00
☐ 24 Time Warp	8.00	12.00
☐ 25 You're Kidding	8.00	12.00
☐ 26 Beam Out	8.00	12.00
☐ 27 Burn Out	8.00	12.00
☐ 28 Interference Out	8.00	12.00
☐ 29 Not So Funny	8.00	12.00
☐ 30 Prisoner Of The Mind	8.00	12.00
☐ 31 Stalking A Killer	8.00	12.00
☐ 32 The Earth Killer	8.00	12.00
☐ 33 Fight For Lithium	8.00	12.00
☐ 34 Destruction Decision	8.00	12.00
☐ 35 "Return My Ship"	8.00	12.00
☐ 36 Frozen At The Controls	8.00	12.00
☐ 37 Christmas Present	8.00	12.00
☐ 38 Amnesia Victim	8.00	12.00
☐ 39 Decoy	8.00	12.00
☐ 40 Beyond Tomorrow	8.00	12.00
☐ 41 Trapped	8.00	12.00
☐ 42 Kirk Outside Spock Inside	8.00	12.00
☐ 43 Spock Takes A Job	8.00	12.00

	Price Range	
☐ 44 Kirk Held Hostage	8.00	12.00
☐ 45 Big Joker	8.00	12.00
☐ 46 A Scream Of Pain	8.00	12.00
☐ 47 Captain's Statue	8.00	12.00
☐ 48 Call Me Senator	8.00	12.00
☐ 49 Into A New World	8.00	12.00
☐ 50 Tranquilized	8.00	12.00
☐ 51 Time For Shore Leave	8.00	12.00
☐ 52 Ice Age	8.00	12.00
☐ 53 Ambushed	8.00	12.00
☐ 54 Pain Of Victory	8.00	12.00
☐ 55 Cornered	8.00	12.00
☐ 56 Jungle Hunt	8.00	12.00
☐ 57 Collision Course	8.00	12.00
☐ 58 Corbomite Maneuver	8.00	12.00
☐ 59 You Give Me A Headache	8.00	12.00
☐ 60 Shore Leave Surprise	8.00	12.00
☐ 61 Killer Aboard	8.00	12.00
☐ 62 Mindless Man	8.00	12.00
☐ 63 Pirates At Bay	8.00	12.00
☐ 64 Off Course	8.00	12.00
☐ 65 Attack By Nothing	8.00	12.00
☐ 66 Funny Little Enemies	8.00	12.00
☐ 67 Poison Attack!	8.00	12.00
☐ 68 Warp Out For Rescue	8.00	12.00
☐ 69 Out Of Control	8.00	12.00
☐ 70 Return To The Living	8.00	12.00
☐ 71 Space Prisoner	8.00	12.00
☐ 72 Raspberries	8.00	12.00
☐ Wrapper	100.00	150.00
☐ Display Box	100.00	200.00

☐ **Topps Photo Cards,** Star Trek, 88 card set, color photos from television show, "captain log" on back with narrative and character profiles, 2½" x 3½", 1976.

☐ Set	30.00	50.00
☐ 1 The U.S.S. Enterprise	.50	1.00

	Price Range	
☐ 2 Captain James T. Kirk	.50	1.00
☐ 3 Dr. "Bones" McCoy	.50	1.00
☐ 4 Science Officer Spock	.50	1.00
☐ 5 Engineer Scott	.50	1.00
☐ 6 Lieutenant Uhura	.50	1.00
☐ 7 Ensign Chekov	.50	1.00
☐ 8 The Phaser—Tomorrow's Weapon	.50	1.00
☐ 9 The Shuttle Craft	.50	1.00
☐ 10 Opponents	.50	1.00
☐ 11 Energize!	.50	1.00
☐ 12 The Alien Mr. Spock	.50	1.00
☐ 13 Men Of The Enterprise	.50	1.00
☐ 14 Story Of Voyage One	.50	1.00
☐ 15 "Live Long And Prosper"	.50	1.00
☐ 16 View From The Bridge	.50	1.00
☐ 17 Toward The Unknown	.50	1.00
☐ 18 Enterprise Orbiting Earth	.50	1.00
☐ 19 The Purple Barrier	.50	1.00
☐ 20 Outwitting A God	.50	1.00
☐ 21 Planet Delta Vega	.50	1.00
☐ 22 Charlies's Law	.50	1.00
☐ 23 Mysterious Cube	.50	1.00
☐ 24 Dwarfed By The Enemy	.50	1.00
☐ 25 Balok's Alter-Ego	.50	1.00
☐ 26 Last Of Its Kind	.50	1.00
☐ 27 Frozen World	.50	1.00
☐ 28 Spock Loses Control	.50	1.00
☐ 29 The Naked Time	.50	1.00
☐ 30 The Demon Within	.50	1.00
☐ 31 "My Enemy ... My Self!"	.50	1.00
☐ 32 Monster Android	.50	1.00
☐ 33 Korby's Folly	.50	1.00
☐ 34 The Duplicate Man	.50	1.00
☐ 35 Balance Of Terror	.50	1.00
☐ 36 Attacked By Spores	.50	1.00
☐ 37 Spock Unwinds!	.50	1.00
☐ 38 Duel At Gothos	.50	1.00
☐ 39 Timeship Of Lazarus	.50	1.00

	Price Range	
☐ 40 Dagger Of The Mind	.50	1.00
☐ 41 The Lawgivers	.50	1.00
☐ 42 Hunting The Tunnel Monster	.50	1.00
☐ 43 Battling The Horta	.50	1.00
☐ 44 Strange Communication	.50	1.00
☐ 45 A Startling Discovery	.50	1.00
☐ 46 McCoy Insane!	.50	1.00
☐ 47 The Guardian Of Forever	.50	1.00
☐ 48 Visit To A Hostile City	.50	1.00
☐ 49 Mystery At Star Base 6	.50	1.00
☐ 50 Fate Of Captain Pike	.50	1.00
☐ 51 The Talosians	.50	1.00
☐ 52 Ordeal On Rigel Seven	.50	1.00
☐ 53 Capturing The Keeper	.50	1.00
☐ 54 Blasted By The Enemy	.50	1.00
☐ 55 Trapped By The Lizard Creature	.50	1.00
☐ 56 The Gorn Strikes!	.50	1.00
☐ 57 Earthman's Triumph	.50	1.00
☐ 58 Specimen: Unknown	.50	1.00
☐ 59 Mirror, Mirror	.50	1.00
☐ 60 Spock's Wedding	.50	1.00
☐ 61 Strangled By Mr. Spock	.50	1.00
☐ 62 Grasp Of The Gods	.50	1.00
☐ 63 The Monster Called Nomad	.50	1.00
☐ 64 The Companion	.50	1.00
☐ 65 Journey To Babel	.50	1.00
☐ 66 Death Ship	.50	1.00
☐ 67 The Tholian Web	.50	1.00
☐ 68 The Architects Of Pain	.50	1.00
☐ 69 The Mugato	.50	1.00
☐ 70 The Deadly Years	.50	1.00
☐ 71 Ancient Rome Revisited	.50	1.00
☐ 72 The Melkotian	.50	1.00
☐ 73 The Vulcan Mind Meld	.50	1.00
☐ 74 Possessed By Zargon	.50	1.00
☐ 75 Creation Of A Humanoid	.50	1.00
☐ 76 Captured By Romulans	.50	1.00
☐ 77 A War Of Worlds	.50	1.00

	Price Range	
☐ 78 Space Of Brains	.50	1.00
☐ 79 I, Yarneg!	.50	1.00
☐ 80 Death In A Single Cell	.50	1.00
☐ 81 The Uninvited	.50	1.00
☐ 82 The Lights Of Zetar	.50	1.00
☐ 83 Invaded By Alien Energy	.50	1.00
☐ 84 Kirk's Deadliest Foe	.50	1.00
☐ 85 The Trouble With Tribbles	.50	1.00
☐ 86 The Nazi Planet	.50	1.00
☐ 87 The Starship Eater	.50	1.00
☐ 88 Star Trek Lives!	.50	1.00
☐ Wrapper	2.00	4.00
☐ Display Box	4.00	8.00
☐ Stickers, Topps Company, correspond with card set, from television show, 1976.		
☐ Set	20.00	30.00
☐ 1 James Kirk	1.00	2.00
☐ 2 Mr. Spock—Unearthly!	1.00	2.00
☐ 3 Spock Of Vulcan	1.00	2.00
☐ 4 Dr. "Bones" McCoy	1.00	2.00
☐ 5 Engineer Scott	1.00	2.00
☐ 6 Lieutenant Uhura	1.00	2.00
☐ 7 Ensign Chekov	1.00	2.00
☐ 8 The Starship Enterprise	1.00	2.00
☐ 9 Kirk Beaming Up!	1.00	2.00
☐ 10 Star Trek Lives!	1.00	2.00
☐ 11 "Highly Illogical!"	1.00	2.00
☐ 12 The Keeper	1.00	2.00
☐ 13 Commander Balok	1.00	2.00
☐ 14 The Mugato	1.00	2.00
☐ 15 Lai, The Interrogator	1.00	2.00
☐ 16 The Parallel Spock	1.00	2.00
☐ 17 Ambassador Gav	1.00	2.00
☐ 18 Alien Possession!	1.00	2.00
☐ 19 Spock Lives!	1.00	2.00
☐ 20 Evil Klingon Kang	1.00	2.00
☐ 21 Spock Forever!	1.00	2.00
☐ 22 The Romulan Vessel	1.00	2.00

STAR TREK: THE MOTION PICTURE

Price Range

☐ **Topps Photo Cards,** series of 88, from Star Trek: The Motion Picture, color photos, with white borders, captioned, 1979.

☐ Set	8.00	12.00
☐ 1 Star Trek: The Motion Picture	.50	1.00
☐ 2 Toward The Unknown	.50	1.00
☐ 3 Space Intruder	.50	1.00
☐ 4 Fate Of The Klingons	.50	1.00
☐ 5 Warning From Space	.50	1.00
☐ 6 "Our Starcrafts—Annihilated!"	.50	1.00
☐ 7 Enterprise in Drydock	.50	1.00
☐ 8 Rebuilding The Enterprise	.50	1.00
☐ 9 Filming 'Drydock' Sequence	.50	1.00
☐ 10 James T. Kirk	.50	1.00
☐ 11 Captain Kirk's Mission	.50	1.00
☐ 12 Dr. 'Bones' McCoy	.50	1.00
☐ 13 Executive Officer Decker	.50	1.00
☐ 14 Navigator Ilia	.50	1.00
☐ 15 Uhura	.50	1.00
☐ 16 Helmsman Sulu	.50	1.00
☐ 17 Engineer Scott	.50	1.00
☐ 18 Security Chief Chekov	.50	1.00
☐ 19 Dr. Christine Chapel	.50	1.00
☐ 20 Janice Rand	.50	1.00
☐ 21 The Vulcan Mr. Spock	.50	1.00
☐ 22 Spock On Planet Vulcan	.50	1.00
☐ 23 The UFP Assembled	.50	1.00
☐ 24 Being From Beyond	.50	1.00
☐ 25 The Face Of Terror	.50	1.00
☐ 26 Lizard-Like Diplomat	.50	1.00
☐ 27 Not Of This Earth	.50	1.00
☐ 28 Alien Insectoid	.50	1.00
☐ 29 The Unearthly	.50	1.00
☐ 30 The Andorians	.50	1.00
☐ 31 Advanced Life Form	.50	1.00
☐ 32 Betel's Attendant	.50	1.00
☐ 33 Andorian—Close-Up	.50	1.00

	Price Range	
☐ 34 The U.S.S. Enterprise	.50	1.00
☐ 35 Back In Operation!	.50	1.00
☐ 36 Refurbished Starship	.50	1.00
☐ 37 Enterprise—Rear View	.50	1.00
☐ 38 Return To The Bridge	.50	1.00
☐ 39 The Senior Officers	.50	1.00
☐ 40 View From The Bridge	.50	1.00
☐ 41 Scotty's Domain	.50	1.00
☐ 42 Fantastic New Devices	.50	1.00
☐ 43 The Engineering Deck	.50	1.00
☐ 44 Investigating A Malfunction	.50	1.00
☐ 45 Heart Of The Starship	.50	1.00
☐ 46 Incredible Explosion!	.50	1.00
☐ 47 Starship Under Attack!	.50	1.00
☐ 48 Assault On Chekov!	.50	1.00
☐ 49 Half Human	.50	1.00
☐ 50 Spock's Fight For Life	.50	1.00
☐ 51 Into The Nameless Void	.50	1.00
☐ 52 Terror In The Transporter Room	.50	1.00
☐ 53 The Surak Craft	.50	1.00
☐ 54 Transporter Malfunction	.50	1.00
☐ 55 Zero Gravity Adventure	.50	1.00
☐ 56 Symbol Of Her People	.50	1.00
☐ 57 Exotically Beautiful Ilia	.50	1.00
☐ 58 Spock's Discovery	.50	1.00
☐ 59 The Phaser Battle!	.50	1.00
☐ 60 Ilia In Sick Bay	.50	1.00
☐ 61 Stamina Of The Alien	.50	1.00
☐ 62 Filming The Shuttlecraft	.50	1.00
☐ 63 Star Explorer	.50	1.00
☐ 64 Alien Menace	.50	1.00
☐ 65 Star Challengers	.50	1.00
☐ 66 "Beam Me Down, Scotty"	.50	1.00
☐ 67 The Landing Party	.50	1.00
☐ 68 Portrait Of A Vulcan	.50	1.00
☐ 69 Beyond Infinity	.50	1.00
☐ 70 The Encounter	.50	1.00
☐ 71 Its Secret Revealed	.50	1.00

	Price Range	
☐ 72 On Spock's Native World	.50	1.00
☐ 73 Spectacular Starship	.50	1.00
☐ 74 Welcoming Dr. McCoy Aboard	.50	1.00
☐ 75 Kirk's Last Stand	.50	1.00
☐ 76 Landscape Of Vulcan	.50	1.00
☐ 77 Klingon Warship—Rear View	.50	1.00
☐ 78 The Final Frontiersmen	.50	1.00
☐ 79 Klingon Warship	.50	1.00
☐ 80 Vulcan Starship—Overhead View	.50	1.00
☐ 81 Pride Of The Starfleet	.50	1.00
☐ 82 Duo For Danger	.50	1.00
☐ 83 The Unearthly Mr. Spock	.50	1.00
☐ 84 Woman From Planet Delta	.50	1.00
☐ 85 New Starfleet Uniforms	.50	1.00
☐ 86 Men With A Mission	.50	1.00
☐ 87 The Deltan Beauty	.50	1.00
☐ 88 Klingon Commander	.50	1.00
☐ Wrapper	.50	1.00
☐ Display Box	1.00	2.00

☐ **Stickers, Topps Company,** correspond with Star Trek: The Motion Picture set, 1979.

☐ Set	4.00	6.00
☐ 1 Engineer Scott	.50	1.00
☐ 2 Janice Rand	.50	1.00
☐ 3 On Spock's Native World	.50	1.00
☐ 4 Security Chief Chekov	.50	1.00
☐ 5 Navigator Ilia	.50	1.00
☐ 6 Helmsman Sulu	.50	1.00
☐ 7 Star Explorer	.50	1.00
☐ 8 Dr. Christine Chapel	.50	1.00
☐ 9 Portrait Of A Vulcan	.50	1.00
☐ 10 Dr. 'Bones' McCoy	.50	1.00
☐ 11 Uhura	.50	1.00
☐ 12 The Deltan Beauty	.50	1.00
☐ 13 The Face Of Terror	.50	1.00
☐ 14 Being From Beyond	.50	1.00
☐ 15 Advanced Life Form	.50	1.00

	Price Range	
☐ 16 Executive Officer Decker	.50	1.00
☐ 17 Betel's Attendant	.50	1.00
☐ 18 Lizard-Like Diplomat	.50	1.00
☐ 19 Pride Of The Starfleet	.50	1.00
☐ 20 Klingon Warship	.50	1.00
☐ 21 The Surak Craft	.50	1.00
☐ 22 Spectacular Starship	.50	1.00

COLLECTOR'S CARDS

Cards in this section were designed to be sold to collectors directly, not through gum sales. This makes these cards much rarer due to limited distribution, but on the other hand most of the cards issued got into the hands of collectors. These cards were designed for the collector so usually are of better quality and more mature subject matter than gum cards.

STAR TREK: THE WRATH OF KHAN

☐ **Fantasy Trading Card Co.,** Star Trek: The Wrath of Khan, 30 card set, color photos, no stickers, no captions, print run limited to 7,500 possible sets, 1982, 5" x 7".

☐ **Set**	15.00	20.00
☐ **Kirk** with book under arm	.50	1.00
☐ **Sulu**	.50	1.00
☐ **Scott**	.50	1.00
☐ **Uhura**	.50	1.00
☐ **Kirk**	.50	1.00
☐ **David Marcus**	.50	1.00
☐ **Khan** inside cargo bay	.50	1.00
☐ **Saavik** on bridge	.50	1.00
☐ **Saavik**	.50	1.00
☐ **Chekov** aiming phaser	.50	1.00
☐ **Khan**	.50	1.00
☐ **Terrell** aiming phaser	.50	1.00
☐ **Kirk And Spock**	.50	1.00
☐ **Carol Marcus, Kirk, David Marcus, and Saavik**	.50	1.00

	Price Range	
☐ **McCoy**	.50	1.00
☐ **Khan** on wrecked bridge of U.S.S. Reliant ...	.50	1.00
☐ **Chekov** in cargo bay holding S. S. Botany Bay belt	.50	1.00
☐ **Carol Marcus,** Genesis control, and David Marcus	.50	1.00
☐ **Saavik** with communicator	.50	1.00
☐ **David Marcus And Kirk**	.50	1.00
☐ **Space Lab Regula I**	.50	1.00
☐ **Khan And Chekov** on Reliant Bridge	.50	1.00
☐ **U.S.S. Reliant**	.50	1.00
☐ **Group Photo,** shows original eight characters	.50	1.00
☐ **Kirk, Spock, and Saavik** on bridge	.50	1.00
☐ **Saavik And Spock**	.50	1.00
☐ **Sulu, Kirk, Uhura, And McCoy** in travel pod	.50	1.00
☐ **McCoy, Scott, And Crewman** holding Kirk back	.50	1.00
☐ **Spock** at bridge station	.50	1.00
☐ **Saavik** at bridge station	.50	1.00
☐ **Wrapper,** 4 different (each)	1.00	2.00
☐ **Display Box**	2.00	4.00

STAR TREK III: SEARCH FOR SPOCK

☐ **FTCC (Fantasy Trading Card Corp.),** Star Trek III: The Search For Spock, 60 scene cards and 20 spaceship cards, no stickers, subject titles on the back of each card, 20 spaceship cards have a glossy finish, 2½″ x 3½″, 1984.

☐ **Set**	8.00	10.00
☐ **1 William Shatner stars as Adml. James T. Kirk**	.50	1.00
☐ **2 Leonard Nimoy as Captain Spock**	.50	1.00
☐ **3 Deforest Kelley stars as Dr. Leonard "Bones" McCoy**	.50	1.00
☐ **4 Chief Engineer M. Scott played by James Doohan**	.50	1.00

	Price Range	
☐ 5 Capt. Hikaro Sulu played by George Takei	.50	1.00
☐ 6 Acting Sci. Officer Commander Pavel Chekov ...	.50	1.00
☐ 7 Nichelle Nichols as the beautiful Uhura	.50	1.00
☐ 8 Introducing Robin Curtis as Lt. Saavik ..	.50	1.00
☐ 9 Ambassador Sarek, Spock's father, portrayed by Mark L.	.50	1.00
☐ 10 Vulcan High Priestess T'Lar played by Dame Judith A.	.50	1.00
☐ 11 Starfleet Comm. Morrow played by Robert Hooks	.50	1.00
☐ 12 Klingon Battle Comm. Kruge played by Christopher Lloyd	.50	1.00
☐ 13 Kruge's pet, Warrigul	.50	1.00
☐ 14 The Enterprise returning home for repairs	.50	1.00
☐ 15 The Enterprise berthed next to the Excelsior ...	.50	1.00
☐ 16 Sarek mind-melds with Kirk	.50	1.00
☐ 17 Kirk replaying the Enterprise's engine room flight record	.50	1.00
☐ 18 Kirk viewing the tape of Spock transferring his katra	.50	1.00
☐ 19 Morrow tells Kirk the bad news—Genesis is off limits	.50	1.00
☐ 20 Conspirators in conference	.50	1.00
☐ 21 Visiting Bones in prison	.50	1.00
☐ 22 Liberating Bones from prison	.50	1.00
☐ 23 Sabotaging the prison's communications console	.50	1.00
☐ 24 Kirk and crew find Saavik and Spock held prisoner	.50	1.00
☐ 25 Commander Chekov at the helm	.50	1.00
☐ 26 Lt. Saavik and Dr. David Marcus ... view the Genesis	.50	1.00
☐ 27 Dr. David Marcus arrives on his creation	.50	1.00

	Price Range	
☐ 28 Locating Spock's torpedo tube coffin	.50	1.00
☐ 29 Spock's burial robe, but no body	.50	1.00
☐ 30 What could have happened to Spock's body?	.50	1.00
☐ 31 Tracking ... Spock?	.50	1.00
☐ 32 The Spock child lost in the snow	.50	1.00
☐ 33 Rescuing the Spock child from the hostile elements	.50	1.00
☐ 34 Uncloaking itself, Kruge's Klingon ship fires	.50	1.00
☐ 35 The Spock child resting in Saavik and David's	.50	1.00
☐ 36 Klingon Landing Party	.50	1.00
☐ 37 Kruge subduing a Genesis mutation ...	.50	1.00
☐ 38 Kruge planning his next strategy against the Ent.	.50	1.00
☐ 39 Deadly enemies crippled in space	.50	1.00
☐ 40 Scotty and Chekov worrying over instrument readings	.50	1.00
☐ 41 Young Spock in the agony of pon farr	.50	1.00
☐ 42 Saavik soothing young Spock from the effects	.50	1.00
☐ 43 Spock, now a young adult, and still aging along with	.50	1.00
☐ 44 Which one shall I execute?	.50	1.00
☐ 45 David attracts the Klingon's fatal hand to save	.50	1.00
☐ 46 Turning certain death into a fighting chance at life	.50	1.00
☐ 47 Watching the Starship Enterprise blaze into history	.50	1.00
☐ 48 Kruge in rage after Kirk outwits him ...	.50	1.00
☐ 49 Kirk and Kruge duel as Genesis convulses	.50	1.00
☐ 50 Fighting on the brink of destruction ...	.50	1.00
☐ 51 The death throes of Genesis	.50	1.00
☐ 52 Kirk bargaining for the lives of his crew	.50	1.00

	Price Range	
☐ 53 Escaping the exploding Genesis planet	.50	1.00
☐ 54 The Ent. crew and their stolen Bird of Prey land	.50	1.00
☐ 55 The Enterprise crew returning Spock to his Vulcan home	.50	1.00
☐ 56 Sarek, at the foot of Mount Seleya asking T'Lar	.50	1.00
☐ 57 McCoy's friendship for Spock is put to the ultimate test	.50	1.00
☐ 58 T'Lar performs the ritual of fal tor pan—the refusion	.50	1.00
☐ 59 Spock and Kirk face to face after fal tor pan	.50	1.00
☐ 60 Spock's memories finally restored; the search is over	.50	1.00
☐ 1 U.S.S. Enterprise NCC–1701 (left view) ..	.50	1.00
☐ 2 U.S.S. Enterprise Rear View	.50	1.00
☐ 3 U.S.S. Enterprise lvg. Spacedock pursued	.50	1.00
☐ 4 U.S.S. Enterprise Front View	.50	1.00
☐ 5 Spacedock orbiting space station Top View	.50	1.00
☐ 6 Spacedock Side View	.50	1.00
☐ 7 NX–2000 U.S.S. Excelsior	.50	1.00
☐ 8 U.S.S. Excelsior Right Rear View	.50	1.00
☐ 9 U.S.S. Excelsior Top View	.50	1.00
☐ 10 U.S.S. Excelsior Bottom View	.50	1.00
☐ 11 The Merchantman merchant ship destroyed	.50	1.00
☐ 12 The Merchantman Bottom View	.50	1.00
☐ 13 The Merchantman Top View	.50	1.00
☐ 14 The Merchantman Rear View	.50	1.00
☐ 15 Kruge's ship Klingon Bird of Prey	.50	1.00
☐ 16 Klingon Bird of Prey captured by Kirk ...	.50	1.00
☐ 17 U.S.S. Grissom NCC-638 Destroyed by Kruge	.50	1.00

	Price Range	
☐ 18 U.S.S. Grissom Rear View	.50	1.00
☐ 19 U.S.S. Grissom Top View	.50	1.00
☐ 20 U.S.S. Grissom Bottom View	.50	1.00
☐ **Wrapper**	1.00	2.00
☐ **Display Box**	2.00	4.00

PROMOTIONAL AND FOREIGN CARDS

These cards were issued in conjunction with the sale of a product in hopes to boost sales. All foreign cards are listed here because not enough information is available about foreign sets to distinguish between gum, collector's and promotional cards. This section is organized chronologically by TV show and movie.

STAR TREK TV SERIES

☐ **Morris, Canadian,** 4½″ x 3¼″, brown-backed stickers on thin stock and mostly black puzzle cards, each sticker is comprised of three or four smaller, numbered stickers depicting TV scenes or new art, the title and Enterprise on a starry black front and a colored puzzle piece behind, copyright 1975 Paramount, issued without gum, per set **15.00 20.00**

☐ **Album For 35 Stickers,** issued with Canadian Morris set, different albums distinguished by the colored centerfold.

☐ **Kirk Portrait**	5.00	7.00
☐ **Spock With Phaser**	5.00	7.00
☐ **Kirk And Gorn**	5.00	7.00
☐ **Robot**	5.00	7.00

☐ **Panini,** made in Italy for European market, 400 stickers plus album, color, TV series, 1979 .. **45.00 85.00**

☐ **Phoenix Candy Company Boxes, United States,** folded box, with all flaps about 8″ x 3½″ when flattened, front photo about 3″ x 2¼″, color photo with number below on front, labeled photo of Enterprise on back of all

Price Range

boxes, copyright 1976 Paramount, issued as individual boxes with candy and two plastic prizes, 8 boxes in set, uncommon 2.00   4.00

☐ **Primrose Confectionery, English,** 2½" x 1⅜", thin white stock with color print on front, number and story on back, all say "Issued A.S. 2307," copyright PPC (Paramount), assumed issued with some type of cookie or pastry, all cards on the market are mint reminders, 12 cards in the set 12.00   15.00

☐ **Topps A And BC, English,** 3¼" x 2¼", color photos, blue border with caption in white, rocket at bottom, story and number on pale bluish-green back, copyright 1969 Paramount, issued in packs with bubble gum, 55 cards in the set, very uncommon, per card 3.00   5.00

☐ **Wrapper** 50.00   75.00

STAR TREK: THE MOTION PICTURE

☐ **General Mills Collector's Series, U.S. And England,** 5⅛" x 3½", plain-backed heavy stock, color photos in silver and white borders, numbered, no issuer information once cut from package, copyright 1979 Paramount, issued on back of General Mills cereal boxes: Cocoa Puffs, Trix, Count Chocula, Frankenberry, Boo-Berry, and Lucky Charms, two vertical cards were on large boxes ("Close-Ups") and one horizontal card on small boxes ("Action Shots"), 18 cards in set, scarce, per card . . .   2.00   4.00

☐ **General Mills Starship Door Signs, U.S. And England,** 6½" x 3½", plain-backed heavy card with angled corners, orange and silver borders around various art and photos with titles, no numbers, no issuer information once cut from

	Price Range	

package, copyright 1979 Paramount, issued on
the back of Cheerios boxes, 7 cards in the set,
scarce.

☐ **Authorized Personnel Only**	3.00	5.00
☐ **Captain's Quarters**	3.00	5.00
☐ **Danger! Keep Out**	3.00	5.00
☐ **Do Not Enter**	3.00	5.00
☐ **Engine Room**	3.00	5.00
☐ **Intermix Chamber**	3.00	5.00
☐ **Medical Officer Dr. Leonard "Bones" McCoy**	3.00	5.00
☐ **U.S.S. Enterprise**	3.00	5.00

☐ **Lyons Maid,** English, 3″ x 1⅜″, color photos,
number and story on back, copyright 1979 Paramount, issued on packs of Lyons Maid ice lol-
lies, wrapper dark blue, flattens out to about 5″
x 3″, 25 with spaces for the cards were issued

as a premium, uncommon, per set	15.00	25.00

☐ **Rainbow Bread,** series of cards numbered
1–33, white borders, either red, blue or yellow
trim, photographs from the first movie, distributed with Rainbow Bread, one card with one
loaf of bread, 3½″ x 2½″, 1979.

☐ **Set**	7.00	10.00
☐ **1 Title Card**	.25	.40
☐ **2 Toward The Unknown**	.25	.40
☐ **3 Space Intruder**	.25	.40
☐ **4 Fate Of The Klingons**	.25	.40
☐ **5 Warning From Space**	.25	.40
☐ **6 "Our Starcrafts Annihilated"**	.25	.40
☐ **7 Enterprise In Drydock**	.25	.40
☐ **8 Rebuilding The Enterprise**	.25	.40
☐ **9 Filming Drydock Sequence**	.25	.40
☐ **10 James T. Kirk**	.35	.50
☐ **11 Captain Kirk's Mission**	.25	.40
☐ **12 Dr. "Bones" McCoy**	.35	.50
☐ **13 Executive Officer Decker**	.35	.50
☐ **14 Navigator Ilia**	.35	.50
☐ **15 Uhura**	.35	.50

	Price Range	
☐ 16 Helmsman Sulu	.35	.50
☐ 17 Engineer Scott	.35	.50
☐ 18 Security Chief Chekov	.35	.50
☐ 19 Dr. Christine Chapel	.35	.50
☐ 20 Janice Rand	.35	.50
☐ 21 The Vulcan Mr. Spock	.50	.60
☐ 22 Spock On Planet Vulcan	.35	.50
☐ 23 The UFP Assembled	.25	.40
☐ 24 Being From Beyond	.25	.40
☐ 25 The Face Of Terror	.25	.40
☐ 26 Lizard-Like Diplomat	.25	.40
☐ 27 Not Of This Earth	.25	.40
☐ 28 Alien Insectoid	.25	.40
☐ 29 The Unearthly	.25	.40
☐ 30 The Andorians	.25	.40
☐ 31 Advance Life Form	.25	.40
☐ 32 Betel's Attendant	.25	.40
☐ 33 Andorian Close-Up	.25	.40
☐ **As above—Kilpatrick's Bread, United States,** like Rainbow Bread issue but with Kilpatrick's Bread logo on back of each card, 33 cards in set, per set	7.00	10.00
☐ **As above,** Colonial Bread, United States, ...	7.00	10.00
☐ **Swizzels Refreshers Stickers, English,** 1¾" x 1¼", stickers with rounded corners, color photos with caption below and number on side, copyright 1979 Paramount, issued in packs of Swizzels Star Trek Refreshers—Flavoured Fizzy Sweets, wrapper black with starburst and rainbow, about 4 1/4" x 3 1/16" when flattened, stickers in set	15.00	17.00

☐ **Topps United Kingdom T.M.P., English,** same format as U.S. cards but on a thinner and whiter stock that gives the red and blue backs a much brighter appearance (backs dull on grayish stock in U.S. cards), some differences in content, no stickers, copyright 1979 Para-

Price Range

mount, wrapper very similar to U.S. but says "Movie Photo Cards Bubble Gum," 88 cards per set, uncommon, per set	15.00	25.00

Note: This set is not identical to the U.S. issue, differing in several cards as follows:

☐ **1 The Final Frontiersmen**	.50	.75
☐ **2 Klingon Ship In Red Border**	.50	.75
☐ **11 Mr. Spock**	.75	1.00
☐ **52 Vulcan Spaceship**	.50	.75
☐ **55 A Pensive McCoy**	.75	1.00
☐ **76 Speeding At Warp Seven**	.75	1.00
☐ **78 Klingon Warship**	.50	.75
☐ **Vending Stickers, United States,** 3 1/8" x 2 1/16", color photos with gold borders, not numbered, no issuer information, backs say only "peel off backing, stick on window or outside of glass," title on front, copyright 1979, Paramount, issued in transparent bubbles (folded) from vending machines at 25¢ each, remainders show no traces of folds, 4 stickers in set. Per set	6.00	10.00
☐ **Enterprise**	2.00	3.00
☐ **Kirk**	2.00	3.00
☐ **Kirk, Spock And Enterprise**	2.00	3.00
☐ **Spock**	2.00	3.00
☐ **Weetabix, United Kingdom,** 3½" x 1⅝", color art with caption on front, color photo in oval on purple back, cards scored at bottom to stand up, issued perforated on one or two long sides, issued in large packs of Weetabix cereal, usually in strips of three cards, 18 cards in the set, uncommon, per set	15.00	25.00
☐ **Andorian Man**	1.00	3.00
☐ **Andorian Woman**	1.00	3.00
☐ **Arcturian,** these six share a common background of blue V'ger floor panels	1.00	3.00

	Price Range	
☐ **Betelgeusian Chief Ambassador**	1.00	3.00
☐ **Captain Kirk**	1.00	3.00
☐ **Commander Decker**	1.00	3.00
☐ **Commander Scott**	1.00	3.00
☐ **Commander Uhuru**	1.00	3.00
☐ **Dr. McCoy**	1.00	3.00
☐ **Klingon Captain**	1.00	3.00
☐ **Lieutenant Chekov**	1.00	3.00
☐ **Lieutenant Ilia**	1.00	3.00
☐ **Lieutenant Sulu**	1.00	3.00
☐ **Megarite,** these six share a common background of Federation Headquarters	1.00	3.00
☐ **Mr. Spock**	1.00	3.00
☐ **Rigellian**	1.00	3.00
☐ **Shamin Priest,** these six share a common background of red panels	1.00	3.00
☐ **Vulcan Master**	1.00	3.00

STAR TREK II: WRATH OF KHAN

☐ **Monty Gum,** Star Trek II: Wrath of Khan, British, 100 cards, smaller than American cards.		
☐ **Set**	25.00	45.00

VIDEO CASSETTES

	Price Range	
☐ **Amok Time/Journey to Babel,** Copyright 1978 Paramount Pictures, issued at $55.95 ..	30.00	40.00
☐ **Balance of Terror/The City on the Edge of Forever,** Copyright 1978 Paramount Pictures, issued at $55.95	30.00	40.00
☐ **Menagerie,** Parts One and Two, Copyright 1978 Paramount Pictures, issued at $55.95 ..	30.00	40.00
☐ **Mirror, Mirror/The Tholian Web,** Copyright 1978 Paramount Pictures, issued at $55.95 ..	30.00	40.00
☐ **Star Trek: The Motion Picture,** original version, 132 minutes, issued at $79.95	50.00	60.00

	Price Range	
☐ **Star Trek: The Motion Picture,** second version, 143 minutes, issued at $39.95	20.00	30.00
☐ **Star Trek II: Wrath of Khan,** issued at $39.95	25.00	30.00
☐ **Star Trek III, The Search for Spock,** Paramount, Home Video	20.00	30.00
☐ **The Trouble With Tribbles/Let That Be Your Last Battlefield,** Copyright 1978 Paramount Pictures, issued at $55.95	30.00	40.00

STAR TREK TV EPISODES (SINGLES) ISSUED AT $14.95 EACH*

☐ **"The Cage"** Pilot episode, black and white, issued at $29.95	28.00	30.00
☐ **"The Man Trap"**	12.00	15.00
☐ **"Charlie X"**	12.00	15.00
☐ **"Where No Man Has Gone Before"**	12.00	15.00
☐ **"The Naked Time"**	12.00	15.00
☐ **"The Enemy Within"**	12.00	15.00
☐ **"Mudd's Women"**	12.00	15.00
☐ **"What Are Little Girls Made Of?"**	12.00	15.00
☐ **"Miri"**	12.00	15.00
☐ **"Dagger Of The Mind"**	12.00	15.00
☐ **"The Carbomite Maneuver"**	12.00	15.00
☐ **"The Menagerie"** (Parts 1 & 2) $29.95	28.00	30.00
☐ **"The Conscience Of The King"**	12.00	15.00
☐ **"Balance of Terror"**	12.00	15.00
☐ **"Shore Leave"**	12.00	15.00
☐ **"The Galileo Seven"**	12.00	15.00
☐ **"The Squire Of Gothos"**	12.00	15.00
☐ **"Arena"**	12.00	15.00
☐ **"Tomorrow Is Yesterday"**	12.00	15.00
☐ **"Court-Marshall"**	12.00	15.00
☐ **"The Return Of The Archons"**	12.00	15.00

*All other episodes have either been issued or are planned to be issued in the near future.

Star Wars

STAR WARS LISTINGS

ACTION FIGURES AND ACCESSORIES

ACTION FIGURES, SMALL

Prices listed for the small action figures are for figures in their original packages. Figures out of their packages are worth only $2 to $4 each unless it is a Star Wars figure that is distinguishable from later versions, in which case it is worth about 50% of the listed value. Sizes vary from 2¼" to 4¼", all by Kenner.

Prices include special collectors' reissues that came with coin. Coins by themselves are worth $.50 to $1.00.

Small Action Figures

Price Range

STAR WARS ACTION FIGURES, 1978

☐ Ben (Obi Wan) Kenobi	5.00	10.00
☐ C-3PO	5.00	10.00
☐ Chewbacca	5.00	10.00
☐ Darth Vader	5.00	10.00
☐ Death Squad Commander	5.00	10.00
☐ Death Star Droid	5.00	10.00
☐ Greedo	5.00	10.00
☐ Hammerhead	5.00	10.00
☐ Han Solo (Vest)	5.00	10.00
☐ Jawa	5.00	10.00
☐ Luke	5.00	10.00
☐ Luke (Stormtrooper)	5.00	10.00
☐ Luke (X-Wing Pilot)	5.00	10.00
☐ Power Droid	5.00	10.00
☐ Princess Leia	5.00	10.00
☐ R5-D4	5.00	10.00
☐ R2-D2	5.00	10.00
☐ Snaggletooth	5.00	10.00
☐ Snaggletooth, Sears version, blue clothing, sil-ver boots	10.00	15.00
☐ Star Destroyer Commander	5.00	10.00
☐ Stormtrooper	5.00	10.00
☐ Tie Fighter Pilot	5.00	10.00
☐ Tuskan Raider	5.00	10.00
☐ Walrus Man	5.00	10.00

EMPIRE STRIKES BACK ACTION FIGURES

☐ AT/AT Commander	5.00	10.00
☐ AT/AT Driver	5.00	10.00
☐ Bespin Security Guard (Black)	5.00	10.00
☐ Bespin Security Guard (White)	5.00	10.00
☐ Boba Fett	5.00	10.00
☐ Boussk	5.00	10.00
☐ C-3PO (Removable Limbs)	5.00	10.00
☐ Cloud Car pilot	5.00	10.00

	Price Range	
☐ **Dengar**	5.00	10.00
☐ **8D8**	5.00	10.00
☐ **EV-9D9**	5.00	10.00
☐ **4-LOM**	5.00	10.00
☐ **FX-7**	5.00	10.00
☐ **Han Solo** (Bespin Outfit)	5.00	10.00
☐ **Han Solo** (Hoth Gear)	5.00	10.00
☐ **IG-88**	5.00	10.00
☐ **Imperial Commander**	5.00	10.00
☐ **Lando Calrussian**	5.00	10.00
☐ **Lobot**	5.00	10.00
☐ **Luke** (Bespin Guard)	5.00	10.00
☐ **Luke** (Hoth Gear)	5.00	10.00
☐ **Princess Leia** (Bespin Gown)	5.00	10.00
☐ **R2-D2** (Sensorscope)	5.00	10.00
☐ **Rebel Commander**	5.00	10.00
☐ **Rebel Commando**	5.00	10.00
☐ **Rebel Soldier**	5.00	10.00
☐ **Ree Yees**	5.00	10.00
☐ **21B**	5.00	10.00
☐ **Stormtrooper** (Hoth Gear)	5.00	10.00
☐ **Ugnaught**	5.00	10.00
☐ **Yoda**	5.00	10.00
☐ **Zuckuss**	5.00	10.00

RETURN OF THE JEDI ACTION FIGURES

☐ **Admiral Ackbar**	5.00	10.00
☐ **Amanaman**	5.00	10.00
☐ **Anakin Skywalker**	5.00	10.00
☐ **AT-ST Driver**	5.00	10.00
☐ **A-Wing Pilot**	5.00	10.00
☐ **Barada**	5.00	10.00
☐ **Bib Fortuna**	5.00	10.00
☐ **Biker Scout**	5.00	10.00
☐ **B-Wing Pilot**	5.00	10.00
☐ **Chief Chirpa**	5.00	10.00

	Price Range	
☐ **Emperor**	5.00	10.00
☐ **Emperor's Guard**	5.00	10.00
☐ **Gamorrean Guard**	5.00	10.00
☐ **General Madine**	5.00	10.00
☐ **Han Solo** (Carbonite)	5.00	10.00
☐ **Han Solo** (Trenchcoat)	5.00	10.00
☐ **Imperial Dignitary**	5.00	10.00
☐ **Imperial Gunner**	5.00	10.00
☐ **Klaatu**	5.00	10.00
☐ **Klaatu** (Skiff Guard)	5.00	10.00
☐ **Lando** (General)	5.00	10.00
☐ **Lando** (Skiff Guard)	5.00	10.00
☐ **Logray**	5.00	10.00
☐ **Luke** (Battle Poncho)	5.00	10.00
☐ **Luke** (Jedi Outfit)	5.00	10.00
☐ **Lumat**	5.00	10.00
☐ **Nien Numb**	5.00	10.00
☐ **Nikto**	5.00	10.00
☐ **Raploo**	5.00	10.00
☐ **Princess Leia** (Boshk Outfit)	5.00	10.00
☐ **Princess Leia** (Poncho)	5.00	10.00
☐ **Prune Face**	5.00	10.00
☐ **R2-D2** (Pop-up Lightsaber)	5.00	10.00
☐ **Racor Keeper**	5.00	10.00
☐ **Romba**	5.00	10.00
☐ **Squid Head**	5.00	10.00
☐ **Teebo**	5.00	10.00
☐ **Warok**	5.00	10.00
☐ **Weequay**	5.00	10.00
☐ **Wicket**	5.00	10.00
☐ **Yak Face**	5.00	10.00

DROIDS ANIMATED ACTION FIGURES, 1985

☐ **Admiral Screed**	2.00	4.00
☐ **A-Wing Pilot**	2.00	4.00

	Price	Range
☐ **Boba Fett**	2.00	4.00
☐ **C-3PO** (figure differs slightly from movie version)	2.00	4.00
☐ **Gaff**	2.00	4.00
☐ **Governor Koong**	2.00	4.00
☐ **Jann Tosh**	2.00	4.00
☐ **Jessica Meade**	2.00	4.00
☐ **Jord Dusat**	2.00	4.00
☐ **Kea Moll**	2.00	4.00
☐ **Kez-Iban**	2.00	4.00
☐ **Kleb Zellock**	2.00	4.00
☐ **Mon Julpa**	2.00	4.00
☐ **Mungo Baobab**	2.00	4.00
☐ **R2-D2** (figure differs slightly from movie version)	2.00	4.00
☐ **Sise Fromm**	2.00	4.00
☐ **Thall Joben**	2.00	4.00
☐ **Tig Fromm**	2.00	4.00
☐ **Uncle Gundy**	2.00	4.00
☐ **Vlix**	2.00	4.00

EWOKS ANIMATED ACTION FIGURES, 1985

☐ **Bondo**	2.00	4.00
☐ **Chief Chirpa**	2.00	4.00
☐ **Chituhr**	2.00	4.00
☐ **Dulok Scout**	2.00	4.00
☐ **Dulok Shaman**	2.00	4.00
☐ **King Gorneesh**	2.00	4.00
☐ **Logray**	2.00	4.00
☐ **Morag**	2.00	4.00
☐ **Paploo**	2.00	4.00
☐ **Urgah Lady Gorneesh**	2.00	4.00
☐ **Weechee**	2.00	4.00
☐ **Wicket W. Warrick** (figure differs slightly from movie version)	2.00	4.00

ACTION FIGURES—LARGE

Price Range

Prices for these dolls are listed with and without boxes. In each case prices are for complete dolls with all accessories. Values for incomplete dolls are much lower.

☐ **Boba Fett,** Kenner Corp., carries a laser rifle and wears a cape and backpack, 13½″ tall

in box	150.00	250.00
no box	75.00	125.00

☐ **C-3PO,** Kenner Corp., 12½″ tall

in box	50.00	75.00
no box	20.00	40.00

☐ **Chewbacca,** Kenner Corp., crossbow laser rifle and ammunition strap, 15″ tall

in box	100.00	150.00
no box	50.00	75.00

☐ **Darth Vader,** Kenner Corp., light saber and cape, 15″ tall

in box	100.00	150.00
no box	50.00	75.00

☐ **Han Solo,** Kenner Corp., hand blaster, belt and medallion, 12½″ tall

in box	150.00	300.00
no box	100.00	200.00

☐ **IG-88,** Kenner Corp., bandolier and 2 rifles, 12½″ tall

in box	200.00	400.00
no box	125.00	250.00

☐ **Jawa,** Kenner Corp., cloth cape, bandolier and laser rifle, 8″ tall

in box	100.00	150.00
no box	50.00	100.00

☐ **Luke Skywalker,** Kenner Corp., light saber, grappling hook and belt, 12″ tall

in box	125.00	250.00
no box	100.00	150.00

☐ **Obi-Wan Kenobi,** Kenner Corp., light saber and cape, 12″ tall

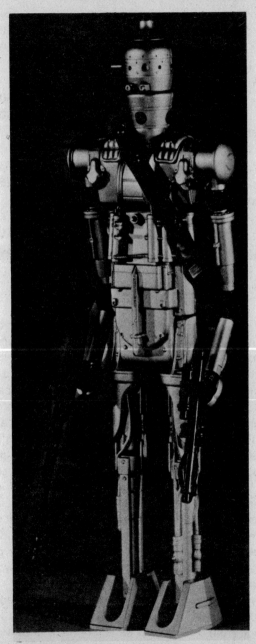

Star Wars: The Empire Strikes Back, IG-88 Large Action Figure, from Kenner

	Price Range	
in box	100.00	150.00
no box	50.00	100.00
☐ **Princess Leia Organa,** Kenner Corp., comb and brush, 11″ tall		
in box	100.00	175.00
no box	50.00	100.00
☐ **R2-D2, Kenner Corp,** internal circuit boards, 8″ tall		
in box	75.00	100.00
no box	25.00	50.00
☐ **Storm Trooper,** Kenner Corp., laser rifle, 12″ tall		
in box	150.00	250.00
no box	50.00	100.00

ARTWORK

As stated in the *Star Trek* section, it would be improper to write a book about collectibles without mentioning original works of art. At the same time, it is impossible to catalog art because it is by nature unique. When considering Star Wars art as a collectible it is, first of all, best to use the same criteria you would use for any other category: does it appeal to you? This might be both difficult and easy at the same time, because Star Wars art is so diverse. The word "art" means a painting to most people, but this overlooks a vast assortment of skills and crafts. At a large Star Wars convention you can find sculptures, ceramics, jewelry, needlepoint, leatherwork, and much more that fits into the category of art.

When buying an item with an eye toward future collectibility, however, you may wish to consider a few things. Is the piece well made? Is the person that made it a good craftsman as well as a good artist? Does the piece have a unique quality? Does it fit in with your other collectibles? Is the artist well known in his or her field? Has the work ever been published, say as a book cover?

Some very well-known artists in the fantasy and science fiction art field have done artwork for published Star Wars items.

Prices range from a few cents for a fan-made craft item to several thousand dollars for a painting by a nationally known artist.

BADGES, BUTTONS AND BUMPER STICKERS

BADGES

**HARD PLASTIC BADGES,
CAME WITH PIN BACK, UNLICENSED**

	Price Range	
☐ **Ambassador to Alderon,** plastic, Star Trek Galore	1.00	3.00
☐ **Brotherhood of the Jedi,** plastic, Star Trek Galore	1.00	3.00
☐ **Droid Technician,** plastic, Star Trek Galore	1.00	3.00
☐ **Imperial Senator,** plastic, Star Trek Galore ..	1.00	3.00
☐ **Jedi Knight,** plastic, Star Trek Galore	1.00	3.00
☐ **Jedi Training Academy,** plastic, Star Trek Galore	1.00	3.00
☐ **Millennium Falcon Crew,** plastic, Star Trek Galore	1.00	3.00
☐ **Sisterhood of the Jedi,** plastic, Star Trek Galore	1.00	3.00
☐ **Terror Squad,** plastic, Star Trek Galore	1.00	3.00
☐ **Wookie translator,** plastic, Star Trek Galore	1.00	3.00
☐ **X-Wing Fighter Pilot,** plastic, Star Trek Galore	1.00	3.00
☐ **Y-Wing Fighter Pilot,** plastic, Star Trek Galore	1.00	3.00

BUTTONS

For reasons explained in the *Star Trek* section of this book, we are listing only licensed buttons. A button should cost between $.75 and $2.00. Size and subject matter have no effect on button prices.

WORD BUTTONS

☐ **Darth Vader Lives,** Word Button, Factors, Etc., 3″	.75	2.00
☐ **May the Force Be With You,** 2¼″	.75	2.00
☐ **May the Force Be With You,** Factors, Etc., 3″	.75	2.00

	Price Range	

☐ **May the Force Be With You,** promotional word button given away at *Star Wars* premier, manufactured for 20th Century Fox by L.A. Button, no value as a collectible due to ease of reproduction, 2¾" .... .75 2.00

PICTURE BUTTONS

Star Wars, Factors, Etc., 3", all with words identifying characters

☐ **Chewbacca**	.75	2.00
☐ **C-3PO**	.75	2.00
☐ **C-3PO/R2-D2,** with Star Wars logo	.75	2.00
☐ **Darth Vader**	.75	2.00
☐ **Luke Skywalker**	.75	2.00
☐ **Obi-Wan**	.75	2.00
☐ **Princess Leia**	.75	2.00
☐ **R2-D2**	.75	2.00

Empire Strikes Back, Factors, Etc., 3", No words

☐ **Boba Fett**	.75	2.00
☐ **Chewbacca**	.75	2.00
☐ **Darth Vader**	.75	2.00
☐ **Luke Skywalker**	.75	2.00
☐ **R2-D2/C-3PO**	.75	2.00
☐ **Yoda**	.75	2.00

Return of The Jedi, Adam Joseph, 2¼", came on cardboard headers.

☐ **Baby Ewok**	.75	2.00
☐ **Chewbacca**	.75	2.00
☐ **Darth Vader,** artwork from prerelease, 1-sheet	.75	2.00
☐ **Darth Vader**	.75	2.00
☐ **Droopy,** from Rebo Band	.75	2.00
☐ **Gamorean Guard**	.75	2.00
☐ **Group shot,** Heroes in woods	.75	2.00
☐ **Imperial Guard**	.75	2.00
☐ **Jabba the Hutt**	.75	2.00

	Price Range	
☐ **Logo from Return of the Jedi**	.75	2.00
☐ **R2-D2 and C-3PO**	.75	2.00
☐ **Yoda**	.75	2.00

STAR WARS FAN CLUB BUTTONS
Picture with logo and character name, 1″, 1978.

FIRST SERIES

☐ **Chewbacca**	.75	2.00
☐ **George Lucas**	.75	2.00
☐ **Han Solo**	.75	2.00
☐ **Luke**	.75	2.00
☐ **Princess Leia**	.75	2.00
☐ **Tusken Raider**	.75	2.00

SECOND SERIES

☐ **Ben Kenobi**	.75	2.00
☐ **Moff Tarkin**	.75	2.00
☐ **Darth Vader**	.75	2.00
☐ **R2-D2**	.75	2.00
☐ **C-3PO**	.75	2.00
☐ **Jawa**	.75	2.00

BUMPER STICKERS

☐ **"Let the Wookie Win"**	1.00	2.00
☐ **"May the Force Be With You"**	1.00	2.00
☐ **"Support the Rebels"**	1.00	2.00
☐ **"Wookies Need Love Too"**	1.00	2.00

BLUEPRINTS

	Price Range	
☐ **Star Wars Blueprints,** shows detailed designs for interior of Death Star. The Millennium Falcon, the Sandcrawler and others, 15 prints in set. Ballantine Books, 13″ x 19″	10.00	15.00

	Price Range	
☐ **Corellian Freighter Blueprints,** Selayana class S starship, interior and exterior details, fan produced, 4 sheets	6.00	8.00
☐ **Imperial Shuttle Blueprints,** L. Miller, Exterior and interior views, fan produced, 3 sheets ...	5.00	7.00
☐ **Star Destroyer,** exteriors, fan produced, 4 sheets	3.00	5.00
☐ **X-Wing Blueprints**	5.00	8.00

BOOKS

	Price Range	
☐ **Art Of The Empire Strikes Back, The,** V. Bullock and V. Hoffman, a celebration of the artistic and technical accomplishment of the famous space epic, oversized softcover, Ballantine, 1981	15.00	20.00
☐ **Art Of Star Wars, The,** C. Titelman, a full script of the original movie illustrated with stills and artist's conceptions, oversized softcover, Ballantine, 1979	15.00	20.00
☐ **Art Of Return Of The Jedi,** a full script of the movie illustrated with storyboards and artists' conceptions, oversized softcover, Ballantine, 1983	18.00	20.00
☐ **Empire Strikes Back, The,** D. Glut, an adaptation of the movie in novel form, following the adventures of Leia, Luke, Han, and Darth Vader, paperback, Ballantine, 1980	2.00	3.00
☐ **Empire Strikes Back, The,** D.F. Glut, an illustrated adaptation of the screenplay, paperback, Del Rey, 1980	5.00	8.00
☐ **Empire Strikes Back, The,** Donald F Glut, hardcover, book club edition, Del Rey, 1980	5.00	10.00
☐ **Empire Strikes Back, The,** Step-up storybook, hardcover, Random House, 1985	4.00	6.00

Price Range

☐ **Empire Strikes Back, The,** Archie Goodwin
and Al Williamson, illustrators, from screenplay
by L. Brackett and L. Kasdan, Marvel Comics
Group, 1980, paperback, 224 pages **5.00**   **7.00**

☐ **Empire Strikes Back,** for British market,
Sphere Publishing, 1980 ....   **5.00**   **10.00**

☐ **Empire Strikes Back,** young readers edition,
for British market, Sphere Publishing, 1980 ..   **5.00**   **10.00**

☐ **Empire Strikes Back, The,** coloring book, features Chewbacca and C-3PO **1.00**   **3.00**

☐ **Empire Strikes Back, The,** coloring book, features Luke Skywalker **1.00**   **3.00**

☐ **Empire Strikes Back, The,** coloring book, features the cast from the movie **1.00**   **3.00**

☐ **Empire Strikes Back,** Kenner, coloring book,
1980, R2-D2 on cover **1.00**   **3.00**

☐ **Empire Strikes Back,** Kenner, coloring book,
1980, Chewie and Leia on cover **1.00**   **3.00**

☐ **Empire Strikes Back,** Kenner, coloring book,
1980, Hans, Chewie, Lando, and Leia on cover   **1.00**   **3.00**

☐ **Empire Strikes Back,** Kenner, coloring book,
1982, Yoda on cover **1.00**   **3.00**

☐ **Empire Strikes Back,** Kenner, coloring book,
1982, Darth Vader and Stormtroopers on cover   **1.00**   **3.00**

☐ **Empire Strikes Back, The,** mix or match story
book, W.D. Barlow, children's puzzle book,
make-your-own story with over 2000 combina-
tions **5.00**   **10.00**

☐ **Empire Strikes Back, The,** pop-up book, Ran-
dom House, 1980 ....   **5.00**   **10.00**

☐ **Empire Strikes Back Notebook, The,** D. At-
tius and L. Smith, contains the complete script
with stage directions and storyboards, soft-
cover, Ballantine, 1980 .... **10.00**   **15.00**

☐ **Empire Strikes Back Panorama Book, The,**
J. Razzi, inside the rebel command, the Dagobah Swamp and the icy planet, Hoth, all in three
dimensions, Random House, 1981 ....   **6.00**   **10.00**

Empire Strikes Back Panorama Book, Random House

	Price Range	
☐ **Empire Strikes Back Portfolio,** 24 prints in a folder, Ralph McQuarrie, Ballantine	10.00	20.00
☐ **Empire Strikes Back Punch Out And Make It Book,** J. Razzi, all the characters and vehicles in the movie, Random House, 1980	5.00	8.00
☐ **Empire Strikes Back Sketch Book, The,** J. Johnston, early artist conceptions of the vehicles, weapons, robots and spaceships, softcover, Ballantine, 1980	8.00	15.00
☐ **Empire Strikes Back Story Book,** the story of the movie illustrated with photos and movie stills, complete pictures of the cast, Lucas film, 1980	5.00	6.00
☐ **Ewoks Join the Fight, The,** Bonnie Bagart, Illustrated by Diane De Groat, softcover, Random House, 1983	2.00	4.00
☐ **Ewoks Save the Day, The,** Kay Carroll, Illustrated by James Woodend, hardcover, Pop-up Book for Children, 1983	2.00	4.00

Price Range

☐ **Force Of Star Wars, The,** Frank Allnutt, compares the Bible and the Force, Bible Voice, 1977, 200 pages **5.00** **10.00**

☐ **425 Questions and Answers About Star Wars and The Empire Strikes Back,** Del Rey, 1982...................................... **4.00** **6.00**

☐ **Guide to the Star Wars Universe, A,** Compiled by Raymond L. Velasco, Ballantine, Del Rey, 1983 .... **3.00** **4.00**

☐ **Han Solo And The Lost Legacy,** Brian Daley, paperback, Del Rey, 1980 .... **6.00** **10.00**

☐ **Han Solo And The Lost Legacy,** Brian Daley, paperback, Ballantine, 1980 .... **2.00** **3.00**

☐ **Han Solo's Rescue,** Kay Carroll, Illustrated by Bryant Eastman, hardcover, Pop-up Book for Children, 1983 .... **3.00** **4.00**

☐ **Han Solo's Revenge,** B. Daley, Solo unknowingly finds himself dealing in slaves, and sentenced to execution, he's rescued and on to more adventures, paperback, Bantam, 1979 **2.00** **3.00**

☐ **Han Solo's Revenge,** B. Daley, Han Solo quits the smuggling game and nothing but trouble comes of it, hardcover, Del Rey Books, 1979 **8.00** **10.00**

☐ **Han Solo At Star's End,** B. Daley, Solo in an adventure about undercover agents and intrigue, paperback, Bantam, 1979 .... **2.00** **3.00**

☐ **Han Solo At Star's End,** B. Daley, Chewbacca is kidnapped and Han can only save himself or his friends, hardcover, Del Rey, 1979 .... **6.00** **10.00**

☐ **How The Ewoks Saved the Trees,** James Woodend, illustrated by Walter Velez, hardcover, Random House, 1984 .... **4.00** **6.00**

☐ **How to Draw Star Wars Heroes, Creatures, Spaceships, and Other Fantastic Things,** Lee J. Ames, A how-to book featuring characters, objects, and scenes from the three films, softcover, Random House, 1984 .... **4.00** **6.00**

	Price Range	
☐ **Jabba's Band,** coloring book	2.00	3.00
☐ **Jedi Master's Quizbook, The,** compiled by Rusty Melter, Del Rey, 1982	2.00	3.00
☐ **Lando Calrissian and the Flamewind of Osceon,** L. Neil Smith, Del Rey, 1983	3.00	4.00
☐ **As above,** hardback, book club edition	5.00	8.00
☐ **Lando Calrissian and the Mindharp of Sharu,** L. Neil Smith, Del Rey, 1983	3.00	4.00
☐ **As above,** hardback, book club edition.	5.00	8.00
☐ **Lando Calrissian and the Starcave of Thonboka,** L. Neil Smith, Del Rey, 1983	3.00	4.00
☐ **Making of Return of the Jedi, The,** John Philip Peecher, Editor, 32 pages of photographs, softcover, Ballantine, 1983	4.00	6.00
☐ **Maverick Moon, The,** Walter Wright, illustrator, Random House, *Star Wars* paperback, 1979	2.00	3.00
☐ **My Jedi Journal,** blank book with small drawings of Yoda, hardcover, Ballantine, 1983 ...	3.00	5.00
☐ **Mystery Of The Rebellious Robot, The,** Mark Corcoran, illustrator, Random House, *Star Wars* paperback, 1979	2.00	3.00
☐ **Once Upon A Galaxy,** Alan Arnold, the making of *The Empire Strikes Back,* softcover, Ballantine, 1980	5.00	8.00
☐ **Probe Droid,** W. Howlett and J. Hazzard, fan produced, satirical look at *Star Wars* and *Empire Strikes Back*	2.00	4.00
☐ **Return Of The Jedi,** James Kahn, Del Rey, 1983	3.00	4.00
☐ **Return of the Jedi,** James Khan, hardback, book club edition	5.00	8.00
☐ **Return Of The Jedi Storybook,** Random House, 1983	6.00	8.00
☐ **Return of the Jedi,** adaptation of *Return of the Jedi* by Elizabeth Levy, a "Step-up Movie AdventureBook," hardcover, Random House, 1983	4.00	6.00

	Price Range	
☐ **Return of the Jedi,** Del Rey, 1983	5.00	7.00
☐ **Return of the Jedi,** British edition, Futura, 1983	5.00	10.00
☐ **Return of the Jedi,** Marvel Comics movie adaptation in novel form, 1983	3.00	5.00
☐ **Return of the Jedi,** Illustrated by John Gambert, engineered by Ib Penick, a pop-up book, adaptation of *Return of the Jedi,* hardcover, Random House, 1983	4.00	6.00
☐ **Return of the Jedi Activity books,** six books of puzzles and games, softcover, Happy House Books, Random House, 1983, each	1.00	2.00
☐ Dot-to-Dot Fun	1.00	2.00
☐ Word Puzzle Book	1.00	2.00
☐ Picture Puzzle Book	1.00	2.00
☐ Things to Do and Make	1.00	2.00
☐ Monster Activity Book	1.00	2.00
☐ Mazes...................................	1.00	2.00
☐ **Return of the Jedi,** Collectors Paradise Press, Compendium, 1983, softcover, 28 pages, 16" x 11"	3.00	5.00
☐ **Return of the Jedi Coloring Books,** three different, Kenner, 1983, each	2.00	3.00
☐ Jabba's Band Coloring Book	2.00	3.00
☐ Lando Calrissian Coloring Book	2.00	3.00
☐ Luke Skywalker Coloring Book	2.00	3.00
☐ **Return of the Jedi Educational Workbooks,** six different, Happy House, 1983, each	1.00	2.00
☐ ABC Readiness	1.00	2.00
☐ Early Numbers	1.00	2.00
☐ Spelling	1.00	2.00
☐ Addition and Subtraction	1.00	2.00
☐ Multiplication	1.00	2.00
☐ Reading and Writing	1.00	2.00
☐ **Return of the Jedi Portfolio,** 20 prints in a folder, Ralph McQuarrie, Ballantine	10.00	20.00

Price Range

☐ **Return of the Jedi,** Paradise Press, Official Collector's Edition, 1983, softcover, 64 pages, the making of the movie 3.00   5.00

☐ **Return of the Jedi Punch-out and Make-it Book,** designed by James Razzi, Illustrated by Daniel Kirk, softcover, Random House, 1983   2.00   5.00

☐ **Return of the Jedi Sketchbook,** Joe Johnston and Nio Radio-Jamero, softcover, Ballantine Books, 1983 ....   5.00   10.00

☐ **Skywalking,** George Lucas's biography, hardback 10.00   20.00

   As above, paperback 2.00   6.00

☐ **Splinter of the Mind's Eye,** Alan Dean Foster, hardcover, book club edition, Del Rey, 1978   5.00   8.00

☐ **Splinter Of The Mind's Eye,** Alan Dean Foster, stranded on an Imperial planet, Luke and Princess Leia search for Kaiburr Crystal, Ballantine, 1978 ....   2.00   3.00

☐ **Star Wars, The Adventures Of Luke Skywalker,** G. Lucas, 16 pages color section, the original story that the saga is based on, Ballantine paperback, 1976.

☐ **First Edition,** no color pages 6.00   10.00

☐ **Later Editions** 2.00   3.00

☐ **Star Wars,** George Lucas, hardback, book club novelization, 1977. ....   6.00   9.00

☐ **Star Wars,** Sphere Publishing, 1977, British Edition 5.00   10.00

☐ **Star Wars Activity Books,** puzzles, games and activities, softcover, Random House, 1979   1.00   3.00

☐ **Artoo Detoo's Activity Book** 1.00   3.00

☐ **Darth Vader's Activity Book** 1.00   3.00

☐ **Luke Skywalker's Activity Book** 1.00   3.00

☐ **Star Wars Album,** Ballantine, official collector's edition, 1977 ....   10.00   15.00

☐ **Star Wars Album,** British collector's edition, softcover, 8½" x 11" 10.00   12.00

	Price Range	
☐ **Star Wars, A Pop-Up Book,** Ib Penick, twelve scenes from the film recreated in cardboard models which pop-up, Random House, 1978	**10.00**	**15.00**
☐ **Star Wars,** R. Thomas and H. Chaykin, the Marvel Comic illustrated version, the story told in comic strip style, paperback, Del Rey	**2.00**	**3.00**
☐ **Star Wars Book About Flight, The,** Caraline Barnes, children's history of flight, softcover, Random House, 1983	**2.00**	**4.00**
☐ **Star Wars Book of Masks, The,** Illustrated by Walter Velez, includes nine masks picturing the faces of *Star Wars* characters to be punched out and worn, softcover, Random House, 1983	**3.00**	**5.00**
☐ **Star Wars: C3PO's Book About Robots,** Joanne Ryder, non-fiction book about robots for children, softcover, Random House, 1983	**2.00**	**4.00**
☐ **Star Wars Intergalactic Passport, The,** Illustrated by Charles R. Bjorkiund, toy passport with seals from planets in the *Star Wars* system, softcover, Ballantine Books, 1983	**1.00**	**3.00**
☐ **Star Wars Iron On Transfer Book,** consists of sixteen color transfers for fabric, Ballantine Books, 1977	**6.00**	**10.00**
☐ **Star Wars Question And Answer Book About Computers,** Fred D'Ignazio, Random House, R2-D2 and C-3PO on softcover, 1983	**4.00**	**6.00**
☐ **Star Wars Question And Answer Book About Space,** Dinah L. Mochi, Scholastic Book Service, R2-D2 and C-3PO on softcover, 1979	**4.00**	**6.00**
☐ **Star Wars Portfolio, The,** Ralph McQuarrie, Production Paintings, Ballantine Books, 1977	**10.00**	**25.00**

Price Range

☐ **Star Wars: Punch-Out And Make-it Book,** Ib Penick, designer, P. Wynne, illustrator, cardboard models you can make of R2-D2, C-3PO, X-Wing fighter and others, Random House, 1978 .... 5.00 8.00

☐ **Star Wars Saga,** Japanese book of photos and information 15.00 20.00

☐ **Star Wars Sketch Book,** Joe Johnston, Ballantine Books, blue cover, silver and white writing and design, 1977 .... 10.00 20.00

☐ **Star Wars, Star Trek And The 21st Century Christians,** Winkie Pratner, Bible Voice, Inc., April, 1984 .... 10.00 12.00

☐ **Star Wars,** Step-Up storybook, hardcover, Random House, 1985 .... 6.00 7.00

☐ **Star Wars Storybook,** G. Richelson, adaptation of movie illustrated with stills and photos, Random House, 1978 .... 6.00 8.00

☐ **Star Wars Word Puzzles,** Linda Quinton, softcover, Random House, 1984 .... 3.00 5.00

☐ **Three Cheers for Kneesaa,** Jane Gerver, Illustrated by Pat Paris, Ewok adventure for young children, softcover, Random House, 1984 ... 2.00 5.00

☐ **Wicket Finds a Way,** Melinda Luke, Illustrated by Pat Paris, Ewok adventure for young children, softcover, Random House, 1984 ...... 2.00 5.00

☐ **Wookiee Storybook, The,** book for young children, detailing the adventures of Chewbacca's son, hardcover, Random House, 1979 ...... 5.00 7.00

☐ **World Of Star Wars,** a compendium of fact and fantasy, 28 color pages, 11″ x 17″ 5.00 7.00

☐ **Yoda's Activity Book,** James Razzi, designer, book of games, puzzles and activities, softcover, Random House, 1981 .... 2.00 4.00

CARDS

TOPPS GUM CARDS

STAR WARS, FIRST SERIES, Blue Borders, Cards 1-66

	Price Range	
☐ Complete set	15.00	25.00
☐ 1 Luke Skywalker	.25	.50
☐ 2 See Threepio And Artoo Detoo	.25	.50
☐ 3 The Little Droid, Artoo Detoo	.25	.50
☐ 4 Space Pirate Han Solo	.25	.50
☐ 5 Princess Leia Organa	.25	.50
☐ 6 Ben (Obi-Wan) Kenobi	.25	.50
☐ 7 The Villainous Darth Vader	.25	.50
☐ 8 Grand Moff Tarkin	.25	.50
☐ 9 Rebels defend their standard	.25	.50
☐ 10 Princess Leia captured	.25	.50
☐ 11 Artoo is imprisoned by the Jawas	.25	.50

Topps Series I Cards

	Price Range	
☐ 12 The Droids are reunited	.25	.50
☐ 13 A sale on Droid	.25	.50
☐ 14 Luke checks out his new Droid	.25	.50
☐ 15 Artoo Detoo is left behind	.25	.50
☐ 16 Jawas of Tatooine	.25	.50
☐ 17 Lord Vader threatens Princess Leia	.25	.50
☐ 18 Artoo Detoo is missing	.25	.50
☐ 19 Searching for the little Droid	.25	.50
☐ 20 Hunted by the Sand People	.25	.50
☐ 21 The Tusken Raiders	.25	.50
☐ 22 Rescued by Ben Kenobi	.25	.50
☐ 23 See Threepio is injured	.25	.50
☐ 24 Stormtroopers seek the Droids	.25	.50
☐ 25 Luke rushed to save his loved ones . . .	.25	.50
☐ 26 A horrified Luke sees his family killed . .	.25	.50
☐ 27 Some repairs for See Threepio	.25	.50
☐ 28 Luke agrees to join Ben Kenobi	.25	.50
☐ 29 Stopped by stormtroopers	.25	.50
☐ 30 Han in the Millennium Falcon	.25	.50
☐ 31 Sighting the Death Star	.25	.50
☐ 32 Lord Vader's Guard	.25	.50
☐ 33 The Droids in the Control Room	.25	.50
☐ 34 See Threepio diverts the guards	.25	.50
☐ 35 Luke and Han as stormtroopers	.25	.50
☐ 36 Blast of the laser rifle	.25	.50
☐ 37 Cornered in the labyrinth	.25	.50
☐ 38 Luke and Han in the refuse room	.25	.50
☐ 39 Steel walls close in our heroes	.25	.50
☐ 40 Droids rescue their master	.25	.50
☐ 41 Facing the deadly chasm	.25	.50
☐ 42 Stormtroopers attack	.25	.50
☐ 43 Luke prepares to swing across the chasm	.25	.50
☐ 44 Han and Chewie shoot it out	.25	.50
☐ 45 The Light Saber	.25	.50
☐ 46 A desperate moment for Ben	.25	.50
☐ 47 Luke prepares for the battle	.25	.50

	Price Range	
☐ 48 Artoo Detoo is loaded aboard	.25	.50
☐ 49 The rebels monitor the raid	.25	.50
☐ 50 Rebel leaders wonder about their fate	.25	.50
☐ 51 See Threepio and Princess Leia	.25	.50
☐ 52 Who will win the final Star War?	.25	.50
☐ 53 Battle in outer space	.25	.50
☐ 54 The victors receive their reward	.25	.50
☐ 55 Han, Chewie and Luke	.25	.50
☐ 56 A day of rejoicing	.25	.50
☐ 57 Mark Hamill as Luke Skywalker	.25	.50
☐ 58 Harrison Ford as Han Solo	.25	.50
☐ 59 Alec Guinness as Ben Kenobi	.25	.50
☐ 60 Peter Cushing as Grand Moff Tarkin ...	.25	.50
☐ 61 Mark Hamill in Control Room	.25	.50
☐ 62 Lord Vader's stormtroopers	.25	.50
☐ 63 May the Force be with you!	.25	.50
☐ 64 Governor of Imperial Outlands	.25	.50
☐ 65 Carrie Fisher and Mark Hamill	.25	.50
☐ 66 Amazing robot See Threepio	.25	.50
☐ Wrapper	.25	.50
☐ Display Box	2.00	3.00

STICKERS, FIRST SERIES, 1-11

☐ Complete set	5.00	10.00
☐ 1 Luke Skywalker	.50	1.00
☐ 2 Princess Leia Organa	.50	1.00
☐ 3 Han Solo	.50	1.00
☐ 4 Chewbacca, the Wookie	.50	1.00
☐ 5 See-Threepio	.50	1.00
☐ 6 Artoo-Detoo	.50	1.00
☐ 7 Lord Darth Vader	.50	1.00
☐ 8 Grand Moff Tarkin	.50	1.00
☐ 9 Ben (Obi-Wan) Kenobi	.50	1.00
☐ 10 Tusken Raider	.50	1.00
☐ 11 X-Wing Fighter	.50	1.00

SECOND SERIES, Red Borders, cards 67-132

	Price Range	
☐ Complete set	15.00	25.00
☐ 67 See Threepio	.25	.50
☐ 68 The Millennium Falcon	.25	.50
☐ 69 Threepio's desert trek!	.25	.50
☐ 70 Special mission for Artoo Detoo!	.25	.50
☐ 71 The incredible See Threepio!	.25	.50
☐ 72 Ben Kenobi rescues Luke!	.25	.50
☐ 73 The Droids wait for Luke	.25	.50
☐ 74 Luke Skywalker on Tatooine	.25	.50
☐ 75 Darth Vader strangles a rebel!	.25	.50
☐ 76 Artoo Detoo on the rebel	.25	.50
☐ 77 Waiting in the Control Room	.25	.50
☐ 78 Droids to the rescue!	.25	.50
☐ 79 Preparing to board Solo's spaceship!	.25	.50
☐ 80 "Where has R2-D2 gone?"	.25	.50
☐ 81 Weapons of the Death Star!	.25	.50
☐ 82 A daring rescue!	.25	.50
☐ 83 Aboard the Millennium Falcon	.25	.50
☐ 84 Rebel pilot prepares for the raid!	.25	.50
☐ 85 Luke on the sand planet	.25	.50
☐ 86 A mighty explosion!	.25	.50
☐ 87 The Droids try to rescue Luke!	.25	.50
☐ 88 Stormtroopers guard Solo's ship	.25	.50
☐ 89 The imprisoned Princess Leia	.25	.50
☐ 90 Honoring the victors!	.25	.50
☐ 91 Solo and Chewie prepare to leave Luke	.25	.50
☐ 92 Advance of the Tusken Raider	.25	.50
☐ 93 Stormtroopers blast the rebels!	.25	.50
☐ 94 Interrogated by stormtroopers!	.25	.50
☐ 95 Sighting Artoo-Detoo!	.25	.50
☐ 96 The Droids on Tatooine	.25	.50
☐ 97 Meeting at the cantina	.25	.50
☐ 98 See Threepio	.25	.50
☐ 99 Ben with the light saber!	.25	.50
☐ 100 Our heroes at the spaceport	.25	.50
☐ 101 The Wookie Chewbacca	.25	.50

	Price Range	
☐ 102 Rebels prepare for the big fight!	.25	.50
☐ 103 Stormtroopers attack our heroes!	.25	.50
☐ 104 Luke's uncle and aunt	.25	.50
☐ 105 Imperial soldiers burn through the star-ship!	.25	.50
☐ 106 A message from Princess Leia!	.25	.50
☐ 107 The Tusken Raider	.25	.50
☐ 108 Princess Leia observes the battle!	.25	.50
☐ 109 Ben turns off the Tractor beam	.25	.50
☐ 110 Threepio fools the guards!	.25	.50
☐ 111 Chewie and Han Solo!	.25	.50
☐ 112 Threatened by Sand People!	.25	.50
☐ 113 Ben hides from Imperial stormtroopers!	.25	.50
☐ 114 Planning to escape!	.25	.50
☐ 115 Hiding in the Millennium Falcon!	.25	.50
☐ 116 Honored for their heroism!	.25	.50
☐ 117 Chewbacca poses as a prisoner!	.25	.50
☐ 118 R2-D2 and C-3PO	.25	.50
☐ 119 Threepio, Ben and Luke!	.25	.50
☐ 120 Luke destroys an Imperial ship!	.25	.50
☐ 121 Han Solo and Chewbacca	.25	.50
☐ 122 The Millennium Falcon speeds through space!	.25	.50
☐ 123 Solo blasts a stormtrooper!	.25	.50
☐ 124 Threepio searches for R2-D2	.25	.50
☐ 125 Luke in disguise!	.25	.50
☐ 126 A quizzical Threepio!	.25	.50
☐ 127 The Rebel Fleet	.25	.50
☐ 128 Roar of the Wookies!	.25	.50
☐ 129 "May The Force be with you!"	.25	.50
☐ 130 Pursued by the Jawas!	.25	.50
☐ 131 Spectacular battle!	.25	.50
☐ 132 Lord Vader and a soldier	.25	.50
☐ Wrapper	.25	.50
☐ Display Box	2.00	3.00

STICKERS, SECOND SERIES, 12-22

	Price Range	
☐ Complete set	6.00	12.00
☐ 12 Han and Chewbacca	.50	1.00
☐ 13 Alec Guinness as Ben	.50	1.00
☐ 14 The Tusken Raider	.50	1.00
☐ 15 See-Threepio	.50	1.00
☐ 16 Chewbacca	.50	1.00
☐ 17 Tusken Raider and Luke on Tatooine	.50	1.00
☐ 18 Hanger deck at Rebel base	.50	1.00
☐ 19 Chewbacca at docking base 94	.50	1.00
☐ 20 R2-D2 and C-3PO	.50	1.00
☐ 21 The Millennium Falcon	.50	1.00
☐ 22 X-Wing and Tie Fighter near The Death Star	.50	1.00

THIRD SERIES, Yellow Borders, cards 133-198

☐ Complete set	12.00	20.00
☐ 133 Ben and Luke help C-3PO to his feet	.25	.50
☐ 134 Luke dreams of being a star pilot	.25	.50
☐ 135 Cantina troubles!	.25	.50
☐ 136 Danger from all sides!	.25	.50
☐ 137 Luke attacked by a strange creature!	.25	.50
☐ 138 On the track of the Droids	.25	.50
☐ 139 Han Salo ... hero or mercenary?	.25	.50
☐ 140 "R2-D2, where are you?"	.25	.50
☐ 141 Some quick thinking by Luke!	.25	.50
☐ 142 Darth Vader inspects the throttled ship	.25	.50
☐ 143 Droids on the sand planet	.25	.50
☐ 144 Harrison on the sand planet	.25	.50
☐ 145 Escape from the Death Star!	.25	.50
☐ 146 Luke Skywalker's aunt preparing dinner	.25	.50
☐ 147 Bargaining with the Jawas!	.25	.50
☐ 148 The fearsome stormtroopers!	.25	.50
☐ 149 The evil Grand Moff Tarkin	.25	.50
☐ 150 Shoot-out at the chasm!	.25	.50
☐ 151 Planning an escape!	.25	.50
☐ 152 Spirited Princess Leia!	.25	.50

	Price Range	
☐ 153 The fantastic Droid Threepio!	.25	.50
☐ 154 Princess Leia comforts Luke!	.25	.50
☐ 155 The Escape Pod is jettisoned!	.25	.50
☐ 156 R2-D2 is lifted aboard!	.25	.50
☐ 157 "Learn about the Force, Luke!"	.25	.50
☐ 158 Rebel victory	.25	.50
☐ 159 Luke Skywalker's home	.25	.50
☐ 160 Destroying a world!	.25	.50
☐ 161 Preparing for the raid!	.25	.50
☐ 162 Han Solo cornered by Greedo!	.25	.50
☐ 163 Caught in the tractor beam!	.25	.50
☐ 164 Tusken Raiders capture Luke!	.25	.50
☐ 165 Escaping from stormtroopers!	.25	.50
☐ 166 A close call for Luke and Princess Leia!	.25	.50
☐ 167 Surrounded by Lord Vader's soldiers!	.25	.50
☐ 168 Hunting the fugitives	.25	.50
☐ 169 Meeting at the Death Star!	.25	.50
☐ 170 Luke and the Princess . . . trapped! ...	.25	.50
☐ 171 "The walls are moving!"	.25	.50
☐ 172 Droids in the Escape Pod	.25	.50
☐ 173 The Stormtroopers	.25	.50
☐ 174 Solo aims for trouble!	.25	.50
☐ 175 A closer look at a "Jawa"	.25	.50
☐ 176 Luke Skywalker's dream	.25	.50
☐ 177 Solo swings into action!	.25	.50
☐ 178 The Star Warriors!	.25	.50
☐ 179 Stormtroopers search the spaceport!	.25	.50
☐ 180 Princess Leia honors the victors	.25	.50
☐ 181 Peter Cushing as Grand Moff Tarkin ..	.25	.50
☐ 182 Deadly blasters!	.25	.50
☐ 183 Dave Prowse as Darth Vader	.25	.50
☐ 184 Luke and his uncle	.25	.50
☐ 185 Luke on Tatooine	.25	.50
☐ 186 The Jawas	.25	.50
☐ 187 Threepio and friend	.25	.50
☐ 188 Starship under fire!	.25	.50
☐ 189 Mark Hamill as Luke	.25	.50

	Price	Range
☐ 190 Carrie Fisher as Princess Leia	.25	.50
☐ 181 Life on the desert world	.25	.50
☐ 192 Liberated Princess!	.25	.50
☐ 193 Luke's uncle buys Threepio!	.25	.50
☐ 194 Stormtrooper attack!	.25	.50
☐ 195 Alec Guinness as Ben Kenobi	.25	.50
☐ 196 Lord Darth Vader	.25	.50
☐ 197 Leia blasts a stormtrooper!	.25	.50
☐ 198 Luke decides to leave Tatooine!	.25	.50
☐ Wrapper	.25	.50
☐ Display Box	2.00	3.00

STICKERS, THIRD SERIES, 23-33

☐ Complete set	6.00	12.00
☐ 23 Darth Vader	.50	1.00
☐ 24 C-3PO and R2-D2	.50	1.00
☐ 25 Escape pod	.50	1.00
☐ 26 C-3PO	.50	1.00
☐ 27 Jawa	.50	1.00
☐ 28 Moff Tarkin	.50	1.00
☐ 29 Han Solo	.50	1.00
☐ 30 Stormtroopers	.50	1.00
☐ 31 Luke and Leia	.50	1.00
☐ 32 Y-Wing and X-Wings	.50	1.00
☐ 33 Han Solo w/blaster	.50	1.00

FOURTH SERIES, Green Borders, cards 199-264

☐ Complete set	10.00	15.00
☐ 199 The Star Warriors aim for action	.25	.50
☐ 200 C-3PO searches for his counterpart ...	.25	.50
☐ 201 Raid at Mos Eisley!	.25	.50
☐ 202 Inquiring about Obi-Wan Kenobi	.25	.50
☐ 203 A Band of Jawas	.25	.50
☐ 204 Stalking the corridors of Death Star ..	.25	.50
☐ 205 Desperate moments for our heroes! ..	.25	.50
☐ 206 Searching for the missing Droid	.25	.50
☐ 207 C-3PO (Anthony Daniels)	.25	.50

	Price Range	
☐ 208 Luke Skywalker on the desert planet	.25	.50
☐ 209 The Rebel Troops	.25	.50
☐ 210 Princess Leia blasts the enemy	.25	.50
☐ 211 A proud moment for Han and Luke ...	.25	.50
☐ 212 A stormtrooper is blasted!	.25	.50
☐ 213 Monitoring the battle	.25	.50
☐ 214 Luke and Leia shortly before the raid	.25	.50
☐ 215 Han bows out of the battle	.25	.50
☐ 216 Han and Leia quarrel about the escape plan	.25	.50
☐ 217 The Dark Lord of the Sith	.25	.50
☐ 218 Luke Skywalker's home—destroyed! ..	.25	.50
☐ 219 The Swing to freedom!	.25	.50
☐ 220 "I'm going to regret this!"	.25	.50
☐ 221 Princess Leia (Carrie Fisher)	.25	.50
☐ 222 "Evacuate? In our moment of triumph?"	.25	.50
☐ 223 Han Solo covers his friends	.25	.50
☐ 224 Luke's secret yen for action!	.25	.50
☐ 225 Aunt Beru Lars (Shelagh Fraser)	.25	.50
☐ 226 Portrait of a Princess	.25	.50
☐ 227 Instructing the Rebel pilots	.25	.50
☐ 228 R2-D2 is inspected by the Jawas	.25	.50
☐ 229 Grand Moff Tarkin (Peter Cushing)	.25	.50
☐ 230 Guarding the Millennium Falcon	.25	.50
☐ 231 Discussing the Death Star's future	.25	.50
☐ 232 The Empire strikes back!	.25	.50
☐ 233 Raiding the Rebel starship	.25	.50
☐ 234 Envisioning the Rebel's destruction ...	.25	.50
☐ 235 Luke Skywalker (Mark Hamill)	.25	.50
☐ 236 Readying the Rebel fleet	.25	.50
☐ 237 The deadly grip of Darth Vadar	.25	.50
☐ 238 Uncle Owen Lars (Phil Brown)	.25	.50
☐ 239 The young star warrior	.25	.50
☐ 240 Artoo's desperate mission!	.25	.50
☐ 241 The Rebel fighter ships	.25	.50
☐ 242 Death Star shootout!	.25	.50
☐ 243 Rebels in the trench!	.25	.50
☐ 244 Waiting at Mos Eisley	.25	.50

	Price	Range
☐ 245 Member of the Evil Empire	.25	.50
☐ 246 Stormtrooper—tool of the Empire	.25	.50
☐ 247 Soldier of evil!	.25	.50
☐ 248 Luke suspects the worst about his family	.25	.50
☐ 249 Ben Kenobi (Alec Guinness)	.25	.50
☐ 250 Luke and Ben on Tatooine	.25	.50
☐ 251 An overjoyed Han Solo!	.25	.50
☐ 252 The honored heroes!	.25	.50
☐ 253 R2-D2 (Kenny Baker)	.25	.50
☐ 254 Darth Vader (David Prowse)	.25	.50
☐ 255 Luke poses with his weapon	.25	.50
☐ 256 The marvelous Droid, See Threepio!	.25	.50
☐ 257 A pair of Jawas	.25	.50
☐ 258 Fighting impossible odds!	.25	.50
☐ 259 Challenging the Evil Empire!	.25	.50
☐ 260 Han Solo (Harrison Ford)	.25	.50
☐ 261 Fury of the Tusken Raider	.25	.50
☐ 262 Creature of Tatooine	.25	.50
☐ 263 The courage of Luke Skywalker	.25	.50
☐ 264 Star pilot Luke Skywalker	.25	.50
☐ Wrapper	.25	.50
☐ Display Box	2.00	3.00

STICKERS, FOURTH SERIES, 34-44

☐ Complete set	6.00	10.00
☐ 34 Han and Chewbacca, in fighting pose	.50	1.00
☐ 35 Han Solo holding gun	.50	1.00
☐ 36 Luke Skywalker in fighting gear	.50	1.00
☐ 37 C-3PO	.50	1.00
☐ 38 R2-D2	.50	1.00
☐ 39 Tusken Raider	.50	1.00
☐ 40 Darth Vader	.50	1.00
☐ 41 Jawas	.50	1.00
☐ 42 Luke Skywalker and gun	.50	1.00
☐ 43 Imperial Stormtrooper	.50	1.00
☐ 44 Princess Leia, by targeting board	.50	1.00

FIFTH SERIES, Orange Borders, cards 265-330 **Price Range**

☐ Complete set	10.00	20.00
☐ 265 Anxious moments for The Rebels	.25	.50
☐ 266 Threepio and Leia monitor the battle	.25	.50
☐ 267 No-nonsense privateer Han Solo!	.25	.50
☐ 268 Ben prepares to turn off the tractor beam	.25	.50
☐ 269 Droids on the run!	.25	.50
☐ 270 Luke Skywalker: farmboy-turned-warrior!....................................	.25	.50
☐ 271 "Do you think they'll melt us down, Artoo?"	.25	.50
☐ 272 Corridors of the Death Star	.25	.50
☐ 273 "This is all your fault, Artoo!"	.25	.50
☐ 274 Droids trick the stormtroopers!	.25	.50
☐ 275 Guarding the Millennium Falcon	.25	.50
☐ 276 It's not wise to upset a Wookie!	.25	.50
☐ 277 Bizarre inhabitants of the cantina!	.25	.50
☐ 278 A narrow escape!	.15	.17
☐ 279 Awaiting the Imperial attack	.25	.50
☐ 280 "Remember Luke, The Force will be with you"	.25	.50
☐ 281 A monstrous thrist!	.25	.50
☐ 282 "Hurry up, Luke—we're gonna have company!"	.25	.50
☐ 283 The Cantina musicians	.25	.50
☐ 284 Distracted by Solo's assault	.25	.50
☐ 285 Spiffed-up for the Awards Ceremony ..	.25	.50
☐ 286 Cantina denizens!	.25	.50
☐ 287 Han and Chewie ready for action!	.25	.50
☐ 288 Blasting the enemy!	.25	.50
☐ 289 The Rebel Fighters take off!	.25	.50
☐ 290 Chewie aims for danger!	.25	.50
☐ 291 Lord Vader senses The Force	.25	.50
☐ 292 The stormtroopers assemble	.25	.50
☐ 293 A friendly chat among alien friends! ..	.25	.50
☐ 294 Droids make their way to the Escape Pod	.25	.50

Price Range

☐ 324 Chewie takes a breather between scenes	.25	.50
☐ 325 The Princess gets the brush!	.25	.50
☐ 326 Animating the "chessboard" creatures	.25	.50
☐ 327 Filming the Sandcrawler	.25	.50
☐ 328 X-Wings positioned for the cameras	.25	.50
☐ 329 Sir Alec Guinness and George Lucas	.25	.50
☐ 330 Filming Luke and Threepio in Tunisia	.25	.50
☐ Wrapper	.25	.50
☐ Display Box	2.00	3.00

STICKERS, FIFTH SERIES, 45-55

☐ Complete set	6.00	10.00
☐ 45 Luke Skywalker, in fighter helmet	.50	1.00
☐ 46 Chewbacca, with cross gun	.50	1.00
☐ 47 Droids, in Death Star control room	.50	1.00
☐ 48 Droids, in Sandcrawler	.50	1.00
☐ 49 Luke, in Millennium Falcon gun turrent	.50	1.00
☐ 50 George Lucas and Greedo	.50	1.00
☐ 51 Anthony Daniels being put in C-3PO costume	.50	1.00
☐ 52 Jawas and Sandcrawler on Tatooine	.50	1.00
☐ 53 George Lucas preparing the Cantina Scene	.50	1.00
☐ 54 Luke and Leia say farewell	.50	1.00
☐ 55 Putting on Chewbacca's mask		

THE EMPIRE STRIKES BACK, FIRST SERIES, TOPPS PHOTO CARDS, cards 1-132

☐ Complete set	15.00	25.00
☐ 2 Luke Skywalker	.25	.50
☐ 3 Princess Leia	.25	.50
☐ 4 Han Solo	.25	.50
☐ 5 Chewbacca	.25	.50
☐ 6 See Threepio	.25	.50
☐ 7 Artoo Detoo	.25	.50
☐ 8 Lando Calrissian	.25	.50

	Price	Range
☐ 9 Yoda	.25	.50
☐ 10 Darth Vader	.25	.50
☐ 11 Boba Fett	.25	.50
☐ 12 The Imperial Probot	.25	.50
☐ 13 Planet of Ice	.25	.50
☐ 14 "Where's Luke?"	.25	.50
☐ 15 Droids on Patrol	.25	.50
☐ 16 The Hidden Rebel Base	.25	.50
☐ 17 New Rebel Strategy	.25	.50
☐ 18 General Rieekan	.25	.50
☐ 19 Leia's Plan	.25	.50
☐ 20 Prey of the Wampa	.25	.50
☐ 21 Examined: Luke's Tauntaun	.25	.50
☐ 22 "But Sir, I Mmh ... Mffh ..."	.25	.50
☐ 23 In Search of Luke	.25	.50
☐ 24 Frozen Death	.25	.50
☐ 25 Skywalker's Rescue	.25	.50
☐ 26 Luke's Fight for Life	.25	.50
☐ 27 Rejuvenation Chamber	.25	.50
☐ 28 Surgeon Droid	.25	.50
☐ 29 Artoo's Icy Vigil	.25	.50
☐ 30 Metal Monster	.25	.50
☐ 31 Zeroing in on Chewie!	.25	.50
☐ 32 Han Aims for Action!	.25	.50
☐ 33 Destroying the Probot	.25	.50
☐ 34 Death of Admiral Ozzel	.25	.50
☐ 35 The Freedom Fighter	.25	.50
☐ 36 Rebel Defenses	.25	.50
☐ 37 Armed Against the Enemy	.25	.50
☐ 38 Joined by Dack	.25	.50
☐ 39 The Sound of Terror	.25	.50
☐ 40 Suddenly ... Starfire!	.25	.50
☐ 41 Rattled by the Enemy	.25	.50
☐ 42 Might of the Imperial Forces	.25	.50
☐ 43 The Snow Walkers	.25	.50
☐ 44 Luke ... Trapped!	.25	.50
☐ 45 Escape from Icy Peril	.25	.50
☐ 46 "Retreat! Retreat!"	.25	.50

	Price Range	
☐ 47 Headquarters in Shambles	.25	.50
☐ 48 Solo's Makeshift Escape	.25	.50
☐ 49 Invaded!	.25	.50
☐ 50 Vader and the Snowtroopers	.25	.50
☐ 51 Snowtroopers of the Empire	.25	.50
☐ 52 Millennium Falcon: Getaway Ship!	.25	.50
☐ 53 Emergency Blast Off!	.25	.50
☐ 54 Battle of the Star Destroyer	.25	.50
☐ 55 Fix-It Man Han Solo!	.25	.50
☐ 56 A Sudden Change of Plan	.25	.50
☐ 57 Misty World of Dagobah	.25	.50
☐ 58 The Creature Called Yoda	.25	.50
☐ 59 "Welcome, Young Luke!"	.25	.50
☐ 60 Journey Through the Swamp	.25	.50
☐ 61 Yoda's House	.25	.50
☐ 62 Artoo Peeking Through	.25	.50
☐ 63 The Secret of Yoda	.25	.50
☐ 64 The Princess Lends a Hand	.25	.50
☐ 65 Repairing Hyperdrive	.25	.50
☐ 66 Star Lovers	.25	.50
☐ 67 "Pardon Me Sir, But ... Ohhh!"	.25	.50
☐ 68 Mysterious and Deadly Chamber	.25	.50
☐ 69 Attacked by Badike Creatures!	.25	.50
☐ 70 "Use the Force, Luke!"	.25	.50
☐ 71 Raising Luke's X-Wing	.25	.50
☐ 72 A Need Beyond Reason	.25	.50
☐ 73 A Gathering of Evils	.25	.50
☐ 74 The Bounty Hunters	.25	.50
☐ 75 IG-88 and Boba Fett	.25	.50
☐ 76 Enter Lando Calrissian	.25	.50
☐ 77 Warm Welcome for an Old Buddy	.25	.50
☐ 78 Comming Pals	.25	.50
☐ 79 "Greetings, Sweet Lady"	.25	.50
☐ 80 Calrissian's Main Man	.25	.50
☐ 81 Pretty as a Princess!	.25	.50
☐ 82 A Swarm of ...?	.25	.50
☐ 83 Threepio. ... Blasted to Bits!	.25	.50
☐ 84 A Pile of See Threepio!	.25	.50

	Price Range	
☐ 85 Escorted by Lando	.25	.50
☐ 86 Dinner Guests	.25	.50
☐ 87 Host of Horror	.25	.50
☐ 88 Deflecting Solo's Blasts	.25	.50
☐ 89 Alas, Poor Threepio!	.25	.50
☐ 90 The Ordeal	.25	.50
☐ 91 The Prize of Boba Fett	.25	.50
☐ 92 His Day of Triumph	.25	.50
☐ 93 The Carbon-Freezing Chamber	.25	.50
☐ 94 End of the Star Warriors?	.25	.50
☐ 95 Pawn of the Evil One	.25	.50
☐ 96 "No! This Can't Be Happening!"	.25	.50
☐ 97 The Fate of Han Solo	.25	.50
☐ 98 Boba's Special Delivery	.25	.50
☐ 99 Observed by Luke	.25	.50
☐ 100 Luke Arrives	.25	.50
☐ 101 Ready for Action!	.25	.50
☐ 102 The Search for Vader	.25	.50
☐ 103 "Where Are You, Skywalker?"	.25	.50
☐ 104 Dark Lord of the Sith	.25	.50
☐ 105 Weapon of Light	.25	.50
☐ 106 The Confrontation	.25	.50
☐ 107 Duel of the Lightsabers	.25	.50
☐ 108 Escape from Their Captors	.25	.50
☐ 109 Lando ... Friend or Foe?	.25	.50
☐ 110 Leia Takes Control!	.25	.50
☐ 111 Blasting the Stormtroopers!	.25	.50
☐ 112 Artoo to the Rescue!	.25	.50
☐ 113 Spectacular Battle!	.25	.50
☐ 114 "Embrace the Dark Side!"	.25	.50
☐ 115 "Hate Me, Luke! Destroy Me!"	.25	.50
☐ 116 Luke's Last Stand	.25	.50
☐ 117 "Do You Have a Foot in My Size?"	.25	.50
☐ 118 Probot	.25	.50
☐ 119 Falcon on Hoth	.25	.50
☐ 120 Snow Walkers	.25	.50
☐ 121 The Pursued	.25	.50
☐ 122 Darth Vader	.25	.50

	Price Range	
☐ 123 Swamps of Dagobah	.25	.50
☐ 124 Cloud City	.25	.50
☐ 125 Lando's Greeting	.25	.50
☐ 126 Threepio's Destruction	.25	.50
☐ 127 Luke Battling Darth	.25	.50
☐ 128 The Final Stand	.25	.50
☐ 129 Rescue	.25	.50
☐ 130 Ion Cannon	.25	.50
☐ 131 Checklist 1–66	.25	.50
☐ 132 Checklist 67–132	.25	.50
☐ Wrapper	.25	.50
☐ Display Box	2.00	3.00

STICKERS, FIRST SERIES, 1-33, Alphabet stickers, 2 letters per card, Yellow background

	Price Range	
☐ Complete set	10.00	20.00
☐ 1 F,O	.50	1.00
☐ 2 R,I	.50	1.00
☐ 3 A,E	.50	1.00
☐ 4 B,X	.50	1.00
☐ 5 U,I	.50	1.00
☐ 6 W,U	.50	1.00
☐ 7 M,N	.50	1.00
☐ 8 C,D	.50	1.00
☐ 9 O,U	.50	1.00
☐ 10 H,E	.50	1.00
☐ 11 F,O	.50	1.00
☐ 12 Y,U	.50	1.00
☐ 13 A,K	.50	1.00
☐ 14 A,V	.50	1.00
☐ 15 E,S	.50	1.00
☐ 16 Q,L	.50	1.00
☐ 17 A,I	.50	1.00
☐ 18 I,O	.50	1.00
☐ 19 Z,T	.50	1.00
☐ 20 G,J	.50	1.00
☐ 21 E,I	.50	1.00

	Price	Range
☐ 22 A,P	.50	1.00
☐ 23 Luke, Darth, Luke in Hoth Gear	.50	1.00
☐ 24 C-3PO	.50	1.00
☐ 25 Luke and Yoda, Luke and Tan-Tan	.50	1.00
☐ 26 Stormtrooper and Bobba Fett	.50	1.00
☐ 27 Yoda and Luke	.50	1.00
☐ 28 Various Aliens	.50	1.00
☐ 29 Luke, Leia, Han and Chewbacca	.50	1.00
☐ 30 Full View of Bobba Fett	.50	1.00
☐ 31 Full View of Stormtrooper and Bounty Hunter	.50	1.00
☐ 32 Lando Calrission, R2-D2 and C-3PO	.50	1.00
☐ 33 Darth Vader	.50	1.00

SECOND SERIES, Blue Borders, cards 133-264

☐ Complete set	10.00	15.00
☐ 133 Introduction	.25	.50
☐ 134 Millennium Falcon	.25	.50
☐ 135 Millennium Falcon	.25	.50
☐ 136 The Executor	.25	.50
☐ 137 Imperial Star Destroyer	.25	.50
☐ 138 Twin-Pod Cloud Car	.25	.50
☐ 139 Slave 1	.25	.50
☐ 140 Rebel Armored Snowspeeder	.25	.50
☐ 141 The Avenger	.25	.50
☐ 142 Tie Fighter	.25	.50
☐ 143 Rebel Transport	.25	.50
☐ 144 Tie Bomber	.25	.50
☐ 145 Preparing for Battle	.25	.50
☐ 146 Seeking the Missing Luke	.25	.50
☐ 147 The Searcher	.25	.50
☐ 148 Star Pilot Luke Skywalker	.25	.50
☐ 149 Luke's Patrol	.25	.50
☐ 150 Shelter on Icy Hoth	.25	.50
☐ 151 Imperial Spy	.25	.50
☐ 152 Tracking the Probot	.25	.50
☐ 153 Han Solo, Rescuer	.25	.50

	Price Range	
☐ 154 Medical Treatment	.25	.50
☐ 155 Worried Droids on Hoth	.25	.50
☐ 156 Imperial Assault!	.25	.50
☐ 157 Narrow Escape!	.25	.50
☐ 158 Fighting Against the Empire	.25	.50
☐ 159 Roar of the Wookie	.25	.50
☐ 160 Chewie's Task	.25	.50
☐ 161 Moments Before the Escape	.25	.50
☐ 162 Last Stages of the Battle	.25	.50
☐ 163 Gallant Warrior	.25	.50
☐ 164 "Raise Those Ships!"	.25	.50
☐ 165 The Awesome One	.25	.50
☐ 166 Vader and His Snowtroopers	.25	.50
☐ 167 Takeover of Rebel Base	.25	.50
☐ 168 The Man Called Han Solo	.25	.50
☐ 169 The Falcon in Repairs	.25	.50
☐ 170 Skills of the Star Pilot	.25	.50
☐ 171 "Sir ... Wait for Me!"	.25	.50
☐ 172 Han's Desperate Plan	.25	.50
☐ 173 An Overworked Wookie?	.25	.50
☐ 174 "Oh, Hello There, Chewbacca!"	.25	.50
☐ 175 Artoo's Bumpy Landing	.25	.50
☐ 176 Mysterious Planet	.25	.50
☐ 177 "Luke ... in Trouble?"	.25	.50
☐ 178 Working Against Time	.25	.50
☐ 179 Han and the Princess	.25	.50
☐ 180 Soldiers of the Empire	.25	.50
☐ 181 The Wookies at Work	.25	.50
☐ 182 Vader and a Bounty Hunter	.25	.50
☐ 183 World of Darkness	.25	.50
☐ 184 Taking no Chances!	.25	.50
☐ 185 Farewell to Yoda and Dagobah	.25	.50
☐ 186 Racing to the Falcon	.25	.50
☐ 187 The Ominous Vader	.25	.50
☐ 188 The Dark Pursuer	.25	.50
☐ 189 Young Senator from Alderan	.25	.50
☐ 190 Don't Fool with Han Solo	.25	.50
☐ 191 Kindred Spirits	.25	.50

	Price Range	
☐ 192 Lobot's Task	.25	.50
☐ 193 A Brave Princess	.25	.50
☐ 194 Corridor of Bespin	.25	.50
☐ 195 Lando's Aide, Lobot	.25	.50
☐ 196 "Get Back Quick ... It's Vader!"	.25	.50
☐ 197 Held by the Stormtroopers	.25	.50
☐ 198 Han's Torment	.25	.50
☐ 199 Lando's Game	.25	.50
☐ 200 Deadly Device	.25	.50
☐ 201 In Vader's Clutches	.25	.50
☐ 202 A Tearful Farewell	.25	.50
☐ 203 Han Faces His Fate	.25	.50
☐ 204 Into the Carbon-Freezing Pit!	.25	.50
☐ 205 An Ugnaught	.25	.50
☐ 206 Tears of a Princess	.25	.50
☐ 207 Suspended in Carbon Freeze	.25	.50
☐ 208 Gruesome Fate!	.25	.50
☐ 209 Evil Threatens!	.25	.50
☐ 210 "This Deal is Getting Worse!"	.25	.50
☐ 211 The Captor, Boba Fett	.25	.50
☐ 212 Fear on Cloud City	.25	.50
☐ 213 A Warrior Driven	.25	.50
☐ 214 Courage of Skywalker	.25	.50
☐ 215 The Pursuer	.25	.50
☐ 216 Stalked by Vader!	.25	.50
☐ 217 A Droid Gone to Pieces	.25	.50
☐ 218 Threepio's Free Ride	.25	.50
☐ 219 Stormtrooper Takeover!	.25	.50
☐ 220 Princess Leia Under Guard!	.25	.50
☐ 221 Bounty Hunter Boba Fett	.25	.50
☐ 222 Lando Covers Their Escape!	.25	.50
☐ 223 Tumbling to an Unknown Fate	.25	.50
☐ 224 On the Verge of Defeat	.25	.50
☐ 225 Gifted Performer	.25	.50
☐ 226 Actress Carrie Fisher	.25	.50
☐ 227 Han Solo (Harrison Ford)	.25	.50
☐ 228 Anthony Daniels as C-3PO	.25	.50
☐ 229 Our Favorite Protocol Droid	.25	.50

	Price Range	
☐ 230 R2-D2 (Kenny Baker)	.25	.50
☐ 231 "Mynocks Outside? Oh My!"	.25	.50
☐ 232 Actor Billy Dee Williams	.25	.50
☐ 233 Galaxy's Most Loyal Droids	.25	.50
☐ 234 Dashing Han Solo	.25	.50
☐ 235 The Force and the Fury	.25	.50
☐ 236 Yoda's Squabble with R2-D2	.25	.50
☐ 237 Blasted by Leia!	.25	.50
☐ 238 The Art of Levitation	.25	.50
☐ 239 Snowswept Chewbacca	.25	.50
☐ 240 Dreamworld . . . or Trap?	.25	.50
☐ 241 Swampland Peril!	.25	.50
☐ 242 "Tried, Have You?"	.25	.50
☐ 243 Encounter on Dagobah	.25	.50
☐ 244 Captain Solo Senses a Trap	.25	.50
☐ 245 A Test for Luke	.25	.50
☐ 246 R2-D2 on the Misty Bog	.25	.50
☐ 247 Confronting the Dark Side	.25	.50
☐ 248 Luke Battles . . . Himself?	.25	.50
☐ 249 Blooming Romance	.25	.50
☐ 250 Chewie Retaliates	.25	.50
☐ 251 Stormtrooper Battle	.25	.50
☐ 252 Director Irvin Kershner	.25	.50
☐ 253 Filming the Falcon	.25	.50
☐ 254 Kershner Directs Mark Hamill	.25	.50
☐ 255 Shooting the Exciting Climax	.25	.50
☐ 256 Filming Vader In His Chamber	.25	.50
☐ 257 Dagobah Comes to Life	.25	.50
☐ 258 Building the Falcon	.25	.50
☐ 259 Hoth Rebel Base Sequence	.25	.50
☐ 260 Filming an Explosion	.25	.50
☐ 261 Spectacular Swampland Set	.25	.50
☐ 262 Acting Can be a Dirty Job!	.25	.50
☐ 263 Checklist 133-198	.25	.50
☐ 264 Checklist 199-264	.25	.50
☐ Wrapper	.25	.50
☐ Display Box	2.00	3.00

STICKERS, SECOND SERIES, 34-66, Alphabet stickers, 2 letters per card, blue background

	Price Range	
☐ Complete set	5.00	10.00
☐ 34 F,O	.50	1.00
☐ 35 R,I	.50	1.00
☐ 36 A,E	.50	1.00
☐ 37 B,X	.50	1.00
☐ 38 U,I	.50	1.00
☐ 39 W,U	.50	1.00
☐ 40 M,N	.50	1.00
☐ 41 C,D	.50	1.00
☐ 42 O,U	.50	1.00
☐ 43 H,E	.50	1.00
☐ 44 E,O	.50	1.00
☐ 45 Y,U	.50	1.00
☐ 46 A,K	.50	1.00
☐ 47 A,V	.50	1.00
☐ 48 E,S	.50	1.00
☐ 49 Q,L	.50	1.00
☐ 50 A,I	.50	1.00
☐ 51 I,O	.50	1.00
☐ 52 Z,T	.50	1.00
☐ 53 G,J	.50	1.00
☐ 54 E,I	.50	1.00
☐ 55 A,P	.50	1.00
☐ 56 Darth Vader in Gold Outline	.50	1.00
☐ 57 Boba Fett	.50	1.00
☐ 58 Probot	.50	1.00
☐ 59 Luke Skywalker	.50	1.00
☐ 60 Princess Leia	.50	1.00
☐ 61 Han Solo	.50	1.00
☐ 62 Lando Calrissian	.50	1.00
☐ 63 Chewbacca	.50	1.00
☐ 64 R2-D2	.50	1.00
☐ 65 C-3PO	.50	1.00
☐ 66 Yoda		

THIRD SERIES, Yellow Borders, cards 266-352

	Price Range	
☐ Complete set	10.00	15.00
☐ 266 Han Solo	.25	.50
☐ 267 Princess Leia	.25	.50
☐ 268 Luke Skywalker	.25	.50
☐ 269 C-3PO	.25	.50
☐ 270 R2-D2	.25	.50
☐ 271 Darth Vader	.25	.50
☐ 272 Boba Fett	.25	.50
☐ 273 Probot	.25	.50
☐ 274 Dengar	.25	.50
☐ 275 Bossk	.25	.50
☐ 276 IG-88	.25	.50
☐ 277 FX-7	.25	.50
☐ 278 Chewbacca	.25	.50
☐ 279 Lando Calrissian	.25	.50
☐ 280 Stormtrooper	.25	.50
☐ 281 Yoda	.25	.50
☐ 282 Imperial Ships Approaching!	.25	.50
☐ 283 The Courageous Trench Fighters!	.25	.50
☐ 284 Too-Onebee	.25	.50
☐ 285 Rebel Protocol Droids	.25	.50
☐ 286 Within the Hidden Base	.25	.50
☐ 287 Calrissian of Bespin	.25	.50
☐ 288 Testing the Carbon-Freezing Process	.25	.50
☐ 289 Flight of the X-Wing	.25	.50
☐ 290 Dodging Deadly Laserblasts!	.25	.50
☐ 291 The Lovers Part	.25	.50
☐ 292 Canyons of Death!	.25	.50
☐ 293 Magnificent Rebel Starship	.25	.50
☐ 294 Old Friends ... or Foes?	.25	.50
☐ 295 Power of the Empire	.25	.50
☐ 296 Threepio in a Jam!	.25	.50
☐ 297 Swamp Plane!	.25	.50
☐ 298 A Hasty Retreat!	.25	.50
☐ 299 Hostile World of Hoth	.25	.50
☐ 300 Descent Into Danger!	.25	.50

	Price Range	
☐ 301 Luke ... Long Overdue!	.25	.50
☐ 302 Toward the Unknown	.25	.50
☐ 303 In Search of Han	.25	.50
☐ 304 Luke's Desperate Decision	.25	.50
☐ 305 Emerging from the Pit	.25	.50
☐ 306 Busy as a Wookie	.25	.50
☐ 307 Portrait of an Ugnaught	.25	.50
☐ 308 The Wizard of Dagobah	.25	.50
☐ 309 Emergency Repairs!	.25	.50
☐ 310 Han on the Icy Wasteland	.25	.50
☐ 311 The Walkers Close In!	.25	.50
☐ 312 Toward Tomorrow	.25	.50
☐ 313 In the Path of Danger!	.25	.50
☐ 314 The X-Wing Cockpit	.25	.50
☐ 315 Hero of the Rebellion	.25	.50
☐ 316 Vader's Private Chamber	.25	.50
☐ 317 Aboard the Executor	.25	.50
☐ 318 The Ominous One	.25	.50
☐ 319 Lord Vader's Orders	.25	.50
☐ 320 "He's Still Alive!"	.25	.50
☐ 321 Lando's Warm Reception	.25	.50
☐ 322 The Landing	.25	.50
☐ 323 Their Last Kiss?	.25	.50
☐ 324 Bounty Hunter IG-88	.25	.50
☐ 325 The Icy Plains of Hoth	.25	.50
☐ 326 Luke Astride His Tauntaun	.25	.50
☐ 327 Rebel Snowspeeders Zero In!	.25	.50
☐ 328 Champions of Freedom	.25	.50
☐ 329 Inside the Falcon	.25	.50
☐ 330 The Training of a Jedi	.25	.50
☐ 331 Yoda's Instruction	.25	.50
☐ 332 The Warrior and the Jedi Master	.25	.50
☐ 333 Imperial Snow Walker Attack!	.25	.50
☐ 334 The Asteroid Chase	.25	.50
☐ 335 Approaching Planet Dagobah	.25	.50
☐ 336 Power Generators	.25	.50
☐ 337 Beauty of Bespin	.25	.50
☐ 338 Dreamlike City	.25	.50

	Price Range	
☐ 339 Luke's Training	.25	.50
☐ 340 Snow Walker Terror	.25	.50
☐ 341 Tauntaun	.25	.50
☐ 342 Cloud City Reactor Shaft	.25	.50
☐ 343 Yoda's Home	.25	.50
☐ 344 Escape from Bespin	.25	.50
☐ 345 Deadly Stompers	.25	.50
☐ 346 Snow Walker Model	.25	.50
☐ 347 Of Helmets and Costumes	.25	.50
☐ 348 Filming the Star Destroyer	.25	.50
☐ 349 Millennium Falcon Miniature	.25	.50
☐ 350 Launching an X-Wing	.25	.50
☐ 351 Model Star Destroyer	.25	.50
☐ 352 Checklist 265-352	.25	.50
☐ Wrapper	.25	.50
☐ Display Box	2.00	3.00

STICKERS, THIRD SERIES, 67-88, Alphabet stickers, 2 letters per card, Green background

☐ Complete set	4.00	8.00
☐ 67 F,O	.50	1.00
☐ 68 R,I	.50	1.00
☐ 69 A,E	.50	1.00
☐ 70 B,X	.50	1.00
☐ 71 U,I	.50	1.00
☐ 72 W,U	.50	1.00
☐ 73 M,N	.50	1.00
☐ 74 C,D	.50	1.00
☐ 75 O,U	.50	1.00
☐ 76 H,E	.50	1.00
☐ 77 E,O	.50	1.00
☐ 78 Y,U	.50	1.00
☐ 79 A,K	.50	1.00
☐ 80 A,V	.50	1.00
☐ 81 E,S	.50	1.00
☐ 82 Q,L	.50	1.00
☐ 83 A,I	.50	1.00

	Price	Range
☐ 84 I,O	.50	1.00
☐ 85 Z,T	.50	1.00
☐ 86 C,J	.50	1.00
☐ 87 E,I	.50	1.00
☐ 88 A,P	.50	1.00

THE RETURN OF THE JEDI, FIRST SERIES, TOPPS PHOTO CARDS, cards 1-132

☐ Complete set	15.00	20.00
☐ 1 Title Card	.25	.50
☐ 2 Luke Skywalker	.25	.50
☐ 3 Darth Vader	.25	.50
☐ 4 Han Solo	.25	.50
☐ 5 Princess Leia Organa	.25	.50
☐ 6 Lando Calrissian	.25	.50
☐ 7 Chewbacca	.25	.50
☐ 8 C-3PO and R2-D2	.25	.50
☐ 9 The New Death Star	.25	.50
☐ 10 The Inspection	.25	.50
☐ 11 Toward The Desert Palace	.25	.50
☐ 12 Bib Fortuna	.25	.50
☐ 13 Court Of Evil	.25	.50
☐ 14 Jabba The Hutt	.25	.50
☐ 15 Intergalactic Gangster	.25	.50
☐ 16 Salacious Crumb	.25	.50
☐ 17 A Message for Jabba The Hutt	.25	.50
☐ 18 Dungeons Of Jabba The Hutt	.25	.50
☐ 19 Beedo And A Jawa	.25	.50
☐ 20 Sy Snootles And The Rebo Band	.25	.50
☐ 21 Droopy McCool	.25	.50
☐ 22 Sy Snootles	.25	.50
☐ 23 Watched By Boba Fett	.25	.50
☐ 24 Boushh's Captive	.25	.50
☐ 25 The Bounty Hunter Boushh	.25	.50
☐ 26 The Villains Confer	.25	.50
☐ 27 Han Solo's Plight	.25	.50
☐ 28 The Rescuer	.25	.50
☐ 29 Decarbonized!	.25	.50

	Price Range	
☐ 30 Princess Leia To The Rescue!	.25	.50
☐ 31 Heroes In Disguise	.25	.50
☐ 32 The Princess Enslaved	.25	.50
☐ 33 Luke Skywalker Arrives	.25	.50
☐ 34 The Young Jedi	.25	.50
☐ 35 The Court in Chaos!	.25	.50
☐ 36 The Rancor Pit	.25	.50
☐ 37 Facing Jabba The Hutt	.25	.50
☐ 38 The Sail Barge And The Desert Skiff ...	.25	.50
☐ 39 Jabba The Hutt's New Dancing Girl	.25	.50
☐ 40 On The Sail Barge	.25	.50
☐ 41 A Monstrous Fate!	.25	.50
☐ 42 The Battle Begins	.25	.50
☐ 43 Lando Calrissian's Fight For Life	.25	.50
☐ 44 Fury Of The Jedi!	.25	.50
☐ 45 Princess Leia Strikes Back!	.25	.50
☐ 46 The Demise Of Jabba The Hutt	.25	.50
☐ 47 Boba Fett's Last Stand	.25	.50
☐ 48 The Rescue	.25	.50
☐ 49 Gamorrean Guard	.25	.50
☐ 50 The Deadly Cannon	.25	.50
☐ 51 The Raging Battle	.25	.50
☐ 52 Princess Leia Swings Into Action!	.25	.50
☐ 53 Swing To Safety	.25	.50
☐ 54 On The Death Star	.25	.50
☐ 55 Guards Of The Emperor	.25	.50
☐ 56 The Deciders	.25	.50
☐ 57 The Emperor	.25	.50
☐ 58 Yoda The Jedi Master	.25	.50
☐ 59 A Word With Ben (Obi-Wan) Kenobi	.25	.50
☐ 60 The Allies Meet	.25	.50
☐ 61 A New Challenge	.25	.50
☐ 62 Pondering The Raid	.25	.50
☐ 63 Mission: Destroy The Death Star!	.25	.50
☐ 64 Mon Mothma	.25	.50
☐ 65 The Friends Depart	.25	.50
☐ 66 Benevolent Creature	.25	.50
☐ 67 The Plan Begins	.25	.50

	Price Range	
□ 68 Forest Of Endor	.25	.50
□ 69 Droids On The Move	.25	.50
□ 70 Blasting A Speeder Bike	.25	.50
□ 71 Approaching The Princess	.25	.50
□ 72 A New Found Friend	.25	.50
□ 73 Princess Leia's Smile	.25	.50
□ 74 Under Attack!	.25	.50
□ 75 Imperial Scout Peril!	.25	.50
□ 76 Entering The Throne Room	.25	.50
□ 77 The Skywalker Factor	.25	.50
□ 78 Captured By The Ewoks	.25	.50
□ 79 The Netted Droid	.25	.50
□ 80 All Hail See-Threepio!	.25	.50
□ 81 Royal Treatment	.25	.50
□ 82 Sitting With Royalty	.25	.50
□ 83 Levitated By Luke	.25	.50
□ 84 The Ewok Leaders	.25	.50
□ 85 Logray and Chief Chirpa	.25	.50
□ 86 Help From Princess Leia	.25	.50
□ 87 Will Han Solo Be Dinner?	.25	.50
□ 88 The Baby Ewok	.25	.50
□ 89 The Forest Creatures	.25	.50
□ 90 The Droid And The Ewok	.25	.50
□ 91 R2-D2 Meets Wicket	.25	.50
□ 92 Unexpected Allies	.25	.50
□ 93 Serious Situation	.25	.50
□ 94 Luke Skywalker's Destiny	.25	.50
□ 95 Quiet, See-Threepio!	.25	.50
□ 96 Imperial Biker Scout	.25	.50
□ 97 Biker Scout And The Battlefield	.25	.50
□ 98 Han Solo's Approach	.25	.50
□ 99 The Ultimate Mission	.25	.50
□ 100 Ready For Action!	.25	.50
□ 101 Ambushed By The Empire	.25	.50
□ 102 Observed By The Ewoks	.25	.50
□ 103 The Courageous Ewoks	.25	.50
□ 104 Prisoners!	.25	.50
□ 105 Revising Their Plan	.25	.50

	Price Range	
☐ 106 AT-ST (All Terrain Scout Transport) ...	.25	.50
☐ 107 The Forest Fighters!	.25	.50
☐ 108 Break For Freedom!	.25	.50
☐ 109 Artoo-Detoo—Hit!	.25	.50
☐ 110 Chewbacca Triumphant!	.25	.50
☐ 111 Ewoks To The Rescue!	.25	.50
☐ 112 Battle In The Forest	.25	.50
☐ 113 Stormtrooper Attack!	.25	.50
☐ 114 The Victorious Rebels	.25	.50
☐ 115 Time Out For Love	.25	.50
☐ 116 Facing The Emperor	.25	.50
☐ 117 Master Of Terror	.25	.50
☐ 118 The Emperor's Offer	.25	.50
☐ 119 Battle Of The Jedi	.25	.50
☐ 120 Lightsaber Battle!	.25	.50
☐ 121 Darth Vader Is Down!	.25	.50
☐ 122 The Confrontation	.25	.50
☐ 123 The Death Star Raid	.25	.50
☐ 124 Military Leader Admiral Ackbar	.25	.50
☐ 125 Within The Death Star	.25	.50
☐ 126 Victory Celebration!	.25	.50
☐ 127 Congratulating Wedge	.25	.50
☐ 128 The Triumphant Trio	.25	.50
☐ 129 The Heroic Droids	.25	.50
☐ 130 Toward Brighter Tomorrows	.25	.50
☐ 131 Checklist I	.25	.50
☐ 132 Checklist II	.25	.50
☐ Wrapper	.25	.50
☐ Display Box	2.00	3.00

STICKERS, FIRST SERIES, 1-33

☐ Complete set	8.00	15.00
☐ 1 Yoda	.50	1.00
☐ 2 Ewok	.50	1.00
☐ 3 Musician from Jabba's Court	.50	1.00
☐ 4 Jabba the Hut	.50	1.00
☐ 5 Alien from Jabba's Court	.50	1.00

	Price Range	
☐ 6 Admiral Ackbar	.50	1.00
☐ 7 Princess Leia dressed as Bounty Hunter	.50	1.00
☐ 8 Han Solo	.50	1.00
☐ 9 Princess Leia	.50	1.00
☐ 10 Luke Skywalker	.50	1.00
☐ 11 Han Solo	.50	1.00
☐ 12 C-3PO	.50	1.00
☐ 13 Chewbacca the Wookie	.50	1.00
☐ 14 Sy Snoddles	.50	1.00
☐ 15 Baby Ewok	.50	1.00
☐ 16 Lando Calrissian's Co-pilot	.50	1.00
☐ 17 Lando Calrissian	.50	1.00
☐ 18 R2-D2	.50	1.00
☐ 19 Obi Wan Kenobi (Ben)	.50	1.00
☐ 20 Luke Skywalker on Jabba's ship	.50	1.00
☐ 21 Luke Skywalker	.50	1.00
☐ 22 Gammorean Guard	.50	1.00
☐ 23 Salacious Crumb (Jabba's Jester)	.50	1.00
☐ 24 Treebo the Ewok	.50	1.00
☐ 25 Boba Fett on Tatooine	.50	1.00
☐ 26 Wicket the Ewok	.50	1.00
☐ 27 Jabba the Hut	.50	1.00
☐ 28 Lando Dressed as One of Jabba's Guard	.50	1.00
☐ 29 Max Rebbo, One of Jabba's Musicians	.50	1.00
☐ 30 Princess Leia Dressed in Forest Attire on Endor	.50	1.00
☐ 31 Princess Leia	.50	1.00
☐ 32 Han Solo	.50	1.00
☐ 33 Stormtrooper on Endor	.50	1.00

SECOND SERIES, cards 133-221

☐ Complete set	12.00	15.00
☐ 133 Title Card	.25	.50
☐ 134 Path To Destiny	.25	.50
☐ 135 Captured!	.25	.50
☐ 136 The Courageous Jedi	.25	.50
☐ 137 The Victors	.25	.50

	Price Range	
☐ 176 Aboard The Sail Barge	.25	.50
☐ 177 Confronting Their Destiny	.25	.50
☐ 178 "Where's Princess Leia?"	.25	.50
☐ 179 Horror From The Pit	.25	.50
☐ 180 "Give In To Your Hate!"	.25	.50
☐ 181 Awaiting His Majesty	.25	.50
☐ 182 A Mother Ewok And Child	.25	.50
☐ 183 A Concerned Princess Leia	.25	.50
☐ 184 Lead Singer Sy Snootles	.25	.50
☐ 185 The Arrival Of Boushh	.25	.50
☐ 186 Master Of His Child	.25	.50
☐ 187 Star Lovers	.25	.50
☐ 188 Luke Skywalker ... Now A Jedi!	.25	.50
☐ 189 Battle Of The Bunker!	.25	.50
☐ 190 Portrait Of Wicket	.25	.50
☐ 191 Trapped By The Empire	.25	.50
☐ 192 Their Secret Revealed	.25	.50
☐ 193 Rethinking The Plan	.25	.50
☐ 194 Snagged By The Ewoks	.25	.50
☐ 195 Han Solo's In Trouble!	.25	.50
☐ 196 Is Han Solo Giving Up?	.25	.50
☐ 197 The Royal Droid	.25	.50
☐ 198 Princess Leia Intercedes	.25	.50
☐ 199 Rescuing Han Solo	.25	.50
☐ 200 Father Versus Son	.25	.50
☐ 201 Luke Skywalker, Jedi Warrior	.25	.50
☐ 202 The Young Jedi Knight	.25	.50
☐ 203 Han Solo Is Alive!	.25	.50
☐ 204 Lando Calrissian Undercover	.25	.50
☐ 205 Horrendous Creature	.25	.50
☐ 206 Corridors Of The Imperial Destroyer!	.25	.50
☐ 207 Surrounded By Ewoks	.25	.50
☐ 208 Gamorrean Guard Profile	.25	.50
☐ 209 Hulking Gamorrean Guard	.25	.50
☐ 210 Guests Of Jabba The Hutt	.25	.50
☐ 211 A Full-Fledged Jedi!	.25	.50
☐ 212 Bizarre Alien Creatures	.25	.50

	Price Range	
☐ 213 Headquarters Frigate	.25	.50
☐ 214 Tie Interceptor (¾ View)	.25	.50
☐ 215 The Nearly Completed Death Star	.25	.50
☐ 216 Rebel Cruiser	.25	.50
☐ 217 Tie Interceptor (Front View)	.25	.50
☐ 218 The Emperor's Shuttle	.25	.50
☐ 219 Portrait Of Chewbacca	.25	.50
☐ 220 Checklist	.25	.50
☐ Wrapper	.25	.50
☐ Display Box	2.00	3.00

STICKERS, SECOND SERIES, 34-55

☐ Complete set	6.00	10.00
☐ 34 Darth Vader	.50	1.00
☐ 35 Luke Skywalker	.50	1.00
☐ 36 Han Solo	.50	1.00
☐ 37 Princess Leia	.50	1.00
☐ 38 C-3PO	.50	1.00
☐ 39 R2-D2	.50	1.00
☐ 40 Wicket the Ewok	.50	1.00
☐ 41 Admiral Ackbar of the Rebel Forces ...	.50	1.00
☐ 42 Chewbacca the Wookie	.50	1.00
☐ 43 The Emperor	.50	1.00
☐ 44 The Millennium Falcon	.50	1.00
☐ 45 R2-D2 and C-3PO at Jabba's Fortress ..	.50	1.00
☐ 46 Han Tied to a Branch on Endor by the Ewoks	.50	1.00
☐ 47 Luke, Leia, Han and Chewbacca on Jabba's Cutter on Tatooine	.50	1.00
☐ 48 Lando Calrissian and His Co-pilot in the Millennium Falcon	.50	1.00
☐ 49 Princess Leia and Jabba the Hut in Jabba's Throne Room	.50	1.00
☐ 50 Luke, Leia, Han, Chewbacca, and the Droids on Endor	.50	1.00
☐ 51 Leia Shushing C-3PO, Chewbacca Laughing in the Background	.50	1.00

	Price Range	
☐ 52 Darth Vader	.50	1.00
☐ 53 R2-D2 and Ewoks on Endor	.50	1.00
☐ 54 Han Solo at Door of Stormtrooper Bunker on Endor	.50	1.00
☐ 55 Salacious Crumb (Jabba's Jester)	.50	1.00

GIANT PHOTO CARDS

	Price Range	
☐ **Topps, Empire Strikes Back,** 5″ x 7″, 1–30, photos on the front with no lettering, cards 1–15 checklist with small photos for first half of set, cards 16–30 checklist for second half of set, sold by the set	15.00	25.00
☐ 1 Darth Vader	.50	1.00
☐ 2 Lando Calrissian	.50	1.00
☐ 3 Chewbacca	.50	1.00
☐ 4 Princess Leia and Han Solo	.50	1.00
☐ 5 Luke Skywalker and Darth Vader	.50	1.00
☐ 6 Darth Vader and Lando Calrissian	.50	1.00
☐ 7 Han Solo and C-3PO	.50	1.00
☐ 8 Luke Skywalker and Yoda	.50	1.00
☐ 9 Inside The Millennium Falcon	.50	1.00
☐ 10 Chewbacca and Princess Leia	.50	1.00
☐ 11 Darth Vader Interviews Bounty Hunters	.50	1.00
☐ 12 Yoda	.50	1.00
☐ 13 Luke Rides His Tauntaun	.50	1.00
☐ 14 Tie fighter and the Millennium Falcon ..	.50	1.00
☐ 15 The Imperial Snow Walkers	.50	1.00
☐ 16 Darth Vader	.50	1.00
☐ 17 Yoda	.50	1.00
☐ 18 Darth Vader's Flagship	.50	1.00
☐ 19 Luke Skywalker Rides his Tauntaun	.50	1.00
☐ 20 X-Wing and Planet Dagobah	.50	1.00
☐ 21 Luke, Princess Leia, C-3PO, and R2-D2	.50	1.00
☐ 22 Snow Speeders Battle the Imperial Snow Walkers	.50	1.00
☐ 23 Darth Vader	.50	1.00
☐ 24 Han Solo	.50	1.00

	Price Range	
☐ 25 Stormtrooper	.50	1.00
☐ 26 Luke Skywalker	.50	1.00
☐ 27 Luke Being Trained by Yoda	.50	1.00
☐ 28 C-3PO and R2-D2	.50	1.00
☐ 29 Yoda	.50	1.00
☐ 30 Luke, Princess Leia, Han Solo and Chewie Prepare to Defend Themselves	.50	1.00

FOREIGN AND PROMOTIONAL

STAR WARS

☐ **Culturama De Centro America, Costa Rica,** small size with collector's album, set of 187	35.00	45.00
☐ **Dixie Cups, United States,** back of box cut-out photos, 5″ x 6″, set of eight	12.00	20.00
☐ **General Mills Cereal, United States,** 1977 Series, one sticker in each box of cereal, set of 16	30.00	50.00
☐ **General Mills Cereal, United States,** 1978 Series, one card per box, set of 18	6.00	12.00
☐ **Kellogg's Star Wars Sticker/Trading (Jedi) Issue,** distributed inside boxes of C-3PO Cereal, 1984. Peel-away sticker on top, trading card underneath. Pictures from Empire Strikes Back and Return of the Jedi. Set of 10	15.00	30.00
☐ **Luke Skywalker,** sticker, Luke with lightsaber card	1.00	2.00
☐ **Han Solo,** sticker, Han, Luke, Leia, Chewbacca, and C-3PO in Imperial Shuttle, card ..	1.00	2.00
☐ **R2-D2,** sticker	1.00	2.00
☐ **C-3PO,** sticker; C-3PO being repaired by R2-D2, card	1.00	2.00
☐ **C-3PO and R2-D2,** sticker; C-3PO with Ewoks, cards	1.00	2.00
☐ **Ewok,** sticker; R2-D2 and Ewoks, card	1.00	2.00
☐ **Yoda,** sticker; Luke and Yoda training, card ..	1.00	2.00

	Price Range	
☐ **Darth Vader,** sticker; Darth with Boba Fett and Lando Calrissian, card	1.00	2.00
☐ **Chewbacca,** sticker; Chewbacca, Boussh and Gamorrean Guard, card	1.00	2.00
☐ **Princess Leia,** sticker; Leia, C-3PO and Chewbacca on Endor, card	1.00	2.00
☐ **Complete set**	5.00	12.00
☐ **Opeechee Chewing Gum, Canada,** same as Topps Series I, II and III, card information in French and Spanish, set of 264	30.00	50.00
☐ **Pacosa Dos International, Spain,** small size with collector's album, set of 187	35.00	45.00
☐ **Panini, Italy,** same size as Topps, with collector's album, set of 256 stickers, 1977	50.00	75.00
☐ **Streets Ice Cream Ltd., Australia,** shaped bottom, cut-outs, set of 12	20.00	35.00
☐ **Tip Top Ice Confections, New Zealand,** one sticker inside each wrapper of R2-D2 ice cream, set of 15	20.00	25.00
☐ **Topps Chewing Gum, England,** same as Series I and II, but with whiter backs, set of 132	20.00	30.00
☐ **Topps Chewing Gum, Mexico,** same as American Series I, except card information is in Spanish, set of 66	20.00	30.00
☐ **Topps Chewing Gum, United States,** Star Wars sugar-free bubble gum, wrapper has picture of different characters, inside wrapper contains a movie photo pin-up, 1978, set of 56	20.00	45.00

EMPIRE STRIKES BACK

☐ **Bibb Linen Co., United States,** side of box cut-outs, 5″ x 5″, set of six	8.00	15.00
☐ **Burger King/Coca-Cola 1980,** *The Empire Strikes Back* and *Star Wars,* Series 1–36 cards, attached by threes with perforations, photo-		

	Price Range	

graphs from the film, red lettering at base, no numbering, distributed to customers 12 years old and younger, 3½" x 2½", set **3.00** **6.00**

☐ **Battle of the Lightsabers** .... **.25** **.50**
☐ **The Bounty Hunters** .... **.25** **.50**
☐ **Cantina Denizens** .... **.25** **.50**
☐ **Captured by the Jawas,** snowswept Chewbacca .... **.25** **.50**
☐ **Chase Through the Asteroids, Space Adventurer Han Solo** .... **.25** **.50**
☐ **The Dark Lord of the Sith** .... **.25** **.50**
☐ **Darth Vader and Boba Fett** .... **.25** **.50**
☐ **The Dashing Han Solo** .... **.25** **.50**
☐ **The Defenders of Freedom** .... **.25** **.50**
☐ **Flight of the Millennium Falcon** .... **.25** **.50**
☐ **Han and Chewie Mean Business** .... **.25** **.50**
☐ **Han Solo in Action** .... **.25** **.50**
☐ **Dixie, United States,** Empire Strikes Back story cards, 4 per box, set of 24, 1981 ...... **10.00** **25.00**

RETURN OF THE JEDI

☐ **Topps,** 180 cards, 1983, Italian Market set .. **15.00** **25.00**

CLOTHING AND ACCESSORIES

	Price Range	

CLOTHING

☐ **Cap,** Imperial Forces with medallion, Thinking Cap Co. **20.00** **25.00**
☐ **Cap,** official rebel forces, beige cap with yellow, red and blue decal with "Star Wars Rebel Forces" caption, The Thinking Cap Co. **15.00** **20.00**
☐ **Cap,** Star Wars fan club **15.00** **20.00**
☐ **Cap,** The Empire Strikes Back, Thinking Cap Co. **10.00** **12.00**
☐ **Cap,** Yoda with ears and patch, Thinking Cap Co. **15.00** **20.00**

Imperial Forces Cap

	Price Range	
☐ **Cap,** Admiral Ackbar, blue with design, Sales Corporation of America, 1983	5.00	8.00
☐ **Cap,** Darth Vader and Emperor's Guards, red and white with design, Sales Corporation of America, 1983	5.00	8.00
☐ **Cap,** Return of the Jedi, black and white with design, Sales Corporation of America, 1983	5.00	8.00
☐ **Fatigue Jacket,** features Luke Skywalker and Bespin Guard	30.00	40.00
☐ **Flight Crew Cap,** Star Wars flight crew, authentic emblem on front, sturdy visor, elasticized headband, one size fits all	5.00	8.00
☐ **Ice Skates,** Wicket and Star Wars logo	15.00	30.00
☐ **Jogging Shorts,** navy blue with red trim, logo from Return of the Jedi, Sales Corporation of America, 1983	5.00	8.00
☐ **Pajamas,** Star Wars, C-3PO, X-Wing, gold . . .	5.00	12.00
☐ **Pajamas,** Star Wars, C-3PO, Darth Vader, R2-D2, blue	5.00	12.00

Price Range

☐ **Pajamas,** May the Force be with You, Darth
Vader, R2-D2, Blue 5.00 12.00
☐ **Pattern,** Empire Strikes Back, Wookie, Leia,
Yoda, Jawa or Darth Vader, McCall's, 1981 6.00 15.00
☐ **Pattern,** #8654, Return of the Jedi shirt pat-
tern, McCall's 4.00 10.00
☐ **Poncho,** Return of the Jedi, children's 5.00 10.00
☐ **Raincoat,** Return of the Jedi, children's 5.00 10.00
☐ **Sandals,** flip flop style with Yoda and captioned
"May The Force Be With You" on sides 7.00 12.00
☐ **Shoelaces,** Stride-Rite, repeat of Star Wars,
light blue, 1983 .... 1.50 2.00
☐ **Slippers,** Darth Vader 8.00 12.00
☐ **Slipper Socks,** Return of the Jedi, C3-PO style,
acrylic and nylon, Stride Rite, 1983 .... 5.00 8.00
☐ **Slipper Socks,** Return of the Jedi, Darth Vader
on the front, acrylic and nylon, Stride Rite, 1983 5.00 8.00
☐ **Sneakers,** Star Wars, assorted colors and de-
signs, cutouts of characters in gores, Stride
Rite 15.00 20.00
☐ **Socks,** boys, Star Wars C-3PO 4.00 6.00
☐ **As above,** "Darth Vader Lives" 4.00 6.00
☐ **As above,** Space battle 4.00 6.00
☐ **As above,** R2-D2 .... 4.00 6.00
☐ **As above,** Chewbacca 4.00 6.00
☐ **Socks,** Star Wars, girl's knee socks 2.00 4.00
☐ **Suspenders,** Empire Strikes Back, with plastic
Darth Vader or Yoda head, for ages 4 through
7, Lee Company, New York 5.00 8.00
☐ **Tee Shirt,** Return of the Jedi, Chewbacca/R2-
D2/C-3PO, photo decal, assorted colors,
Junior Stars, 1983 .... 6.00 10.00
☐ **Tee Shirt,** Return of the Jedi, Han Solo/inset
of Sarlacc and Ewok, photo decal, assorted
colors, Junior Stars, 1983 .... 6.00 10.00
☐ **Tee Shirt,** Return of the Jedi, Luke Sky-
walker/Darth Vader, photo decal, assorted col-
ors, Junior Stars, 1983 .... 6.00 10.00

Price Range

☐ **Tee Shirt,** Return of the Jedi, Luke Sky-
walker/Darth Vader/Emperor, photo decal, as-
sorted colors, Junior Stars, 1983 . . . .   6.00   10.00

☐ **Tee Shirt,** Return of the Jedi, Princess
Leia/inset of Princess Leia and Han Solo,
photo decal, assorted colors, Junior Stars,
1983 . . . .   6.00   10.00

☐ **Tee Shirt,** Return of the Jedi, R2-D2/Wicket,
photo decal, assorted colors, Junior Stars,
1983 . . . .   6.00   10.00

☐ **Tee Shirt,** Return of the Jedi, Wicket the Ewok,
photo decal, assorted colors, Junior Stars,
1983 . . . .   6.00   10.00

☐ **Tee Shirt,** Luke Skywalker against view port in
throne room 6.00   10.00

☐ **Tee Shirt,** official Star Wars shirt, with "Star
Wars" on the front, "May the force be with
you" on the back 15.00   20.00

☐ **Tee Shirt,** Return of the Jedi, features Ewoks   6.00   10.00

☐ **Tee Shirt,** Return of the Jedi, features R2-D2
and Wicket the Ewok 6.00   10.00

☐ **Tee Shirt,** Star Wars, shows Darth Vader and
fighters 6.00   10.00

☐ **Tee Shirt,** Star Wars, sword design 6.00   10.00

☐ **Tee Shirt,** features Luke and C-3PO 6.00   10.00

☐ **Tee Shirt,** shows robots 6.00   10.00

☐ **Tee Shirt,** Star Wars Fan Club with Bantha logo   10.00   15.00

☐ **Tee Shirt and Cap,** available through Hi-C promotional offer until 5/31/84. White with navy
blue trim, cap has illustration of Luke and Darth
Vader, shirt has a montage of characters from
Return of the Jedi. 15.00   20.00

☐ **Underoos,** Boba Fett 6.00   9.00

☐ **Underoos,** C-3PO 6.00   9.00

☐ **Underoos,** Darth Vader 6.00   9.00

☐ **Underoos,** Luke Skywalker 6.00   9.00

☐ **Underoos,** Princess Leia 6.00   9.00

☐ **Underoos,** R2-D2 . . . .   6.00   9.00

	Price Range	
☐ **Underoos,** Yoda	6.00	9.00
☐ **Vest,** similar to the vest worn by Han Solo in the Empire Strikes Back, distributed by Star Wars Fan Club	30.00	40.00

ACCESSORIES

☐ **Backpack,** Return of the Jedi, nylon, red background, Yoda Force design, Adam Joseph Ind., 1983	10.00	20.00
☐ **Barrel Bay,** Return of the Jedi, red background with a Yoda Force design, Adam Joseph Ind., 1983	10.00	20.00
☐ **Belt,** Lee, stretch, metal buckle says "Return Of The Jedi," belt is red and black with "Star Wars/Return Of The Jedi" repeated around it, 1982	2.50	3.50
☐ **Belt,** Return of the Jedi cast, blue	4.00	6.00
☐ **Belt,** Return of the Jedi, brown	4.00	6.00
☐ **Belt,** Star Wars, elastic with "May The Force Be With You" caption, one size fits all	6.00	8.00
☐ **Belt,** Star Wars/Empire Strikes Back, blue ...	4.00	6.00
☐ **Belt,** Star Wars/Empire Strikes Back, brown	4.00	6.00
☐ **Belt,** Star Wars logo, elastic, tan or navy, Lee, 1981	4.00	6.00
☐ **Belt Buckle,** C-3PO & R2-D2, brass, Basic Tool & Supply Co., 1977	8.00	15.00
☐ **Belt Buckle,** Darth Vader, brass, Basic Tool & Supply Co., 1977	8.00	15.00
☐ **Belt Buckle,** Star Wars Logo, brass, Basic Tool & Supply Co., 1977	8.00	15.00
☐ **Belt Buckle,** X-Wing with Star Wars logo, brass, Basic Tool & Supply Co., 1977	8.00	15.00
Billfolds, Return of the Jedi, snap front, plastic, three different designs, Adam Joseph Ind., 1983		
☐ **R2-D2 and C-3PO**	2.00	5.00
☐ **Darth Vader and Emperor's Guards**	2.00	5.00
☐ **Yoda**	2.00	5.00

Price Range

Billfolds, Return of the Jedi, Velcro, plastic, three different designs, Adam Joseph Ind., 1983

☐ **R2-D2 and C-3PO**	3.00	6.00
☐ **Yoda**	3.00	6.00
☐ **Darth Vader**	3.00	6.00

Coin Holders, Return of the Jedi, Velcro, three different designs, Adam Joseph Ind., 1983

☐ **R2-D2**	1.00	3.00
☐ **Yoda**	1.00	3.00
☐ **Darth Vader**	1.00	3.00
☐ **Ditty Bag,** Adam Joseph, R2-D2 and C-3PO on clear vinyl	8.00	15.00
☐ **Duffle Bag,** features R2-D2 and C-3PO on blue bag, Adam Joseph, 1983	10.00	12.00
☐ **Space Commander's Flight Bag,** rugged canvas bag, with famous Hildebrandt Star Wars poster design	10.00	20.00
☐ **Knapsack,** Return of the Jedi, features Darth Vader and Imperial Guards on red bag, Adam Joseph Industries, 1983	8.00	10.00
☐ **Knapsack,** Return of the Jedi, features R2-D2 and C-3PO on blue bag, Adam Joseph Industries, 1983	8.00	10.00

IRON-ON T-SHIRT TRANSFERS

STAR WARS DESIGNS

☐ "Darth Vader Lives" with Vader's Helmet	1.00	2.00
☐ R2-D2 & C-3PO in ship corridor	1.00	2.00
☐ "May the Force be With You"	1.00	2.00
☐ Han Solo & Chewbacca	1.00	2.00
☐ Chewy	1.00	2.00
☐ Droids, blue background	1.00	2.00
☐ Poster Art, Hildebrandt	1.00	2.00
☐ Vader's helmet with ships	1.00	2.00
☐ Jawas	1.00	2.00

	Price Range	
☐ **Darth Vader, full figure**	1.00	2.00
☐ **Star Wars Logo (Glitter)**	1.00	2.00
☐ **"May the Force be with You,"** rainbow glitter, unlicensed, 1977	1.00	2.00
☐ **"Star Wars," rainbow glitter,** unlicensed, 1977	1.00	2.00
☐ **Star Wars Iron-on Transfer Book,** Twentieth Century Fox, a book of decals to personalize T-shirts including Darth Vader, R2-D2 and C-3PO, and Luke Skywalker, 1977	10.00	15.00

EMPIRE STRIKES BACK DESIGNS

☐ **Empire Strikes Back Logo**	1.00	2.00
☐ **Poster Art (Kissing scene)**	1.00	2.00
☐ **Lando Calrissian**	1.00	2.00
☐ **Han Solo**	1.00	2.00
☐ **Star Destroyer**	1.00	2.00
☐ **X-Wing Fighter**	1.00	2.00
☐ **TIE Fighter**	1.00	2.00
☐ **Millennium Falcon**	1.00	2.00
☐ **Boba Fett**	1.00	2.00
☐ **The Way of The Force**	1.00	2.00
☐ **Yoda**	1.00	2.00

   Pocket Pals, Return of the Jedi, Velcro, three different designs, Adam Joseph Industries

☐ **R2-D2**	1.00	3.00
☐ **Darth Vader**	1.00	3.00
☐ **Yoda**	1.00	3.00
☐ **Tote Bag,** Return of the Jedi, red background with drawing of Yoda, "May the Force be with you" pattern behind him, Adam Joseph Industries, 1983	10.00	15.00
☐ **Tote Bag,** Return of the Jedi, blue background, red logo, pictures of C-3PO and R2-D2, Adam Joseph Industries, 1983	10.00	15.00
☐ **Umbrella,** Return of the Jedi, features Darth Vader, Adam Joseph Industries	8.00	10.00

	Price Range	
☐ **Umbrella,** Return of the Jedi, features R2-D2 and C-3PO, Adam Joseph Industries	8.00	10.00

MISCELLANEOUS

☐ **Space Trunks,** scenes from Empire Strikes Back, metal with lids, 2 different, Metal Box Co., 1980	5.00	10.00
☐ **Storage Container,** square, scenes from Empire Strikes Back, Metal Box Co., 1980	5.00	10.00
☐ **Storage Container,** oval, scenes from Empire Strikes Back, Metal Box Co., 1980	5.00	10.00
☐ **String Dispenser,** R2-D2, Sigma	20.00	35.00
☐ **Suncatchers,** makit and bakit, Fundimensions, 1983		
☐ **Gamorrean Guard**	4.00	6.00
☐ **R2-D2**	4.00	6.00
☐ **Darth Vader**	4.00	6.00
☐ **Jabba the Hutt**	4.00	6.00
☐ **Switcheroo, C-3PO,** Kenner, glow-in-the-dark light switch, red eyes glow yellow at night ...	2.00	3.00
☐ **Switcheroo, Darth Vader,** Kenner, glow-in-the-dark snap-on light switch cover, fluorescent pink eyes glow yellow at night	2.00	3.00
☐ **Switcheroo, R2-D2,** Kenner, glow-in-the-dark light switch, blue fluorescent eyes glow yellow at night	2.00	3.00
☐ **Tape Carrier,** Return of the Jedi Take-a-Tape-Along, Disneyland-Vista, photos from film, holds six tapes, 1983	5.00	10.00
☐ **Tape Dispenser,** C-3PO, Sigma	10.00	20.00
☐ **Tape Dispenser,** red plastic, picture of Darth Vader, Return of the Jedi	2.00	4.00
☐ **Telephone,** Darth Vader Speakerphone, produced by ATC (AT&T Branch), 1983, 14", extremely high quality collectible, limited production	100.00	150.00

	Price Range	
☐ **Tissues,** photos on box, cut-out on back, 6 different, Puff's, each	1.00	2.00
☐ **Transistor Radio,** R2-D2, Kenner Corp.	20.00	30.00
☐ **Vase,** Yoda, ceramic, Sigma	15.00	30.00
☐ **Wallpaper,** Return of the Jedi, double roll ...	30.00	35.00
☐ **Wallpaper,** Star Wars, 20th Century Fox, brown and tan, with several scenes of the movie, Han Solo and Leia, Obi with R2-D2 and C-3PO, Jedi warriors and ships, Darth fighting with Obi, portrait of the stars, colorful, detailed graphics, per roll	35.00	40.00

COLLECTOR PLATES

Plates in this Hamilton Collection series are 8¼" diameter and limited to 14 firing days. Artist is Thomas Blackshear.

	Price Range	
☐ **Han Solo,** first plate in series, shows Han seated in Mos Eisley cantina	30.00	35.00
☐ **Luke and Darth Vader,** third plate in series, shows the fight scene in Emperor's chamber from Return of the Jedi	30.00	35.00
☐ **R2-D2 and Wicket,** second plate in series, shows characters and Endor background ...	30.00	35.00

COMIC BOOKS

MARVEL COMICS GROUP, 7/77-PRESENT

	Price Range	
☐ **1** (30 cents edition)	5.00	10.00
☐ **1** (35 cents edition)	10.00	30.00
☐ **2–4**	4.00	8.00
☐ **5–10**	3.00	5.00
☐ **11–16**	2.00	4.00
☐ **17–19**	1.50	3.00

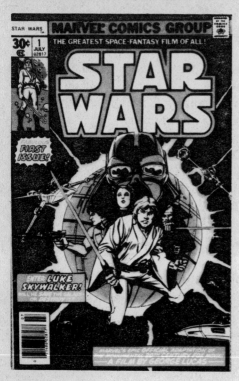

Marvel Star Wars #1

	Price Range	
☐ **20–30**	.90	1.80
☐ **31–37**	.80	1.60
☐ **38,** special edition	1.00	2.00
☐ **39,** Empire Strikes Back	3.00	5.00
☐ **40–44**	1.45	1.90
☐ **45–49**	1.25	1.75
☐ **50** (75 cents edition)	3.00	5.00
☐ **51–55**	.75	1.00
☐ **56–107**	.50	.75
☐ **1,** Star Wars Annual, Marvel Comics, 1979 ...	1.00	2.00
☐ **2, As above,** 1980	1.00	2.00
☐ **3, As above,** 1981	1.00	2.00

MARVEL COMICS, FEBRUARY 8, 1978-PRESENT

Price Range

☐ **1–160** Star Wars Weekly, British edition, still being published, now monthly, each 1.00   2.00

MARVEL ILLUSTRATED BOOKS

☐ **Empire Strikes Back,** Marvel Super Special No. 2, complete story, 11″ x 14″, 1980 . . . . .   2.00   4.00

☐ **Return of the Jedi,** Marvel Comics Group, Volumes 1–4, October 1983 to January 1984, four issue limited series, set 2.00   4.00

☐ **Star Wars,** Four New Adventures in Full Color (Way of the Wookie, The Day After the Death Star, Weapons Master, War on Ice), first edition, November 1981 . . . .   3.00   6.00

☐ **Star Wars 2,** World of Fire, first edition, October 1982. . . . .   2.00   4.00

☐ **Star Wars Treasury 1,** story of Episode IV (part one of two), Marvel Comics Group, includes black and white photos from film on inside front and inside back covers, large size, 11″ x 14″ 1977. . . . .   2.00   4.00

☐ **Star Wars Treasury 2,** story of Episode IV (part two of two), Marvel Comics Group, includes black and white photos from film on inside front and inside back covers, large size, 11″ x 14″, 1977. . . . .   2.00   4.00

☐ **Star Wars Treasury 3,** story of Episode IV complete in one issue, Marvel Comics Group, large size, 11″ x 14″, 1978 . . . .   2.00   4.00

STAR COMICS (JUVENILE DIVISION OF MARVEL)

☐ **Droids,** based on the animated TV series # 1–6   .25   .75

☐ **Ewoks,** based on the animated TV series # 1–12 25   .75

COSMETICS

	Price Range	
☐ **Beauty Bag,** Princess Leia, contains creme rinse, cologne, shampoo, soap and comb, Omni Cosmetics, 1982	10.00	15.00
☐ **Belt Kit,** Luke Skywalker, contains two 2 oz. bottles (shampoo and bubble bath), one bar orange soap with Luke's picture and Star Wars logo, orange comb and toothbrush, Omni Cosmetics, 1982	6.00	10.00
☐ **Bubble Bath,** Chewbacca, Omni Cosmetics, 1981	4.00	6.00
☐ **Bubble Bath,** Darth Vader, Omni Cosmetics, 1981	4.00	6.00
☐ **Bubble Bath,** Jabba the Hut, Omni Cosmetics, 1983	4.00	6.00
☐ **Bubble Bath,** Luke Skywalker, Omni Cosmetics, 1981	4.00	6.00
☐ **Bubble Bath,** Princess Leia, Omni Cosmetics, 1981	4.00	6.00
☐ **Bubble Bath,** R2-D2, Omni Cosmetics, 1981	4.00	6.00
☐ **Bubble Bath,** Star Wars Refueling Station, 8 oz. refill for bubble bath figures, Omni Cosmetics, 1982	6.00	10.00
☐ **Bubble Bath,** Wicket the Ewok, Omni Cosmetics, 1983	4.00	6.00
☐ **Bubble Bath,** Yoda, Omni Cosmetics, 1981 . .	4.00	6.00
☐ **Comb,** Return of the Jedi, pop-up in Darth Vader case, Adam Joseph Industries, 1983 . .	3.00	4.00
☐ **Comb,** Return of the Jedi, pop-up, Princess Leia, Adam Joseph Industries, 1983	3.00	4.00
☐ **Comb,** Return of the Jedi, pop-up, R2-D2, C-3PO, Adam Joseph Industries, 1983	3.00	4.00
☐ **Comb and Keeper,** featuring Max Rebo band, Adam Joseph Industries, 1983	4.00	6.00
☐ **Comb and Keeper,** C-3PO & R2-D2 in landspeeder, Adam Joseph Industries, 1982	4.00	6.00
☐ **Shampoo,** Chewbacca, Omni Cosmetics, 1981	5.00	6.00

	Price Range	
☐ **Shampoo,** Darth Vader, Omni Cosmetics, 1981	5.00	6.00
☐ **Shampoo,** Jabba the Hutt, Omni Cosmetics, 1983	4.00	5.00
☐ **Shampoo,** Luke Skywalker, Omni Cosmetics, 1981	5.00	6.00
☐ **Shampoo,** Princess Leia, Omni Cosmetics, 1981	5.00	6.00
☐ **Shampoo,** R2-D2, Omni Cosmetics, 1981	5.00	6.00
☐ **Shampoo,** Wicket, Omni Cosmetics, 1983	3.00	4.00
☐ **Shampoo,** Yoda, Omni Cosmetics, 1981	5.00	6.00
☐ **Shampoo,** Star Wars refueling station, refill	5.00	6.00
☐ **Soap,** Chewbacca, Omni Cosmetics, 1981, 4oz. bars, came boxed individually and in assortments.	2.00	3.00
☐ **Soap,** C-3PO, Omni Cosmetics, 1981	2.00	3.00
☐ **Soap,** Darth Vader, Omni Cosmetics, 1981	2.00	3.00
☐ **Soap,** Lando Calrissian, Omni Cosmetics, 1981	2.00	3.00
☐ **Soap,** Leia, Omni Cosmetics, 1981	2.00	3.00
☐ **Soap,** Luke, Omni Cosmetics, 1981	2.00	3.00
☐ **Soap,** R2-D2, Omni Cosmetics, 1981	2.00	3.00
☐ **Soap,** Yoda, Omni Cosmetics, 1983	2.00	3.00
☐ **Soap,** Wicket, Omni Cosmetics, 1983	2.00	3.00
☐ **Soap,** Lando, Omni Cosmetics, 1983	2.00	3.00
☐ **Soap,** Gamorrean Guard, Omni Cosmetics, 1983	2.00	3.00
☐ **Soap Dish,** Luke's Sandspeeder, Sigma	20.00	30.00
☐ **Toothbrush,** Kenner, battery operated with power unit and two toothbrushes, painted scenes from Empire Strikes Back on sides, 1980	10.00	15.00
☐ **Toothbrush,** Kenner, battery operated with scenes from the movie and captioned "Star Wars"	12.00	20.00
☐ **Toothbrush,** Kenner, battery operated, Ewok	10.00	20.00
☐ **Toothbrushes,** Oral B, Return Of The Jedi, six different characters: Luke, The Ewoks, Darth Vader, Han Solo, C-3PO and Leia, 1983, each	2.00	4.00
☐ **Toothbrush Holder,** Snowspeeder, Sigma	20.00	30.00

COSTUMES

	Price Range	
☐ **Costume,** Boba Fett, child's, Halloween, with mask, Ben Cooper Co.	5.00	10.00
☐ **Costume,** C-3PO, Halloween, with mask, Ben Cooper	5.00	10.00
☐ **Costume,** Darth Vader, Halloween, with mask, Ben Cooper Co.	5.00	10.00
☐ **Costume,** Klattu, Halloween type, suit reads "Revenge of the Jedi," Ben Cooper, 1983. . .	5.00	10.00
☐ **Costume,** Luke Skywalker, Halloween type, with mask	5.00	10.00
☐ **Costume,** Obi-Wan Kenobi, Halloween type, with mask	5.00	10.00
☐ **Costume,** Princess Leia Organa, Halloween type, with mask	5.00	10.00
☐ **Costume,** R2-D2, Halloween type, with mask	5.00	10.00
☐ **Mask,** Admiral Ackbar, Don Post Studios, 1983	40.00	60.00
☐ **Mask,** Cantina Band member, Don Post Studios, 1978	40.00	60.00
☐ **Mask,** C-3PO, Don Post, soft vinyl helmet, painted gold	40.00	60.00
☐ **Mask,** Chewbacca, by Don Post, soft latex, hand-applied hair	40.00	60.00
☐ **Mask,** Darth Vader, Don Post, rigid helmet, smoked plastic eyes, fits over entire head . . .	40.00	60.00
☐ **Mask,** Emperor, by Don Post	40.00	60.00
☐ **Mask,** Gamorrean Guard, by Don Post	40.00	60.00
☐ **Mask,** Klaatu, by Don Post	40.00	60.00
☐ **Mask,** Stormtrooper, by Don Post, rigid helmet, smoked plastic eyes, fits over entire head, white and black	40.00	60.00
☐ **Mask,** Yoda, Don Post Studios, 1980	40.00	60.00
☐ **Mask,** Weequay, Don Post Studios, 1983	40.00	60.00
☐ **Mask,** Wicket by Don Post, 1983	40.00	60.00
☐ **Mask,** Tusken Raider, Don Post Studios, 1980	40.00	60.00

	Price Range	
☐ **Mask,** Ugnaught, Don Post Studios, 1980	40.00	60.00
☐ **Pattern,** McCalls 7772, Chewbacca, Leia, Yoda, Jawa, Darth Vader, 1981	4.00	6.00
☐ **Pattern,** to make Ewok costume, McCalls, 1983	4.00	6.00

FAN CLUBS

The following is a partial list of fan clubs devoted to *Star Wars.* Most are soliciting new members. Don't forget your SASE when writing for information.

The Alliance For Star Wars Fans
846 Carrol
Akron, OH 44305

The Official Star Wars Fan Club
P.O. Box 2202
San Rafael, CA 94912

The Dave Prowse Fan Club
12 Marshalsea Road
London SE1 4YB England

On The Mark (Mark Hamill)
P.O. Box 5276
Orange, CA 92667

Ford's Fabulous Fans
1335 S. Garret St.
Anaheim, CA 92804

FANZINES

As with *Star Trek* fanzines, several different types of *Star Wars* fanzines exist: Action/Adventure (AA), Mixed Media (MM), and Adult. Lucasfilm was not very happy with the subject matter of some fanzines and has taken an active part in directing fanzine editors *not* to produce Adult *Star Wars* stories. As a result, the vast majority of *Star Wars* fanzines are Action/Adventure. Because of this, Adult *Star Wars* fanzines that do exist sell for much more than comparable *Star Trek* fanzines.

Below are some of the more collectible fanzines. Some are currently available while others are long out of print. The prices listed are for single issues of ORIGINAL issue copies only.

	Price	Range
☐ **Against the Sith,** by N. Duncan (AA)	12.00	15.00
☐ **Alderaan,** by Kzinti Press (AA)	8.00	10.00
☐ **Besbin Times,** by P. Nolan (AA)	8.00	10.00
☐ **Beta Antares,** by Interplanetary Fizbin Society (MM)	8.00	10.00
☐ **Combining Forces,** by K. Gianna (AA)	12.00	15.00
☐ **Crossed Sabres,** by K. Harkins (AA)	15.00	18.00
☐ **Empire Review,** by S. Barrett (AA)	10.00	12.00
☐ **Esper!,** by T'Kuhtian Press (AA)	8.00	10.00
☐ **Facets,** by J. Firmstone (AA)	15.00	18.00
☐ **Far Realms,** by J. Hennig (MM)	15.00	18.00
☐ **Imperial Entanglements,** by K. Osman (AA)	10.00	15.00
☐ **Incident on Ardnor,** by N. White (AA)	15.00	18.00
☐ **Jedi Journal,** by E. Dougherty (AA)	10.00	12.00
☐ **Kessell Run,** by M. Malkin (AA)	15.00	18.00
☐ **Legends of Light,** by S. Voll (AA)	18.00	20.00
☐ **Lighter Side of the Force,** by S. Crites (AA)	8.00	10.00
☐ **Mos Eisley Tribune,** (AA)	15.00	18.00
☐ **Multiverse,** by N. White (AA)	12.00	15.00
☐ **Outland Chronicles,** by C. Jeffords (AA)	12.00	15.00
☐ **Pegasus,** Series by J. Hendricks (AA)	35.00	40.00
☐ **Princess Tapes,** (2) by J. Lowe (AA)	25.00	30.00
☐ **Showcase Special,** by S. Emily	12.00	15.00
☐ **Skywalker,** by B. Deer (AA)	50.00	60.00
☐ **Slaysu,** Series by C. Siebrant (Adult)	20.00	25.00
☐ **Thunderbolt,** by J. Hicks (AA)	10.00	12.00
☐ **Twin Suns,** by J. Hicks (AA)	12.00	15.00

The list below is only partially representative of the short stories, novels, newsletters, commentaries and correspondence circulating around the world of *Star Wars.* If you would like to contact any on this list, please enclose a self-addressed stamped envelope for ordering or submitting information.

Alderaan
Jeff Johnston
Box 8554
Toledo, OH

Bad Karma And Other Fallacies
K. Shepherd Tibbetts
5861 Keeneland Parkway
Dallas, TX 75211

Bantha Tracks
Maureen Garrett
P.O. Box 2202
San Rafael, CA 94912

Bellerophon
Judy Schenkofsky
P.O. Box 1433
Daly City, CA 94014

Bespin Times
Pat Nolan
3284 Hull Ave.
Bronx, NY 10467

Circle of Light
Jumeau Press
2720 Exuma Rd.
West Palm Bch, FL 33406

Collected Circle Of Fire
Pat Nusskan
5851-C Western Run Drive
Baltimore, MD 21209

Comlink
Regina Gottesman
100 West 94th St.
New York, NY 10025

Dark Lord
Lucinda C. Brown
521 S. Frederick Avenue, No. 204
Gaithersburg, MD 20877

Docking Bay
Cyndi Hartman
3702 Fairway Place
Rock Ford, IL 61107

A Galaxy Far Away
Debbie Gitschlag
Box 5137
Greeley, CO 80631

H.A.M.I.L.L.S
Star Wars Appreciation Society of
Australia
Denise Cunningham
P.O. Box 669
Campbelltown, 2560
N S.W. Australia

Hoth Or Bust
Cathi Brown
205 S. Winnebago
Lake Mills, IA 50450

The Jedi Journal
Eileen Dougherty
1414 Stallion Lane
West Chester, PA 19380

Massteria
Meg Garrett
910 W. Rosewood Court
Ontario, CA 91762

Outlands Chronicles
Christine Jeffords
Phanton Press
630 Bloomfield Ave.
Verona, NJ 07044

Phasers And Lightsabers
Eliana B. Cortez
12311 Glynn
Downey, CA 90242

Princess Tapes
Krystarion Press
JA Low
2500 Fontaine Rd.
Greensboro, NC 27407

Skywalker
Bev Clark
744 Belmont Place East, #203
Seattle, WA 98102

Sons And Daughters Of The Force
Debbie Stoy
21 Marion Avenue
Sumter, SC 29150

Southern Nights
Ann Wortham
1402 Allison Ave.
Alt. Springs, FL
32701

Trackless Voids
Shelley Ward
5960 Odessa Avenue
La Mesa, CA 92041

FIGURINES

	Price Range	
☐ **Bantha,** Star Trek Galore Inc., metal, originally made by Heritage, miniature, painted or plain	15.00	20.00
☐ **Bib Fortuna,** by Sigma, handpainted bisque porcelain, 1983	10.00	15.00
☐ **Biker Scout,** by Sigma, handpainted bisque porcelain, 1983	15.00	20.00
☐ **Boba Fett,** by Sigma, handpainted bisque porcelain, 1983	10.00	15.00
☐ **C-3PO,** Star Trek Galore Incorporated, metal (originally made by Heritage), miniature, gold finish or plain	8.00	12.00
☐ **C-3PO and R2-D2,** by Sigma, handpainted bisque porcelain, 1983	10.00	15.00

	Price Range	
☐ **Darth Vader,** by Sigma, handpainted bisque porcelain, 1983	10.00	15.00
☐ **Galactic Emperor,** by Sigma, handpainted bisque porcelain, 1983	10.00	15.00
☐ **Gamorrean Guard,** by Sigma, handpainted bisque porcelain, 1983	10.00	15.00
☐ **Han Solo,** by Sigma, handpainted bisque porcelain, 1983	15.00	20.00
☐ **Han Solo,** Star Trek Galore Inc., metal, painted or plain	5.00	10.00
☐ **Jabba the Hut,** by Sigma, handpainted bisque porcelain, 1983	15.00	20.00
☐ **Jawas,** Star Trek Galore Incorporated, metal (originally made by Heritage), miniature, painted or plain	8.00	12.00
☐ **Klaatu,** by Sigma, handpainted bisque porcelain, 1983	10.00	15.00
☐ **Lando Calrissian,** by Sigma, handpainted bisque porcelain, 1983	10.00	15.00
☐ **Luke Skywalker,** by Sigma, handpainted bisque porcelain, 1983	15.00	20.00
☐ **Luke Skywalker,** Star Trek Galore Incorporated, metal (originally made by Heritage), miniature, silver finish or painted	5.00	10.00
☐ **Obi-Wan Kenobi,** Star Trek Galore Incorporated, metal (originally made by Heritage), miniature, painted or plain	8.00	12.00
☐ **Princess Leia,** Star Trek Galore Incorporated, metal (originally made by Heritage), miniature, painted or plain	8.00	12.00
☐ **Princess Leia Organa,** by Sigma, handpainted bisque porcelain, 1983	10.00	15.00
☐ **R2-D2,** Star Trek Galore Incorporated, metal (originally made by Heritage), miniature, painted or plain	8.00	12.00
☐ **Sand Person,** Star Trek Galore Incorporated, metal (originally made by Heritage), miniature, painted or plain	8.00	12.00

	Price Range	
☐ **Snitch,** Star Trek Galore Incorporated, metal (originally made by Heritage), miniature, painted or plain	8.00	12.00
☐ **Storm Trooper,** Star Trek Galore Incorporated, metal (originally made by Heritage), miniature, painted or plain	8.00	12.00
☐ **Sy Snootles and the Rebo Band,** by Sigma, handpainted bisque porcelain, 1983	15.00	20.00
☐ **Wicket W Warrick,** by Sigma, handpainted bisque porcelain, 1983	10.00	15.00

FILMS AND VIDEO CASSETTES

	Price Range	
☐ **Film,** Star Wars, super 8 mm, Ken Films, 8 min., 1977	15.00	25.00
☐ **Film,** Star Wars, super 8 mm, Ken Films, 17 min., 1977	25.00	30.00
☐ **Film,** Star Wars, super 8 mm, Ken Films, sound, 17 min., 1977	25.00	35.00
☐ **Film,** Empire Strikes Back, super 8 mm, Ken Films, 8 min.	10.00	20.00
☐ **Film,** Empire Strikes Back, super 8 mm, Ken Films, 16 min.	15.00	25.00
☐ **Film,** Empire Strikes Back, super 8 mm, sound, Ken Films, 17 min.	25.00	35.00
☐ **Movie Cassette Color Show,** Star Wars, snaps into Star Wars cassette viewer, four cassettes, Kenner, 1977		
☐ **Destroy Death Star**	8.00	15.00
☐ **Battle in Hyperspace**	8.00	15.00
☐ **Danger at the Cantina**	8.00	15.00
☐ **Assault on Death Star**	8.00	15.00
☐ **Teaser,** Star Wars, released through JEF Films	15.00	30.00
☐ **Teaser,** Empire Strikes Back, JEF Films	10.00	25.00
☐ **Teaser,** Revenge of the Jedi, JEF Films	5.00	15.00

	Price Range	
☐ **Video cassette,** Star Wars, CBS Fox Video . .	25.00	45.00
☐ **Video cassette,** Empire Strikes Back, CBS Fox Video	25.00	45.00
☐ **Video cassette,** Return of the Jedi, CBS Fox Video	25.00	45.00
☐ **Video cassette,** Making of Star Wars, The, plus sp FX: The Empire Strikes Back, CBS Fox Video	25.00	45.00

GAMES

	Price Range	
☐ **Adventures Of R2-D2 Game,** Kenner, color coded game spinner, no counting or reading, colorful game board and four R2-D2's	10.00	15.00
☐ **Battle at Sarlacc's Pit,** Parker Brothers, 1983	5.00	10.00
☐ **Destroy Death Star,** board game and 12 color coded fighters, Kenner Corp.	10.00	20.00
☐ **Electric Battle Command,** Kenner, intergalactic combat game, move and fire X-Wing and Tie fighters, play alone or with up to three opponents	30.00	40.00
☐ **Electronic Laser Battle Game, Race to the Death Star,** Kenner, players fly these X-Wing fighters away from Death Star, lights and sounds, includes AC adapter	50.00	100.00
☐ **Escape From Death Star,** Kenner, a game of strategy, follows movie, in order to win, players must spin their way out of the trash compactor, and fight their way through enemy fighters, two to four players	10.00	20.00
☐ **Hoth Ice Planet Adventure Game,** Kenner, strategic battle with Boba Fett and the stormtroopers, spinner and board	7.00	15.00
☐ **Return of the Jedi,** the play-for-power card games, five games in one, 36 cards, 45 cards, 4 guide cards, Parker Brothers, 1983	2.00	5.00

Price Range

☐ **Star Wars,** the ultimate space adventure game, you must fly your Rebel fighter from Hoth to Dantooine to escape the Empire, Parker Brothers, 1982 . . . .   **7.00   15.00**

☐ **X-Wing Aces Target Game,** Kenner, shooting gallery, Tie fighter image flashes across screen, lights and sounds, electric **75.00 150.00**

☐ **Yoda The Jedi Master Game,** Kenner, based on the planet of Dagobah, win by becoming a Jedi Knight **10.00   15.00**

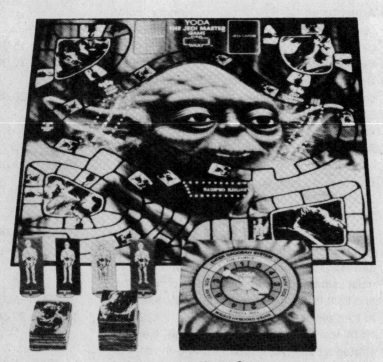

Yoda the Jedi, Master Game

GREETING CARDS

STAR WARS BIRTHDAY AND EVERYDAY CARDS,
Drawing Board, 1977, full-color scenes from *Star Wars* with text on front and inside

	Price Range	
☐ **Darth Vader on cover,** text "Don't Play Games with Me ... WRITE!!!"	2.00	3.00
☐ **Blank cover,** text "Lost Without T You" Obi-Wan Kenobi on cover; text "May the Force Be with You!"	2.00	3.00
☐ **Luke and C-3PO on cover,** text "They Don't Make Them Like You Anymore!"	2.00	3.00
☐ **C-3PO on cover,** text "Sorry I Haven't Written ... But I'm Only Human!"	2.00	3.00
☐ **Millennium Falcon on cover,** text "Greetings from Tatooine!"	2.00	3.00
☐ **Ships battling on cover,** text "Would Have Written Sooner ... But I Just Haven't Had A Minute!"	2.00	3.00
☐ **Chewy on cover,** text "You're Weird ... But Wonderful!"	2.00	3.00
☐ **Darth Vader on cover,** text "Happy Birthday, Earthling!"	2.00	3.00
☐ **Luke in trash compactor on cover,** text "There's No Escaping ... Another Birthday!"	2.00	3.00
☐ **Chewy on cover,** text "Not Feeling Well? May You Soon Have the Strength of a Wookie!"	2.00	3.00
☐ **C-3PO on cover,** text "Feeling Kinda Rusty? How About a Warm Lubrication Bath? Get Well Soon!"	2.00	3.00
☐ **Darth Vader on cover,** text "When I say 'Have a Nice Day, I *mean* Have a Nice Day!"	2.00	3.00
☐ **R2-D2/C-3PO on cover,** text "Have a Happy Birthday ... it's the human thing to do!"	2.00	3.00

Price Range

☐ **R2-D2 on cover,** text "From your faithful Droid;" inside the card "Within me is a message expressly beamed to you from one of your fellow humanoids, Happy Birthday." 2.00 3.00

☐ **Luke on cover,** text "Hold it Right There! ... and have a Happy Birthday!" 2.00 3.00

☐ **R2-D2/C-3PO on cover,** text "29 again? ... It boggles the memory bank! Oh well, Happy Birthday!" 2.00 3.00

STAR WARS BIRTHDAY AND EVERYDAY CARDS,
Drawing Board, 1977, diecut cards with full color artist conceptions of text inside

☐ **Chewbacca on cover,** text "That's Wookie Talk for Happy Birthday!" 2.00 3.00

☐ **Darth Vader on cover,** text "The Empire Commands You to Have a Happy Birthday!" 2.00 3.00

☐ **Ben on cover,** text "Happy Birthday and May the Force Be With You!" 2.00 3.00

☐ **Luke/Leia/Han on cover,** text "Happy Birthday from the Alliance!" 2.00 3.00

☐ **Stormtrooper on cover,** text "Have a Happy Birthday! Darth Vader Wants it that Way!" ... 2.00 3.00

☐ **C-3PO on cover,** text "Happy Birthday from Your Friendly Droid!" 2.00 3.00

☐ **R2-D2 on cover,** text "That's Droid Talk for Happy Birthday!" 2.00 3.00

☐ **R2-D2/C-3PO on cover,** text "Sorry to hear about your malfunction! Hope all systems are functioning soon!" 2.00 3.00

STAR WARS CHRISTMAS CARDS,

Price Range

Drawing Board, 1977, full-color pictures or artwork on the covers, text inside, 6 different

☐ **C-3PO on cover,** text "For an out-of-this-world Grandson . . . from our galaxy to your galaxy, Happy Holidays!"	2.00	3.00
☐ **Chewbacca on cover,** text "Merry Christmas Earthling"	2.00	3.00
☐ **Droids on cover,** text "PEACE and GOODWILL towards all mankind . . . and to their faithful androids!"	2.00	3.00
☐ **Leia/R2-D2 on cover,** text "For an out-of-this-world granddaughter . . . The code is broken and the message is clear—Have a Merry Christmas and a Happy New Year!"	2.00	3.00
☐ **Luke, Han and Chewbacca on cover,** text "From the Alliance . . . Happy Holidays"	2.00	3.00
☐ **Obi-Wan on cover,** text "MERRY CHRISTMAS . . . and may the Force be with you!"	2.00	3.00
☐ **R2-D2 on cover,** text "VREEP ADOOT BLEEP . . . That's Droid talk for Happy Holidays!"	2.00	3.00
☐ **R2-D2/C-3PO on cover,** text "For an Earthling Girl . . . In keeping with the ancient humanoid custom, Christmas kisses to you!"	2.00	3.00
☐ **X-Wings on cover,** text "To an out-of-this-world boy . . . Intergalactic Greetings and May the Force be with you"	2.00	3.00

STAR WARS JUVENILE BIRTHDAY CARDS

☐ **C-3PO on cover,** "You're 12 . . . Hope it's the best day on Earth since you were born!"	2.00	3.00
☐ **Chewbacca on cover,** "Now that you're 7 . . . Wishing you 7 gronks and one to grow on."	2.00	3.00
☐ **Darth Vader on cover,** "I've uncovered information that says you are 11 . . . And I will see to it that it's celebrated throughout the far reaches of the galaxy!"	2.00	3.00

	Price Range	

☐ **Obi-Wan on cover,** "Honored one, now that you are 10 ... May the Force be with you on your birthday and for many years to come." — 2.00 / 3.00

☐ **R2-D2 on cover,** "Earthling, my calculations confirm that you are 9 ... Hope it's your finest day on the planet yet." .... — 2.00 / 3.00

☐ **Stormtrooper on cover,** "You're 8 ... So join the troops and have the best birthday in the universe!" .... — 2.00 / 3.00

STAR WARS HALLOWEEN CARDS, Drawing Board, 1977, full-color pictures or artwork on cover, text inside, 9 different

☐ **Luke on cover,** text "For an out-of-this-world son ... May your deflector shields protect you this Halloween!" .... — 2.00 / 3.00

☐ **Darth on cover,** text "This is my MY kind of holiday! Happy Halloween!" .... — 2.00 / 3.00

☐ **C-3PO on cover,** text "Trick or Treat, Earthling!" .... — 2.00 / 3.00

☐ **Chewy on cover,** text "Do Not Fear ... Your Wookie friend is here!" .... — 2.00 / 3.00

☐ **Leia on cover,** text "For an out-of-this-world daughter ... Intergalactic wishes for a Happy Halloween!" .... — 2.00 / 3.00

☐ **Millennium Falcon on cover,** text "For an Earthling girl ... All Hallows Eve greetings from Tatooine!" .... — 2.00 / 3.00

☐ **Ben on cover,** text "Happy Halloween ... and may the Force be with You!" .... — 2.00 / 3.00

☐ **Han/Luke/Chewy on cover,** text "From the Alliance ... Happy Halloween!" .... — 2.00 / 3.00

☐ **Ships fighting on cover,** text "For an Earthling boy ... Intergalactic greetings for a Happy Halloween!" .... — 2.00 / 3.00

EMPIRE STRIKES BACK GREETING CARDS, Drawing Board, diecut, 1980

Price Range

☐ **Boba Fett on cover,** text "May you get your share of bounty on your birthday!" 1.50 2.00

☐ **Luke on tauntaun,** "Wishing you the happiest birthday in the galaxy!" 1.50 2.00

☐ **Yoda on cover,** text "Happy Birthday . . . and may you live to be 800!" 1.50 2.00

RETURN OF THE JEDI GREETING CARDS, Drawing Board, 1983

☐ **C-3PO/Ewoks on cover,** text "Hope you have a Royal time! Happy Birthday!" 1.50 2.00

☐ **Darth Vader on cover,** "I want *you* to have a happy birthday." 1.50 2.00

☐ **Darth and Imperial Guards,** "May the Force be with you." 1.50 2.00

☐ **Ewoks on cover,** text "Have a Birthday filled with happy surprises!" 1.50 2.00

☐ **Ewoks/R2-D2 on cover,** text "Happy Birthday to a wonderful friend!" 1.50 2.00

☐ **Luke/Leia on speeder bike on cover,** text "It's your Birthday . . . Have a thrilling day!" 1.50 2.00

☐ **Mogaar and Leia on cover,** text "It's so special having a friend like you!" 1.50 2.00

☐ **Rebo Band on cover,** text "Droopy, Sy, Max and I hope your birthday strikes a happy note!" 1.50 2.00

BIRTHDAY CARD GAMES. Fold-out birthday card games, Drawing Board, 1980, 3 different

☐ **Happy Birthday Maze Card,** Leia, Chewy, Han on Cloud City 2.00 3.00

☐ **Birthday Greetings Maze Card,** Darth Vader in asteroid belt 2.00 3.00

☐ **Yoda Birthday Puzzle Card,** Hidden objects in Dagobah swamp 2.00 3.00

HOUSEHOLD WARES

FURNITURE

	Price Range	
☐ **Bookcase,** Return of the Jedi, fiberboard/hardboard, 20″ x 18″ x 41″	15.00	30.00
☐ **Bookcase/Toy Chest,** Return of the Jedi, chalkboard doors with chalk and eraser, shows painted Ewoks, R2-D2 and C-3PO, 32″ x 18″ x 41″	20.00	45.00
☐ **Nightstand,** Return of the Jedi, scalloped front, sides and back show scenes from the film, 20″ x 16½″ x 25″	15.00	30.00
☐ **Table and Chair Set,** child's, Return of the Jedi, two chairs, 25½″ round table, table top features characters from the film, American Toy and Furniture Company, 1983	15.00	30.00
☐ **Waste Basket,** metal, shows characters and scenes from Return of the Jedi, 1983	5.00	15.00

KITCHENWARE

☐ **Bowl,** Star Wars, plastic, cereal, Deka, 1978	5.00	10.00
☐ **Bowl,** Empire Strikes Back, plastic, cereal, Deka, 1980	3.00	8.00
☐ **Bowl,** Empire Strikes Back, plastic, soup, Deka, 1980	3.00	8.00
☐ **Bowl,** Return of The Jedi, plastic, cereal, Deka, 1983	2.00	5.00
☐ **Cake Decorating Kit,** R2-D2, includes pan, Wilton, 1980	10.00	20.00
☐ **Cake Decorating Kit,** Boba Fett, includes pan and candles, Wilton, 1983	10.00	20.00
☐ **Cake Decorating Kit,** Chewbacca, Wilton, 1980	10.00	20.00
☐ **Cake Decorating Kit,** C-3PO, Wilton, 1983 ..	10.00	20.00
☐ **Cake Decorating Kit,** Darth Vader, Wilton, 1980	10.00	20.00

	Price Range	
☐ **Cake Put-Ons,** kit contains C-3PO and R2-D2, Wilton, 1980	4.00	5.00
☐ **Cake Toppers,** set of C-3PO and R2-D2 cake decorations, Wilton, 1983	2.00	3.00
☐ **Cake Toppers,** Set of Darth Vader and Stormtrooper cake decorations, Wilton, 1983	2.00	3.00
☐ **Candy Molds,** Wilton, transparent plastic, detailed shapes of Darth Vader, R2-D2, Chewbacca, C-3PO, Yoda, Stormtrooper, two mold sheets, 8⅛″ x 7¾″	2.00	3.00
☐ **Candy Mold, hard,** white plastic, 7½″ x 8″ sheet mold for making Darth Vader, R2-D2, C-3PO, Chewbacca, Stormtrooper, Ewok and Yoda suckers, Wilton, stock numbers, 1983	2.00	3.00
☐ **Candy Mold,** R2-D2, mold for making large 4″ high R2-D2, Wilton	2.00	3.00
☐ **Cereal Boxes,** C-3PO cereal, 6 different cutout masks, Kelloggs, each	1.00	2.00
☐ **Cookie Box,** The Imperial Forces, chocolate with pictures of Darth Vader, Gamorrean Guard, Jabba the Hutt, Emperor's Royal Guard, 8 oz. box, Pepperidge Farm, 1983 . . .	2.00	3.00
☐ **Cookie Box,** The Rebel Alliance I, vanilla, with pictures of Luke Skywalker, Yoda, Princess Leia, Han Solo, 8 oz. box, Pepperidge Farm, 1983	2.00	3.00
☐ **Cookie Box,** The Rebel Alliance II, peanut butter, with pictures of Chewbacca, R2-D2, Admiral Ackbar, Max Rebo, 8 oz. box, Pepperidge Farm, 1983	2.00	3.00
☐ **Cookie Jar,** C-3PO, handcrafted by Roman, upper body, head and shoulder lift off, gold paint over ceramic	40.00	75.00
☐ **Cookie Jar,** Roman Ceramics Corp., R2-D2, ceramic, blue and white	40.00	75.00
☐ **Cookie Jar,** Darth Vader, ceramic, blue and white, Sigma	50.00	75.00

Cookie Jar, C-3PO, Roman Ceramics

	Price Range	
☐ **Decanter,** Star Wars, plastic, Deka, 1978	10.00	20.00
☐ **Decanter,** Empire Strikes Back, plastic, Deka, 1980	8.00	15.00
☐ **Decanter,** Return of the Jedi, plastic, 1983 ..	5.00	10.00
☐ **Glasses,** E. S. B., Burger King/Coca-Cola, set of four with pictures on the front and description on the back: Luke Skywalker, Lando Calrissian, Darth Vader, R2-D2 and C-3PO, height 6″, 1977, set	20.00	35.00
☐ **Glasses,** Burger King/Coca-Cola, set of four drinking glasses of scenes from the movie: Luke Skywalker, Han Solo, Darth Vader, R2-D2 and C-3PO (Burger King also issued matching posters), height 5¾″, 1977	30.00	45.00

Price Range

☐ **Glasses,** Burger King/Coca-Cola, set of four, Han Solo in Sand Barge fight scene, the court of Jabba the Hutt, Ewok Village and Return of the Jedi logo, 1983 . . . . **15.00** **25.00**

☐ **Glasses,** set of three, made for European market **20.00** **30.00**

☐ **Lunchbox,** Thermos, Star Wars, metal, painted pictures of characters and scenes, including panel of the entry into Mos Eisley, plastic thermos pictures R2-D2 and C-3PO, 1977. . . . . **15.00** **25.00**

☐ **Lunchbox,** Star Wars, Thermos, metal, X-Wing and Tie fighter, plastic thermos, 1977 . . . . **15.00** **25.00**

☐ **Lunchbox,** Star Wars, plastic thermos, Darth Vader, C-3PO, R2-D2, 1977 . . . . **15.00** **25.00**

☐ **Lunchbox,** Star Wars, plastic thermos, came with decals, 1977 . . . . **10.00** **20.00**

☐ **Lunchbox,** Thermos, metal, The Empire Strikes Back, 1980 . . . . **8.00** **15.00**

☐ **Lunchbox,** Empire Strikes Back, Thermos, plastic, space scene, 1981 . . . . **5.00** **12.00**

☐ **Lunchbox,** Empire Strikes Back, Thermos, metal, Han, Leia, Chewbacca, and C3-PO, 1981 . . . . **8.00** **15.00**

☐ **Lunchbox,** Empire Strikes Back, Thermos, metal, Luke and R2-D2, 1981 . . . . **8.00** **15.00**

Glasses, Coca-Cola, Burger King, SW, set of four

Price Range

☐ **Lunchbox,** Thermos, Empire Strikes Back, plastic, red with photographs of Luke, Leia, Han and Chewbacca on Hoth, thermos has a photograph of Yoda, 1980	5.00	12.00
☐ **Lunchbox,** Return of the Jedi, thermos, metal, characters and scenes, 1983	5.00	10.00
☐ **Lunchbox,** Thermos, Return of the Jedi, plastic, red with side panel of Wicket and R2-D2, cartoon style, thermos features Wicket, 1983	4.00	8.00
☐ **Mug,** Ben (Obi-Wan) Kenobi, California Originals, ceramic, head only, brown	25.00	50.00
☐ **Mug,** Chewbacca, California Originals, ceramic, head only, brown	25.00	50.00
☐ **Mug,** Darth Vader, ceramic, head only, California Originals	25.00	50.00
☐ **Mug,** Star Wars, plastic, Deka, 1978	5.00	8.00
Mugs, Empire Strikes Back, four designs, 10 oz., Deka Plastics, 1980		
☐ Luke, Leia and Han	2.00	5.00
☐ Darth Vader and Boba Fett	2.00	5.00
☐ R2-D2, Chewbacca and C-3PO	2.00	5.00
☐ Yoda	2.00	5.00
☐ **Mug,** Return of the Jedi, 2 different scenes, plastic, 1983	2.00	5.00
☐ **Mugs,** white with four different scenes painted on the side in color from the triology, Sigma, 1983		
☐ R2 and 3PO in control room	7.00	15.00
☐ Leia (in Empire snow outfit) captured by stormtroopers and Darth Vader	7.00	15.00
☐ Luke and X-Wing in bog on Dagobah, with Yoda	7.00	15.00
☐ Chewbacca and Boba Fett on Cloud City . . .	7.00	15.00
Mugs, Empire Strikes Back, stoneware, set of 4, Sigma, 1981		
☐ Chewbacca	5.00	10.00
☐ C-3PO	5.00	10.00
☐ Darth Vader	5.00	10.00
☐ Yoda	5.00	10.00

	Price Range	
Mugs, ceramic character mugs, Sigma, R.O.J.		
☐ Han	8.00	15.00
☐ Luke	8.00	15.00
☐ Leia	8.00	15.00
☐ Darth Vader	8.00	15.00
☐ C-3PO	8.00	15.00
☐ R2-D2	8.00	15.00
☐ Yoda	8.00	15.00
☐ Chewbacca	8.00	15.00
☐ Klaato	8.00	15.00
☐ Gamorrean Guard	8.00	15.00
☐ Lando	8.00	15.00
☐ Wicket	8.00	15.00
☐ **Placemats,** Empire Strikes Back, plastic, set of four, AT-AT, Luke and Vader, ship and Yoda. Dixie	5.00	10.00
☐ **Placemats,** vinyl, features different scenes from Return of the Jedi, set of four, 11″ x 17″, Darth Vader and Princess Leia, Luke Skywalker and Yoda, R2-D2 and C-3PO, Chewbacca and Boba Fett, per set	16.00	20.00
☐ **Place Setting,** mug, bowl, plate, ceramic, scenes from Star Wars, Sigma, 1978	45.00	75.00
☐ **Place Setting,** mug, bowl and plate, shows Ewoks, Deka, per set, 1983	8.00	15.00
☐ **Place Setting,** mug, bowl and plate in box, ceramic, Sigma	30.00	50.00
☐ **Plate,** Star Wars, plastic, Deka, 1978	5.00	8.00
☐ **Plate,** Return of the Jedi, plastic, 1980	2.00	5.00
☐ **Salt and Pepper Shaker Sets,** Yoda or R2-D2, Sigma	20.00	35.00
☐ **Soup Bowl,** Return of the Jedi, plastic bowl, 14 oz., Deka, 1983	2.00	5.00
☐ **Teapot,** Luke and Tauntaun, Sigma	65.00	100.00
☐ **Tin,** Return of the Jedi, Chein Industries, C-3PO/R2-D2 on lid, circular, 3½″ x 1″	1.00	3.00

	Price Range	
☐ **Same as above,** 3½" x 3½"	2.00	5.00
☐ **Tin,** Return of the Jedi, Chein Industries, Darth Vader on lid, circular, 3½" x 1"	1.00	3.00
☐ **Same as above,** 3½" x 3½"	2.00	5.00
☐ **Tin,** Return of the Jedi, Chein Industries, Ewoks on lid, circular, 3½" x 1"	1.00	3.00
☐ **Same as above,** 3½" x 3½"	2.00	5.00
☐ **Tin,** Return of the Jedi, Chein Industries, Jabba the Hutt on lid, circular, 3½" x 1"	1.00	3.00
☐ **Same as above,** 3½" x 3½"	2.00	5.00
☐ **Tin,** Return of the Jedi, Chein Industries, Luke Skywalker/Han Solo/Princess Lei/Yoda on lid, circular, 3½" x 1"	1.00	3.00
☐ **Same as above,** 3½" x 3½"	2.00	5.00
☐ **Tin,** Return of the Jedi, Chein Industries, photo montage on lid, circular, 3" x 5"	3.00	8.00
☐ **Same as above,** 3½" x 3½"	2.00	5.00
☐ **Tin,** Return of the Jedi, Chein Industries, The Rebo Band on lid, circular, 3½" x 1"	1.00	3.00
☐ **Tote Tin,** Return of the Jedi, Chein Industries, montage photo, has lid and handles, 4½" x 5½" x 4"	5.00	12.00
☐ **Tray,** Return of the Jedi, Chein Industries, tin, montage photo, 12" x 14½"	5.00	15.00
Tumblers, Star Wars, plastic, Deka, 1978		
☐ 6 oz......................................	2.00	5.00
☐ 11 oz	2.00	5.00
☐ 17 oz	2.00	5.00
☐ **Tumblers,** Empire Strikes Back, plastic, Deka, 1980, same size as above	1.00	3.00
☐ **Tumblers,** Return of the Jedi, plastic, Deka, 1983, same size as above	1.00	3.00
☐ **Tumblers,** Pepperidge Farm, free with purchase of Star Wars cookies, plastic, four different pictures	1.00	2.00

LINENS

Price Range

☐ **Beach Towel,** Yoda	8.00	10.00
☐ **Beach Towel,** two different towels with scenes from Return of the Jedi, Bibb Co., 1983	5.00	8.00
☐ **Bed Sheet,** Return of the Jedi	12.00	15.00
☐ **Bedspread,** Empire Strikes Back, shows Lord Vader's Chamber, 63″ x 108″, Bibb, 1980 ...	20.00	30.00
☐ **Bedspread,** Empire Strikes Back, pictures assorted characters from the movie, 80″ x 108″	30.00	35.00
☐ **Bedspread,** same as above, 94″ x 108″	35.00	40.00
☐ **Bedspread,** Return of the Jedi, cast, twin size	15.00	25.00
☐ **Bedspread,** Star Wars, pictures Princess Leia and Luke Skywalker, twin size	30.00	35.00
☐ **Blanket,** features Star Wars movie characters	30.00	35.00
☐ **Blanket,** features scenes and characters from Return of the Jedi	15.00	20.00
☐ **Drapes,** Star Wars movie characters for children's bedroom	20.00	25.00
☐ **Hand Towel,** features the Empire Strikes Back movie characters	4.00	6.00
☐ **Pillow,** Return of the Jedi, die-cut, Darth Vader, Adam Joseph Industries, 1983	5.00	15.00
☐ **Pillow,** Return of the Jedi, die-cut, R2-D2, Adam Joseph Industries, 1983	5.00	15.00
☐ **Pillow Case,** Return of the Jedi	5.00	10.00
☐ **Pillow Case,** Star Wars movie characters	10.00	20.00
☐ **Pillow Case,** The Empire Strikes Back movie characters	8.00	15.00
☐ **Sheet Set,** Empire Strikes Back, comes with pillow cases, Black Falcon, Ltd	25.00	30.00
☐ **Sheet Set,** Return of the Jedi, white background, characters in color, twin set, Marimekko, 1983	15.00	30.00
☐ **Slumber Bag,** Empire Strikes Back, features characters from the movie, Marimekko, 1983	25.00	30.00
☐ **Slumber Bag,** features Princess Leia and Luke Skywalker, Marimekko, 1983	30.00	35.00

	Price Range	
☐ **Slumber Bag,** Return of the Jedi featuring Darth Vader, Bibb Co.,1983	20.00	25.00
☐ **Towel,** Star Wars imprinted in red, also shown with their names imprinted are Darth Vader, C-3PO and R2-D2, 1977	15.00	25.00
☐ **Towel Set,** Empire Strikes Back, includes Yoda washcloth, Darth and Fett hand towel, bath towel and beach towel with characters, Cannon, 1979–80	20.00	35.00
☐ **Washcloth,** R2-D2, 1977	5.00	10.00

LATCH HOOK RUGS, available through Lee Wards

☐ **C-3PO and R2-D2**	10.00	20.00
☐ **R2-D2**	10.00	20.00
☐ **Darth Vader**	10.00	20.00
☐ **Chewbacca**	10.00	20.00
☐ **Yoda**	10.00	20.00
☐ **Stormtrooper**	10.00	20.00

MACRO TINS, METAL BOX CO., 1980

☐ **Chewbacca**	2.00	5.00
☐ **Darth**	2.00	5.00
☐ **Han**	2.00	5.00
☐ **Imperial cruiser**	2.00	5.00
☐ **Leia**	2.00	5.00
☐ **Luke**	2.00	5.00
☐ **Probot**	2.00	5.00
☐ **Yoda**	2.00	5.00
☐ **Magnets,** set, four magnets featuring Darth Vader, Chewbacca, R2-D2, and Yoda, Adam Joseph Industries, 1983	2.00	6.00

MICRO TINS, METAL BOX CO., 1980

☐ **Boba Fett**	1.00	3.00
☐ **Imperial Walkers**	1.00	3.00

	Price	Range
☐ **Lando**	1.00	3.00
☐ **Luke and Darth**	1.00	3.00
☐ **Luke and Tauntaun**	1.00	3.00
☐ **Yoda**	1.00	3.00

MISCELLANEOUS

☐ **Alarm Clock,** Star Wars Talking Alarm, three-dimensional R2-D2 and C-3PO, the Robot's voices are alarm, clock is 30-hour manual wind, 4″ x 6¾″ x 7¾″	35.00	50.00
☐ **Back Pack Box,** Yoda, ceramic, sigma	25.00	40.00
☐ **Bank,** combination, Metal Box Co., 1980, Yoda	15.00	20.00
☐ **Bank,** combination, Metal Box Co., 1980, Darth Vader	15.00	20.00
☐ **Bank,** Return of the Jedi, Darth Vader, Adam Joseph Industries, 1983	5.00	8.00
☐ **Bank,** Return of the Jedi, Emperor's Royal Guard, Adam Joseph Industries, 1983	5.00	8.00
☐ **Bank,** Return of the Jedi, Gamorrean Guard, Adam Joseph Industries, 1983	25.00	35.00
☐ **Bank,** Return of the Jedi, Kneesaa the Ewok, Adam Joseph Industries, 1983	5.00	8.00
☐ **Bank,** Return of the Jedi, R2-D2, Adam Joseph Industries, 1983	5.00	8.00
☐ **Bank,** Return of the Jedi, Wicket the Ewok, Adam Joseph Industries, 1983	5.00	8.00
☐ **Bank,** C-3PO, ceramic, Roman Ceramics	35.00	75.00
☐ **Bank,** Darth Vader, ceramic, Roman Ceramic	35.00	75.00
☐ **Bank,** Chewbacca, ceramic, Sigma	25.00	35.00
☐ **Bank,** Obi-Wan, ceramic, Sigma	25.00	35.00
☐ **Bank,** Yoda, ceramic, Sigma	15.00	30.00
☐ **Bank,** ceramic, R2-D2, Roman Ceramics Corporation, painted white and blue	20.00	50.00
☐ **Bookends,** Darth Vader and Chewbacca	25.00	40.00
☐ **Box,** stormtrooper, ceramic, Sigma	15.00	25.00
☐ **Calculator-Clock,** Return of the Jedi, LCD ..	10.00	20.00
☐ **Candle,** Chewbacca, for cake	3.00	5.00

	Price	Range
☐ **Candle,** Darth Vader, for cake	3.00	5.00
☐ **Candle,** R2-D2, for cake	3.00	5.00
☐ **Candleholder,** Yoda, Sigma	10.00	15.00
☐ **Christmas Ornaments,** one set of five different Return of the Jedi ornaments	10.00	20.00
☐ **Clock,** Star Wars, round in blue case, battery operated, shows R2-D2 and C-3PO, Welby-Elgin	30.00	50.00
☐ **As above,** electric	25.00	50.00
☐ **Clock,** Empire Strikes Back, square, in blue case, battery operated, shows Darth Vader and stormtroopers, Welby-Elgin	35.00	60.00
☐ **As above,** electric	30.00	60.00
☐ **Clock/Radio,** quartz clock with R2-D2 and C-3PO on face and built-in AM/FM radio, Bradley Time, 1984	30.00	35.00
☐ **Lamp,** Chewbacca, 9½″, fan produced	20.00	40.00
☐ **Lamp,** Darth Vader, 12″, fan produced	20.00	40.00
☐ **Lamp,** R2-D2, 8¼″, fan produced	20.00	40.00
☐ **Mirror,** Darth Vader, Sigma	10.00	20.00
☐ **Music Box,** Ewoks, ceramic, Sigma	25.00	40.00
☐ **Music Box,** Hoth Turret, Sigma	25.00	40.00
☐ **Music Box,** Max Rebo Band, Sigma	25.00	40.00
☐ **Nightlight,** Return of the Jedi, C-3PO, Adam Joseph, 1983		
☐ Dimensional	3.00	5.00
☐ Dome	5.00	8.00
☐ **Nightlight,** Return of the Jedi, Darth Vader, Adam Joseph, 1983	3.00	5.00
☐ Dome	5.00	8.00
☐ **Nightlight,** Return of the Jedi, R2-D2, dimensional, Adam Joseph Ind., 1983	3.00	5.00
☐ **Nightlight,** Return of the Jedi, Yoda, Adam Joseph Ind., 1983		
☐ Dimensional	3.00	5.00
☐ Dome	5.00	8.00
☐ **Picture Frame,** C-3PO, ceramic, Sigma	10.00	20.00
☐ **Picture Frame,** R2-D2, ceramic, Sigma	10.00	20.00

	Price Range	
☐ **Radio,** AM headset, Kenner, 9V battery	20.00	30.00
☐ **Record Tote,** box for storing 45s with pictures from Empire Strikes Back on sides, Disney records, 1982.	5.00	10.00
☐ **Sceni-Clock,** Star Wars, quartz, Tie fighter displays time, R2-D2, C-3PO in three dimension, reads "May the force be with you," 8¼" x 4" x 7"	25.00	50.00

JEWELRY

	Price Range	
☐ **Belt Buckle,** C-3PO and R2-D2, 3", blue enamel background, Lee Co., 1979	5.00	10.00
☐ **Belt Buckle,** Darth Vader, 3", oval, brass, the Leather Shop, San Francisco Inc., 1977	5.00	10.00
☐ **Belt Buckle,** Darth Vader, in relief of bust, "Lord Vader" embossed on each side, decorative border, black with silver, Star Trek Galore	10.00	15.00
☐ **Belt Buckle,** Darth Vader, oval 2½", head and mane in relief, black enamel background, came packaged with leather belt in Empire Strikes Back box, Lee Company, 1980	5.00	10.00
☐ **Belt Buckle,** Empire Strikes Back logo	5.00	10.00
☐ **Belt Buckle,** "May the Force be with you," 3", brass, probably unlicensed	5.00	10.00
☐ **Belt Buckle,** Return of the Jedi logo, brass with enamel, 3", rectangular, came with adjustable stretch SW/ROJ logo belt. Lee Company, 1982	5.00	10.00
☐ **Belt Buckle,** Return of the Jedi, Darth Vader, Brass head with tan enamel square, 1¼", came with adjustable stretch SW/ROJ logo belt, Lee Co., 1983	5.00	10.00
☐ **Belt Buckle,** Return of the Jedi, Jabba the Hut, Brass, 2½", rectangular, came with leather belt. Lee Company, 1983	5.00	10.00

	Price Range	
☐ **Belt Buckle,** Return of the Jedi, Jabba the Hut, picture, round, 1¼", came with adjustable stretch SW/ROJ logo belt. Lee Co., 1983 ...	5.00	10.00
☐ **Belt Buckle,** Return of the Jedi, Yoda, round, brass, 2", came packaged with leather belt in Empire Strikes Back box. Lee Company, 1980	5.00	10.00
☐ **Belt Buckle,** R2-D2 & C-3PO with Star Wars logo	7.00	12.00
☐ **Belt Buckle,** Star Wars logo, heavy metal, 2"x 3"	7.00	12.00
☐ **Belt Buckle,** Return of the Jedi, Wicket the Ewok, picture, round, 1¼", came with adjustable stretch SW/ROJ logo belt, Lee Co., 1983	5.00	10.00
☐ **Bracelet,** gold link chain, with Darth Vader, C-3PO and R2-D2	6.00	10.00
☐ **Charm Bracelet,** with C-3PO, R2-D2, and Chewbacca	5.00	7.00
☐ **Earrings,** C-3PO heads, gold, pierced, Factors Etc., 1977	8.00	10.00
☐ **Earrings,** C-3PO, full figure, clip-on, Factors Etc., 1977	8.00	10.00
☐ **Earrings,** Chewbacca, pierced, Factors Etc., 1977	8.00	10.00
☐ **Earrings,** Darth Vader, black finish, pierced, Factors Etc., 1977	8.00	10.00
☐ **Earrings,** Darth Vader, clip-on, Factors Etc., 1977	8.00	10.00
☐ **Earrings,** R2-D2, silver, pierced, Factors Etc., 1977, small	8.00	10.00
☐ **Earrings,** R2-D2, silver, movable legs, Factors Etc., 1977	8.00	10.00
☐ **Key Chain,** Boba Fett	3.00	5.00
☐ **Key Chain,** C-3PO	3.00	5.00
☐ **Key Chain,** Chewbacca	3.00	5.00
☐ **Key Chain,** "Darth Vader Lives"	3.00	5.00
☐ **Key Chain,** Han on Hoth	3.00	5.00
☐ **Key Chain,** Lando Calrissian	3.00	5.00

	Price	Range
☐ **Key Chain,** Leia on Hoth	3.00	5.00
☐ **Key Chain,** Luke on Hoth	3.00	5.00
☐ **Key Chain,** R2-D2	3.00	5.00
☐ **Key Chain,** Yoda	3.00	5.00
☐ **Key Ring,** maker unknown, clear plastic, shows Wicket in center	3.00	5.00
☐ **Key Ring,** stormtrooper figurine, silver finish	3.00	5.00
☐ **Key Ring,** Male Ewok Baby, three-dimensional, solid rubber, Adam Joseph Ind., 1983	3.00	4.00
☐ **Key Ring,** Female Ewok Baby, three-dimensional, solid rubber, Adam Joseph Ind., 1983	3.00	4.00
☐ **Key Ring,** Darth Vader, brass, Adam Joseph Ind.	5.00	8.00
☐ **Key Ring,** 4 plastic cards with McQuarrie art from Jedi on each side	1.00	2.00
☐ **Key Ring,** Millennium Falcon, brass, Adam Joseph Ind., 1983	5.00	8.00
☐ **Key Ring,** R2-D2, brass, Adam Joseph Ind., 1983	5.00	8.00
☐ **Key Ring,** Yoda, brass, Adam Joseph Ind., 1983	5.00	8.00
☐ **Pendant,** C-3PO, in relief, movable arms, gold finish, Factors Etc.	6.00	10.00
☐ **Pendant,** C-3PO, enamel, 1¼″	5.00	10.00
☐ **Pendant,** C-3PO and R2-D2, Empire Strikes Back, enamel, came boxed, Wallace Berrie ..	5.00	15.00
☐ **Pendant,** Chewbacca, in relief, brown with gold belt, moveable arms, Factors Etc., 1977	6.00	10.00
☐ **Pendant,** Darth Vader, bust in relief, black, Factors Etc., 1977	6.00	10.00
Pendant, E.S.B., Wallace Berrie, 1980, came boxed, enamel		
☐ **Chewbacca**	5.00	15.00
☐ **Darth Vader**	5.00	15.00
☐ **R2-D2**	5.00	15.00
☐ **R2-D2/C-3PO**	5.00	15.00
☐ **Pendant,** Jawa, in relief, silver or gold	6.00	10.00
☐ **Pendant,** Millennium Falcon, small	8.00	15.00

	Price	Range
☐ **Pendant,** R2-D2, enamel, ¾"	5.00	10.00
☐ **Pendant,** R2-D2, Empire Strikes Back, enamel, 1", came boxed, Wallace Berrie	5.00	15.00
☐ **Pendant,** R2-D2 in relief, silver finish, movable legs, Factors Etc., 1977	6.00	10.00
☐ **Pendant,** lettering of "Star Wars" and stars cut-out and connected, silver finish	4.00	6.00
☐ **Pendant,** "Star Wars" logo, trapezoid shape, silver or gold finish, Star Trek Galore, 1977	4.00	6.00
☐ **Pendant,** stormtrooper, white bust in relief, white and black	6.00	10.00
☐ **Pendant,** TIE Fighter, small	8.00	15.00
☐ **Pendant,** X-Wing Fighter, silver finish, Factors Etc., 1977	6.00	10.00
☐ **Pendant,** C-3PO bust in relief gold, Adam Joseph Ind., 1983	3.00	5.00
☐ **Pendant,** R2-D2, gold, in relief, Adam Joseph Ind., 1983	3.00	5.00
☐ **Pendant,** Yoda, gold, in relief, Adam Joseph Ind., 1983	3.00	5.00
☐ **Pendant,** Ewok, gold, in relief, Adam Joseph Ind., 1983	3.00	5.00
☐ **Pendant,** Salacious Crumb, gold, in relief, Adam Joseph Ind., 1983	3.00	5.00
☐ **Pendant,** Emperor's Guard, gold, in relief, Adam Joseph Ind., 1983	3.00	5.00
☐ **Pendant,** R2-D2, in relief, painted, Adam Joseph Ind., 1983	3.00	5.00
☐ **Pendant,** Darth Vader, in relief, painted, Adam Joseph, 1983	3.00	5.00
☐ **Pendant,** Yoda, in relief, painted, Adam Joseph Ind., 1983	3.00	5.00
☐ **Pendant,** May the Force Be With You, photo-etched, Adam Joseph Ind., 1983	2.00	4.00
☐ **Pendant,** Return Of The Jedi, photo-etched, Adam Joseph Ind., 1983	2.00	4.00
☐ **Pendant,** X-Wing Fighter, photo-etched, Adam Joseph Ind., 1983	2.00	4.00

	Price Range	

Pin, lapel, promotional item with Atari Cartridges, metal, black and silver.

☐ **C-3PO**	2.00	5.00
☐ **Darth Vader**	2.00	5.00
☐ **R2-D2**	2.00	5.00

Pins, 2-piece medals hooked together with jump ring, Wallace Berrie Co., 1980

☐ **Boba Fett,** from The Empire Strikes Back	5.00	15.00
☐ **Chewbacca,** from The Empire Strikes Back	5.00	15.00
☐ **Darth Vader,** from The Empire Strikes Back	5.00	15.00
☐ **Millennium Falcon,** from The Empire Strikes Back	5.00	15.00
☐ **X-Wing Fighter,** from The Empire Strikes Back	5.00	15.00
☐ **Yoda,** from The Empire Strikes Back	5.00	15.00
☐ **Pins,** C-3PO, bust, in relief, Adam Joseph Ind., 1983	3.00	5.00
☐ **Pins,** R2-D2, gold, in relief, Adam Joseph Ind., 1983	3.00	5.00
☐ **Pins,** Yoda, gold, in relief, Adam Joseph Ind., 1983	3.00	5.00
☐ **Pins,** Ewok, gold, in relief, Adam Joseph Ind., 1983	3.00	5.00
☐ **Pins,** Salacious Crumb, gold, in relief, Adam Joseph Ind., 1983	3.00	5.00
☐ **Pins,** Emperor's Guard, gold, in relief, Adam Joseph Ind., 1983	3.00	5.00
☐ **Pins,** May the Force be With You, photo-etched, Adam Joseph Ind., 1983	2.00	4.00
☐ **Pins,** Return of the Jedi, photo-etched, Adam Joseph Ind., 1983	2.00	4.00
☐ **Pins,** X-Wing Fighter, photo-etched, Adam Joseph Ind., 1983	2.00	4.00
☐ **Pins,** Star Wars, photo-etched, Adam Joseph Ind., 1983	2.00	4.00
☐ **Pins,** The Force, photo-etched, Adam Joseph Ind., 1983	2.00	4.00
☐ **Pins,** Male Ewok Baby, in relief, plastic, Adam Joseph Ind., 1983	2.00	4.00

Price Range

☐ **Pins,** Female Ewok Baby, in relief, plastic, Adam Joseph Ind., 1983 ....   2.00   4.00

Rings, Wallace Berrie Co., 1980, came boxed

☐ **C-3PO and R2-D2,** from The Empire Strikes Back 3.00   5.00

☐ **Darth Vader,** from The Empire Strikes Back   3.00   5.00

☐ **R2-D2,** from The Empire Strikes Back 3.00   5.00

☐ **The Empire Strikes Back,** features an X-Wing Fighter 3.00   5.00

☐ **The Empire Strikes Back,** "May the Force be with You" 3.00   5.00

☐ **Yoda,** from The Empire Strikes Back 3.00   5.00

☐ **X-Wing Fighter Pilot,** photo-etched, Adam Joseph Ind., 1983 ....   2.00   4.00

☐ **Stickpins,** C-3PO in relief, gold finish, Factors Etc., 1977 ....   3.00   5.00

☐ **Stickpins,** Darth Vader, bust in relief, black, Factors Etc., 1977 ....   3.00   5.00

☐ **Stickpins,** R2-D2, in relief, silver finish, Factors Etc., 1977 ....   3.00   5.00

☐ **Watch,** Bradley, quartz LCD, C-3PO and R2-D2 on dial, plays Star Wars theme, all black 20.00   25.00

☐ **Watch,** Bradley, quartz LCD, R2-D2 and C-3PO on face, silvertone with black strap 20.00   25.00

☐ **Watch,** Bradley, R2-D2 and C-3PO on dial, sweep second hand, stainless case with black strap 20.00   25.00

☐ **Watch,** Bradley, quartz LCD, R2-D2, C-3PO and two ships on blue face, musical alarm, black case and strap 20.00   25.00

☐ **Watch,** Darth Vader double image with words Star Wars, picture of Vader and words switch back and forth as watch is moved, digital, Bradley, 1982 ....   25.00   30.00

☐ **Watch,** digital, came with 11 different picture stickers for face, Texas Instruments, 1977 ..   20.00   25.00

☐ **Watch,** wind-up, C-3PO and R2-D2 on a black background 20.00   25.00

	Price Range	
☐ **Watch,** wind-up, C-3PO and R2-D2 on a light blue background	20.00	25.00
☐ **Watch,** LCD, Darth Vader's head on a gray background, Bradley Time	20.00	25.00
☐ **Watch,** wind-up, Darth Vader's head on a gray background	20.00	25.00
☐ **Watch,** wind-up, Darth Vader full figure on gray background, Bradley Time, 1977	20.00	25.00
☐ **Watch,** wind-up, Jabba the Hutt	20.00	25.00
☐ **Watch,** wind-up, Yoda head on a gray background	20.00	25.00

MAGAZINES

	Price Range	
☐ **American Cinematographer,** Star Wars issue	75.00	100.00
☐ **American Cinematographer,** R2-D2 and C-3PO on cover, profiles Return of the Jedi inside	4.00	5.00
☐ **Best of Starlog, The,** Vol. 1, Luke Skywalker with blaster in photographs from Empire Strikes Back on cover, assorted articles	2.00	3.00
☐ **Best of Starlog, The,** Vol. 2, Yoda on cover, assorted articles	2.00	3.00
☐ **Best of Starlog,** #4, Jabba on cover.	2.00	3.00
☐ **Best of Starlog,** #5, Luke and Vader fighting scene on cover.	2.00	3.00
☐ **Cinefantastique,** F.S. Clark Publishers, the magazine with a "sense of wonder," Vol. 12, No. 5 and 6, July/August, 1982, "Star Trek II" and "The Revenge of the Jedi"	5.00	8.00
☐ **Vol. 6, No. 4, Vol. 7, No. 1,** double issue, "Making Star Wars," 23 interviews with the actors, technicians and artists	15.00	20.00
☐ **Vol. 1, No. 26,** May/July, behind the scenes with Star Wars material, a color Star Wars center spread	5.00	8.00

Magazine, American Cinematographer, Star Wars issue

	Price Range	
☐ **Vol. 1, No. 30,** Oct./Nov., 1977, Star Wars follow-up with news of the sequel	5.00	8.00
☐ **Comic Collector's Magazine,** No. 139, Oct. 1977, this issue devoted to Star Wars, interviews, behind the scenes and comic art	5.00	8.00
☐ **Cracked,** No. 173, November 1980, "The Empire Strikes it Out"	2.00	4.00
☐ **Cracked,** No. 174, December 1980, "The Empire Strikes it Rich"	2.00	4.00
☐ **Cracked,** No. 199, November 1983, "Returns of the Jed Eye"	2.00	4.00
☐ **Creative Computing,** Vol. 8, No. 8, August 1982, cover photograph of Darth Vader	2.00	4.00

Price Range

☐ **Delap's F and SF Review,** a review of fantasy and science fiction, Fredric Pattern Publisher, Vol. 3, No. 7, July 1977, a cover story on Star Wars plus reviews of the movie 8.00 12.00

☐ **Discover,** Vol. 5, No. 8, August 1984, Lucus, C-3PO and R2-D2 on cover, contains article entitled "Computerizing the Movies" 2.00 4.00

☐ **Dynamite,** No. 76, 1980, Scholastic Magazines, Luke with sabre on cover, article on The Empire Strikes Back 2.00 4.00

☐ **Dynamite,** No. 114, Luke and Leia on cover, 1983 .... 2.00 4.00

☐ **Electric Company, The,** April/May 1983, Yoda on cover, Star Wars articles 2.00 4.00

☐ **Empire Strikes Back Official Collector's edition** 5.00 8.00

☐ **Famous Monsters Issue No. 137,** Star Wars special issue, Sept., 1977 .... 5.00 8.00

☐ **Issue No. 165,** Empire Strikes Back special issue, May, 1980 .... 3.00 6.00

☐ **Fantascene,** Fantascene Productions, No. 3, copyright 1977, "The Star Wars," an article on the technical aspects of the film 10.00 15.00

☐ **Fantastic Films,** the magazine of fantasy and science fiction in the cinema, Blake Publishing Company, Chicago, IL

☐ **Vol. 1, No. 1,** April 1978, Star Wars, "Let the Wookie win," "The Ships of Star Wars," "Interview with Rick Baker" and "Animating the Death Star trench" 4.00 5.00

☐ **Vol. 1, No. 3,** May 1978, the latest on behind the scenes at Paramount during the making of Star Wars 4.00 5.00

☐ **Vol. 1, No. 8.,** April 1979, "Star Wars strikes back," news on the sequel 3.00 4.00

☐ **Vol. 2, No. 2,** June 1979, Star Wars: "One last time down the death trench" with never before seen photos 3.00 4.00

Price Range

☐ **Vol. 3, No. 2,** July 1980, "An Interview with Larry Kasdan, the screenwriter for Empire Strikes Back," "An Interview with special effects photographer Dennis Muren" 3.00 4.00

☐ **Vol. 3, No. 3,** Sept. 1980, "Gary Kurtz Interviewed," the producer of Star Wars and Empire Strikes Back, a Wookie on the cover 3.00 4.00

☐ **Vol. 3, No. 4,** Oct. 1980, "The Empire Talks Back," "Painting the Empire," Yoda on the cover 3.00 4.00

☐ **Vol. 3, No. 5,** Dec. 1980, "Speculation concerning the future history of the Star Wars saga," clone wars explained 3.00 4.00

☐ **Vol. 3, No. 7,** Feb. 1981, "From Star Wars to Empire," "The Weapons of Star Wars," "Rich Baker," "Animating the Death Star Trench," "The Best of Fantastic Films" 3.00 4.00

☐ **Vol. 3, No. 8,** April 1981, part two of "From Star Wars to Empire," "The Mystery behind Darth Vader's prosthetic armor" 3.00 4.00

☐ **Vol. 3, No. 9,** June 1981, "Star Wars comes to radio," illustrated cover of characters making radio program 3.00 4.00

☐ **Vol. 4, No. 1,** August 1981, "The Voice of Vader," "Nevana Limited," "From Star Wars to Empire" 3.00 4.00

☐ **Vol. 4, No. 4,** April 1982, "From Star Wars to Empire to Revenge of the Jedi" 3.00 4.00

☐ **Films And Filming,** Hansom Books, London, Vol. 23, No. 11, August 1977, preview of Star Wars 6.00 10.00

☐ **Future,** the magazine of science adventure, Future Magazine, Inc., New York, No. 1, April 1978, advertising posters of Star Wars 3.00 4.00

☐ **Hollywood Studio Magazine,** D. Denny Publisher, Vol. 12, No. 5, June 1978, "New 15 million Star Trek movie," "Star Wars, a sequel" 6.00 10.00

	Price Range	
☐ **Kuifje,** (Belgian), Vol. 38, No. 5, Return of the Jedi issue	3.00	5.00
☐ **Ladies Home Journal,** September 1983, contains article entitled "Jedimania: Why we love those Star Warriors"	2.00	4.00
☐ **L'ecran Fantastique,** (French), No. 13, Empire Strikes Back issue	3.00	5.00
☐ **As above,** No. 33, Empire Strikes Back cover	3.00	5.00
☐ **As above,** No. 37, Return of the Jedi cover ..	3.00	5.00
☐ **As above,** No. 38, Return of the Jedi cover ..	3.00	5.00
☐ **L'Express,** (French), No. 1519, 23 August 1980, cover story, "La Guerre Pour Rire," Star Wars II	4.00	6.00
☐ **Life,** Vol. 4, No. 1, January 1981, features Yoda on cover, title: "The Year in Pictures"	4.00	6.00
☐ **Life,** Vol. 6, No. 6, June 1983, article: "George Lucas: A man and his Empire"	4.00	6.00
☐ **Mad,** No. 196, January 1978, "Star Bores," Mad plot synopsis	3.00	5.00
☐ **Mad,** No. 197, March 1979, "A 'Mad' look at 'Star Wars'"	3.00	5.00
☐ **Mad,** No. 203, December 1978, "The Mad 'Star Wars' musical"	3.00	5.00
☐ **Mad,** No. 220, January 1981, "The Empire Strikes Out"	2.00	4.00
☐ **Mad,** No. 230, April 1982, "The Star Wars Log"—*Mad's* version of Lucas' personal log.	2.00	4.00
☐ **Mad,** No. 242, October 1983, "Star Bores—Re-Hash of the Jedi"	2.00	4.00
☐ **Mad Movies,** (French), No. 20, Empire Strikes Back cover, 1980	3.00	5.00
☐ **Mediascene Preview,** the magazine of tomorrow's entertainment, Supergraphics, Reading, PA		
☐ **Vol. 1, No. 22,** Nov. 1976, the first Star Wars feature news, color cover and center spread art	12.00	15.00

Price Range

☐ **Vol. 2, No. 4,** August 1980, The Empire Strikes Back, an interview with Mark Hamill, a profile of Harrison Ellenshaw, creator of unknown worlds 8.00   12.00

☐ **Vol. 2, No. 11,** "Darth Vader returns with a new ally, Boba Fett" and new costume designs . .   6.00   10.00

☐ **Vol. 3, No. 2,** Star Wars interview with Brian Johnson, special effects 4.00   6.00

☐ **Military Modeler,** Vol. 7, No. 11, November 1980, cover photograph of Millennium Falcon, "Han Solo's Millennium Falcon" 4.00   6.00

☐ **Movie Monsters,** Vol. 1, No. 3, Fall 1981, Darth and Bounty Hunters on cover, article entitled: "Star Wars: The legend of Darth Vader" 2.00   4.00

☐ **Muppet Magazine,** Vol. 1, No. 3, Summer 1983, cover features Kermit as Luke, Gonzo as Darth, Piggy as Leia, article: "Super Star War: Battle of the Space Heroes" 2.00   4.00

☐ **National Enquirer,** June 21, 1983, cover photograph of stolen shuttle scene from Return of the Jedi, contains article "Top Psychiatrists Explain the Amazing Appeal of Return of the Jedi" 3.00   6.00

☐ **Newsweek,** Newsweek, Inc., Vol. 89, No. 22, May 30, 1977, "Fun in space," a review of Star Wars 15.00   20.00

☐ **People,** July 18, 1977, contains article entitled "The Talented Folks Who Gave Us C-3PO And The Summer's Box Office Sizzler," with photographs 3.00   5.00

☐ **People,** Vol. 8, No. 26, "The 25 most Intriguing People of 1977," R2-D2 on cover, "The Shyest guy in Hollywood creates 'Star Wars' " 3.00   5.00

☐ **People,** June 6, 1983, cover shows Carrie Fisher from Return of the Jedi 2.00   4.00

☐ **People,** Vol. 19, No. 24, June 20, 1983, Darth Vader on cover, "Match wits with the Jedi Quiz Kid" 2.00   4.00

	Price Range	
☐ **People,** Vol. 16, No. 9, August 31, 1981, Mark Hamill and Yoda on cover, story on Mark Hamill	2.00	4.00
☐ **People,** August 14, 1978, contains article about Carrie Fisher entitled "Star Wars Strikes Again," cover photo shows Carrie and Darth Vader	3.00	5.00
☐ **People,** June 9, 1980, contains article entitled "Star Wars Strikes Back," cover shows Yoda	2.00	4.00
☐ **Questar,** the new magazine of science fiction and fantasy, William Wilson Publisher, Jefferson, PA		
☐ **No. 1,** c. 1978, "The Triumph of Star Wars," "Close Encounters With Star Wars"	8.00	12.00
☐ **No. 20,** August 1980, cover story, "The Making of an Empire: Star Wars Returns"	3.00	5.00
☐ **Review,** Vol. 2, No. 14, interview with Billy Dee Williams, Rogue's eye view of Star Wars Adventure	3.00	4.00
☐ **Review,** Vol. 2, No. 12, double length interview with Richard Marquand, Luke and Leia on cover	3.00	4.00
☐ **Return Of The Jedi Official Collector's Edition,** Lucasfilm, 1983	4.00	6.00
☐ **Return of the Jedi Giant Collector's Compendium,** magazine with poster and stories on production and the actors	4.00	6.00
☐ **Rolling Stone,** No. 322, July 24, 1980, cover features Luke, Leia, Han and Lando in street clothes, article entitled: "Slaves to (of) the Empire"	6.00	8.00
☐ **Rolling Stone,** No. 400/401, Darth Vader, Jedi monsters and Princess Leia on cover, "George Lucas: The Rolling Stone Interview;" "Space Cadet: A Few Words with Carrie Fisher"	4.00	6.00
☐ **Science And Fantasy,** R. Finton, publisher, no date, interviews with the stars of Star Wars and an article on the music	4.00	6.00

Price Range

☐ **Science Fiction, Horror And Fantasy,** Douglas Wright Publishing, Los Angeles, CA, Star Wars collector edition, Vol. 1, No. 1, Fall 1977, the making of Star Wars: the secrets behind the special effects, official blueprints, discussions with all the main characters 4.00   6.00

☐ **Scintillation,** the magazine of science fiction people, Carl Bennet, Publisher, No. 13, June 1977, "George Lucas brings the excitement back" 6.00   10.00

☐ **Starfix,** (French), Return of the Jedi special issue, 1980 ....   3.00   5.00

☐ **Star Force,** Vol. 1, No. 2, October 1980, features Star Wars, Empire Strikes Back and other creepy crawlies 2.00   4.00

☐ **Star Force,** Vol. 2, No. 3, August 1981, Darth Vader, Lando and scenes from Empire Strikes Back on cover, contains article "Star Wars III: The Sci-Fi Success Story Continues" 2.00   4.00

☐ **Starlog #7,** features an X-Wing fighter and a Tie fighter on the cover 6.00   10.00

☐ **Starlog #19,** Cantina Creatures on cover, Star Wars TV Special 3.00   4.00

☐ **Starlog #31,** ESB on cover, report on movie inside 3.00   4.00

☐ **Starlog #35,** Darth Vader on cover 3.00   4.00

☐ **Starlog #36,** Vader and Boba Fett on cover   3.00   4.00

☐ **Starlog #37,** Millennium Falcon on cover ...   3.00   4.00

☐ **Starlog #40,** features Luke Skywalker and Yoda on cover 3.00   4.00

☐ **Starlog #41,** cover photograph of Luke and Yoda on Dagobah, interview with Mark Hamill   3.00   4.00

☐ **Starlog #48,** features Luke Skywalker and Yoda on cover 3.00   4.00

☐ **Starlog #50,** features Boba Fett on cover ...   3.00   4.00

☐ **Starlog #51,** features Luke Skywalker on cover 3.00   4.00

☐ **Starlog #56,** features Darth Vader on cover   3.00   4.00

Starlog #7

	Price Range	
☐ **Starlog #65,** cover photograph of Luke with Lightsabre; interview with Mark Hamill, "I was Mark Hamill's Stand-in," December 1982	3.00	4.00
☐ **Starlog #69,** features Return of the Jedi cast on cover	3.00	4.00
☐ **Starlog #71,** assorted articles on Return of the Jedi, interviews with Carrie Fisher and Richard Marquand, cover photograph of Han, Luke, and Leia, June 1983	3.00	4.00
☐ **Starlog Poster Magazine,** Vol. 2, 1984, contains ten 16″ x 21″ color posters, includes close-up of Darth Vader	3.00	4.00
☐ **Star Wars Album,** Bantam Books 1977, official pictorial behind-the-scenes look at the making of the movie, sold at theaters	8.00	12.00

Price Range

☐ **Star Wars Compendium, Vol. II,** June 1981, compilation of information on the Star Wars poster book (minus the posters) 6.00 8.00

☐ **Vol. III,** June 1982, reset of the poster book on The Empire Strikes Back 4.00 6.00

☐ **Star Wars Newspaper,** Starfleet Productions Inc., publisher, 1977 .... 2.00 3.00

☐ **Star Wars, The Making Of The World's Greatest Movie,** Paradise Press, Inc., 1977, an entire magazine devoted to the making of Star Wars, with special effects, who's who in Star Wars 6.00 8.00

☐ **Star Wars Spectacular,** a Warren magazine, special edition of Famous Monsters, 1977, issue devoted to the motion picture, articles on robots, special effects, a tribute to George Lucas 6.00 8.00

☐ **Time Magazine,** R. Davidson Publishing, Vol. 109, No. 22, May 30, 1977, "The Year's Best Movie—Star Wars," profile of the movie and stars 15.00 20.00

☐ **Time Magazine,** R. Davidson, Vol. 115, No. 20, May 19, 1983, "The Empire Strikes Back," profiles of the movie, behind-the-scenes production and George Lucas 6.00 8.00

☐ **Time Magazine,** Vol. 121, No. 21, May 23, 1983, "Star Wars III: The Return of the Jedi," profiles the movie and its stars, a second article profiles George Lucas 4.00 6.00

☐ **True,** UFOs and Outer Space Quarterly, No. 19, Fall 1980, AT-ATS on cover, story: "The Empire Strikes Back ... But Not Out!" 2.00 4.00

☐ **US,** Vol. 4, No. 7, July 22, 1980, cover story: "The Good Guys of Star Wars" 2.00 4.00

☐ **US,** Vol. 8, No. 13, June 20, 1983, cover photograph and articles on Return of the Jedi 2.00 4.00

	Price Range	
☐ **Video Games,** Vol. 2, No. 2.	2.00	4.00
☐ **Videogaming Illustrated,** February 1983, cover illustration of Darth Vader, Articles: "Star Wars Spectacular: First look at the Jedi Arena Videogame," "Revenge of the Jedi Film and Videogame," "Darth Vader Interviewed"	2.00	4.00
☐ **World of "Star Wars,"** A Compendium of Fact and Fantasy From Star Wars and The Empire Strikes Back, Paradise Press, 1981	4.00	6.00

MODELS

Many model kits were reissued by the manufacturer as newer movies were released. A model in a Star Wars box can add up to 50% to the value, as in the case of some of the early ships that were equipped with lights. Please note, these prices are for complete, unassembled models in the original box. Assembled models are practically worthless.

	Price Range	
☐ **Artoo-Detoo Van,** snap-together, molded in color, MPC, 1977	5.00	12.00
☐ **AT-AT,** glue or snap-together, MPC, 1982 . . .	10.00	15.00
☐ **AT-AT Structor Kit,** motorized walking model kit, MPC, 1984	6.00	10.00
☐ **AT-ST,** 6″-high snap-together, plastic model, MPC, 1983	5.00	8.00
☐ **AT-ST Structor Kit,** motorized walking model kit, MPC, 1984	5.00	10.00
☐ **A-Wing Fighter Model,** snap-together, MPC, 1983	5.00	8.00
☐ **Battle on Ice Planet Hoth,** glue or snap-together, diorama, 11¾″ x 17¾″, MPC, 1982	20.00	30.00
☐ **B-Wing Fighter Model,** snap-together, MPC, 1983	5.00	8.00
☐ **C-3PO,** plastic	5.00	10.00
☐ **C-3PO Structor Kit,** motorized walking model kit, MPC, 1984	6.00	10.00

	Price Range	
☐ **Darth Vader,** head, plastic	25.00	50.00
☐ **Darth Vader's Tie Fighter,** plastic	5.00	10.00
☐ **Darth Vader Model,** Fundimensions, General Mills Fun Group, molded in black, glow-in-the-dark light saber, movable arm, height 11¼", 1979	10.00	20.00
☐ **Encounter With Yoda On Dagobah,** glue or snap-together, 5¾" x 10", MPC, 1982	15.00	20.00
☐ **Imperial Cruiser,** plastic	15.00	20.00
☐ **Jabba's Throne Room,** plastic diorama, MPC, 1983	15.00	20.00
☐ **Luke Skywalker Van,** snap-together, molded in color, MPC, 1977	5.00	12.00
☐ **Millennium Falcon,** glue or snap-together, MPC, 1982	20.00	35.00
☐ **Mirr-A-Kits,** snap-together models of space-crafts, from Return of the Jedi, MPC, 1984		
☐ **AT-ST**	3.00	5.00
☐ **Shuttle Tyderium**	3.00	5.00
☐ **Speeder Bike**	3.00	5.00
☐ **Tie Interceptor**	3.00	5.00
☐ **Y-Wing**	3.00	5.00
☐ **X-Wing**	3.00	5.00
☐ **Rebel Base,** glue or snap-together, diorama, Fundimensions, 1982	20.00	30.00
☐ **R2-D2,** flying model, Estes Industries, 1977 ..	10.00	15.00
☐ **R2-D2 Model Kit,** MPC, 1977, 1980, 1983 ...	5.00	12.00
☐ **Shuttle Tyderium,** MPC, 1983	15.00	20.00
☐ **Slave I Model Kit,** MPC, 1982	15.00	25.00
☐ **Snow Speeder Model Kit,** MPC, 1980	15.00	25.00
☐ **Speeder Bike Vehicle,** model kit, MPC, 1983	8.00	12.00
☐ **Tie Fighter,** glue or snap-together, MPC, 1982	5.00	8.00
☐ **Tie Fighter,** flying model, Maxi-Brute, Estes Industries, 1977	10.00	20.00
☐ **Tie Interceptor Model Kit,** MPC, snap-together, 1983	10.00	15.00
☐ **X-Wing Fighter,** glue or snap-together, 12½", MPC, 1982	8.00	12.00

Millennium Falcon Model, Star Wars box, MPC

	Price Range	
☐ **X-Wing Fighter,** flying model rocket, Maxi-Brute, Estes Ind., 1977	15.00	20.00
☐ **X-Wing Fighter,** snap-together (smaller than glue-together version), MPC, 1983	5.00	8.00
☐ **Yoda,** plastic	5.00	10.00

PARTY GOODS

	Price Range	
☐ **Balloons,** Empire Strikes Back, package of ten, assorted colors, Drawing Board	3.00	5.00
☐ **As above,** Ewok, package of six, assorted colors, Drawing Board, 1983	2.00	4.00
☐ **Banner,** Empire Strikes Back, design-ware, pictures characters from the movie, says "Happy Birthday," Drawing Board, 1981	3.00	5.00

	Price Range	
☐ **Blowouts,** Empire Strikes Back, Darth Vader's head on a blue background with white stars, package of four, Drawing Board, 1981	1.00	2.00
☐ **Blowouts,** Return of the Jedi, pictures Darth Vader, Drawing Board	1.00	2.00
☐ **Cake Decorating Kit,** features candles and writing implements to create Darth Vader cake	8.00	15.00
☐ **Cake Decorating Kit,** R2-D2 cake pan	4.00	7.00
☐ **Cake Pan,** shaped like Darth Vader head, 9½" x 11"	4.00	7.00
☐ **Candles,** for birthday cake, 3½" high, Wilton, 1980		
☐ Candles, Chewbacca	2.00	5.00
☐ Candles, R2-D2	2.00	5.00
☐ Candles, Darth Vader	2.00	5.00
☐ **Centerpiece,** Empire Strikes Back, shows Bespin scene, Drawing Board, 1981	2.00	5.00
☐ **Centerpiece,** Return of the Jedi, Drawing Board	2.00	5.00
☐ **Gift Tags,** Star Wars, self-stick, pack of 5, R2-D2/C3-PO, Drawing Board	1.00	3.00
☐ **Gift Tag,** Star Wars, birthday scenes, Drawing Board	1.00	2.00
☐ **Gift Tag,** Star Wars, R2-D2, C-3PO, Drawing Board	1.00	2.00
☐ **Gift Tag,** Star Wars, space battle, Drawing Board	1.00	2.00
☐ **Gift Tag,** Star Wars, characters from the movie, Drawing Board	1.00	2.00
☐ **Gift Tag,** Empire Strikes Back, Drawing Board	1.00	2.00
☐ **Hats,** pictures Boba Fett, Darth Vader, R2-D2, and C-3PO, eight in a package, Drawing Board, 1981	5.00	8.00
☐ **Invitations,** Star Wars, pictures R2-D2/C-3PO pack of 8, Drawing Board, 1978	1.00	3.00
☐ **Invitations,** Star Wars, die-cut, pictures R2-D2/C-3PO, pack of 8, Drawing Board, 1978	2.00	5.00

	Price Range	
☐ **Invitations,** Star Wars, postcard, pack of 16, Drawing Board, 1978	**1.00**	**2.00**
☐ **Invitations,** characters from Empire Strikes Back, two styles, one with "2" fold, other with color envelopes, Drawing Board, 1980	**1.00**	**3.00**
☐ **Name Badges,** Star Wars, pictures Darth Vader, pack of 16, Drawing Board, 1978	**1.00**	**2.00**
☐ **Napkins,** beverage size, paper, Star Wars, pack of 16, Drawing Board, 1978	**1.00**	**2.00**
☐ **Napkins,** Star Wars, luncheon size, pack of 16, Drawing Board, 1978	**1.00**	**2.00**
☐ **Napkins,** Empire Strikes Back, beverage size, set of 16, Drawing Board, 1980	**1.00**	**2.00**
☐ **Napkins,** Empire Strikes Back, pictures Bespin, Darth Vader, Boba Fett, R2-D2 and C-3PO, set of 16, Drawing Board, 1980	**1.00**	**2.00**
☐ **Napkins,** Beverage, Return of the Jedi, shows Luke and Darth, pack of 16	**1.00**	**2.00**
☐ **Napkins,** Luncheon, same as above	**1.00**	**2.00**
☐ **Package Decoration,** R2-D2, Drawing Board	**1.00**	**2.00**
☐ **Package Decoration,** Yoda, Drawing Board	**1.00**	**2.00**
☐ **Paper Cups,** Star Wars, pictures R2-D2, C-3PO, pack of 8, Drawing Board, 1978	**2.00**	**5.00**
☐ **Paper Cups,** Dixie Cup, series of scenes from Star Wars, miniature size	**2.00**	**5.00**
☐ **Paper Cups,** Dixie Cup, pictures scenes from Empire Strikes Back, miniature size	**2.00**	**5.00**
☐ **Paper Cups,** Empire Strikes Back, pictures Bespin, Darth Vader, Boba Fett, R2-D2 and C-3PO, set of 8, 9 oz, Drawing Board, 1980 ...	**2.00**	**5.00**
☐ **Paper Cups,** Return of the Jedi, shows Luke and Darth, pack of 8, Drawing Board	**2.00**	**5.00**
☐ **Paper Hats,** Return of the Jedi, shows Luke and Darth, pack of 8	**2.00**	**5.00**
☐ **Paper Plates,** Star Wars, luncheon size, pictures Darth Vader, pack of 8, Drawing Board, 1978	**1.00**	**3.00**

Price Range

☐ **Paper Plates,** Star Wars, dinner size, pictures C-3PO/R2-D2, set of 8, Drawing Board, 1978 — 1.00 / 3.00

☐ **Paper Plates,** Empire Strikes Back, pictures Chewbacca, set of 8, Drawing Board, 1980 .. — 1.00 / 3.00

☐ **Paper Plates,** Empire Strikes Back, pictures Yoda and Jedi, set of 20 .... — 1.00 / 3.00

☐ **Paper Plates,** Empire Strikes Back, dinner size, plastic coated, pictures Darth Vader, Boba Fett, R2-D2 and C-3PO in color, set of 8, Drawing Board, 1980 .... — 2.00 / 4.00

☐ **Paper Plates,** Return of the Jedi, shows Darth Vader and Luke Skywalker, pack of 8, 7″, Drawing Board .... — 1.00 / 3.00

☐ **Paper Plates,** Return of the Jedi, shows Luke and Darth, pack of 8, 9″, Drawing Board .... — 1.00 / 3.00

☐ **Party Bags,** Return of the Jedi, shows Luke and Darth, pack of 8 .... — 1.00 / 3.00

☐ **Party Hats,** Star Wars, pack of 8, Drawing Board, 1978 .... — 2.00 / 5.00

☐ **Party Name Badges,** inscription: Star Wars, in lower left corner, Drawing Board .... — 1.00 / 2.00

☐ **Perk-up Seals,** Empire Strikes Back, 3 sheets to a pack, bad guys or good guys, Drawing Board .... — 1.00 / 3.00

☐ **Perk-up Seals,** Return of the Jedi, 3 sheets to a pack, 3 different sets, Drawing Board ..... — 1.00 / 3.00

☐ **Place Cards,** Star Wars, pictures R2-D2/C-3PO, pack of 8, Drawing Board, 1978 .... — 1.00 / 2.00

☐ **Place Mats,** Star Wars, set of 8, Drawing Board, 1978 .... — 2.00 / 6.00

☐ **Puffy Stickers,** Empire Strikes Back, plastic, 1 sheet per pack, bad guys or good guys, Drawing Board .... — 2.00 / 4.00

☐ **Puffy Stickers,** Return of the Jedi, 3 sheets to a pack, 3 different sets, Drawing Board ..... — 2.00 / 4.00

☐ **Table Cover,** 60″ x 96″, pictures R2-D2, C-3PO and X-Wings, Star Wars, Drawing Board, 1978 — 1.00 / 5.00

	Price Range	
☐ **Table Cover,** Empire Strikes Back, pictures Bespin, Darth Vader, Boba Fett, R2-D2 and C-3PO, 60″ x 90″, Drawing Board, 1980	1.00	5.00
☐ **Table Cover,** Empire Strikes Back movie characters, paper	1.00	5.00
☐ **Table Cover,** Return of the Jedi, shows Luke and Darth, pack of 8	1.00	5.00
☐ **Thank-You Notes,** Empire Strikes Back, pictures R2-D2, 8 to a package, Drawing Board, 1981	1.00	3.00
☐ **Wrapping Paper,** Star Wars, space battle scenes, roll or sheets, Drawing Board, 1978	1.00	4.00
☐ **Wrapping Paper,** Star Wars, R2-D2/C-3PO, roll or sheets, Drawing Board, 1978	1.00	4.00
☐ **Wrapping Paper,** Star Wars, characters from the movie, Drawing Board, 1978	1.00	4.00
☐ **Wrapping Paper,** Empire Strikes Back, pictures Yoda and Obi-Wan Kenobi	1.00	4.00
☐ **Wrapping Paper,** Empire Strikes Back, Drawing Board	1.00	4.00
☐ **Wrapping Paper,** Star Wars, birthday paper, rolls or sheets, Drawing Board, 1978	1.00	4.00

PATCHES

	Price Range	
☐ **Embroidered Patch,** Factors, etc., says "Brotherhood of the Jedi," black on white ...	2.00	5.00
☐ **Embroidered Patch,** Factors, etc., says "Darth Vader lives," white on black	2.00	5.00
☐ **Embroidered Patch,** Factors, etc., says "May the force be with you," white on black	2.00	5.00
☐ **Embroidered Patch,** Factors, etc., says "Star Wars," black on white	2.00	5.00
☐ **Embroidered Patch,** Factors, etc., says "Star Wars," white on black, 2″ x 4″	2.00	5.00

	Price Range	
☐ **Embroidered Patch,** Thinking Cap Co., "Empire Strikes Back"	2.00	5.00
☐ **Embroidered Patch,** captioned "Star Wars—A New Hope," shows orange planet of Yavin and Luke Skywalker with light saber in hand, various colors, triangular shape, 3¾" x 5", original	25.00	40.00
☐ **As above,** Fan Club reissue	10.00	15.00
☐ **Embroidered Patch,** Star Wars, Lucasfilm Fan Club, pentagonal shape	2.00	4.00
☐ **Embroidered Patch,** patch worn by cast and crew of The Empire Strikes Back during filming of ice planet Hoth scenes in Norway, pictures Darth Vader in flames, embroidered in seven colors, 3" x 4½", original	20.00	35.00
☐ **As above,** Fan Club reissue	8.00	12.00
☐ **Embroidered Patch,** from Revenge of the Jedi, original from shooting set, with first title of newest movie	25.00	50.00
☐ **Embroidered Patch,** authentic Return Of The Jedi patch, multi-colored, highly detailed embroidered portrait of Yoda, various colors, 3¼" x 5½", Fan Club reissue	5.00	10.00

POSTERS

This section on posters is divided into three sections. The first section covers theatrical release posters. These are designed for display at theatres or other locations advertising the movies. The second section lists posters used in other types of promotions, i.e., food or drink promotions, educational or other special events. The last section covers posters that were offered for sale to the general public, including poster books.

Prices listed are for rolled posters, unless otherwise noted. The lower price is for a poster in good condition showing wear but basically intact. The higher price is for a poster in original or mint condition.

THEATRE POSTERS

In this section, posters are arranged chronologically by movie. You will find *Star Wars* first, followed by *Empire Strikes Back* and then *Return of the Jedi*. The *Ewok Adventure* TV movie is also included.

All movie posters are printed at contracted printing plants called National Screen Services, which are generally located near areas of distribution. These distribution points have been sending out advertising material for films from most studios since 1942. Today, movie posters come in five basic sizes. The one-sheet (27 x 41 inches) is usually printed on a thin clay-coated paper stock, in use since 1970. The insert size (14 x 36 inches) is printed on a heavy card stock paper which lends itself to greater durability. The half-sheet or display poster is also printed on the more durable paper stock and is the only movie poster format with a horizontal composition. The thirty-forty (30 x 40 inches) is printed on the heavy card stock paper. In most cases, the printing plates used to print the one-sheets are also used for the thirty-forty. The last of the standard movie poster sizes is the forty-by-sixty (40 x 60 inches) and it, too, is printed on the heavy card stock paper. Larger sizes exist, usually for sign and billboard use. These are usually designated as a multiple of one-sheets (three-sheet or six-sheet), each being three or six times the standard size of a one-sheet.

Special thanks to Jeff Killian of L'Affiche for descriptions and pricing in this section. His magazine is highly recommended: L'Affiche, 2352 S. Osage, Wichita, KS 67213.

STAR WARS FIRST ADVANCE POSTER (FIRST VERSION)

This was the first one-sheet size poster to be released for *Star Wars*. It was printed on silver mylar paper which has a chrome finish and is very reflective. It features the phrase, "COMING TO YOUR GALAXY THIS SUMMER—STAR WARS." The *Star Wars* logo featured on this poster is different than the standardized logo that was adopted a few months later.

	Price	Range
☐ **One-Sheet rolled**	200.00	400.00
☐ **One-Sheet folded**	100.00	200.00

STAR WARS FIRST ADVANCE (SECOND VERSION)

Price Range

Similar to first version but on white paper and with standard trademark logo.

☐ **One-sheet rolled**	80.00	200.00
☐ **One-sheet folded**	25.00	100.00

STAR WARS ADVANCE (STYLE 'B')

Blue ink on white paper, "A LONG TIME AGO IN A GALAXY FAR, FAR AWAY ... STAR WARS"

☐ **One-sheet rolled**	60.00	200.00
☐ **One-sheet folded**	30.00	80.00

Poster, Star Wars style 'A,' 1-sheet

STAR WARS STYLE 'A'

Price Range

Illustration by Tom Jung. Luke with light sabre and Leia in front of large Darth Vader helmet.

☐ One-sheet rolled	30.00	100.00
☐ One-sheet folded	25.00	80.00
☐ Insert rolled	30.00	50.00
☐ Insert folded	15.00	25.00
☐ 30 x 40 rolled	40.00	80.00
☐ 30 x 40 folded	20.00	30.00
☐ 40 x 60 rolled	40.00	75.00
☐ 40 x 60 folded	20.00	30.00
☐ Three-sheet folded	30.00	50.00
☐ Six-sheet folded	50.00	100.00
☐ Standee	60.00	100.00

STAR WARS STYLE 'A,' HALF-SHEET

Different artwork from regular style 'A'

☐ Half-sheet rolled	40.00	75.00
☐ Half-sheet folded	20.00	50.00

STAR WARS STYLE 'C'

Illustrated by Tom Cantrell. Artwork used on many foreign posters.

☐ One-sheet rolled	80.00	150.00
☐ One-sheet folded	75.00	125.00

STAR WARS STYLE 'D'

Illustration by Drew Struzan & Charles White III. Done in 1930s style of circus posters.

☐ One-sheet rolled	75.00	150.00
☐ One-sheet folded	20.00	50.00
☐ 30 x 40 rolled	45.00	85.00
☐ 30 x 40 folded	25.00	40.00
☐ 40 x 60 rolled	60.00	100.00
☐ 40 x 60 folded	30.00	50.00
☐ Standee	50.00	100.00

STAR WARS HAPPY BIRTHDAY

Price Range

At the end of the first year of Star Wars distribution, a special birthday poster was released to theatres still playing the movie. Probably less than 500 printed.

☐ **One-sheet rolled**	200.00	400.00
☐ **One-sheet folded**	150.00	300.00

STAR WARS 1979 REISSUE

Cropped version of style 'A' artwork with bright red band across the middle containing information on new Star Wars toys.

☐ **One-sheet rolled**	50.00	75.00
☐ **One-sheet folded**	40.00	60.00

STAR WARS 1981 REISSUE

Cropped style 'A' artwork with red banner proclaiming that "The Force will be with you for two weeks only."

☐ **One-sheet rolled**	20.00	35.00
☐ **One-sheet folded**	10.00	25.00
☐ **Half-sheet rolled**	20.00	35.00
☐ **Half-sheet folded**	10.00	20.00
☐ **Insert rolled**	20.00	35.00
☐ **Insert folded**	10.00	20.00
☐ **30 x 40 rolled**	25.00	40.00
☐ **30 x 40 folded**	10.00	20.00
☐ **40 x 60 rolled**	25.00	40.00
☐ **40 x 60 folded**	10.00	20.00
☐ **Standee**	30.00	50.00

STAR WARS 1982 REISSUE

"Star Wars is Back" with "Revenge of the Jedi" trailer advertisement.

☐ **One-sheet rolled**	25.00	35.00
☐ **One-sheet folded**	15.00	20.00
☐ **Half-sheet rolled**	25.00	40.00
☐ **Half-sheet folded**	10.00	20.00
☐ **Insert rolled**	25.00	40.00
☐ **Insert folded**	10.00	20.00

	Price Range	
☐ 30 x 40 rolled	25.00	40.00
☐ 30 x 40 folded	10.00	20.00
☐ 40 x 60 rolled	30.00	45.00
☐ 40 x 60 folded	15.00	25.00
☐ Standee	35.00	55.00

THE EMPIRE STRIKES BACK ADVANCE STYLE 'A'

Darth Vader's Helmet superimposed on a field of stars.

☐ One-sheet rolled	40.00	100.00
☐ One-sheet folded	25.00	75.00

EMPIRE STRIKES BACK STYLE 'A'

Illustration by Rodger Kastel. Dubbed the "Love Story" or "Kissing Scene" poster due to the "Gone With the Wind" style artwork.

☐ One-sheet rolled	40.00	80.00
☐ One-sheet folded	30.00	70.00
☐ Half-sheet rolled	30.00	60.00
☐ Half-sheet folded	10.00	20.00
☐ Insert rolled	25.00	40.00
☐ Insert folded	20.00	30.00
☐ 30 x 40 rolled	30.00	70.00
☐ 30 x 40 folded	20.00	35.00
☐ 40 x 60 rolled	40.00	80.00
☐ 40 x 60 folded	25.00	40.00
☐ Standee	50.00	100.00

EMPIRE STRIKES BACK STYLE 'B'

Illustration by Tom Jung. Light blue background.

☐ One-sheet rolled	25.00	40.00
☐ One-sheet folded	20.00	35.00
☐ Half-sheet rolled	20.00	40.00
☐ Half-sheet folded	10.00	20.00
☐ Insert rolled	20.00	40.00
☐ Insert folded	10.00	20.00
☐ 30 x 40 rolled	25.00	45.00
☐ 30 x 40 folded	10.00	24.00
☐ 40 x 60 rolled	30.00	50.00

	Price Range	
☐ 40 x 60 folded	12.00	25.00
☐ Standee	20.00	60.00

EMPIRE STRIKES BACK 1981 SUMMER RE-RELEASE

☐ One-sheet rolled	20.00	30.00
☐ One-sheet folded	15.00	25.00
☐ Half-sheet rolled	20.00	35.00
☐ Half-sheet folded	8.00	18.00
☐ Insert rolled	20.00	35.00
☐ Insert folded	8.00	18.00
☐ 30 x 40 rolled	20.00	40.00
☐ 30 x 40 folded	10.00	20.00
☐ 40 x 60 rolled	30.00	45.00
☐ 40 x 60 folded	12.00	24.00
☐ Standee	30.00	55.00

EMPIRE STRIKES BACK 1982 RE-RELEASE

☐ One-sheet rolled	10.00	20.00
☐ One-sheet folded	10.00	20.00
☐ Half-sheet rolled	15.00	25.00
☐ Half-sheet folded	8.00	12.00
☐ Insert rolled	15.00	25.00
☐ Insert folded	8.00	12.00
☐ 30 x 40 rolled	20.00	30.00
☐ 30 x 40 folded	10.00	15.00
☐ 40 x 60 rolled	25.00	35.00
☐ Standee	20.00	40.00

REVENGE OF THE JEDI ADVANCE (FIRST VERSION)

No release date on bottom.

☐ One-sheet rolled	80.00	200.00
☐ One-sheet folded	50.00	100.00

REVENGE OF THE JEDI ADVANCE (SECOND VERSION)

Release date May 25, 1983 on bottom. Most of the print run was distributed through the Star Wars Fan Club.

	Price Range	
☐ One-sheet rolled	60.00	150.00
☐ One-sheet folded	60.00	125.00

Note: Counterfeit versions of the two posters above exist. Printing quality is poor so the poster looks muddy and out of focus.

RETURN OF THE JEDI STYLE 'A'

Illustration by Tim Reamer. Lightsaber artwork.

☐ One-sheet rolled	20.00	35.00
☐ One-sheet folded	10.00	25.00
☐ Half-sheet rolled	15.00	30.00
☐ Half-sheet folded	10.00	25.00
☐ Insert rolled	15.00	30.00
☐ Insert folded	10.00	20.00
☐ 30 x 40 rolled	20.00	35.00
☐ 30 x 40 folded	10.00	20.00
☐ 40 x 60 rolled	25.00	35.00
☐ 40 x 60 folded	15.00	25.00
☐ Standee	25.00	40.00

RETURN OF THE JEDI STYLE 'B'

Illustration by Kazuhiko Sano.

☐ One-sheet rolled	20.00	35.00
☐ One-sheet folded	15.00	25.00
☐ Half-sheet rolled	25.00	35.00
☐ Half-sheet folded	10.00	20.00
☐ Insert rolled	25.00	35.00
☐ Insert folded	10.00	20.00
☐ 30 x 40 rolled	30.00	40.00
☐ 30 x 40 folded	10.00	25.00
☐ 40 x 60 rolled	20.00	40.00
☐ 40 x 60 folded	10.00	20.00
☐ Standee	30.00	50.00

RETURN OF THE JEDI 1985 REISSUE

Illustration by Tom Jung.

☐ One-sheet rolled	10.00	25.00

	Price Range	
☐ **One-sheet folded**	10.00	20.00
☐ **Half-sheet rolled**	10.00	25.00
☐ **Half-sheet folded**	10.00	20.00
☐ **Insert rolled**	10.00	20.00
☐ **Insert folded**	8.00	15.00
☐ **30 x 40 rolled**	15.00	25.00
☐ **30 x 40 folded**	10.00	15.00
☐ **40 x 60 rolled**	20.00	30.00
☐ **40 x 60 folded**	15.00	20.00
☐ **Standee**	25.00	40.00

THE CARAVAN OF COURAGE STYLE 'A'

Illustration by Kazuhiko Sano. Foreign release and distribution by Star Wars Fan Club.

☐ **One-sheet rolled**	20.00	30.00
☐ **One-sheet folded**	15.00	25.00

THE CARAVAN OF COURAGE STYLE 'B'

Illustration by Drew Struzan. Fan club distribution and foreign release.

☐ **One-sheet rolled**	20.00	30.00
☐ **One-sheet folded**	15.00	25.00

FOREIGN THEATRICAL POSTERS

Often in different sizes, sometimes with different art. This listing is not complete but should give a feel for pricing.

☐ **Star Wars,** British, Quad poster, 30″ x 40″ . .	75.00	100.00
☐ **As above,** Italian, 54″ x 39″	50.00	75.00
☐ **As above,** German, Style 'A'	50.00	75.00
☐ **As above,** German, Style 'B'	50.00	75.00
☐ **As above,** Japanese, Teanser	30.00	50.00
☐ **As above,** Japanese, Reissue	15.00	20.00
☐ **As above,** French	50.00	75.00
☐ **Empire Strikes Back,** German, Style 'A'	30.00	50.00
☐ **As above,** Italian, 54″ x 39″	30.00	50.00
☐ **As above,** Japanese, Style 'A' or 'B'	15.00	20.00
☐ **Return of the Jedi,** British, Quad, 30″ x 40″	20.00	30.00
☐ **Triple Feature,** British, Quad, 30″ x 40″	15.00	20.00

PROMOTIONAL POSTERS

Many of these posters are much rarer than some of the theatrical posters. Limited or regional distribution adds to their desirability and value. Many were only available for a short period of time.

Posters are listed chronologically by movie.

STAR WARS

☐ **Luke Skywalker Poster,** Howard Chaykin artist. Star Wars in red letters on lower right. Images of Luke, Leia and others superimposed over aqua and orange circle, black background. First promotional poster, distributed at the World Science Fiction Convention in Kansas City. Star Wars Corporation, 1976, 20″ x 29″

Rolled	75.00	250.00
Folded	40.00	100.00

☐ **Star Wars Style 'A' Record Promotion Poster,** Tom Jung artist. Design is basically the same as regular style 'A' with the rearranging of the credits at the bottom and the enlargement of the phrase, "Original Motion Picture Soundtrack on 20th Century Record and Tapes," 1977, 27″ x 41″

Rolled	50.00	90.00
Folded	40.00	60.00

☐ **Star Wars Style 'D' Record Promotion Poster,** Drew Struzan & Charles White III artists. Similar to style 'D' theatre poster with record promo added, 1978, 27″ x 41″

Rolled	60.00	90.00
Folded	40.00	75.00

Price Range

☐ **Star Wars Concert Poster,** Illustrated by John Alum. Sold only at Hollywood Bowl on November 30, 1978. 20th Century Fox, 1978, 24″ x 37″

Rolled	75.00	200.00
Folded	25.00	75.00

☐ **Star Wars Radio Drama Poster,** Illustration by Celia Strain. Sent only to National Public Radio Stations for promotion. Lucasfilms Ltd., 1979, 17″ x 29″

Rolled	25.00	75.00
Folded	20.00	50.00

☐ **Burger Chef/Coca-Cola Promotional Posters,** set of four full-color posters (Luke Skywalker, Darth Vader, C-3PO and R2-D2, Chewbacca and Han Solo). 20th Century Fox, 1977, 18″ x 24″

Each	3.00	5.00
Set of four	10.00	20.00

☐ **Burger King/Coca-Cola Promotional Posters,** set of four with same art as above but with white borders. 20th Century Fox, 1977, 18″ x 24″

Each	3.00	4.00
Set of four	10.00	15.00

☐ **General Mills,** 2-sided, set of 4, Star Destroyer, R2-D2 and C-3PO, Space Battle, Hildebrandt art, 1978, 9″ x 14½″ 6.00 10.00

☐ **Immunization Poster,** from U.S. Department of Health, Education and Welfare/Public Health Service, promotes immunization of children. Features R2-D2 and C-3PO, 1979. .... 5.00 10.00

☐ **Kenner Promotional Poster,** captioned "Star Wars is forever," montage on one side and Star Wars Toys advertised on the back 3.00 5.00

Price Range

☐ **Proctor and Gamble Promotional Posters,** set of three (Ben Kenobi and Vader fighting, C-3PO and R2-D2, Leia, Han, Chewbacca and Luke collage). 20th Century Fox, 1978, 17½″ x 23″

Each	3.00	5.00
Set of three	10.00	15.00

☐ **Star Wars Record Mylar Poster,** included in Star Wars Soundtrack Album. Darth Vader's helmet in mylar, black background

Rolled	4.00	6.00
Folded	3.00	4.00

☐ **Topps Bubble Gum Press Sheets,** often the gum card art is printed first on paper to test it. Sometimes offered as a promotion on gum wrappers, often 22″ x 28″

☐ **Star Wars**	15.00	25.00
☐ **Empire Strikes Back**	15.00	25.00
☐ **Return of the Jedi**	15.00	25.00

EMPIRE STRIKES BACK

☐ **American Library Association Promotional Poster,** captioned "Read and the Force is with you." Features Yoda, 22″ x 34″ 5.00   6.00

☐ **Coca-Cola Boris Poster,** art By Boris Valejo. Sold in theatres, Lucasfilm, 1980, 24″ x 33″   8.00   12.00

☐ **Coca-Cola Promotional Posters,** set of three by famous artist Boris Valejo. (Darth Vader, Luke of Dagobah, Luke and Han on Hoth). Lucasfilm Ltd., 1980, 17″ x 23″

Each	3.00	5.00
Set of three	10.00	15.00

☐ **Proctor and Gamble Promotional Posters,** set of four (Luke, Darth Vader, C-3PO and R2D2, Han and Leia in Bespin Freeze Chamber). Photographic, Lucasfilm Ltd., 1980 17″ x 23″

Proctor and Gamble Empire Strikes Back Poster

	Price Range	
Each	3.00	4.00
Set of four	10.00	15.00
☐ **Empire Strikes Back Radio Drama Poster,** illustration by Ralph McQuarrie. Sent only to National Public Radio Stations for publicity. Much rarer than Star Wars version. Lucasfilm Ltd., 1982, 17″ x 28″		
Rolled	35.00	70.00
Folded	25.00	45.00
☐ **Star Wars Fan Club, Empire Issue,** kissing scene. Membership kit. 22″ x 28″	5.00	6.00
☐ **Video Promotion,** main characters and AT-AT battle scene, given to video shops to promote cassette	5.00	8.00
☐ **Weekly Reader Book Club,** montage of characters, 1980, 14½″ x 20½″	4.00	6.00

RETURN OF THE JEDI

	Price Range	

☐ **Return of the Jedi Hi-C Promotional Poster,** front: painted Jedi montage; back: selection of photographs from the film. Free with purchase of 4 cans of Hi-C, 1983, 17″ x 22″ **3.00   4.00**

☐ **Marvel Comics, Jedi Promotional Poster,** issued to promote Marvel Super Special No. 27, 1983

Rolled **4.00   6.00**

Folded **3.00   4.00**

☐ **Oral-B Toothbrush Jedi Poster,** free with purchase of 2 Oral-B adult toothbrushes. **4.00   6.00**

☐ **Proctor and Gamble Jedi Posters,** set of four, (Leia and Jabba, Lando and Skiff guard; Luke with blaster at Jabba's, R2 and Teebo the Ewok). 1983, 18″ x 22″

Each **4.00   6.00**

Set **10.00   15.00**

☐ **Scholastic Inc.,** mother and baby Ewok, 1983, 22″ x 15″ **4.00   6.00**

☐ **Star Wars Fan Club, Jedi Issue,** Death Star, B-Wing, and other vehicles. In membership kit. 22″ x 28″ **4.00   6.00**

☐ **Weekly Reader Book Club,** montage of characters, 1983, 14½″ x 20½″ **4.00   6.00**

☐ **Weekly Reader Book Club,** Wicket the Ewok, 14½″ x 20½″, 1983 . . . . **4.00   6.00**

GENERAL PUBLIC

FACTORS, ETC.

The first *Star Wars* poster licensee, full-color, 20″ x 28″.

STAR WARS

☐ **Hildebrandt Artwork**	**3.00**	**4.00**
☐ **Cantina Band Poster, limited distribution** . .	**6.00**	**10.00**

	Price Range	
☐ **Ship Battle Scene, limited distribution**	6.00	10.00
☐ **Darth Vader**	3.00	5.00
☐ **Princess Leia**	3.00	5.00
☐ **Luke Skywalker**	3.00	5.00
☐ **C-3PO and R2-D2**	3.00	5.00

EMPIRE STRIKES BACK

☐ **Darth Vader and Stormtroopers**	3.00	5.00
☐ **Boba Fett**	3.00	5.00
☐ **Montage of characters**	3.00	5.00
☐ **R2-D2, C-3PO w/Empire Logo**	3.00	5.00
☐ **Yoda**	3.00	5.00
☐ **Darth Vader Poster,** 3-D, came with 3 pens, glue and parts sheet. 17" x 22", 1978	10.00	15.00
☐ **Paint a Poster: Star Wars,** 5 different, 15" x 23" posters.	10.00	15.00
☐ **Pen a Poster: Star Wars,** 2 posters, 17" x 22", 6 pens	8.00	12.00
☐ **Sales Corporation of America, Animated TV Posters,** each is full color, 17" x 22"		
☐ **Droids, the adventures of R2-D2 and C-3PO, Ewoks.** Friends come in all shapes and sizes	3.00	5.00

SALES CORPORATION OF AMERICA (FULL-COLOR, 22" X 34")

☐ **Star Wars, style 'D'**	3.00	5.00
☐ **Empire Strikes Back, advance**	3.00	5.00
☐ **Return of the Jedi, teaser**	3.00	5.00
☐ **Return of the Jedi, style 'A'**	3.00	5.00
☐ **Darth Vader montage**	3.00	5.00
☐ **Vehicle battle scene**	3.00	5.00
☐ **Ewok montage**	3.00	5.00
☐ **Endor portrait**	3.00	5.00
☐ **Return of the Jedi, style 'B'**	3.00	5.00

SALES CORPORATION OF AMERICA (FULL-COLOR, 24″ X 72″)

Price Range

☐ **Darth Vader door poster** 4.00   6.00

SALES CORPORATION OF AMERICA (RETURN OF THE JEDI POSTER ART MINI-POSTERS, FULL-COLOR, 11″ X 14″, 1983)

☐ **#0021 Jabba & Friends** 1.00   3.00
☐ **#0023 Vehicle battle scene** 1.00   3.00
☐ **#0025 Jedi teaser** 1.00   3.00
☐ **#0027 Vehicle shuttle landing** 1.00   3.00
☐ **#0029 Laser, one-sheet** 1.00   3.00
☐ **#0031 Ewok montage** 1.00   3.00
☐ **#0033 Darth Vader montage** 1.00   3.00
☐ **#0035 Luke Skywalker** 1.00   3.00
☐ **#0037 Emperor montage** 1.00   3.00
☐ **#0039 Creature M montage** 1.00   3.00
☐ **#0041 Speeder bike** 1.00   3.00
☐ **#0043 Montage, one-sheet** 1.00   3.00

STAND-UP POSTERS (COLOR SILHOUETTES BACKED WITH CARDBOARD, FACTORS, ETC.)

☐ **Boba Fett,** 69″ x 26″ 15.00   25.00
☐ **Chewbacca,** 69″ x 30″ 15.00   25.00
☐ **C-3PO,** 69″ x 26″ 15.00   25.00
☐ **Darth Vader,** 69″ x 43″ 15.00   25.00
☐ **R2-D2,** 41″ x 30″ 15.00   25.00

STAND-UP POSTERS (RETURN OF THE JEDI, SALES CORPORATION OF AMERICA)

☐ **Darth Vader with Imperial Guards** 10.00   15.00
☐ **Ewoks** 10.00   15.00
☐ **R2-D2/C-3PO** 10.00   15.00

☐ **Star Wars** *Poster* Monthly, giant poster on back
　 of interviews, stories, inside looks at production
　 and special effects. No. 1, R2-D2 and C-3PO,
　 plus the stories of the stars 5.00   8.00

Price Range

☐ **As above,** No. 2, Darth Vader, plus how the dogfights were made 5.00 8.00

☐ **As above,** No. 3, R2-D2 and C-3PO in the Death Star, plus Han Solo, rogue space pilot 5.00 8.00

☐ **As above,** No. 4, Chewbacca, plus soldiers of the Empire and the building of R2-D2 .... 5.00 8.00

☐ **As above,** No. 5, Darth Vader, portrait of evil, plus inside stories of Chewbacca and Tarkin 5.00 8.00

☐ **As above,** No. 6, C-3PO, plus the secrets of Artoo Detoo and the spaceships 5.00 8.00

☐ **As above,** No. 7, R2-D2, plus the Droids of Star Wars 5.00 8.00

☐ **As above,** No. 8, Imperial stormtrooper, plus Ben Kenobi, man or legend, also space travel secrets 5.00 8.00

☐ **As above,** No. 9, the dark lord, plus the brains of the Droids 5.00 8.00

☐ **As above,** No. 10, Star Wars montage, plus what it takes to be a space pilot and the return of evil..................................... 5.00 8.00

☐ **As above,** No. 11, R2-D2, plus the men behind the masks 5.00 8.00

☐ **As above,** No. 12, space dogfight, plus the cantina aliens and the Soundmaster 5.00 8.00

☐ **As above,** No. 13, Luke and C-3PO, plus the shooting of Star Wars and the model squad 5.00 8.00

☐ **As above,** No. 14, attacking the Death Star, plus the machines that made lines move 5.00 8.00

☐ **As above,** No. 15, C-3PO, plus "Empire latest" and the Orbiter 102 Space Freighter 5.00 8.00

☐ **As above,** No. 16, R2-D2 with C-3PO, plus the Star Wars quiz and fan club facts 5.00 8.00

☐ **Empire Strikes Back Poster Album.** Bantha tracks, an official Star Wars fan club publication, featuring all the characters 5.00 8.00

	Price Range	
☐ **Empire Strikes Back Poster Book,** giant poster with editorials and information on back, issue one, "Back in Action," Princess Leia, Han Solo and Chewbacca on bridge.	5.00	8.00
☐ **As above,** issue two, "The Dark Lord, The Forces of the Empire," Darth Vader	5.00	8.00
☐ **As above,** issue three, "The mysteries of Yoda, the indignities of Artoo Detoo"	5.00	8.00
☐ **As above,** issue four, "AT-AT attack, the magic factory"	5.00	8.00
☐ **As above,** issue five, "Han Solo—Hero and Scoundrel, laser weapons"	5.00	8.00
☐ **Return of the Jedi Poster Book,** Paradise Press #1	4.00	8.00
☐ **As above,** #2	4.00	8.00
☐ **As above,** #3	4.00	8.00

PROMOTIONAL ITEMS, STUDIO

Note: See individual sections for commercial promotional items.

	Price Range	
☐ **Art Portfolio, ESB Promotional Item,** not available to the general public, contains two prints by R. McQuarrie of scenes from the movie, inner envelope sealed with lead Darth Vader medallion, outer envelope embossed with Vader, silkscreen	75.00	120.00
☐ **Cardboard Cutout,** from Burger King glasses promotion, lifesize Darth Vader, 1983, height 6'2"	10.00	20.00
☐ **Cardboard Cutout,** from Butterfly Originals display, Emperor's Royal Guard, height 54"	6.00	12.00
☐ **Decal,** Ralph McQuarrie, Bounty Hunters, given with renewal of membership in fan club, 4"x 5"	2.00	4.00
☐ **Decal,** Ralph McQuarrie, Yoda on Dagobah, given with renewal of membership in fan club, 4"x 5"	2.00	4.00

	Price Range	
☐ **Flyer,** Star Wars, blue with white and light blue lettering, no pictures, Twentieth Century Fox, 1977	2.00	3.00
☐ **Flyer,** The Empire Strikes Back, Japanese version, colorful collage of scenes from the second movie, one sheet, 7″ x 10″	3.00	4.00
☐ **Flyer,** Revenge of the Jedi, full-color fold-out, 44″ x 15″	20.00	30.00
☐ **Flyer,** Revenge of the Jedi, one page, logo front, toy list on back, release date 5/27/83	10.00	15.00
☐ **As above,** Return of the Jedi, 5/25/83	2.00	5.00
☐ **Intergalactic Passport,** hand-made, numbered, stamped, in silver-embossed hard cover. Used as set pass for Empire Strikes Back	40.00	60.00
☐ **Kit,** Kenner, including letter from Luke Skywalker, poster with scenes from the three films, action figure, $1 rebate coupon, coupon for free action figure, 1984	10.00	15.00
☐ **Lobby Card,** Empire Strikes Back, 11″ x 14″, set of 8	20.00	35.00
☐ **8″ x 10″ still set**	15.00	25.00
☐ **Lobby Cards,** Star Wars, 11″ x 14″, set of 8	25.00	50.00
☐ **8″ x 10″ still set, color**	20.00	35.00
☐ **Lobby Cards,** Return of the Jedi, 11″ x 14″, set of 8	15.00	30.00
☐ **8″ x 10″ still set**	10.00	20.00
☐ **Masks,** cut-outs from boxes of C-3PO Cereal by Kellogg, six different, set	5.00	8.00
☐ **Membership Card,** Official Star Wars Fan Club, Jedi issue, place for name and force number to be filled in	1.00	2.00
☐ **Pamphlet,** The Empire Strikes Back, German version, folded, photos and brief description of main characters in the film	4.00	5.00
☐ **As above,** The Ewoks, German version, folded	3.00	4.00

Price Range

☐ **Paperweight,** pewter, Empire Strikes Back, made by Lucasfilm for employees, cast, and crew 40.00   60.00

☐ **Planetary Maps,** came with some Kenner "Power of the Force" toys, 17½" x 18", set of 3, Death Star, Tatooine, and Endor 2.00   5.00

☐ **Promotional Posters—see "Posters"**

☐ **Press Kit,** Empire Strikes Back, 11 glossy stills plus production notes, biographies of stars and a nice folder, usually only available to the press for publicity 40.00   75.00

☐ **Press Kit,** Star Wars, rare and important collectible 100.00   150.00

☐ **Press Kit,** Return of the Jedi 25.00   50.00

☐ **Promotion Guide,** Revenge of the Jedi, produced in 1982 by Lucas Films, artwork by R. McQuarrie, all white cover with Revenge of the Jedi imprinted on it 50.00   75.00

☐ **Star Wars Program Books,** 20th Century Fox, biography of the stars, the robots, the villains, and behind-the-scenes look at the production, sold in theatre lobbies

Star Wars Program Book

	Price	Range
☐ **1st Printing,** slick cover	10.00	25.00
☐ **Reprint,** pebble-tone cover	5.00	10.00
☐ **Star Wars Promotional Book,** unusual because it was released as a book rather than a press kit, opens to 11″ x 28″, 11″ x 14″ closed, black cover	100.00	150.00
☐ **T-Shirt and Cap,** available through Hi-C promotional offer, until May 31, 1984, white with navy blue trim, cap has illustration of Luke and Darth Vader, shirt has montage of characters from Return of the Jedi.	10.00	15.00
☐ **Stills,** 8″ x 10″, Star Wars, given by fan club to members	1.00	2.00
☐ **As above,** for Empire Strikes Back	1.00	2.00
☐ **As above,** for Return of the Jedi	1.00	2.00
☐ **Storyboard replica,** given by fan club to members	2.00	5.00

Star Wars Promotional Book

	Price Range	
☐ **Tumbler,** Pepperidge Farm, C-3PO/R2-D2/Wicket, plastic, store premium given with purchase of Star Wars Cookies	1.00	3.00
☐ **Videotape Box,** CBS/Fox, 14″ x 8″ x 2″, given to video stores to advertise Empire Strikes Back on home video cassettes. Pictures Star Wars scene on one side, Empire Strikes Back on other.	3.00	5.00

PUZZLES, JIGSAW

	Price Range	

CRAFT MASTER (70 PIECES, 12″ X 18″, 1983)

☐ #33603, Jedi scenes	2.00	3.00
☐ #33604, Jabba the Hut throne room	2.00	3.00
☐ #33605, Death Star scene	2.00	3.00

CRAFT MASTER (8″ X 11″)

☐ Scenes from Return of the Jedi, each	2.00	3.00

KENNER (140 PIECES, 14″X 18″, 1977)

☐ C-3PO & R2-D2, at award ceremony	3.00	5.00
☐ Han Solo & Chewbacca	3.00	5.00
☐ Jawas capture R2-D2	3.00	5.00
☐ Luke & Han in garbage pit	3.00	5.00
☐ Luke at Mos Eisley	3.00	5.00
☐ Luke with Jawas & Droids	3.00	5.00
☐ Tusken Raider on Bantha	3.00	5.00
☐ Tusken Raider, standing	3.00	5.00
☐ X-Wing and Tie Fighter	3.00	5.00

KENNER (500 PIECES, 15½″ X 18″, 1977)

☐ Awards Ceremony	4.00	6.00
☐ Ben and Vader dueling	4.00	6.00
☐ Cantina scene...........................	4.00	6.00
☐ Leia & Luke on Death Star	4.00	6.00

	Price Range	
☐ Luke on Tatooine	4.00	6.00
☐ Luke, Uncle Owen, Jawas	4.00	6.00
☐ Rebel hanger on moon of Yavin	4.00	6.00
☐ Space battle	4.00	6.00
☐ Victory celebration	4.00	6.00
☐ X-Wing fighter	4.00	6.00

KENNER (1000 PIECES, 1977)

☐ Ben, Luke, Chewy and Han, in cockpit of Falcon	6.00	10.00
☐ Hildebrandt artwork, poster design	6.00	10.00

KENNER (1500 PIECES, 1977)

☐ Millennium Falcon, in Hyperspace	8.00	12.00
☐ Stormtrooper, in detention corridor	8.00	12.00

WADDINGTON, BRITISH

☐ Star Wars, 150 pieces, R2-D2 and C-3PO, 1977	8.00	15.00
☐ Return of the Jedi, 150 pieces, 11″ x 17″, 1983		
☐ No. 159A, Jabba's Throne Room	5.00	10.00
☐ No. 159B, Luke With Blaster	5.00	10.00
☐ No. 159C, Group on Millennium Falcon	5.00	10.00
☐ No. 159D, Darth Vader	5.00	10.00

RECORDS AND TAPES

The records are divided into two sections: (1) soundtracks and music, and (2) records with stories on them. Values are for records in excellent condition with dust jackets.

STAR WARS SOUNDTRACKS AND MUSIC

	Price Range	
☐ **Bienvenido, E. T.,** arranged and directed by Rafael Acosta, contains theme from *Star Wars,* 12-inch LP album, Orfeon Records, #LP-20-TV-019, Spanish album	10.00	15.00
☐ **Big Daddy,** contains theme from *Star Wars,* 12-inch LP album, Rhino Records, #RHI(S) 852	9.00	11.00
☐ Also available on cassette—Rhino RNC 852	9.00	11.00
☐ **Classic Space Themes,** including music from *The Empire Strikes Back,* performed by The Birchwood Pops Orchestra. Contains *Star Wars,* main theme from *The Empire Strikes Back, The Imperial March (Darth Vader's Theme)* and *Yoda's Theme,* 12-inch LP album, Pickwick Records, #SPC-3772, stereo, 1980	9.00	10.00
☐ **Classic Space Themes,** includes *Star Wars Theme* (Disco version), 12-inch LP album, Pickwick Records, #SPC-3172, stereo, 1980	9.00	11.00
☐ **Chewie, The Rookie Wookie,** from the album *Living in These Star Wars,* performed by The Rebel Force Band, 7-inch 45 rpm, Bonwhit Records	5.00	7.00
☐ **Close Encounters of the Third Kind and Star Wars,** composed by John Williams, performed by the National Philharmonic Orchestra, conducted by Charles Gerhardt. Contains *Main Title, The Little People Work, Here They Come!, Princess Leia Theme, The Final Battle, The Throne Room,* and *End Title,* 12-inch LP album, RCA Red Seal Record, #ARL 1-2698, stereo, 1978	12.00	15.00
☐ **Disco Excitement,** performed by Enock Light and His Light Brigade, contains Disco version of theme from *Star Wars,* 12-inch LP album, Lakeshore Music, #LSM 107, 1978	15.00	18.00
☐ Also available on 8-track tapes and cassettes	15.00	18.00

Price Range

☐ **Dune,** arranged by David Matthews, contains *Princess Leia's Theme* and the main theme from *Star Wars,* 12-inch LP album, CTI Records, #7-5005, 1977 .... **9.00 12.00**

☐ Also available on stereo 8-track tape and cassette **9.00 12.00**

☐ **Empire Jazz,** produced and arranged by Ron Carter from the original soundtrack from the motion picture *Star Wars/The Empire Strikes Back,* composed by John Williams. Contains *The Imperial March (Darth Vader's Theme) The Asteroid Field, Han Solo and the Princess (Love Theme), Lando's Palace, Yoda's Theme,* 12-inch LP album, RSO Records, #RS-1-3085, 1980 .... **8.00 10.00**

☐ Also available in 8-track tape, RS-8T-1-3085 **8.00 10.00**

☐ Also available in cassette, RS-CT-1-3085 .... **8.00 10.00**

☐ **The Empire Strikes Back,** the original soundtrack from the motion picture, composed and conducted by John Williams with The London Symphony Orchestra, 2 12-inch LP album, RSO Records, #RS-2-4201, 1980 .... **12.00 15.00**

☐ Also available on 8-track tape, RS-8T-2-4201 **12.00 15.00**

☐ Also available on cassette, RS-CT-2-4201 ... **12.00 15.00**

☐ **The Empire Strikes Back (Medley),** performed by Meco. Contains *Darth Vader's Theme, Yoda's Theme* and *The Force Theme,* RSO Records, #RS-1038, stereo, 7-inch 45 rpm, 1980 .... **3.00 5.00**

☐ **The Empire Strikes Back,** performed by Boris Midney and His Orchestra. Contains *Yoda's Theme, The Imperial March (Darth Vader's Theme), Han Solo and the Princess (Love Theme)* and *Star Wars (Main Theme),* RSO Records, #RS-1-3079 .... **8.00 10.00**

☐ Also available on 8-track tape, RSO Records 8T-1-3079, and cassette, RSO Records CT-1-3079 .... **8.00 10.00**

Price Range

☐ **The Empire Strikes Back,** (Meco Plays Music From), contains *The Empire Strikes Back (Medley), Darth Vader/Yoda's Themes, The Battle in the Snow, The Force Theme, The Asteroid Field/Finale,* 10-inch LP album, RSO Records, #RO-1-3086, 1980 . . . .   8.00   10.00

☐ **The Empire Strikes Back,** music from the original soundtrack of the motion picture. Music composed and conducted by John Williams, performed by The London Symphony Orchestra, 12-inch LP album, RSO Records, #RSO Super RSS-23, 1980, British Pressing 10.00   12.00

☐ **The Empire Strikes Back, Symphonic Suite,** from the original motion picture soundtrack, performed by The National Philharmonic Orchestra, conducted by Charles Gerhardt, 12-inch LP album, Chalfont Digital Records, #SDG 313, 1980, Pressed in Japan 15.00   17.00

☐ **Flip Side of Red Seal,** performed by Tomita, contains theme from Star Wars, 12-inch LP album, Victor (S) Records, #XRL1-5173 . . . .   9.00   10.00

☐ **Greatest Science Fiction Hits II,** conducted by Neil Norman and His Cosmic Orchestra. Contains *Star Wars: The Empire Strikes Back (Medley),* 12-inch LP album, GNP Crescendo Records, #GNPS-2133, 1980 . . . .   9.00   12.00

☐ Also available on cassette, GNP Crescendo Record, #GNPS-2133 . . . .   9.00   12.00

☐ **Great Movies—There's Something Going On Out There,** contains main title from Star Wars, performed by the National Philharmonic Orchestra, 12-inch LP album, His Masters Voice Record, #OPL 1-0003 . . . .   13.00   16.00

☐ **Hörspiel Nach Dem Gleichnamigen Film Mit Den Originalsprechern Krieg Der Sterne.** (*The Story of Star Wars* in German), with music and sound effects from the original soundtrack

Price Range

from the motion picture, 12-inch LP album, Fontana Records, #9199535, full-color, 8-page photo booklet **10.00**   **12.00**

☐ **The Imperial March (Darth Vader's Theme) and The Battle In The Snow,** performed by The London Symphony Orchestra, conducted by John Williams. From the original soundtrack of the motion picture *The Empire Strikes Back,* 12-inch LP album, RSO Record, #RS-1033, 1980 ....   **9.00**   **12.00**

☐ **John Williams Symphonic Suites—E. T., The Extra-Terrestrial, Close Encounters of the Third Kind, and Star Wars,** performed by The London Symphony Orchestra and The National Philharmonic Orchestra, conducted by Frank Barber, 12-inch LP album, EMI-Angel Records, #RL-32109, British Recording **12.00**   **15.00**

☐ **La Guerre Des Etoiles** (*Star Wars* in French), 7-inch 33⅓ rpm, Buena Vista Records, #LLP-455F **10.00**   **12.00**

☐ **Living In These Star Wars,** Country-Western version of *Star Wars,* performed by the Rebel Force Band, 12-inch LP album, Bonwhit Records **10.00**   **12.00**

☐ **Main Theme—Star Wars,** performed by David Matthews, from the album *Dune,* 7-inch 45 rpm, CTI Records #7-5005, CTI Records #OJ-39, 1977 ....   **5.00**   **7.00**

☐ **Main Title Themes From The Empire Strikes Back, Star Wars, 2001, A Space Odyssey And Close Encounters,** 12-inch LP album, Peter Pan Records, #1116 ....   **8.00**   **10.00**

☐ **Meco—Ewok Celebration,** contains themes from *Star Wars: The Motion Picture,* 12-inch LP album, Arista Records, #AL 8-8098 ....   **8.00**   **10.00**

Price Range

☐ **Music From John Williams—Close Encounters Of The Third Kind And Star Wars,** performed by The National Philharmonic Orchestra, conducted by Charles Gerhardt, 12-inch LP album, RCA Records, #AGLI-3650, stereo .. 10.00 12.00

☐ **Music From Other Galaxies And Planets,** featuring *The Main Theme* and *Princess Leia's Theme* from *Star Wars,* performed by Don Ellis and Survival, 12-inch LP album, Atlantic Records, #SD 18227, 1977 .... 10.00 12.00

☐ **Music From Star Wars,** performed by The Electric Moog Orchestra, arranged and conducted by Jimmy Wisner, 12-inch LP album, Musicor Records, #MUS-8801 .... 8.00 10.00

☐ **1084—A Space Odyssey,** performed by John Williams conducting The Boston Pops Orchestra. Includes *Parade Of The Ewoks* from *Return Of The Jedi, Star Wars Main Theme, The Empire Strikes Back, The Asteroid Field, The Forrest Battle* from *Return Of The Jedi, Star Trek, The Main Theme From TV,* and *The Main Theme From Star Trek: The Motion Picture,* 12-inch LP album, J & B Records, #JB-177 ... 9.00 11.00

☐ **Pops In Space,** performed by The Boston Pops Orchestra, conducted by John Williams. Contains *The Asteroid Field, Yoda's Theme,* and *The Imperial March* from *The Empire Strikes Back,* 12-inch LP album, Philips Digital Record, #9500 921, 1980, European Pressing 12.00 15.00

☐ **Pops In Space,** The Boston Pops Orchestra, conducted by John Williams, contains *Star Wars Main Theme* and *The Princess Leia Theme,* 12-inch LP album, Philips Digital Record, #9500 921, 1980 .... 12.00 15.00

☐ **Princess Leia's Theme,** from *Star Wars,* performed by David Matthews. From the album, *Dune,* 7-inch 45 rpm, CTI Records, #7-5005, CTI Records #OJ-40, 1977 .... 5.00 7.00

	Price Range	
☐ **Return of the Jedi,** soundtrack, RSO	10.00	15.00
☐ **Return of the Jedi,** symphonic rendition, National Philharmonic, RCA Red Seal	15.00	20.00
☐ **Space Organ,** performed by Jonas Nordwall, contains medley from *Star Wars—Main Title, Princess Leia's Theme, Cantina Band,* 12-inch LP album, Crystal Clear Records, #CCS-6003, 1979	10.00	12.00
☐ **Spaced Out Disco Fever,** contains theme from *Star Wars, Star Trek Theme, Bionic Woman Theme, Six Million Dollar Man Theme, Theme From 2001, A Space Odyssey, Beyond The Outer Limits, Rocket Man, Space Race,* and *Star Light,* 12-inch LP album, Wonderland Records, #315, stereo	6.00	8.00
☐ **Spectacular Space Hits,** performed by The Odyssey Orchestra, includes themes from *2001, Star Trek, Star Wars, Superman, Close Encounters,* and *The Empire Strikes Back,* 12-inch LP album, Sina Qua Non Records, No. SQN 7808, stereo	10.00	12.00
☐ **Star Tracks,** performed by Erich Kunzel and The Cincinnati Pops Orchestra. Includes *Main Title* from *Star Wars, The Imperial March* from *The Empire Strikes Back, Luke and Leia (Love Theme)* from *Return of the Jedi* and *Main Theme From Star Trek TV,* 12-inch LP album, Telarc Digital Record, #DG-10094, stereo . .	12.00	15.00
☐ **Star Trek—Main Theme From The Motion Picture,** performed by The Now Sound Orchestra, contains *Theme From Star Wars, Part I* and *Theme From Star Wars, Part II,* 12-inch LP album, Synthetic Plastic Records, #6001	9.00	10.00
☐ **Star Trek—21 Space Hits,** contains theme from *Star Wars,* 12-inch LP album, Music World Ltd. Record, #EMS-1003, 1979 (This is a New Zealand record album.)	12.00	15.00

Price Range

☐ **Star Wars And Close Encounters Of The Third Kind,** Suite conducted by Zubin Mehta and The Los Angeles Philharmonic Orchestra. *Star Wars Suite* contains *Main Title, Princess Leia's Theme, The Little People, Cantina Band, The Battle, Throne Room,* and *End Title,* 12-inch LP album, London Records, #7M1001, 1978 . . . .   **10.00   12.00**

☐ **Star Wars/Close Encounters,** performed by Richard "Groove" Holmes, contains *Theme From Star Wars,* 12-inch LP album, Versatile Records, #P 798, 1977 . . . .   **10.00   12.00**

☐ **Star Wars,** selections from the film, performed by Patrick Gleeson on the world's most advanced synthesizer. Contains *Star Wars Theme, Luke's Theme, The Tatooine Desert, Death Star, Star Wars Cantina Music, Princess Leia's Theme, Droids,* and *Ben Kenobi's Theme,* Mercury Records, #SRM-1-1178, 1977 . . . .   **10.00   12.00**

☐ **Also available on 8-track tape and cassette**   **10.00   12.00**

☐ **Star Wars,** John Rose playing the Great Pipe Organ at the Cathedral of St. Joseph in Hartford, Conn., 12-inch LP album, Delos Records, #DEL/F 25450 . . . .   **9.00   11.00**

☐ **Star Wars, Main Title,** from the 20th Century-Fox film, *Star Wars,* performed by Maynard Ferguson, 7-inch 45 rpm, Columbia Records, #3-10595 . . . .   **3.00   5.00**

☐ **Star Wars Main Theme,** from the album *Not Of This Earth* by Neil Norman and His Cosmic Orchestra, 7-inch 45 rpm, GNP Crescendo Records, #GNP 813, 1977 . . . .   **4.00   6.00**

☐ **Star Wars And Other Galactic Funk,** performed by Meco, 12-inch LP album, Casablanca Records, #MNLP-8001 (Meco Millennium Record Co., Inc.) 1977 . . . .   **8.00   12.00**

Price Range

☐ **The Star Wars Stars,** 7-inch 45 rpm, Lifesong
Records, #LS 45031 . . . .   5.00   7.00

☐ **Star Wars/The Empire Strikes Back,** special
in-store play disc, featuring excerpts from *Star
Wars/The Empire Strikes Back,* 12-inch LP
album (promotion copy—not for sale), RSO
Records, #RPO-1025 . . . .   10.00   15.00

☐ **Star Wars Dub,** English recording, Burning
Sounds Record, #BS-1019 . . . .   10.00   12.00

☐ **Star Wars,** music from the Sci-Fi Film, composed by John Williams, performed by the London Philharmonic Orchestra, conducted by
Colin Frechter. Contains *Main Titles, Imperial
Attack, Princess Leia's Theme, Fighter Attack,
Land Of The Sand People, The Return Home,*
12-inch LP album, Damil Records, #SGA
1000, 1977 . . . .   15.00   20.00

☐ Also available on cassette, Ahed Records, #C-
SGA 1000 . . . .   15.00   20.00

☐ Also manufactured in the United Kingdom by
Damont Records, Ltd., Hayes, Middlesex, 12-
inch LP album, Damont Records, #DMT-2001   9.00   11.00

☐ **Star Wars,** performed on two pianos by Ferrante & Teicher, contains *Main Title* from *Star
Wars,* 12-inch LP album, United Artists Record,
#UA LA 855-G 10.00   12.00

☐ **Star Wars,** original soundtrack composed and
conducted by John Williams, performed by The
London Symphony Orchestra. The first pressing contains a poster of the *Star Wars* fighting
ships and a program from the motion picture,
12-inch LP album, 20th Century Records, #2T-
541, 1977 . . . .   20.00   25.00

☐ Also available on cassette, 20th Century Rec-
ords, #RSO-541 . . . .   20.00   25.00

Price Range

☐ **Star Wars—Main Title and Cantina Band,** from the original soundtrack performed by The London Symphony Orchestra, conducted by John Williams, 7-inch 45 rpm, 20th Century Records, #TC-2345, 1977, play time 2:20 ..   **5.00**   **7.00**

☐ **As above,** longer version, play time 5:20 ....   **7.00**   **10.00**

☐ **Star Wars—Main Title,** from the original soundtrack of the motion picture, performed by The London Symphony Orchestra, conducted by John Williams, 7-inch 45 rpm, 20th Century Records, #TC-2358, 1977 ....   **5.00**   **7.00**

☐ **The Star Wars Trilogy—Return of the Jedi, The Empire Strikes Back, and Star Wars.** Music by John Williams from the original motion picture scores. Varuan Kojian conducting the Utah Symphony Orchestra, 12-inch LP album, Varese Sarabande Digital Record, #704.210, 1983 (Contains *Darth Vader's Death* and *Fight With The Tie Fighters*—only available recording of these two themes.) ...   **17.00**   **20.00**

☐ **The Star Wars Trilogy—Star Wars, The Empire Strikes Back and The Return of the Jedi,** digital recording by The Utah Symphony Orchestra, conducted by Varuan Kojian, 12-inch LP album, Victor Records, #VIC-28124, Japanese Pressing **17.00**   **20.00**

☐ **Themes From The Movie**, contains *Main Theme* from *Star Wars* an *Princess Theme,* 12-inch LP album, Pet an Records, #8201 ....   **7.00**   **9.00**

☐ **Themes From Star Wars, New York, New York, The Deep, Black Sunday, The Greatest, A Bridge Too Far, Annie Hall, Exorcist II, The Heretic and Roller Coaster,** performed by The Birchwood Pops Orchestra, contains *Main Theme From Star Wars,* 12-inch LP album, Pickwick Record, #SPC-3582, stereo **8.00**   **10.00**

STAR WARS STORY RECORDS

Price Range

☐ **The Adventures of Luke Skywalker,** from *The Empire Strikes Back,* featuring the voices of Mark Hamill, Harrison Ford, Carrie Fisher, Billy Dee Williams, Anthony Daniels, James Earl Jones, and Frank Oz. Music performed by The London Symphony Orchestra, conducted by John Williams, 12-inch LP album, RSO Records, #RS-1-3081, 1980 .... 10.00 15.00

☐ Also available on 8-track tape, RSO Records, RS-8T-1-3081 .... 10.00 15.00

☐ Also available on cassette, RSO Records, RS-CT-1-3081 .... 10.00 15.00

☐ **Christmas in the Stars,** *Star Wars* Christmas album, featuring the original cast: R2-D2 (Anthony Daniels) and C-3PO. Album concept by Meco Monardo, 12-inch LP album, RSO Records, #RS-1-3093 .... 10.00 12.00

☐ **Droid World—The Further Adventures of Star Wars,** adapted from Marvel Comics, story by Archie Goodwin, illustrated by Dick Foes, 7-inch 33⅓ rpm record and 24-page full-color illustrated booklet, Buena Vista Records, #453   5.00   7.00

☐ Also available on cassette, Buena Vista Records, #153-DC, 1983 .... 5.00   7.00

☐ **The Empire Strikes Back,** read-along book and record. Story, music, sound effects, and photos from the original motion picture, 7-inch 33⅓ rpm record and 24-page full-color illustrated book, Buena Vista Records, #451, 1979   5.00   6.00

☐ Also available on cassette, Buena Vista Records, #151-DC 5.00   6.00

☐ **L'Empire Contre-Attaque (The Empire Strikes Back), in French,** 7-inch 33⅓ rpm, Buena Vista Records, #LLP-458-F 10.00 12.00

	Price Range	
☐ **La Guerre Des Etoiles, L'Empire Contre-Attaque,** raconte par Dominique Paturel, livre-disque, 24-pages du film, 12-inch LP album, Buena Vista, #ST-3984-F	10.00	12.00
☐ (Star Wars—The Empire Strikes Back. Narrated by Dominique Paturel. Book and Record. 24 pages of photos from the original motion picture.)		
☐ **La Guerra De Las Galaxias (Star Wars),** story, music and sound effects from the original motion picture (in Spanish), 7-inch 33⅓ record and 24-page full-color illustrated booklet, Buena Vista Records, #450-M, 1979	5.00	7.00
☐ Also available on cassette, Buena Vista Records, #150-SC	5.00	7.00
☐ **La Guerra De Las Galaxias,** read-along book and record (in Spanish), story, music and sound effects from the original motion picture, 7-inch 33⅓ rpm record with 24-page full-color illustrated booklet, Buena Vista Records, #450-S	7.00	10.00
☐ Also available on cassette, Buena Vista Records, #150-SC	7.00	10.00
☐ **L'Histoire De La Guerre Des Etoiles,** raconte par Dominique Paturel. Bande originale de la musique et des effets sonores du film, 12-inch LP album, Buena Vista Records, #ST-3893-F	10.00	12.00
☐ (The Story of Star Wars, narrated by Dominique Paturel. Music and sound effects from the original soundtrack of the motion picture, in French.)		
☐ Also available on cassette	10.00	12.00
☐ **Planet of the Hogibs—The Further Adventures of Star Wars,** adapted from Marvel Comics, story by David Micheline, illustrated by Greg Winters, 7-inch 33⅓ rpm record and 24-page full-color illustrated booklet, Buena Vista Records, #454	5.00	7.00

	Price Range	
☐ Also available on cassette, Buena Vista Records, #154-DC, 1983	5.00	7.00
☐ **Rebel Mission to Ord Mantell, A Story From The Star Wars Saga,** script by Brian Daley, author of *Star Wars* and *The Empire Strikes Back* radio series, Buena Vista Records, #2104 . .	8.00	12.00
☐ Also available on cassette, Buena Vista Records, #2104-B, 1983	8.00	12.00
☐ **Return of the Jedi,** picture disk, story record, RSO	10.00	15.00
☐ **Return of the Jedi,** story record, RSO	8.00	10.00
☐ **Star Wars,** read-along adventure series. Story, music and photos from the original motion picture, 7-inch 33⅓ rpm record and 24-page full-color illustrated booklet, Buena Vista Records, #450	5.00	7.00
☐ Also available on cassette, Buena Vista Records, #150-DC, 1979	5.00	7.00
☐ **Star Wars Adventures in Colors and Shapes,** 7-inch 33⅓ record, Buena Vista Records, #480	5.00	5.00
☐ **Star Wars Adventures in ABC,** 7-inch 33⅓ rpm record, Buena Vista Records, #481	5.00	7.00
☐ **Star Wars and The Story of Star Wars,** two 4-track reel-to-reel tapes with beautifully illustrated full-color 16-page booklet and program, 20th Century Records, #RN-541 (This is an extremely rare item. The record manufacturer that bought out 20th Century Records has no record of its existence.)	100.00	125.00
☐ **Star Wars Cassette Storybook,** book and cassette, Black Falcon Ltd.	10.00	12.00
☐ **The Story of The Empire Strikes Back,** dialogue, music and sound effects from the original motion picture soundtrack. Includes 16-page full-color souvenir photo booklet. Features the voices of Mark Hamill, Harrison Ford, Carrie Fisher, Billy Dee Williams, Anthony Dan-		

	Price Range	
iels, James Earl Jones, Alec Guiness, and Frank Oz. Narration by Malachi Throne, 12-inch LP album, Buena Vista Records, #62102, 1983	8.00	10.00
☐ **The Story of Star Wars,** dialogue, music and sound effects from the original motion picture soundtrack. Includes 16-page full-color souvenir photo book, audio tape cassette, Buena Vista Records, #6101B, 1977	10.00	15.00
☐ **The Story of Star Wars,** from the original soundtrack. Contains 12-inch LP record and 16-page full-color photo booklet. Narration by Roscoe Lee Browne. Contains voices, music and sound effects from original motion picture, 12-inch LP album with booklet, 20th Century-Fox Records, #T-550	15.00	20.00

SCRIPTS

It is virtually impossible to distinguish between an original and a duplicated script. Most scripts today are reproduced by photocopy machines so there is usually only one original. Even the actors use photocopied scripts. Unless you can trace the history of a script and are convinced of its originality, assume it is a copy. Often an original will have notations and changes penciled in by the user.

	Price Range	
☐ **Script,** Star Wars, authenticated original	50.00	200.00
☐ **Script,** Star Wars, copy	15.00	20.00
☐ **Script,** Empire Strikes Back, authenticated original	50.00	150.00
☐ **Script,** Empire Strikes Back, copy	15.00	20.00
☐ **Script,** Return of the Jedi, authenticated original	50.00	150.00
☐ **Script,** Return of the Jedi, copy	15.00	20.00
☐ **Script,** Star Wars Radio Drama, 13 chapters, authenticated original, per chapter	50.00	100.00

	Price Range	
☐ **Script,** Star Wars Radio Drama, copy, all 13 chapters	25.00	35.00
☐ **Script,** Star Wars Radio Drama, copy, all 13 chapters, autographed by Anthony Daniels. Copy of his original script with notations and changes.	40.00	60.00
☐ **Script,** Empire Strikes Back Radio Drama, authenticated original, per chapter	50.00	100.00
☐ **Script,** Empire Strikes Back Radio Drama, copy	25.00	35.00

SHEET MUSIC

	Price Range	
☐ **Music Book,** The Empire Strikes Back. Lucasfilm Ltd., 1980, includes "Star Wars" (main theme), "The Imperial March" (Darth Vader's theme), "Yoda's Theme," "Han Solo and the Princess," "May The Force Be With You," and "Finale," numerous pictures with captions ...	8.00	10.00
☐ **Music Book,** Star Wars, 20th Century Fox Film Corporation, 1977, includes "Main Title" (piano solo), "Main Title" (sketch score), "Princess Leia's Theme" (piano solo), "Cantina Band" (sketch score), numerous pictures with extensive cutlines	8.00	10.00
☐ **Music Book,** The Star Wars Saga, 100 pages, music and black and white photos	10.00	12.00
☐ **Sheet Music,** "The Empire Strikes Back Medley" (Darth Vader/Yoda's theme) by John Williams, Fox Fanfare Music Inc., and Bantha Music, 1980	2.00	3.00
☐ **Sheet Music,** "Han Solo and The Princess" by John Williams, from The Empire Strikes Back. Fox Fanfare Music, Inc., 1980	2.00	3.00
☐ **Sheet Music,** "Princess Leia's Theme" by John Williams, from Star Wars. Fox Fanfare Music, Inc., 1977	2.00	3.00

	Price Range	
☐ **Sheet Music,** "Star Wars" (main theme), by John Williams, from the movie The Empire Strikes Back, Fox Fanfare Music, Inc., 1977	2.00	3.00
☐ **Star Wars Picture Music Book,** 26 pages ...	5.00	10.00

STATIONERY AND SCHOOL SUPPLIES

	Price Range	

BINDERS (3-Ring, 8½" x 11", Stuart Hall)

☐ **Yoda**	2.00	3.00
☐ **Boba Fett**	2.00	3.00
☐ **Darth Vader**	2.00	3.00
☐ **C-3PO/R2-D2**	2.00	3.00
☐ **Luke**	2.00	3.00
☐ **Book Covers,** Butterfly Originals, return of the Jedi, laminated, 1983, two per pack	2.00	3.00

BOOKMARKS

Sixteen different designs from Return of the Jedi, Random House, 1983.

☐ **Luke**	.75	1.50
☐ **Darth Vader**	.75	1.50
☐ **Leia**	.75	1.50
☐ **R2-D2**	.75	1.50
☐ **Lando**	.75	1.50
☐ **Chewbacca**	.75	1.50
☐ **Yoda**	.75	1.50
☐ **Admiral Ackbar**	.75	1.50
☐ **Ben Kenobi**	.75	1.50
☐ **Han Solo**	.75	1.50
☐ **Boba Fett**	.75	1.50
☐ **Wicket the Ewok**	.75	1.50
☐ **Emperor's guard**	.75	1.50
☐ **Stormtrooper**	.75	1.50
☐ **Jabba the Hutt**	.75	1.50

BOOKPLATES

Price Range

Four different designs from Return of the Jedi, all have the caption: "This book belongs to," Random House, 1983.

☐ **Darth Vader,** black border	.50	1.50
☐ **Yoda,** green	.50	1.50
☐ **C-3PO and R2-D2,** blue	.50	1.50
☐ **Wicket,** brown	.50	1.50

BULLETIN BOARDS (Cork, Glow-In-The-Dark, 11″ x 17″, 6 Different, Manton, E.S.B., 1981)

☐ **AT-AT**	5.00	10.00
☐ **Chewbacca**	5.00	10.00
☐ **C-3PO/R2-D2**	5.00	10.00
☐ **Darth Vader**	5.00	10.00
☐ **Luke Skywalker**	5.00	10.00
☐ **Yoda**	5.00	10.00

BULLETIN BOARDS (Cork, Manton Co., 1980)

☐ **Darth Vader,** 14″ x 23″	6.00	12.00
☐ **C-3PO and R2-D2** (sold as a set)	6.00	12.00
☐ **Yoda**	6.00	12.00
☐ **Bad Guys,** 17″ x 23″, Darth Vader, Boba Fett, Stormtroopers	6.00	12.00
☐ **Good Guys,** 17″ x 23″, Luke, Leia, Han, Chewbacca, C-3PO, R2-D2	6.00	12.00
☐ **Star Wars Logo,** 17″ x 23″, bordered by Millennium Falcon, X-Wing	6.00	12.00
☐ **Tie Fighters**	6.00	12.00

BULLETIN BOARDS (Manton Cork Co.)

☐ **Main Characters and Ewoks,** in Ewok village, 17″ x 23″	6.00	12.00
☐ **Jabba's Throne Room,** 17″ x 23″	6.00	12.00
☐ **Jabba's Throne Room,** 11″ x 17″	5.00	10.00
☐ **Max Rebo's Band,** 11″ x 17″	5.00	10.00
☐ **Darth Vader and Luke Skywalker,** dueling, 11″ x 17″	5.00	10.00

	Price Range	
☐ **C-3PO, R2-D2, and Ewoks,** 11″ x 17″	5.00	10.00
☐ **Business Cards,** one set of 12 different Star Wars scenes	2.00	5.00
☐ **Calendar,** Ballantine Books, photos from the movie, 12¼″ x 13″, 1978, came boxed	25.00	30.00
☐ **Calendar,** Ballantine Books, cover black and red, large photos from the movie, 12¼″ x 13″, 1979	20.00	25.00
☐ **Calendar,** 1980, poster art from Star Wars, Ballantine Books	10.00	15.00
☐ **Calendar,** Ballantine Books, photos from The Empire Strikes Back, 12¼″ x 13″, 1981	5.00	12.00
☐ **Calendar,** Return of the Jedi, with photographs from film, Ballantine Books, 1984.	5.00	8.00
☐ **Calendar,** Return of the Jedi, the 1984 Ewok, illustrated by Pat Paris, cartoon style color pictures, with 48 peel-off stickers. Random House.	4.00	7.00

1981 Empire Strikes Back Calendar

	Price Range	

☐ **Chalkboard,** R2-D2 and Ewok in corner, Manton Cork Co., 11″ x 17″ . . . . — 5.00 / 10.00

☐ **Compass,** C-3PO, R2-D2, Fundimensions, 1983 . . . . — 2.00 / 5.00

☐ **Construction Paper,** 12″ x 9″, Biker Scout, Stuart Hall, R.O.J. . . . . — 1.00 / 3.00

☐ **Crayon Holder and Sharpener,** Darth Vader, Fundimensions, 1983. . . . . — 2.00 / 4.00

☐ **Doodle Pad,** 12″ x 7″, Max Rebo Band, Stuart Hall, R.O.J. . . . . — 1.00 / 2.00

☐ **Empire Strikes Back Super Scene Collection,** Lucasfilm, Inc., premium from Burger King and Coca-Cola, free to children under twelve, 1980 . . . . — 5.00 / 10.00

☐ **Envelope Seals,** 24 free for membership in stamp club, Bunker Hill . . . . — 2.00 / 3.00

☐ **Erasers,** Butterfly Originals, Return of the Jedi, 1983, glow-in-the-dark spaceships, three per card . . . . — 2.00 / 3.00

☐ **Erasers,** Butterfly Originals, figurines of Wicket, R2-D2, Darth Vader, Yoda and Emperor's Royal Guard, Jabba the Hutt, Max Reebo, Bib Fortuna, Gamorrean Guard, and Admiral Ackbar, one per card, each . . . . — 1.00 / 2.00

☐ **Growth Chart,** paper characters from Star Wars, with their heights recorded on the chart — 2.00 / 5.00

☐ **Lap Pack,** portfolio with stationery and envelopes, Drawing Board . . . . — 5.00 / 8.00

☐ **Learn to Letter and Write Tablets,** 7″ x 12″, Stuart Hall

☐ **Boba Fett** . . . . — 1.00 / 2.00

☐ **Yoda** . . . . — 1.00 / 2.00

☐ **Darth Vader** . . . . — 1.00 / 2.00

☐ **Stormtroopers** . . . . — 1.00 / 2.00

☐ **Luke Skywalker** . . . . — 1.00 / 2.00

☐ **Ewoks in Flyer** . . . . — 1.00 / 2.00

☐ **Magnifying Glass,** Wicket, Fundimensions, 1983 . . . . — 3.00 / 6.00

	Price Range	
☐ **Markers,** Jedi logo in silver, one blue, one black, Butterfly Originals, 1983	1.00	2.00
Notebooks, Stuart Hall, spiral bound, covers depict scenes and characters from The Empire Strikes Back, each book contains 50 ruled sheets, ten different styles.		
☐ **Yoda**	1.00	2.00
☐ **Luke Skywalker**	1.00	2.00
☐ **Darth Vader, Stormtroopers**	1.00	2.00
☐ **C-3PO And R2-D2**	1.00	2.00
☐ **Hoth, Bespin Scenes**	1.00	2.00
☐ **Boba Fett**	1.00	2.00
☐ **Han, Leia and Luke**	1.00	2.00
☐ **Darth Vader**	1.00	2.00
☐ **Star Destroyer**	1.00	2.00
☐ **Bounty Hunter, Probot 2-1B**	1.00	2.00
☐ **Note Pads,** Star Wars, Drawing Board, 2 different, 1977		
☐ **Wookie Doodle Pad**	1.00	2.00
☐ **Official Duty Poster**	1.00	2.00
☐ **Notes,** Star Wars, boxed, Hildebrandt drawing, box of 10, Drawing Board, 1977		5.00
☐ **Notes,** Star Wars, boxed, C-3PO/R2-D2, box of 10, Drawing Board, 1977		5.00
☐ **Notes,** Star Wars, assorted, Drawing Board, 1977		5.00
☐ **Notes,** Star Wars, Foldover, set of 12, Drawing Board, 1977		5.00
☐ **Pen,** maker unknown, printed with "May the Force Be With You," cap has Darth Vader's head on shirt pocket tab, length 5", ...	1.00	2.00
☐ **Pencil,** The Empire Strikes Back, printed in large red letters, red strip with heads of major characters	1.00	2.00
☐ **Pencils,** Jedi logo, Darth Vader or C-3PO, package of four, Butterfly Originals, 1983	2.00	4.00

Price Range

☐ **Pencils,** Pop-a-point, glittery red, "May the Force be with you" in silver, two pencils to a card, 22 pencil point rechargers, Butterfly Originals, 1983 . . . .   2.00   4.00

☐ **Pencils,** red, with Darth Vader, package of four, Butterfly Originals, 1983 . . . .   2.00   4.00

☐ **Pencil Cup,** Yoda, ceramic, Sigma, 1983 . . . .   15.00   25.00

☐ **Pencil Heads,** C-3PO, Darth Vader, Emperor's Royal Guard, Ewok, Butterfly Originals, 1983   .50   1.50

☐ **Pencil Pouch,** Return of the Jedi, blue background, Luke and Darth dueling, Butterfly Originals, 1983 . . . .   2.00   5.00

☐ **Pencil Sharpener,** special figure collection, R2-D2, Yoda or Darth Vader, Butterfly Originals, 1983 . . . .   1.00   2.00

☐ **Pencil Tablet,** 8″ x 10″, R2-D2/Ewok, Stuart Hall, R.O.J. 1.00   2.00

Pencil Tablets, 8″ x 10″, 50 sheets, Stuart Hall

☐ C-3PO, R2-D2 . . . .   1.00   2.00

☐ Space vehicles 1.00   2.00

☐ Planet scenes 1.00   2.00

☐ **Pencil Tablets** (four scenes, 8″ x 10″, Stuart Hall, 1980)

☐ **Probot** 1.00   2.00

☐ **21-B** 1.00   2.00

☐ **Bounty Hunters** 1.00   2.00

☐ **Bespin Characters,** Star Destroyer, and Millennium Falcon 1.00   2.00

Pencil Tins (metal with hinged lids, Metal Box Co., 1980)

☐ **R2-D2 and C-3PO** 1.00   3.00

☐ **Yoda** 1.00   3.00

☐ **Darth Vader** 1.00   3.00

☐ **Chewbacca** 1.00   3.00

Pencil Tops, H. C. Ford and Sons Ltd., made in Macao for British market, 1982, 48 pieces to a box

	Price Range	
Set One—Star Wars Box		
☐ **Chewbacca**	2.00	5.00
☐ **Darth Vader**	2.00	5.00
☐ **Han Solo** (Hoth gear)	2.00	5.00
☐ **Luke** (flight suit)	2.00	5.00
☐ **R2-D2**	2.00	5.00
☐ **Yoda**	2.00	5.00
Set Two—Return of the Jedi Box		
☐ **Admiral Ackbar**	2.00	5.00
☐ **Bib Fortuna**	2.00	5.00
☐ **Darth Vader**	2.00	5.00
☐ **Gamorrean Guard**	2.00	5.00
☐ **Imperial Guard**	2.00	5.00
☐ **Wicket**	2.00	5.00
☐ **Pencil Tray,** C-3PO, ceramic, Sigma, 1981 ..	15.00	30.00
☐ **Pen,** Darth Vader felt-tip marker, 3½″, red felt-tip marker, shape of Darth Vader, Butterfly Originals, 1983	1.00	2.00
☐ **Pens,** two pens on card, picture of Jedi logo and circular picture of characters in blue on white background, Butterfly Originals, 1983	2.00	4.00
Pocket Memos (3″ x 5″, 70 sheets, Stuart Hall)		
☐ **C-3PO and R2-D2**	.75	1.50
☐ **Yoda**	.75	1.50
☐ **Darth Vader**	.75	1.50
☐ **Stormtroopers**	.75	1.50
☐ **Boba Fett**	.75	1.50
☐ **Luke Skywalker**	.75	1.50
☐ **Aliens**	.75	1.50
Portfolios, Stuart Hall, five different scenes from The Empire Strikes Back, each portfolio has inside pocket.		
☐ **Luke Skywalker**	1.00	2.00
☐ **Darth Vader, Stormtroopers**	1.00	2.00
☐ **C-3PO and R2-D2**	1.00	2.00
☐ **Bounty Hunters, Probot 2-1B**	1.00	2.00

	Price Range	
☐ **Yoda**	1.00	2.00
Portfolios (R.O.J., Stuart Hall, 9¾″ x 11″)		
☐ **Luke and Darth**	1.00	2.00
☐ **Jabba the Hut**	1.00	2.00
☐ **Biker Scouts**	1.00	2.00
☐ **C-3PO/R2-D2/Wicket**	1.00	2.00
☐ **Rebo Band**	1.00	2.00
☐ **Battle Scene**	1.00	2.00
☐ **Postcards,** package of 20 Star Wars postcards featuring C-3PO and R2-D2 on cover, Drawing Board, 1977	5.00	10.00
☐ **Prestomagix,** American Publishing Corp., rub-down transfers that allow you to create your own scenes, series of six, 1980	1.00	3.00
☐ **Puffy Stickers,** Empire Strikes Back, Topps Chewing Gum Co., peel-off, three-dimensional stickers, eight to a set with all the characters, 1980	3.00	5.00
☐ **Puffy Stickers,** peel-off, three-dimensional, two different sets, Drawing Board Greeting Cards, 1983	2.00	4.00
☐ **Puffy Stickers,** two sets, 7 stickers in one set, 6 stickers in the other, made in Taiwan, proba-bly unlicensed, R.O.J.	2.00	4.00
☐ **Puffy Stickers,** two sets, 6 stickers in each set, made in Taiwan, probably unlicensed, Happy-mates Division Electro-Plastics Inc.	2.00	4.00
☐ **Puffy Stickers** (Return of the Jedi, water-proof, set, Decal Specialties/Drawing Board, 1983) Death Star, X-Wing, Tie, Falcon, Imperial Shut-tle	2.00	4.00
☐ AT-AT, B-Wing, Sail Barge, Speeder Bike Scout	2.00	4.00
☐ **Reinforcements,** Butterfly Originals, foil, 48 per pack	1.00	2.00
☐ **Rubber Stamps,** Return of the Jedi, boy or girl Ewok on card with 3 interchangeable stamps, Adam Joseph, 1983	1.00	3.00

	Price Range	
Rubber Stamps (Return of the Jedi, Adam Joseph Ind., 1983)		
☐ **X-Wing Fighter Pilot**	.75	1.50
☐ **Gamorrean Guard**	.75	1.50
☐ **Darth Vader**	.75	1.50
☐ **C-3PO**	.75	1.50
☐ **Imperial Guard**	.75	1.50
☐ **Yoda**	.75	1.50
☐ **Chewbacca**	.75	1.50
☐ **Wicket**	.75	1.50
☐ **Tie Fighter**	.75	1.50
☐ **Biker Scout**	.75	1.50
☐ **Admiral Ackbar**	.75	1.50
☐ **Millennium Falcon**	.75	1.50
☐ **Ruler,** Butterfly Originals, blue and white, cast, 12",	1.00	3.00
☐ **School Kit,** 6" ruler, pencil sharpener, eraser, and pencil pouch, Return of the Jedi, Butterfly Originals	5.00	10.00
☐ **Scissors,** red plastic, changing inset picture of Darth Vader and Imperial Shuttle, Butterfly Originals, 1983	2.00	4.00
☐ **Star Wars Stamp Collection Kit,** H.E. Harris and Co., album, 24 Star Wars seals plus miscellaneous stamps, 1977	10.00	15.00
☐ **Stationery,** Drawing Board, die-cut, R2-D2, 1977	2.00	5.00
☐ **Stationery,** Drawing Board, Star Wars, boxed, 1977	2.00	5.00
☐ **Stationery,** Drawing Board, Star Wars, padded, 1977	2.00	5.00
Themebooks, 8" x 10½" or 8½" x 11", Stuart Hall		
☐ **Boba Fett**	1.00	2.00
☐ **Yoda**	1.00	2.00
☐ **Han/Luke/Leia**	1.00	2.00
☐ **Darth and Boba Fett**	1.00	2.00

Star Wars Stamp Collecting Kit, H.E. Harris

	Price Range	
☐ **Space Vehicles**	1.00	2.00
☐ **Chewbacca**	1.00	2.00
☐ **Heroes**	1.00	2.00
☐ **Themebooks,** R.O.S., Stuart Hall, 8½″ x 11″		
☐ **Luke and Darth**	1.00	2.00
☐ **Jabba the Hut**	1.00	2.00
☐ **Biker Scouts**	1.00	2.00
☐ **C-3PO/R2-D2/Wicket**	1.00	2.00
☐ **Rebo Band**	1.00	2.00
☐ **Battle Scene**	1.00	2.00
☐ **Transfer Set,** Return of the Jedi, "Battle on Endor," includes 12″ x 24″ action poster, transfer sheet with over 40 transfers, special magic stick, Prestomagix, 1983	4.00	10.00
☐ **Valentines,** one box of Return of the Jedi Valentines	5.00	10.00
☐ **Wrapping Paper,** Empire montage in color, 30″ x 5′ roll, Drawing Board, 1981	2.00	5.00

TOYS

	Price Range	
☐ **Action Play Doh Set,** Kenner, Empire Strikes Back, molds of the characters plus snow speeder	15.00	25.00
☐ **Action Play Doh Set,** Kenner, Ewok village . .	8.00	15.00
☐ **Action Play Doh Set,** Kenner, Luke, Leia, Jabba and five other characters plus castle and plastic skiff, 1983	8.00	15.00
☐ **Action Play Doh Set,** Kenner, Star Wars, molds of Luke, Leia, Darth, R2-D2, X-Wing fighter and playmate of Death Star	20.00	30.00
☐ **Action Play Doh Set,** Kenner, Yoda, molds of Yoda, Luke, R2-D2, Darth, X-Wing plus Dagobah playmate	15.00	25.00
☐ **Biker Scout Laser Pistol,** Kenner, 1983	10.00	20.00
☐ **Bop Bag,** Kenner, R2-D2, heat-sealed vinyl returns to standing position after each bop, height 36″	10.00	20.00
☐ **Bop Bag,** Kenner, Chewbacca, 1978, 50″ . . .	10.00	20.00
☐ **Bop Bag,** Kenner, Darth Vader, 50″	10.00	20.00
☐ **Bop Bag,** Kenner, Jawa, 36″, 1979	10.00	20.00
Candy Heads, Topps, The Empire Strikes Back, series one, plastic figurine heads, filled with candy, each:		
☐ Darth Vader	1.00	2.00
☐ C-3PO	1.00	2.00
☐ Chewbacca	1.00	2.00
☐ Rebel fighter	1.00	2.00
☐ Stormtrooper	1.00	2.00
Candy Heads, Topps, the Empire Strikes Back, Yoda series, filled with candy, each:		
☐ Yoda	.75	1.50
☐ Taun-taun	.75	1.50
☐ Bounty Hunter Bossk	.75	1.50
☐ 2-1B	.75	1.50
Candy Heads, Topps, Return of the Jedi:		
☐ Darth Vader	.50	1.50

	Price Range	
☐ Admiral Ackbar	.50	1.50
☐ Wickett	.50	1.50
☐ Sy Snootles	.50	1.50
☐ Jabba the Hut	.50	1.50
☐ Baby Ewok	.50	1.50
☐ **Chewbacca,** Kenner, large furry stuffed polyester with bandolier	20.00	35.00
☐ **Color and Clean Machine,** 50″, action scenes for continuous coloring, four crayons and wipe-off cloth	4.00	8.00
☐ **Darth Vader Action Kit,** battery powered, breathing sound	10.00	20.00
☐ **Darth Vader Communicator,** mirror-backed communicator for sending light signals through deep space, round disc has picture of Darth	3.00	5.00
☐ **Die-Cast Imperial Tie Fighter,** Kenner	15.00	25.00
☐ **Die-Cast Landspeeder,** Kenner, rolling wheels simulate floating motion, miniature Luke and C-3PO	25.00	40.00
☐ **Die-Cast Millennium Falcon,** Kenner, transparent cockpit with Han and Chewbacca in cockpit, laser cannon and radar dish	35.00	50.00
☐ **Die-Cast Slave I,** Kenner, spaceship has laser cannon and Boba Fett in cockpit, retractable landing gear	20.00	40.00
☐ **Die-Cast Snow Speeder,** Kenner, movable laser cannon, retractable landing gear, rebel soldiers	20.00	40.00
☐ **Die-Cast Star Destroyer,** Kenner, includes captured rebel ship	25.00	50.00
☐ **Die-Cast Tie Bomber,** Kenner, rare	150.00	250.00
☐ **Die-Cast Tie Fighter,** Kenner, miniature Darth	15.00	25.00
☐ **Die-Cast Twin Pod Cloud Car,** Kenner, retractable landing gear, orange, Bespin guards in cockpit	25.00	40.00
☐ **Die-Cast X-Wing,** Kenner, plastic wings open, Luke in cockpit	25.00	40.00

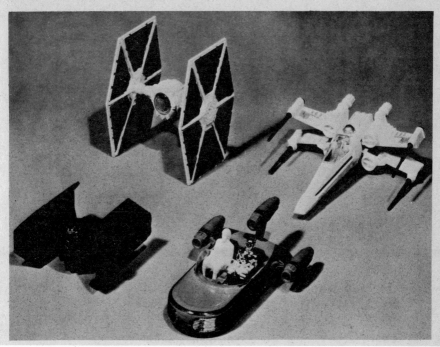

Star Wars Die-Cast Vehicles (Series I), from Kenner

	Price Range	
☐ **Die-Cast Y-Wing,** Kenner, laser cannon swivels, rear engine pods detachable, laser bomb, retractable landing gear	25.00	40.00
☐ **Dip Dots,** Kenner, Star Wars painting set, set of eight water colors in non-spill tray with 16 posters from the movie	10.00	15.00
☐ **Ewok Watercolor Set**	4.00	8.00
☐ **Figurines,** Fundimensions, 1980, Yoda, Leia or Luke on Taun-taun, all approx. 5½", 4 colored paints, brush and painting instructions	5.00	8.00
☐ **Force Light Saber,** Kenner, Empire Strikes Back version with glow-in-the-dark plastic, low humming sound when swung, needs no batteries.	10.00	20.00

Price Range

☐ **Frisbee,** Empire Strikes Back, shows Darth Vader's head, C-3PO and R2-D2, promotional give-away from Burger King and Coca-Cola   4.00   6.00

☐ **Give a Show Projector,** Kenner, Empire Strikes Back, set of 16 strips of 112 slides ..   15.00   20.00

☐ **Give a Show Projector,** Kenner, Ewok projector 10.00   15.00

☐ **Give a Show Projector,** Kenner, 16 color strips of 112 slides tell Star Wars story 25.00   40.00

☐ **Kite,** Darth Vader, 1983, 55″ figure kite, Spectra Star 4.00   5.00

☐ **Kite,** Droids, 1985, 80″ streamer kite, Spectra Star 4.00   5.00

☐ **Kite,** Ewoks on Hang Glider, 1985, 80″ mylar octopus, Spectra Star 6.00   8.00

☐ **Kite,** Luke Skywalker, 1983, 55″ Spectra Star   6.00   8.00

☐ **Kite,** Star Wars, 1983, 42″ Delta Wing, Spectra Star 3.00   4.00

☐ **Laser Pistol,** Kenner, black gun, action button activates 2-speed laser sounds, replica of pistol used by Han Solo came with Star Wars, Empire, and Jedi decals 20.00   30.00

☐ **Laser Rifle,** Kenner, black plastic, two electronic sounds by activating trigger and rapid fire button, with scope uses one 9 volt battery, 1978 ....   35.00   40.00

☐ **Light Saber,** Kenner, has vinyl inflatable blade that lights up, comes with patch kit, uses two "AA" batteries 25.00   40.00

☐ **Light Saber,** "The Force" light saber, Empire Strikes Back and Return of the Jedi, manual noisemaker, no batteries needed, Kenner ...   9.00   15.00

☐ **Light Saber,** Droids animated TV, 1985. Battery operated, Kenner 12.00   18.00

☐ **Movie Viewer,** Kenner, scenes of Star Wars, hand crank, forward or reverse, super eight, color film cassettes 20.00   30.00

Star Wars Electronic Laser Rifle, from Kenner

	Price Range	
☐ **Movie Viewer,** Kenner, scenes from Empire Strikes Back, forward or reverse, focal control	15.00	20.00
☐ **Music Box Radio,** Ewok, Kenner	10.00	20.00
☐ **Paint By Number,** Fundimensions, 1983, 8″ x 10″ scene from Return of the Jedi. Includes paints, four different sets	10.00	12.00
☐ **Paint By Number,** Fundimensions, acrylic, glow-in-the-dark paint, each: Darth Vader, Princess Leia, Luke Yoda, each	5.00	8.00
☐ **Playnts Poster Set,** Kenner, tip-proof paints with posters of Luke Skywalker, Princess Leia, Darth Vader, R2-D2, and scenes from Star Wars, 16″ x 24″	8.00	12.00
☐ **Radio,** Luke Skywalker AM headset radio, styled like pilot's headset with Star Wars decals	25.00	45.00
☐ **Radio Controlled R2-D2,** Kenner, replica of popular robot, beeping sound, automated, height 8″, 1978	50.00	100.00
☐ **R2-D2,** stuffed, Kenner, movable legs and squeeker	20.00	30.00
☐ **R2-D2 Toy Toter,** American Toy and Furniture Co., 17″ x 28″	15.00	25.00

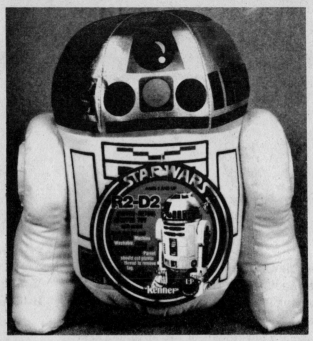

Stuffed R2–D2, from Kenner

	Price Range	
☐ **Rub-On Transfers,** Letrasett, printed in U.K. for European market, 1977, 3 panoramas and transfer sheets	10.00	25.00
☐ **Scout Walker Command Tower,** Gym-Dandy, has speeder bike ride and sound effects	100.00	300.00
☐ **Sit 'N' Spin,** Ewok from Return of the Jedi ...	15.00	25.00
☐ **SSP Van,** Kenner, Darth Vader featured on black van with headers, mags, custom grilles, sparks and sound	20.00	30.00
☐ **SSP Van,** Kenner, white van features Luke, Leia, R2-D2 and C-3PO, sounds and sparks	20.00	30.00
☐ **SSP Van Set,** includes both vans listed above	40.00	50.00

Price Range

☐ **Star Wars Duel at the Death Star Auto Racing Set,** Power Passers, Darth Vader on 19″ x 20″ box, equipped with track, ramps and two electric cars shaped like a Tie-fighter and an X-Wing fighter, 1978 .... 100.00 150.00

☐ **Stuffed Figures,** large, Kenner, 1983: Latara, Paploo, Princess Kneesa, Wicket, each: 20.00 30.00

☐ **Stuffed Figures,** small, Kenner, 1983, Leeni, Mookiee, Nippet, Gwig Malani Wiley, each .. 15.00 20.00

☐ **As above,** four pack of small plush figures .. 50.00 75.00

☐ **Sy Snootles and the Rebo Band,** Kenner, 1983 .... 10.00 15.00

☐ **Talking Telephone,** Ewok, Kenner 25.00 40.00

☐ **Teaching Clock,** Ewok, Kenner 15.00 25.00

☐ **Yoda Hand Puppet,** painted plastic, 8½″, came boxed 12.00 20.00

☐ **Yoda the Jedi Master,** Kenner, 1981, approx. 5¼″ tall, ask any question, turn him upside-down and receive one of twenty answers ... 10.00 15.00

MICRO COLLECTIONS

Micro Collections were an attempt by Kenner to diversify their *Star Wars* line. These sets came with posed, painted die-cast metal figures approximately 1¼ inches in height. These sets should not be confused with those made for the larger action figures.

☐ **Bespin Control Room,** Kenner, breakaway window, remote lever and platform, comes with 4 die-cast figures 15.00 20.00

☐ **Bespin Freeze Chamber,** platform lowers figure into chamber, remote claw, escape hatch, 4 figures 15.00 20.00

☐ **Bespin Gantry,** Kenner, remote door, rotating platform, comes with 4 figures 15.00 20.00

☐ **Bespin World,** Kenner, Control Room, Freeze Chamber and Gantry plus 16 figures 25.00 40.00

	Price Range	
☐ **Death Star Compactor,** Kenner, trash compactor, escape hatch, blast door plus 8 die-cast figures.	15.00	20.00
☐ **Death Star Escape,** Kenner, bridge, exploding cannon, elevator and rope assembly, six figures.	15.00	20.00
☐ **Death Star World,** Kenner, Death Star Compactor, Death Star Escape plus 14 figures. . .	25.00	40.00
☐ **Hoth Generator Attack,** Kenner, exploding generator, scout walker and 6 die-cast figures	10.00	20.00
☐ **Hoth Ion Cannon,** Kenner, cannon, observation tower and blast doors, 8 figures	10.00	20.00
☐ **Hoth Turret Defense,** Kenner, two exploding gun turrets and 6 die-cast figures	10.00	20.00
☐ **Hoth Wampa Cave,** Kenner, includes 4 figures	10.00	20.00
☐ **Hoth World,** Hoth Generator Attack, Hoth Ion Cannon, Hoth Turret Defense, Hoth Wampa Cave plus 19 figures	30.00	40.00
☐ **Millennium Falcon,** Kenner, top comes off to reveal secret compartments, 6 figures	30.00	50.00
☐ **Imperial Tie Fighter,** break-apart feature, 1 figure	15.00	25.00
☐ **Rebel Armored Snow Speeder,** Kenner, cockpit opens, harpoon gun, break-apart feature, includes 2 die-cast figures	15.00	25.00
☐ **X-Wing Fighter,** Kenner, break-apart feature, 1 figure	15.00	25.00

TOYS, ACTION-FIGURE RELATED

All the toys in this section were designed to be used with the small action figures (3¾"). Values listed are for complete toys in the original boxes. Toys without boxes are worth about 50% less. Toys "Mint in Box" are worth 25% more!

	Price Range	
☐ **Action Figure Collector's Case,** black vinyl, illustrated cover, holds 24 figures, Kenner, 1979	5.00	10.00

Price Range

☐ **Action Figure Collector's Stand,** plastic stand for action figures with cardboard backdrop, done before action figures were produced to get Star Wars merchandise out as soon as possible, Kenner, 1977 . . . .   20.00   30.00

☐ **Armoured Sentinel Transport,** Kenner, mini-rig collection, moveable laser cannon from the Return of the Jedi 6.00   10.00

☐ **AT-AT (All-Terrain Armored-Transport) Model,** also called the Imperial Snow Walker, Lucasfilm, Ltd., poseable legs, moveable control center, includes two snow speeders and two laser turrets, height 17½" 50.00   75.00

☐ **ATL (Air to Land) Interceptor Vehicle,** from Droids animated, Kenner, 1985 . . . .   8.00   10.00

☐ **AST-5,** anti-gravity vehicle, mini-rig, has moveable laser cannons 6.00   10.00

☐ **A-Wing Fighter,** battery-operated sound, Kenner, 1985 . . . .   15.00   20.00

☐ **Battle Damaged Tie Interceptor,** releaseable solar panels, lights and sounds, Kenner, 1983   30.00   40.00

AT-AT, Empire Strikes Back Box

Price Range

☐ **Battle-Damaged X-Wing Fighter,** Kenner, set of labels lets kids choose to make Luke's spaceship look battle damaged, retractable landing gear and laser lights and sounds 30.00   40.00

☐ **B-Wing Fighter,** Kenner, 1983 . . . .   20.00   30.00

☐ **Cantina Adventure Set,** Kenner Corp., includes four action figures: Greedo, Hammerhead, Walrus Man and Snaggle Tooth, 1978   35.00   50.00

☐ **C-3PO Collector's Case,** gold plastic bust of C-3PO, holds 40 figures, Kenner, 1983 . . . . .   8.00   10.00

☐ **Captivator, Cap-2,** Mini-rig, rotating legs with suction cups stick to flat surfaces, rotating arms can grasp action figures, Kenner 6.00   10.00

☐ **Chewbacca Bandolier Strap,** carries 10 action figures 5.00   10.00

☐ **Cloud City Playset,** Kenner, Bespin backdrop and four action figures: Han Solo, Ugnaught, Calrissian and Boba Fett, 1981 . . . .   15.00   25.00

☐ **Creature Cantina,** Kenner Corp., scenic backdrop and action platform, button-operated door, action levers move figures around in simulated battles 20.00   30.00

☐ **Dagobah Action Set,** Kenner, craggy tree house where the master of the Jedi lives, levitation levers, a bog where action figures sink, tree cave, levers to relive light saber battle . .   20.00   30.00

☐ **Darth Vader Collector's Case,** black plastic, shaped like bust of Darth, holds 24 figures, Kenner, 1980 . . . .   8.00   15.00

☐ **Darth Vader's Tie Fighter,** solar panels pop off, movable cockpit, sound, batteries, Kenner   25.00   40.00

☐ **Death Star Space Station,** elevator, 4 floors, laser cannon bridge, control area & trash compactor, Kenner, 1978 . . . .   50.00   75.00

☐ **Desert Sail Skiff,** Mini-rig, Kenner 6.00   10.00

☐ **Desert Skiff Vehicle,** from Droids animated, Kenner, 1985 . . . .   12.00   18.00

Price Range

☐ **Display Arena,** for action figures, four L-shaped plastic stands with cardboard backdrops showing scenes from the Empire Strikes Back, Kenner, 1981 .... 15.00 20.00

☐ **Droid Factory,** Kenner, 33 interchangeable parts, five different robots can be made at a time, crane takes parts from supply to assembly, ramp rolls out the finished product 30.00 40.00

☐ **Empire Strikes Back Rebel Command Center Adventure Set,** Kenner Corp., includes cardboard Rebel base and three action figures, 1981 .... 20.00 25.00

☐ **Endor Forest Ranger,** Mini-rig, movable hatch, Kenner 6.00 10.00

☐ **Ewok Assault Catapult,** Kenner, 1983 ...... 10.00 15.00

☐ **Ewok Battle Wagon,** Kenner, 1984 .... 20.00 30.00

☐ **Ewok Combat Glider,** Kenner, 1983 .... 10.00 15.00

☐ **Ewok Family Hut Playset,** Ewok animated, Kenner, 1985 .... 20.00 30.00

☐ **Ewok Fire Cart Playset,** Ewok animated, Kenner, 1985 .... 20.00 30.00

☐ **Ewok Village Action Playset,** Kenner, net trap, vine elevator, tree escape chute, carrying litter, two huts, campfire 20.00 30.00

☐ **Ewok Woodland Wagon Playset,** Ewok animated, Kenner, 1985 .... 8.00 15.00

☐ **Hoth Ice Planet Adventure Set,** Kenner, cardboard backdrop, AT-AT and battle scenes plus plastic base and action figures, 1980 .... 20.00 25.00

☐ **Hoth Wampa,** movable legs and spring-loaded arms, Kenner 8.00 15.00

☐ **Imperial Attack Base,** Kenner, ice planet Hoth with trenches, mines explode, the command post blows up, laser gun makes firing sound 20.00 30.00

☐ **Imperial Shuttle,** Kenner, 1983, fold-down wings and ramp, many movable features 30.00 50.00

Price Range

☐ **Imperial Shuttle Pod,** Kenner, mini-rig collection, rearview mirror and wing cannons, from Return of the Jedi **6.00** **10.00**

☐ **Imperial Side Gunner,** from Droids animated, Kenner, 1985 .... **12.00** **18.00**

☐ **Imperial Sniper Vehicle,** Kenner, 1985 ..... **5.00** **10.00**

☐ **Imperial Troop Transporter,** Kenner, accommodates two Star Wars figures, with six sounds, rotating laser gun and swiveling radar dish, six compartments for captured figures, two prisoner immobilization units, uses one "C" battery **25.00** **45.00**

☐ **Interceptor Int-4-Minirig,** opening hatch, moveable laser, landing skids and remote controlled wings, Kenner **6.00** **10.00**

☐ **ISP-6,** Imperial Transport, Mini-rig, movable wing cannons, ... **6.00** **10.00**

☐ **Jabba The Hutt Dungeon Action Playset,** Kenner Corp., plastic case and three action figures: 8D-8, Nikto and Klaatu, 1983 .... **25.00** **40.00**

☐ **Jawa Sand Crawler,** radio controlled, operates up to 20 feet away, moves in any direction, roof latch opens on control area, manual elevator, Kenner **75.00** **150.00**

☐ **Land Of Jawas,** Kenner Corp., simulated sand dune base with boulders and cave, action levers move figures around in mock battles, escape pod and sand crawler with elevator ... **35.00** **50.00**

☐ **Landspeeder,** Kenner Corp., special suspension which shifts from non-moving position to a floating ride on spring wheels, room for four action figures, release button pops hood to reveal turbo reactor **25.00** **40.00**

☐ **Landspeeder,** Kenner Corp., battery operated, room for four action figures, hand-held control shaped like R2-D2, larger than other landspeeder **75.00** **100.00**

Price Range

☐ **Laser Rifle Case,** for action figures, holds 19 figures, Kenner, 1984 .... 10.00 20.00

☐ **Millennium Falcon Spaceship,** Kenner, battle alert sounds, cockpit has flip-open canopy, radar dish swivels, retractable landing skids, hidden compartments for attacking storm-troopers 35.00 60.00

☐ **Mobile Laser Cannon, MCL-3,** Kenner, Mini-rig, has cockpit which opens, dome for protection 6.00 10.00

☐ **Multi-terrain Vehicle,** Kenner, spring-loaded legs, moveable laser, has room for action figure 6.00 10.00

☐ **One-Man Sand Skimmer,** Kenner, 1985 .... 5.00 10.00

☐ **Patrol Dewback,** Kenner Corp., Tatooine creature ridden by stormtroopers, tail moved left to right makes head move, saddle and reins included 20.00 30.00

☐ **Personnel Deployment Transport,** Kenner, mini-rig has ramps that open and close, moveable laser gun 6.00 10.00

☐ **Radar Laser Cannon,** Kenner, swivels, clicks, and explodes 6.00 10.00

☐ **Rancor Monster,** Kenner, 1983 .... 10.00 20.00

☐ **Rebel Transport,** Kenner, front and back comes off to expose cockpit and clicking cannons, crew chamber, escape hatch, five back-packs, four gas masks 30.00 50.00

☐ **Security Scout Vehicle,** Kenner, 1985 ...... 5.00 10.00

☐ **Scout Walker Vehicle,** Kenner, head swivels, side cannons turn and click, push button makes legs move, stands unassisted 20.00 50.00

☐ **Slave I,** Kenner, Boba Fett's spaceship, moveable ramps, cockpit has adjustable seat, gravity activated wings move freely, frozen Han Solo included 30.00 50.00

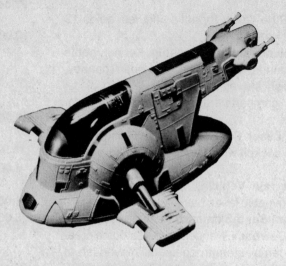

Slave I Action Figure Accessory

Price Range

☐ **Snow Speeder,** Kenner, clear cockpit can hold two action figures, remote landing gear, laser lights pulsate, sound, removable harpoon with string, battery operated 35.00   50.00

☐ **Speeder Bike Vehicle,** Kenner, automatic rear brake flaps, moveable handle bars, blow-apart battle damage 10.00   15.00

☐ **Star Destroyer,** cross section of ship, meditation chamber, movable hatches and guns, Kenner 35.00   60.00

☐ **Tauntaun,** slot in back for action figure to ride, Kenner 5.00   10.00

☐ **Tauntaun With Open Belly,** Kenner, save Luke from freezing by putting him in the open belly rescue feature, sculpted saddle, moveable hind legs 15.00   25.00

☐ **Tie Fighter,** Kenner Corp., has solar panels that come off at the press of a button to simulate battle damage, red laser cannon lights up, with laser sound, uses two "AA" batteries ... 30.00   50.00

Price Range

☐ **Tri-pod Laser Cannon,** Kenner, energizer unit and hose, moveable tripods, makes machine gun sound 6.00   10.00

☐ **Turret And Probot Play Set,** Kenner, recreate Hoth battle scenes with sculpted replica of ice planet, figures can be ejected at flip of a switch, laser gun turret swivels and clicks 20.00   40.00

☐ **Twin Pod Cloud Car,** Kenner, has clear canopy, manually operated landing gear 25.00   50.00

☐ **Vehicle Maintenance,** Kenner, repairs ships, comes with eight tools, two energizers which attach to vehicles 15.00   20.00

☐ **X-Wing Fighter,** Kenner Corporation, rebel space craft, button opens wings to X formation and closes them again, front landing gear locks up during flight, with real laser sound, uses two "AA" batteries 25.00   35.00

☐ **Y-Wing Fighter,** Kenner, Return of the Jedi collection, battery operated laser, cannons and sounds, bomb and landing pads 25.00   35.00

VIDEO GAMES

Price Range

☐ **Jedi Arena,** Parker Bros., for Atari and Sears game systems, 1983 . . . .   15.00   25.00

☐ **Star Wars,** The Empire Strikes Back, Parker Bros., for Atari and Sears video game systems, 1982 . . . .   15.00   25.00

☐ **Star Wars,** The Arcade Game, Parker Bros., 1984 . . . .   400.00 1000.00

☐ **Return of the Jedi,** Death Star Battle, Parker Bros., 1984 . . . .   15.00   25.00

ABOUT THE AUTHORS

Sue Cornwell graduated from Hood College with a Bachelor of Arts degree. She attended the first *Star Trek* convention in New York in 1972 while still in college. In 1974, she was a dealer at a convention and has attended hundreds of conventions since that time.

Mike Kott graduated from Rensselaer Polytechnic Institute with degrees in Physics and Geology. After a short time as an Engineering Geologist, he entered the collectibles field as a comic book dealer.

In 1976, the authors formed Intergalactic Trading Co., Inc., specializing in *Star Trek* and *Star Wars* collectibles. They have attended over 300 conventions as dealers, and sold through the mail for over 10 years. Intergalactic is currently the most active company in the country dealing primarily in *Star Trek* and *Star Wars* collectibles.

The authors were major contributors to the first edition of the *Star Trek and Star Wars Collectibles Guide* and helped with subsequent editions until taking over authorship of the current, larger book.

The HOUSE OF COLLECTIBLES Series

☐ *Please send me the following price guides –*
☐ *I would like the most current edition of the books listed below.*

THE OFFICIAL PRICE GUIDES TO:

☐ 199-3	**American Silver & Silver Plate** 5th Ed.	$11.95
☐ 513-1	**Antique Clocks** 3rd Ed.	10.95
☐ 283-3	**Antique & Modern Dolls** 3rd Ed.	10.95
☐ 287-6	**Antique & Modern Firearms** 6th Ed.	11.95
☐ 738-X	**Antiques & Collectibles** 8th Ed.	10.95
☐ 289-2	**Antique Jewelry** 5th Ed.	11.95
☐ 539-5	**Beer Cans & Collectibles** 4th Ed.	7.95
☐ 521-2	**Bottles Old & New** 10th Ed.	10.95
☐ 532-8	**Carnival Glass** 2nd Ed.	10.95
☐ 295-7	**Collectible Cameras** 2nd Ed.	10.95
☐ 548-4	**Collectibles of the '50s & '60s** 1st Ed.	9.95
☐ 740-1	**Collectible Toys** 4th Ed.	10.95
☐ 531-X	**Collector Cars** 7th Ed.	12.95
☐ 538-7	**Collector Handguns** 4th Ed.	14.95
☐ 748-7	**Collector Knives** 9th Ed.	12.95
☐ 518-2	**Collector Plates** 4th Ed.	11.95
☐ 296-5	**Collector Prints** 7th Ed.	12.95
☐ 001-6	**Depression Glass** 2nd Ed.	9.95
☐ 589-1	**Fine Art** 1st Ed.	19.95
☐ 311-2	**Glassware** 3rd Ed.	10.95
☐ 243-4	**Hummel Figurines & Plates** 6th Ed.	10.95
☐ 523-9	**Kitchen Collectibles** 2nd Ed.	10.95
☐ 291-4	**Military Collectibles** 5th Ed.	11.95
☐ 525-5	**Music Collectibles** 6th Ed.	11.95
☐ 313-9	**Old Books & Autographs** 7th Ed.	11.95
☐ 298-1	**Oriental Collectibles** 3rd Ed.	11.95
☐ 746-0	**Overstreet Comic Book** 17th Ed.	11.95
☐ 522-0	**Paperbacks & Magazines** 1st Ed.	10.95
☐ 297-3	**Paper Collectibles** 5th Ed.	10.95
☐ 529-8	**Pottery & Porcelain** 6th Ed.	11.95
☐ 524-7	**Radio, TV & Movie Memorabilia** 3rd Ed.	11.95
☐ 288-4	**Records** 7th Ed.	10.95
☐ 247-7	**Royal Doulton** 5th Ed.	11.95
☐ 280-9	**Science Fiction & Fantasy Collectibles** 2nd Ed.	10.95
☐	**Sewing Collectibles** 1st Ed.	8.95
☐ 299-X	**Star Trek/Star Wars Collectibles** 1st Ed.	7.95
☐ 248-5	**Wicker** 3rd Ed.	10.95

THE OFFICIAL:

☐ 445-3	**Collector's Journal** 1st Ed.	4.95
☐ 549-2	**Directory to U.S. Flea Markets** 1st Ed.	4.95
☐ 365-1	**Encyclopedia of Antiques** 1st Ed.	9.95
☐ 369-4	**Guide to Buying and Selling Antiques** 1st Ed.	9.95
☐ 414-3	**Identification Guide to Early American Furniture** 1st Ed.	9.95
☐ 413-5	**Identification Guide to Glassware** 1st Ed.	9.95
☐ 448-8	**Identification Guide to Gunmarks** 2nd Ed.	9.95
☐ 412-7	**Identification Guide to Pottery & Porcelain** 1st Ed.	9.95
☐ 415-1	**Identification Guide to Victorian Furniture** 1st Ed.	9.95

THE OFFICIAL (SMALL SIZE) PRICE GUIDES TO:

☐ 309-0	**Antiques & Flea Markets** 4th Ed.	$4.95
☐ 269-8	**Antique Jewelry** 3rd Ed.	4.95
☐ 737-1	**Baseball Cards** 7th Ed.	4.95
☐ 647-2	**Bottles** 3rd Ed.	4.95
☐ 544-1	**Cars & Trucks** 3rd Ed.	5.95
☐ 519-0	**Collectible Americana** 2nd Ed.	4.95
☐ 294-9	**Collectible Records** 3rd Ed.	4.95
☐ 306-6	**Dolls** 4th Ed.	4.95
☐ 359-7	**Football Cards** 7th Ed.	4.95
☐ 540-9	**Glassware** 3rd Ed.	4.95
☐ 526-3	**Hummels** 4th Ed.	4.95
☐ 279-5	**Military Collectibles** 3rd Ed.	4.95
☐ 745-2	**Overstreet Comic Book Companion** 1st Ed.	4.95
☐ 278-7	**Pocket Knives** 3rd Ed.	4.95
☐ 527-1	**Scouting Collectibles** 4th Ed.	4.95
☐ 494-1	**Star Trek/Star Wars Collectibles** 3rd Ed.	3.95
☐ 307-4	**Toys** 4th Ed.	4.95

THE OFFICIAL BLACKBOOK PRICE GUIDES OF:

☐ 743-6	**U.S. Coins** 26th Ed.	3.95
☐ 742-8	**U.S. Paper Money** 20th Ed.	3.95
☐ 741-X	**U.S. Postage Stamps** 10th Ed.	3.95

THE OFFICIAL INVESTORS GUIDE TO BUYING & SELLING:

☐ 534-4	**Gold, Silver & Diamonds** 2nd Ed.	12.95
☐ 535-2	**Gold Coins** 2nd Ed.	12.95
☐ 536-0	**Silver Coins** 2nd Ed.	12.95
☐ 537-9	**Silver Dollars** 2nd Ed.	12.95

THE OFFICIAL NUMISMATIC GUIDE SERIES:

☐ 254-X	**The Official Guide to Detecting Counterfeit Money** 2nd Ed.	7.95
☐ 257-4	**The Official Guide to Mint Errors** 4th Ed.	7.95

SPECIAL INTEREST SERIES:

☐ 506-9	**From Hearth to Cookstove** 3rd Ed.	17.95
☐ 530-1	**Lucky Number Lottery Guide** 1st Ed.	4.95
☐ 504-2	**On Method Acting** 8th Printing	6.95

TOTAL	

SEE REVERSE SIDE FOR ORDERING INSTRUCTIONS.

FOR IMMEDIATE DELIVERY

VISA & MASTER CARD CUSTOMERS
ORDER TOLL FREE!
1-800-638-6460

This number is for orders only; it is not tied into the customer service or business office. Customers not using charge cards must use mail for ordering since payment is required with the order—sorry, no C.O.D.'s.

OR SEND ORDERS TO

THE HOUSE OF COLLECTIBLES
201 East 50th Street
New York, New York 10022

POSTAGE & HANDLING RATES
First Book $1.00
Each Additional Copy or Title $0.50

Total from columns on order form. Quantity_____ $_____

☐ Check or money order enclosed $_____ (include postage and handling)

☐ Please charge $_____to my: ☐ MASTERCARD ☐ VISA

Charge Card Customers Not Using Our Toll Free Number Please Fill Out The Information Below

Account No. _____Expiration Date_____
(All Digits)
Signature_____

NAME (please print)_____PHONE_____

ADDRESS_____APT. #_____

CITY_____STATE_____ZIP_____